Anthropology after Gluckman

MANCHESTER
1824

Manchester University Press

Anthropology after Gluckman

The Manchester School, colonial and postcolonial transformations

Richard Werbner

Manchester University Press

The right of Richard Werbner to be identified as the author of this work has been asserted by him in accordance with the Copyright, Designs and Patents Act 1988.

Published by Manchester University Press
Altrincham Street, Manchester M1 7JA, UK
www.manchesteruniversitypress.co.uk

British Library Cataloguing-in-Publication Data is available

ISBN 978 1 5261 3800 2 hardback
ISBN 978 1 5261 6031 7 paperback

First published by Manchester University Press in hardback 2020

This edition published 2021

The publisher has no responsibility for the persistence or accuracy of URLs for any external or third-party internet websites referred to in this book, and does not guarantee that any content on such websites is, or will remain, accurate or appropriate.

Typeset by New Best-set Typesetters Ltd

To Flora,
who asks the Four Questions

Praise poem

Praise-song of our lord Makapweka, Dokotela Gluckman[1]

(note: Makapweka is a praise-name of God – 'he who is so generous when he gives to the parent, he gives also the child' [*sic*]).

Composed by Mundia, Attendant on the King

Our lord is a snake on top of the marsh-grasses;
He is a fish-eagle shining on the island where he always eats fishes,
Our lord dazzles his subjects because it is for them that he rules.
Our lord is iron burning as it comes out of the fire, when you look
  at him you close your eyes.
And he is the sun when it splits the storm, if we try we cannot see
  him.
His head dazzles us, like the sun shining on the waters of the
  Zambezi at midday.
He does not deny anyone a gift, as soon as he sees a person he
  gives to him.
When he does not give to a wicked person, tomorrow he reforms
  him.
Lord, we praise you Makapweka, you strengthen the people thus.
The people will give you kingship, if you do well by them.
We praise you, Lord Makapweka, but you are unfortunate that
  you find our king speechless [he'd had a stroke, *sic*]; he sickens
  greatly.
But if it is so, may you strengthen the Ngambela [Prime Minister
  sic], it is he of ours.

If you love one another and meet over affairs, your work will go well.

The whole country, if it lays blame, blames you, the Ngambela;

If it gives praise, it praises you also; because you are the healer of all the people.

If they do not obey the laws well, they blame you because you do not know how to rule well.

You have agreed, great lord, to do the work of King Edward [?George *sic*] to act with sense; therefore we praise you.

And your clerk Sianga who helps you in writing the affairs of the land, may he work well.

You, lord, have held your land well, you have strengthened it so that it does not tremble, because you are the rafter of the house of government.

It is you who are the lord of all black people, because when you have given judgment in a case there is no-one who contradicts you,

You who are like a sharp knife cutting affairs.

When you have finished speaking there is silence, because you are the child of God. It is he who gave first, afterwards indeed gave to all the people; also it is who started people that they might speak.[2]

You are the Plain [the heartland of Barotseland – the grassy flood-plain of the Zambezi *sic*] your face and feet are most beautiful.

When you appear standing 'midst the drums of the royal dance, the musicians want to put a cover over your bald head, so that they may play.

Also, when you stand in a gulf of the Lyambai [Zambezi *sic*] the net – fishermen want to trawl in your face because it shines like waters.

Notes

1 Praise-song of our lord Makapweka, Dokotela Gluckman, Gluckman Papers, Royal Anthropological Institute. The occasion for the composition of the praise poem is not known.
2 The praise-singer repeats the first verse, from 'Our lord is a snake' to 'Zambezi at midday'.

Contents

Acknowledgements

I have benefited from much encouragement and support in writing this book, as it has taken me to so many frontiers of research. I am especially grateful to Adam Kuper, Emanuel Marx, Chris Fuller, Flemming Daugard-Hansen, Gobe Matenge, Harri Englund, Isaak Niehaus, James Peters, James Pritchett, John Scott, Keir Martin, Marilyn Strathern, Martin Everett, Oliver House, Ralph Grillo, Richard Fardon, Robert Gordon, Sarah Walpole, Sam Mpotchane, Susan J. Smith and Tjakabaka Matenge. The Satterthwaite Colloquium on African Religion and Ritual has given me the opportunity to get very constructive criticism on parts of this work in progress. Above all, I want to thank my wife Pnina, who has walked the walk, talked the talk, and generously read every word to help make fresher drafts possible.

Parts of the book are revised versions of my earlier work that appeared in the following:

Werbner, R., 'The Manchester School in South-Central Africa', *Annual Review of Anthropology* 13 (1984): 157–85; reprinted as 'South-Central Africa: the Manchester School and after', in Richard Fardon (ed.), *Localizing Strategies* (Edinburgh: Scottish Academic Press, 1990), 152–81.

Werbner, R., 'Cosmopolitan ethnicity: entrepreneurship and the nation: minority elites in Botswana', *Journal of Southern African Studies* 28(4) (2002): 727–49.

Werbner, R., *Reasonable Radicals and Citizenship in Botswana* (Bloomington, IN: Indiana University Press, 2004).

Werbner, R., 'Responding to rooted cosmopolitanism: patriots, ethics and the public good in Botswana', in P. Werbner (ed.), *Anthropology and the New Cosmopolitanism* (Oxford: Berg, 2008).

Werbner, R., 'Anthropology and the postcolonial', in R. Fardon et al. (eds), *The Sage Handbook of Social Anthropology* (London: Sage, 2012).

Werbner, R., '"Down-to-earth": friendship and a national elite circle in Botswana', in M. Guichard (ed.), *Friendship, Descent and Alliance* (Oxford: Berghahn, 2014).

Werbner, R., 'Grassroots ecumenism in conflict – introduction', *Journal of Southern African Studies* 44(2) (2018): 201–20.

Introduction

Rediscovery and exploration

This book rediscovers the many-sidedness of the Manchester School and its continuing impact, through a method of social biography and related intellectual history. The approach focuses on each primary subject as a member of a circle of persons powerfully significant for one another and intensely engaged with a leading member.[1] This is the circle of pioneering social anthropologists around Max Gluckman, known as the Manchester School; and in many ways, having Robert Gordon's monumental biography of Gluckman has deepened my understanding of his engagement with them (Gordon 2018). My own book reveals that members of the circle engaged in deep dialogue, enduring friendships and counterposed creativity, their apparent intent being to collaborate and yet not to trespass, so to speak, on the others' perceived domains. If specially identified with distinctive developments, such as the extended case method and its application to the study of conflict resolution,[2] they were mavericks, who claimed, among themselves, not a unity in research interests or theoretical assumptions but evolving conversations across disciplines and highly personal directions. The rediscovery of the complexity of their engagement, as well as their impact, illuminates an exploration of the frontiers between ethnography, the sociology of knowledge and the anthropology of colonial to postcolonial change and of cosmopolitanism.

My early knowledge of the Manchester School came when I was a Brandeis University undergraduate about to study in the Manchester department, and in preparation I met Elizabeth Colson at

Boston University in 1959. She found the time to give me her
impressions of each of her old colleagues, so varied that I came
away with what she herself might have called a good gossip. It was
a fine introduction not to a harmonious team following their leader,
but to some highly individual, rather argumentative players, critical
of each other, with their own characteristic ways and interests, often
at the frontiers of the social sciences.

My early impression of social anthropology in 1959 came in
the late colonial period, now known to historians as 'The End of
Empire'; and I now write in a postcolonial moment that critics
consider still calls for 'decolonization'. With that in mind, I want
to make it clear, from the very start, that I accept that the present
challenge comes at a time when the old question of 'The School',
Manchester, British or otherwise, is again being urgently asked,
along with another about 'the whole development of social anthropology'. How does this twenty-first-century development fit into
or depend upon the great transformation from our colonial past
into our postcolonial present? What kind of knowledge are we
passing on?

In response, throughout much of this book, I will consider
certain salient issues of the making of anthropology in colonial
times, and then in the next to last chapter, I will address questions
of anthropology and the postcolonial. Some of the questions are
about the past critique of power and coercion and the aftermath of
struggles for liberation. Even further, there is another significant part
of the knowledge needed in our troubled times. This has to illuminate the vulnerability of anthropologists ourselves and the risks
we endure in researching politically sensitive issues, even apparently
everyday matters. It is a strength, continuing from our past, that we
remain committed to anthropology and intensive fieldwork, despite
becoming prohibited immigrants or unwittingly being caught in the
cross-fire of conflict, which disturbs, undoes or completely stops
our research (Gray 2019). Among the lessons to be learned from
the work of the Manchester School is endurance, to keep on
meeting the need for rethinking in our subject, in the light of
sustained and intense fieldwork, and with an informed understanding of where we have come from.

A great deal of ink has been spilt on the question of the 'schoolness' of the Manchester School, and especially its customary focus

on conflict, its house style, and its sophisticated, indeed innovative research methods. It has grown to be a scholarly industry that was fostered very deliberately and with a strong grasp of popular communication by Max Gluckman himself, and it includes my own early account in *The Annual Review of Anthropology* (1984, revised 1990). In this early account I reported alternative perspectives, an outsider's and an insider's. I found it was an outsider, Mary Douglas, who in a review was the first to 'salute [the emergence of] a school of anthropology whose publications are developed through close discussion, and where each worker's work is enhanced by his focus on a common stock of problems' (Douglas 1959a: 168). By contrast, I reported, from the insider's perspective, the view of my own fieldwork supervisor, Clyde Mitchell, who told me: 'Seen from outside, the Manchester School *was* a school. But seen from the inside, it was a seething contradiction. And perhaps the only thing we had in common was that Max was our teacher, and that meant we wrote ethnography rich in actual cases' (Werbner 1990: 152–3). If the insider's perspective was one thing, and the outsider's another, so too was criticism a matter of, to use a favourite Manchester notion, situational selection. The insiders prided themselves on intense argument and direct, open criticism of each other and their works in progress, explicitly in seminars; in public and publications, disagreements sometimes appeared frank, though usually more respectful than in seminar confrontations. Of course, as I show later, the flow of frank, judgemental and telling gossip among the insiders was remarkable, as might be expected from the analysis in Manchester gossip studies (Colson 1953; Gluckman 1963a; Epstein 1969). As for the outsiders, it was Mary Douglas who took on the role of being a prosecutor or unavoidable nemesis. Douglas praised or damned in subsequent reviews monograph after monograph of the Manchester School, and for this reason, among others, I will comment later at some length on her importance for the Manchester School.

Having myself been a PhD student and later colleague of Max Gluckman, Clyde Mitchell and Victor Turner and, as well, a long-time friend of Elizabeth Colson and 'Bill' Epstein, I write, admittedly, from an insider's view, and intentionally with much affection and admiration. Of course, where possible, I have sought to reach a reasonable balance between my memories, personal documents, notes and knowledge of gossip and the correspondence and reports available in the archives, as well as the considerable body of Manchester School publications.

Not surprisingly, being at the centre of a contentious circle, Gluckman found it to be one thing to plan, but another to implement, and still another to provide a full overview of the implementation. His Seven-Year Plan for the Rhodes-Livingstone Institute (RLI), from which the Manchester School arose, provoked this criticism by the American anthropologists George Marcus and Michael Fischer, that it was one of 'ultimately unco-ordinated team projects: making systematic connections (between the studies) was left to individual readers' (1986: 91). Admittedly, it was extremely ambitious plan for comparative research, across a whole region of Africa, that was to be in accord with a typology not of 'tribes' but of rural areas with variation in these factors: 1) the presence or absence of cash crops, 2) the import or export of labour, and 3) the relative proximity to the railway network. Gluckman expected that the research would account for 'the *differential* effects of labour migration and urbanization on the family and kinship organization, the economic life, the political values, the religious and magical beliefs' (Gluckman 1945a: 9, italics mine). It is a breathtaking ambition, and the Plan explicitly took even class differentiation into account, for example, 'a class of peasant farmers emerging among Tonga, with their cash crops' (Gluckman 1945a: 9).

Colson considered the research to be framed by a method for 'the intensive study of small communities'. It was designed to test hypotheses about a limited number of factors, not to provide an account of cultures or whole societies with the same 'tribal' name (Colson 1967). Without denying that Marcus and Fischer are right in a sense – the Plan did fall short of its too ambitious promise – I would argue that in good measure it was actually carried out. Even further, in a whole series of introductions, Gluckman distilled systematically for the reader the fresh, outstanding contributions of each Manchester monograph; and he made many of the findings coherently accessible in his popular works, such as *Custom and Conflict in Africa* (1956) and *Politics, Law and Ritual in Tribal Society* (1965), and in BBC talks. As I will discuss in Chapters 1 and 2, Gluckman was a public intellectual who spoke on behalf of the continuing advance of research in modern social anthropology, and not only by his own 'School'.

Gluckman put a stamp of apparent unity on it all when he introduced the collection of essays, *The Craft of Social Anthropology* (Epstein 1967), which gave a defining representation of his colleagues' methods and modes of analysis in relation to current theoretical problems:

> The contributors are anthropologists who have had the opportunity of working closely together for many years as officers of the Rhodes-Livingstone Institute, or in the Department of Social Anthropology at Manchester University, or both. They are thus able to discuss within a common framework modern fieldwork methods, not simply as a set of techniques *per se*, but rather as tools for examining a number of problems that have come to interest them. But we would like to stress that we see our own work as firmly set in the whole development of social anthropology. (Gluckman 1967: xi)

Strategies for destabilizing ethnography

Of all the ethnographic strategies that destabilize ethnography in order to reinvigorate it with fresh life and insights, the one most cultivated by Gluckman himself – for example, on the Nuer, in *Custom and Conflict* (1960) – and some of his students (Uberoi 1962; Werbner 1967, 1969, 1979a, 1981, 1990, 1992, 2015; Handelman 1990) belongs in the mainstream known as 're-analysis'. I offer an example of re-analysis in Chapter 9. Here I want to introduce re-analysis as one destabilizing strategy among others – deconstruction and redescribing – in order to enhance our knowledge of the heuristic value of each, but especially re-analysis in relation to the others and in the fresh elucidation of a classic among Manchester School studies, Victor Turner's *Chihamba, the White Spirit* (1975).

Although under the rubric 'deconstruction' I see an ethnographic strategy, I am well aware that after Derrida (1974), literary critics see and disagree under that rubric with regard to many things and approaches about which I am not competent to speak. I am taking the licence to apply 'deconstruction' to a destabilizing strategy that had its heyday following the publication of *Writing Culture* (Marcus and Clifford 1986). Deconstruction is, above all, the critical uncovering of concealment in the text of an ethnography. Hidden through rhetoric, through the appealing style of writing, through the seductive, often apparently simple and realistic narrative voice of the writer, are presuppositions, in particular about power and inequality. As Pnina Werbner reminds us, the deconstructive critiques of the Nuer in *Writing Culture* seemed to liberate the reader from politically significant complicity, unwitting entanglement in colonial domination being disguised or glossed over (P. Werbner 2018: 81). For example, James Clifford deconstructed 'an allegory of Anglo-Saxon democracy' in *The Nuer*, the people themselves being represented as 'the vanishing primitive' (Clifford 1986: 111–12). Renato Rosaldo critically uncovered the concealment of domination in a 'literary pastoral style': Evans-Pritchard described the Nuer as embodying 'democratic values, rugged individualism, fierce pride, and a warrior spirit … idealized characteristics of a certain masculine imagination … an ideal of human liberty, even in the midst of colonial domination' (Rosaldo 1986: 96). Ethnographers felt the challenges, first to interrogate political bias in their own texts as well as in anthropological classics, and in so doing to effect a critique of their own culture and its narrative arts for collusion in the domination of others. So overwhelming did this interrogation trend become that it led many to something like a failure of nerve, with doubt about whether ethnography, especially writing but also research in fieldwork, was still credible and valid or even possible.

The destabilizing strategy of redescribing, like deconstruction, aims against concealment and in favour of some liberation. Unlike deconstruction, however, redescribing turns away from power and inequality to a concern for displacement. What is it that has to be displaced? Or, perhaps exorcised? As Roy Wagner would have it:

> The future of Western society lies in its ability to create social forms that will make distinctions between classes and segments of society, so that these distinctions do not come of themselves as implicit racism, discrimination, corruption, crisis, riots, necessary 'cheating' and 'finagling' and so on. The future of anthropology lies in its ability to exorcise 'difference' and make it conscious and explicit. (Wagner 1975: 158)

I cite this passage particularly because of its signal significance in the development of redescribing. Marilyn Strathern places it on the flyleaf of *The Gender of the Gift* (1988), to indicate a starting point for her own first contribution in a major and comparative work of redescribing.

Wagner was not himself given to redescribing; it was, of course, for the future. Hence, reading his *Invention of Culture* (1975) in about 1978 (well before *Writing Culture*) 'was like a door opening' for Marilyn Strathern (Viveiros de Castro, Fausto and Strathern 2017: 44). Her remarkable body of many, richly varied studies now gives the most productive and substantial, if individual and often highly personal, examples of actually redescribing ethnography. How these bear the hallmark of redescribing is intricately revealed in the reflexive accounts and interviews, the debates and commentaries, especially on ways of rethinking and reimagining sociality, in Ashley Lebner's illuminating collection, *Redescribing Relations* (2017). I refer the reader to it as a whole, while I will regard a very small part in due course.

Strathern has a gift of redescribing that appears to be paradoxical: intensely serious and, sometimes at once, deliberately and admittedly playful and tricky. It is a gift of argument and narrative. Here, I present some attention to the argument, as explicitly described for redescribing, and I offer very little attention to the substantial narrative, revealing the complexities of social life, the idioms surprisingly true to themselves, and the fine disclosure of difference in metaphysics, 'Melanesian' vs. 'Western'. I want to extract bits of her earliest account of her attempt at making the argumentative gift in her chapter on 'Anthropological Strategies' (Strathern 1988: ch. 1). Later, in my Chapter 5, I take up the substantial question of any dialogue around relational thought and social relations that might be or might have been sustained between Strathern and members of the Manchester School in their concern with the development of social network analysis.

Above all, redescribing turns to awaken consciousness of premises, to call for the unexamined to be examined, for constructs not to be taken for granted. It is no good going on pretending, for the sake of convenience in analysis, that disparate things are commensurate. If we cannot avoid the use of fictions in analysis, we have to be vigilant in learning how they may be rooted in Western metaphysics, and in letting readers be clear about the fictional problematics involved. In question, for a start, are what Strathern identifies 'as the premises on which much writing on Melanesia (though *not of course restricted* to it) has been based' (1986: 7, italics mine). The caveat in italics hints at an extended aspect of this destabilizing strategy, which Strathern takes care immediately to make explicit: 'These premises belong to a particular cultural mode of knowledge and explanation' (1986: 7). *They are ours*, as is the mode itself, but if we cannot wholly extract ourselves from them – *we are also theirs*, so to speak – we have the potential to be critical about them by making them visible, even as the metaphysical roots of our thought. Hence for Strathern redescribing is something of a wake-up call to reflect on how accounts deploy fundamental oppositions – we might say common-sense logic – in appearing to be cogent.

To engage as a Westerner in having to think and write about how Melanesians think is to have to come to terms with and find a language for fundamental disparity, the difference being in math-ematics as in metaphysics. According to Strathern, for the Melane-sian, no one is less than two. But the Westerner thinks and talks about one being one, as in any opposition, which is one in oppo-sition to another. In Melanesian thought, as Strathern constructs it, the one person is no less than a composite of two opposites. Hence to engage with this dual predicament within a Western mode of knowledge and explanation, Strathern turns to two per-spectives, feminist and anthropological, which, if both Western, are alternatives, sometimes overlapping, sometimes at odds with each other. Being conflicted, they are just right for a running argu-ment that may apprehend difference without occluding it. The one ethnographer as author becomes the two sparring partners, highly appropriate for a 'Melanesianist'; if a straddler, she does not sit on the fence but takes one side against the other, in turns, even for ironic and playful effect. Strathern elucidates the critical expo-sure directed towards academics and members of her own society, through what emerges as a shifting 'contextualist' perspective of her own: 'I choose to show the contextualized nature of indigenous constructs by exposing the contextualized nature of analytical ones. For members of that society [her own], of course, such a laying bare of assumptions will entail a laying bare of purpose and intent' (1986: 8).[3] Notably, by contrast to deconstruction's destructive force, its unnerving of ethnographers with critical and self-doubt about ethnography, redescribing in its destabilizing of ethnography has elicited an efflorescence, known to Strathern's credit as the New Melanesian Ethnography.

By comparison to both deconstruction and redescribing, re-analysis is hardly novel. That is, in good measure, because it shares very simply with much academic practice in puzzling about what is mistaken in a text, argument or received analysis. In such practice, re-analysis is pragmatic, on the creative way to ethnographic renewal. The appeal is this. Hunt for the mistake and track it down; and crucial in such detection, perhaps most fun, is the recovery, for purposes of further creativity, of both the accidental and the missing. The accidental could be a bit of fieldwork observation, information or odd data, not integral to the argument or explanation, and apparently unimportant, but given in the ethnography for the sake of a more complete record. The missing is not assumed, as in deconstruction, to have been kept out or silenced in the service of power and domination. Instead, to be learned through re-analysis is how and why the missing is missing. Sometimes, it gets recognized in comparison from one ethnography to others, and along with the accidental becomes at once destabilizing and constructive in further learning as to where a theoretical orientation constitutes blinkers and bias in ethnography. So far, to my knowledge, the engagement with theory in re-analysis has avoided coming to terms with a boldly philosophical drive, as in redescribing, rooted in 'Western metaphysics', or in the foundational ideas and oppositions of 'Euro-Americans'.[4] Instead, more within the workmanlike practice, familiar in academic scholarship, re-analysis does advance debate by pitching one theoretical tradition against another, as well as by arguing within the frame of a theoretical orientation for mistakes or shortcomings in the construction of an account.

At the heart of my re-analysis in Chapter 9, on Victor Turner's masterpiece *Chihamba, the White Spirit* (1975), I address questions of perspectival ethnography, and of the extent to which Turner's familiar ideas (on performance, liminality, semiotics and the ritual process) shed light on *Chihamba* as a ritual drama. My account speaks to a new generation of reflexive ethnographers, to close the distance between them and the radical experiments in perspectival plurality that twentieth-century ethnographies advanced. Into the foreground emerge tricks and fantasy, Bacchanalia and the preoccupation of magicians with playful sexuality for the arousal of fertility and well-being in harmony with the ancestors, male and female.

More into the background goes the 'ritual man' preoccupied with cosmic principles.

The re-analysis puts arguments to proof in a way that opens out interpretation to alternative theory. In line with Thomist philosophy, Turner gave short shrift to playful oppositions, so important for his own arguments in *The Ritual Process* (1969). He became preoccupied with isolated monism. A single principle overwhelmed his view, the essence by itself as the transcendent *Kavula*, the source of all being. In terms of *spirituality*, Turner decontextualized *Kavula* and thus misapprehended 'the pure act-of-being'. Against that, my re-analysis captures *Kavula* and the ghost, husband and wife, in their opposition, and thus conceptualizes the dynamics of their duality. In terms of *sacrifice* and an apparent ritual climax in the beheading of a victim, Turner gave us no development. My re-analysis clarifies a progression towards exorcism informed by a simple cultural axiom, namely: *the production and consumption of food and the reproduction of life are two sides of the same thing.*

In accord with that, I document in my own day-to-day account the dramatization of playful sex and reproduction in and through the means of production and consumption. The climactic moment – a rite of beheading followed by an appearance of emptiness – is sexual, good to the point of orgiastic overcoming for a satisfied ghost or her apparition, not at all like the spectral, sexless moment of emptiness at the tomb of Jesus: Turner's resurrection comparison is fundamentally mistaken.

The cultic importance of gender bias, playful sexuality and histrionic impression management raises a challenge to the relation between Turner's very rich record of vernacular texts and ritual practice and his religious and philosophical advocacy. To advance a view of 'ritual man' and his creativity in ritual drama, Turner brought together the Thomist reasoning about the pure act-of-being and Arthur Rimbaud's French surrealist theory of *voyance* – the reasoned disordering of all the senses. If much performance creates an esoteric mystery, about which an Ndembu magician boasts that it is terrifying and awesome, there is no direct observation by Turner to back his claim that it is actually so bewildering that there is the 'disordering of all of the senses' (1975: 185). In Chapter 9, I unpack the phases in the ritual process which disclose the familiar and the matter-of-fact in the ordering of the senses and the ecstatic, sensuous play on and with sexuality. Moments of Bacchanalia surge, but not *voyance*. Here the culmination of re-analysis is recognition of the continuing rich interest in an ethnography as an open text.

The renewed challenge, present coverage

Where, in *The Craft of Social Anthropology*, Gluckman saw for his colleagues the opportunity and ability 'to discuss within a common framework', the challenge I take up in *Anthropology after Gluckman* is to go back to being, as it were, the native having that first encounter with a social anthropologist, Elizabeth Colson, and hopefully, also, having a reasonable respect for his elders. It is to present my early impression refreshed; that is, to attend to significant difference and diversity in intellectual histories, personal dispositions and careers, while also recognizing Manchester's living legacies for 'the whole development of social anthropology'.

My coverage of contributions and their contributors is broad, though of course partial – urban and village studies, early directors of the Rhodes-Livingstone Institute (Gluckman, Colson and Mitchell) and the first Manchester PhDs (Epstein and Turner), interests in politics, law, kinship, history and social change, symbolism and ritual, methodology, urbanism, networks and relational thought. I show the linkage between their distinctive theoretical directions and their personal dispositions and special careers. On this basis, I show also some of the development of ideas and interests from generation to generation at Manchester through the work of the early School's students and some students of students.

Adam Kuper (2015) argues trenchantly for an outsider's critical view in the fourth edition of what is now perhaps the most popular textbook on twentieth-century British social anthropology's Great Men and (some) Women.[5] A brief comment on that view prepares the way for rethinking beyond the textbook and towards our own approach in *Anthropology after Gluckman*. If once a young man's amusing anti-establishment shocker, Kuper's history, now with its no less lively retrospection, has become an elder's standard textbook, in plentiful second-hand supply on Amazon. Yet as a perspective on the development of the Manchester School and, more broadly, modern social anthropology, there are remarkable shortcomings. It is hard to think of a historian of social anthropology better placed than Kuper to illuminate the important strands in the work of his Cambridge teacher, Meyer Fortes.[6] But Kuper sheds no light on Fortes's constructive response to field and process theories and turmoil in 1930s science, his wrestling with the conceptual ambiguities of his times, his use of heuristic fictions. In Chapters 2 and 5, I present a better perspective on that, and elsewhere I take up the archaeological evidence that over the *longue durée* of more than a millennium, the sacred centre of Tallensi in the Tong Hills has been a central meeting place for disparate ritual congregations (Werbner 2009). Better appreciated on this basis is Fortes's view of long-term Tallensi stability in the past and what has been seen as his alleged blind spot on history, despite his concern for the suffering and dislocation that colonial violence imposed on Tallensi.

My point is this. Kuper's history is too much in step with a growing trend to rewrite our past simply as a Golden Era of social anthropology, much influenced by *African Political Systems* (Fortes and Evans-Pritchard 1940) and segmentary lineage theory, but without an exemplary strand of connective relationality from Fortes (for examples, see Barth 2005; Eriksen and Nielsen 2013). This relational strand lies in still vital contributions distinctively by Fortes, and not by Evans-Pritchard, on unbounded relations, personal networks, overlapping fields of social ties, powerfully felt collaboration in cross-cutting ritual performance, and central place or nodal religious organizations, which I call regional cults (Werbner 1977a). It is a relational strand that is not the novelty it appears to be in recent work on arguments about the need to displace received and apparently unexamined formulations of an opposition between the Individual and Society and to rethink sociality in terms of relations and relations between relations (Lebner 2017). Recovering this strand, in its connective and relational significance, rather than as obscured by stereotypes of the 'isolated, closed society', enables me to show in Chapters 2, 5, 7 and 10 how influential this strand has been and still is for social anthropology, and in particular for the Manchester School.

In a further shortcoming, Kuper turns the stereotype of exclusion and closure on to the Manchester School itself. True, members of the Manchester department, like members of other British anthropology departments, now as in the past, did publish some edited collections consisting mainly of essays by fellow members

(Gluckman and Devons 1964; Epstein 1967a), but other collections were more inclusive (Colson and Gluckman 1951; Gluckman 1962b; Turner 1971). What the stereotype obscures, contrary to any fresh understanding of the Manchester School, is the actual engagement by its members in collaboration at frontiers in anthropology and across disciplines. Much of *Anthropology after Gluckman* documents this in chapter after chapter: to be an insider of the circle was to be also a critical and influential contributor as a frontiersman or frontierswoman distinctively and in one's own right. It is to that interaction on the inside and at the frontiers that we owe the distinction and the distinctiveness of the Manchester School.

Gluckman fostered a toxic loyalist milieu around himself, imagines Kuper, partly in macho, no-holds-barred seminars. In Kuper's first edition, and only somewhat revised in the fourth, the story is that 'deviants and turn-coats were tolerated with great ferocity, but no criticism was tolerated from outsiders' (Kuper 1973: 160). Others have told the Mancunian story differently (see Gordon 2018: 368–70). A. L. Epstein recalled the difference between the LSE seminars when he was a student, under Firth, who would 'spring on people' so that 'I was shaken rigid', and, under Gluckman, the Manchester seminars: 'If you didn't feel you had anything to say, you could be quiet throughout the seminar' (Yelvington 1997: 293). Kuper's textbook history hides what Frederick Barth, like others knowing the seminars well, perceived first-hand: 'Gluckman had an unusual ability to wrestle directly with the ethnographic data of others as presented in their papers, and he used it with great skill during seminar discussions' (Barth 2005: 38). About the RLI seminars, Clyde Mitchell recalled that Gluckman would ask what appeared to be irrelevant questions, and then 'slowly a pattern would begin to emerge and soon we were all agog with excitement as he showed us how it would all fit together in a meaningful way' (Gordon 2018: 337). In Chapter 2 and later discussions, I offer further understanding of argument and academic life, in its more creative, if sometimes fierce, intensity under Gluckman's leadership at Manchester.[7]

Notes

1 In that circle, John Barnes was a prominent member of a primary triad, along with Elizabeth Colson and J. Clyde Mitchell. Of the members of

the Manchester School I discuss, Barnes was the only one with whom I had no personal contact, and I was never his student or friend. For this reason, and my intention to build my account on first-hand knowledge and personal relations – as it were, my inclusion in the same 'thick' or effective network – I mention some of his important contributions but I do not devote a chapter primarily to his life and intellectual history

2 See Douglas 1959a, 1959b; Kapferer 1987, 2006; Evens and Handelman 2006; Mills 2008; Kuper 2015; Englund 2018; Gordon 2018: 367–8.

3 See Strathern 1996 for a more recent clarification of this strategy in her view of how 'Euro-American concepts of hybrid and network' might be extended with social imagination: 'That includes seeing how they are put to work in their indigenous context as well as how they might work in an exogenous one. It also includes attention to the way they become operationalized as manipulable or usable artefacts in people's pursuit of interests and their construction of relationships' (1996: 521).

4 In redescribing, 'Euro-Americans' is not a term for an actual population but a shorthand personification for convenience in exposition: 'I personify a discourse for expositional convenience' (Strathern 1996: 531 n.2).

5 Regrettably, Kuper pushes his stimulating intellectual argument into a personal attack and a paranoid imaginary of Manchester seminars and departmental life. Contrary to reality, Gluckman appears to be a mad boss, rather than an inspiring, charismatic and, of course, argumentative, even awkward one, with great vitality.

6 For a valuable, in-depth re-evaluation of Meyer Fortes's thought and works, with a fine, amicable touch of ancestor worship, see Kuper 2016.

7 For a perceptive account of 'cohesion and solidarity' within Gluckman's 'team' at the RLI, see Gordon 2018: 334–6.

1

Max Gluckman in South Africa: role model, early leadership

A monumental biography, social anthropology as a modern discipline

Max Gluckman is now the subject of one of the most monumental, gossip-rich and finely, even contentiously, documented biographies of a modern anthropologist, *The Enigma of Max Gluckman* by Robert Gordon (2018).[1] This biography reveals remarkable turns in Gluckman's life, while he played a leading part in the making of social anthropology as a modern discipline. In this chapter, I will draw freely on Gordon's biography, but highlight certain aspects of Gluckman's personal and intellectual history that call into question received wisdom about his contributions and their value for social anthropology in the past and for the future. I will argue that his formative years were highly important for his development and long-term projects as a social anthropologist. For this reason, in this chapter, I consider his formative years closely, in detail, and in relation to his father's significance as a much-admired role model, a public-spirited lawyer, a cosmopolitan and liberal anglophile, who himself fought, documented and analysed a remarkable legal and political struggle under colonial rule.

The son of Jewish immigrants – his father Emanuel from Latvia (1881–1953), his mother Katie (née Cohen, 1884–1968) born in Odessa in Russia but Lithuanian by citizenship – Max was born in Johannesburg, South Africa in 1911. If Zionism was a difficult mother's milk for Max – and Katie was a founding, highly successful organizer of South African women Zionists – it was under the influence of his father, Emanuel, that talk of legal cases, the law

and the public good was the stuff of everyday life in Max's family
of three brothers and one sister. Their motivation to excel, to be
distinguished, was remarkable. His was a family of liberal, progressive, public-spirited lawyers, with his father and one brother, Philip,
in the family firm, defending causes, often with little or no pay,
such as that of the pioneer African trade unionist Klements Kadalie.
Frail Barrier, Philip's novel inspired by his father's example and his
own experience of coping with the quest for justice under the so-
called colour bar, tells some of the family story (Gillon 1952). Their
elder brother, Colin, became the state prosecutor of Israel, who
famously brought Israeli soldiers to justice for their criminal responsibility in the Kafr Kassim massacre of Arab villagers.

Max Gluckman was, in my view, a public intellectual, who
throughout his career reached beyond the academic world to speak,
especially in many often-controversial radio broadcasts, to very wide
audiences. In the 1940s he made it a major goal of the Rhodes-
Livingstone Institute (RLI), under his direction, to translate 'the
knowledge gained through research into a form that would be
understood by those responsible for policy, and by "everyman"'
(Colson 1977: 288). A liberal and radical during the 1930s in the
days of his South African student politics, in colonial Northern
Rhodesia he found it necessary as a fieldworker and RLI director
to negotiate, to compromise, to avoid political confrontations. He
had not only suspicious enemies but also sympathetic allies among
those colonial officials who were progressive for their times, some
of whom remained his lifelong friends; the colonial administration
was, like any bureaucracy, divided. Nevertheless, hardly ever did his
findings or suggestions make a significant difference in the implementation of colonial rule. Against a dominant trend among social
anthropologists of his time, Gluckman became a political activist,
openly and forcefully anti-colonial. When he was based in the University of Manchester, he gave his highly vocal, strong and prominent support to the anti-apartheid and anti-colonial movements.

Gluckman could be a formidable presence, a big, athletic man,
well over six foot two and, as his praise-singer Mundia tells, bald.
He was a deeply engaged and charismatic figure, apparently loving
a fight or wrestling with his own towering rage, yet wondrously
charming, even if sometimes aggressive and fiercely adversarial.

To local research assistants and novice fieldworkers, like me as his supervisee, his advice – which he feared he had himself not always followed – was 'Keep your eyes and your ears open, but your mouth shut.' He had an Achilles heel which, in reporting on his role in the Rhodes-Livingstone Institute, Elizabeth Colson has described and perhaps understated: 'Gluckman did not easily relinquish direction of the work he had initiated' (Colson 1977: 293). This flaw of trying to keep control of his old Institute and later his Manchester University department, when the time had come for his successors to take over, brought him much grief in quarrels with old friends and close colleagues. My own relations with him as his student and colleague were often stormy, though towards the very end of his life they were full of amity and mutual understanding, after I married his niece, Pnina, in 1971.[2]

Gluckman's masterpiece in process

Gluckman's masterpiece is, of course, *The Judicial Process among the Barotse*, published in 1955. A central part of it, from four of his 1954 BBC lectures, appears in an outstanding essay, 'The Reasonable Man in Barotse Law', which now speaks very usefully to the growing anthropological interest in ethics and morality.[3] We can gauge its wider reception from the warning he was given at the time by George Homans, the American sociologist: 'You have reached the top now. All that is left is a long, slow, coast downhill' (Gluckman 1963b: 178). Accompanying Gluckman on this downhill coast were almost none of his Manchester School colleagues. The fact is, as I discuss in Chapter 6, only A. L. 'Bill' Epstein, himself a trained lawyer, engaged in any major, serious debate with the ideas and arguments of *The Judicial Process among the Barotse*.

In *The Judicial Process* and in later studies, 'Max influenced the work of others', Elizabeth Colson argued, 'but did not inspire his own students' (Colson 2008a: 335). Her guess is that they did not address his law studies because they 'may have feared being seen as intellectual rivals'. It is a telling remark, though unpacking the whole story would demand a book in itself, to accompany Gordon's monumental biography. I think it could also be argued that *The Judicial Process* marked a departure from Gluckman's earlier sociological work that was problematic for his old students and established Manchester School colleagues. At the core of *The Judicial Process* was an interest in situated logic and reasoning, in ambiguity and semantics, in the importance of imprecision in words. For all its regard for 'the social framework' in which judges' arguments proceed, it seemed to veer too much towards a universalist version of 'interpretive anthropology'; for example, it argued that all legal concepts have the same five broad characteristics, summed up under the rubric 'flexible' (Gluckman 1955: 293–4). More fundamentally, Gluckman asserted, 'My study of the Lozi judicial process, which is akin to our own judicial process, faithfully depicts modes of reasoning which are probably found wherever men apply norms to varied disputes' (1955: 33).[4] Clarifying forensic skill is important throughout Gluckman's exposition of actual cases. Gluckman's motive is unmistakable, and now well known, and yet still worth restating: to honour the intellectual sophistication of Lozi reasoning, which he admired, on a par with practice considered to be judicious in English courts and elsewhere.[5]

It is remarkable that what we now see as the exceptional strength of *The Judicial Process* – the close analysis through a very substantial body of cases – was held to be a weakness at the time Gluckman was writing. He was under pressure to pare down the cases from Meyer Fortes, Evans-Pritchard and Radcliffe-Brown, who urged him, remarked Gluckman, 'to cut down my cases in the book, and I just had to tell them that I cannot do my analysis except out of cases' (MG to CM, 5 February 1956, MBPL). Gluckman went on to complain that people 'brought up on abstract analysis which EP does will not appreciate case material' (MG to CM, 5 February 1956, MBPL).

Writing in 2008, Colson recalled that in the early 1950s, Gluckman was much engrossed in reading and talking about legal realism and the 'work of legal theorists in conjunction with his study of Lozi jurisprudence' (Colson 2008a: 335). As Gluckman later explained, this was his view of the American legal realists: 'they were arguing that a study of the rules of law alone was inadequate; it was essential also to study the *processes* by which facts in evidence became facts-in-law, and the *processes* by which problems of uncertainty not covered clearly by specific rules were met' (Gluckman 1973a: 614, italics mine).

Processes, processes, *The Judicial Process* – why did Gluckman drum in *process?* The answer must be obvious: process mattered, and above all. The drumming registered his sense of being embattled, perhaps with very good reason; his approach was later to be caricatured as 'rule-centred', and working within a 'rule-centred paradigm' (Comaroff and Roberts 1981: 8).[6] Against that, I think Bruce Kapferer is correct when he discerns a fundamental turn in a lasting preoccupation of Gluckman's: the study of events. It is the turn to 'processual analysis', which Kapferer aptly prefers to 'situational analysis', the more familiar label attached to much of Gluckman's methodology (Kapferer 2006: 321). For the affinity that Gluckman found between his stance and the legal realists, however, there is a challenge, somewhat beyond Kapferer's recognition – namely, a commitment to science; and to address that, I want to open out, later in Chapter 2, the lasting impact from Gluckman's formative years in the 1930s of 'process theory' derived from physicists and philosophers of science.

Gluckman's role model and his celebrated cause

For Max, his father Emanuel was a role model: the much-loved, heroic and esteemed man Max had to live up to. Knowledge of a celebrated cause in Emanuel Gluckmann's career as an advocate is highly significant, and for the sake of my argument about Max's formative years, my account unpacks that closely. It illuminates the emergence of concerns with ethics and the moral imagination, equity and the allocation of responsibility, the rule of law and due process, power and resistance, and race relations that, over Max's lifetime, continued to be fundamental in his anthropology.

This celebrated cause is the one Emanuel as advocate himself publicized for a mass audience in a series of *Rand Daily Mail* articles, and later his widely distributed booklet, *The Tragedy of the Ababirwas, and some Reflections on Sir Herbert Sloley's Report* (Gluckmann 1922; see also Tlou and Campbell 1997: 257–60; Molosiwa 2013; Gordon 2018: 25–6). If the family law firm had a manifesto, it was this. *The Tragedy of the Ababirwas* has two parts, according to the title, starting with narrative history and concluding with analytic argument; for short, I refer to it as *The Tragedy*. The first part traces the political and legal history of a case that Emanuel as advocate tried and failed to bring to a fair, impartial court on behalf of the Birwa tribe or ethnic group (then called Ababirwas) in the early 1920s Bechuanaland Protectorate; more than a thousand Birwa were violently forced to abandon their looted and destroyed homes in an area known as the Tuli Block. The second part is a critique of a Commission of Inquiry, headed not by an advocate but a colonial official, Sir Herbert Sloley, a former Resident Commissioner in Basutoland, who in an unrelated, earlier inquiry, apparently a whitewash, had already satisfied the Protectorate Administration as being 'a safe pair of hands'. In the inquiry that was supposed to redress the complaints of the Birwa, Emanuel was not allowed to represent the people as their attorney, and this part of his essay documents and proves a miscarriage of justice – his close analysis exposes shortcomings, contrary to the rule of law, in denied cross-examination, lack of due process, judicial bias, intimidation of witnesses and even the prejudicial theatrics of the inquiry (it appeared to have been more than anything else a *pitso*, a public assembly called by the chief at the centre of his own court in the midst of a vast multitude of his followers); the inquiry was so unsafe, so unjust, that it unwittingly exposed, Emanuel argued, a pernicious system of government under the Protectorate Administration. Emanuel's story reveals how he fought tenaciously, in and out of court, and was eventually left unpaid a large sum of money, in defence of his clients' right to live in peace, free of despotic abuse of power.

In the early twentieth century, the Tuli Block was at a frontier between, on one side, the bounded land recognized by the Protectorate authorities to be in a Tswana tribal reserve under Chief Khama and, on the other side, what was then the settler state of Southern Rhodesia. As Emanuel reported, in a fresh initiative to sell its land to white farmers, the British South Africa Company pushed to dislocate Africans from the Tuli Block and resettle them in the nearby Tswana tribal reserve. For Khama, this was a most welcome opportunity. Blocked by defined boundaries from territorial expansion, Khama wanted immigrants who would advance his old objective for a great kingdom, including lesser tribes, and expanding with more subjects, more taxpayers (Molosiwa 2013): the more the people, the greater the chief. For the people in the Tuli Block, who were ethnically not Tswana but Birwa with origins among Kalanga and relatives in the Transvaal and Zimbabwe, Khama's opportunity was their hated disaster, Emanuel revealed. Their dislocation came to be severe and intolerable. They had been living in what they regarded as ancestral lands to which they had returned at the end of the pre-colonial wars, some four decades earlier – they had been people outlying in what I call the shatter zone; the dislocation put them under the domination of one of Khama's men as an appointed governor, not a chief of their own people. They were treated as tenants-at-will, expelled at the Company's instruction to go back to being subjects of their paramount chief. As they saw it, Khama was not and never had been their chief; they had never paid him tribute; furthermore, they had never been tenants, for after their return to their ancestral homes, some forty years earlier, they only paid Protectorate hut-tax, never Company rent. After initial unsuccessful attempts by Khama to order them to resettle, at his command they were forced to move. In the Tuli Block, well beyond the tribal reserve, and near a police station, with the full knowledge of the Protectorate official in charge, the responsible sergeant, an armed regiment sent by Khama ran amok, behaving as was customary, in Khama's own words, like 'a pack of wild dogs' (Gluckmann 1922: 19). If Khama's people had ever been 'unwarlike', this was their ironic moment for a break-out: 'Scenes ensued which usually accompany the sack of a hostile settlement by a licentious soldiery' (Gluckmann 1922: 4). Khama's regiment looted, raped, burned down Birwa homes, and drove them on a six-day forced march to the reserve. Later, the Protectorate Administration publicly offered its cover-up, taking ultimate responsibility: 'Khama at the request of the Resident Commissioner agreed to invite the Mabirwa to return to the Bamangwato Reserve' (Gluckmann 1922: 4).

Remarkably, in the first of Emanuel's newspaper articles, while he held Paramount Chief Khama responsible for his despotic excesses, he took care not to belittle or vilify him, or accuse him of financial greed as a tax collector for the British and more to blame for evicting the Birwa than the British South Africa Company – a contention now raised in revisionist history (see Wylie 1990: 241; Molosiwa 2013: 154). That would not have helped his clients, or even, perhaps, occurred to Emanuel in his historical moment; after all, for a progressive public at that time in the British Empire,

the Paramount Chief was 'The Great Khama', rare among chiefs
under British rule in being allowed to have his own standing army:

> Khama is a remarkably dignified and romantic figure ... He is the
> Bismarck of South African native diplomacy in the same degree as
> Chaka was the Napoleon of its native military science ... His wonder-
> ful gifts have enabled him to withstand the encroachments of both the
> indomitable Matabele and, later, the all-conquering whites.
>
> Khama early recognised the impossibility of maintaining complete
> independence against the whites; he embraced Christianity, allowed
> missionaries to settle in his territory, and employed their influence as
> well as the thunder of English artillery in preserving his unwarlike
> tribe from the attacks of his two deadly enemies: the Boers and the
> Matabeles. (Gluckmann 1922: 4)

Dominant as Khama was in his own domain, he was a formidable political adversary. Emanuel came to learn, at serious personal
cost and with great difficulty through moments of despair, that
Khama was all the more formidable given his highly revered standing and trusted place in the Administration, and his cosy alliance
with Administration officials and with British South Africa Company
agents:

> This extraordinary man exercises a tremendous, and frequently baleful,
> influence on the Administration of the territory; I do not attack the
> rectitude of its officials, but Khama, in their eyes, can do no wrong;
> he has to be maintained as if part of the constitution. (Gluckmann
> 1922: 2)

In Khama's own eyes, Emanuel Gluckmann was an unworthy nui-
sance, not a Christian gentleman like himself. Khama harangued
Emanuel's clients at the inquiry:

> Khama had attempted to impress on them the futility of proceeding
> against him. He told them that he was a great chief, and that I could
> do him nothing, as I was only an insignificant Jew, and that he had
> no fear of the result of any action which might be taken against him.
> (Gluckmann 1922: 17)

Khama insisted he could not be sued by any subject of his. In fact,
the Birwa, led by their own chief Malema, were the first to hire

a lawyer to take a Paramount Chief to court, although others in the Protectorate 'had used South African lawyers to look after their financial interests and defend them against legal charges lodged by whites' (Morton and Ramsay 1987: 67). Even further, when the possibility of a suit in some tribunal or special court was initially being considered, Emanuel was led to believe that the 'Imperial Government would be financing Khama' (Gluckmann 1922: 10). As a Jew, Emanuel was suspected of being a money-grubber, not 'a serious advocate for oppressed subjects' (Gordon 2018: 26), and, to put him off, he was warned that he risked coming away without any costs for a trial. At one point, Emanuel was himself threatened with a personal suit for alleged slander against Captain G. E. Nettleton, the Resident Magistrate in Khama's capital, Serowe, later the Government Secretary and second highest official in Bechuanaland.

Such threats and allegations were not to budge Emanuel. He had an adversarial streak, as did his son Max after him, being all the more dedicated to his cause when he felt his honour and manhood under attack. Yet Emanuel also recorded his vulnerability, his feeling that 'my confidence in the justice and impartiality of the Administration had been greatly shaken by that allegation' (Gluckmann 1922: 11). He reluctantly had to realize that the game was getting dirty, and was not going to be played by the rules: 'officialdom was prejudiced' against him; red herrings were being thrown in the way of his investigation; the Resident Commissioner was 'casting an accusation against my honour as practitioner and my veracity as a man' (Gluckmann 1922: 12). Eventually, Emanuel was completely blocked, after a series of manoeuvres in bad faith by Administration officials in the face of his offers to negotiate, to seek a reasonable settlement out of court or to have an advocate head an impartial tribunal. With obvious cunning, Sir Herbert, the Special Commissioner, tried to persuade Emanuel to become merely an adviser, a whisperer without professional standing in the inquiry and thus subject to punishment if he interfered to speak out or cross-examine on behalf of his clients. When Sir Herbert abruptly refused to allow Emanuel to represent the Birwa as their attorney, he left the inquiry and boycotted the proceedings, lest he appear to acquiesce in a travesty, a mockery of a trial. He had become aware that the dislocated Birwa were treated like slaves and starving in

their new village within the tribal reserve; before he left Bechuanaland, he had a message sent to them:

> all such as were hungry should come to my cattle post and I shall feed
> them for so long as I shall be able; I am sending them periodical sup-
> plies of grain out of my pocket; I have given instructions to my
> representative at Palapye to slaughter my cattle and distribute the meat
> among the sufferers. (Gluckmann 1922: 20)

In his first article, Emanuel offered his understanding of how
and why the British South Africa Company had got a Concession
on land apparently belonging to Paramount Chief Khama:

> I understand that, in order the better to prevent the depredations of
> the Boers across the Limpopo into Bechuanaland, Khama agreed to
> transfer a strip of land along that river to the British South Africa
> Company, several miles in width, known as Tuli Block, and, although
> ... the property of the British South Africa Company, it is governed
> by the Administration of the Bechuanaland Protectorate. (Gluckman
> 1922: 4)

Emanuel's understanding was received wisdom at the time, the official version held for practical purposes by the Administration and
in dealings with its officials. But it is an understanding that he
himself came to doubt, in the light of his further research on the
legal history of land tenure, which he reported in the last articles
of *The Tragedy* (Gluckmann 1922: 29; for Khama's land negotiations
in London during his visit to Queen Victoria and the consequences,
see Molosiwa 2013: 113–74).

Dubious, a land-grab – that is my own understanding of this
British South Africa Company concession for the Tuli Block. The
details are intricate. Below I quote Emanuel Gluckmann's report at
length to show how dealing with the Birwa dislocation called for
an appreciation of its entanglement in imperial geopolitics. Apparently, Emanuel himself reached this view fully in the critique he
wrote only after he was blocked from representing the Birwa as
their attorney, at the Commission of Inquiry headed by the Special
Commissioner, Sir Herbert Sloley.

In the following account I offer a broad view of the early
history, including Emanuel's evidence, to clarify what moved the

people themselves to resistance. In the pre-colonial and early colonial period, the little communities of an ambiguous, ill-defined area,
now roughly western Zimbabwe and eastern Botswana, had constituted a shatter zone; in it, the more or less independent peoples
and their polities or petty chiefdoms, many being outlying tributar-
ies of more ancient states in disarray, were sometimes on the move
or in forced migration between the currently bigger states, Tswana
and Ndebele; these more centralized tributary kingdoms, based on
great capital towns, competed for expansion, for the petty chiefdoms' tribute or uncertain loyalties, often in raids, even in longer
wars. In that context, the actual extent of the Tswana state under
Khama was ill-defined at its frontiers in relation to outlying communities or chiefdoms; not only did Khama not hold a compact
territory, but what land he did hold he had no power to alienate
forever as freehold. With the declaration of the Bechuanaland Protectorate came bounded territory for Khama's state as a recognized
tribe, and along with that his drive to consolidate his power and
authority over outlying communities through special governors.
When the Company gained its provisional hold over the buffer
strip, it was for a railway line, not a freehold property or an enclave
for white settlers only. Emanuel reported this history of colonial
tenure and limited Company ownership as well as tribal affiliation
to a chief:

> In 1895, the shadow of impending war was straining the relations
> between England and the Transvaal Republic, and the Imperial Gov-
> ernment considered it advisable to obtain from Khama and the other
> Bechuanaland Chiefs, then on a visit in London, a cession of a strip
> of country between the Limpopo and the Protectorate. Tuli Block
> was thus ceded not to the Company, as contended by Sir Herbert
> [the Special Commissioner], but to the Crown. The district was then
> largely no-man's land, but the Bechuanaland Chiefs had a number of
> cattle-posts strung between Palla to Tuli, and those they undertook
> to recall to their own side of the line as soon as the boundaries would
> be marked off. The raison d'etre for the corridor passed with the
> conquest of the Republic, Tuli Block became an Imperial Reserve,
> and such it remained until it was transferred to the Company by the
> High Commissioner's Proclamation, No. 13, promulgated in the
> Bechuanaland Protectorate on the 30th June, 1905. In its preamble
> the Proclamation asserts that the lands in question are vested in the

High Commissioner, and only a limited ownership is transferred by the enactment to the Company; special provision is made in Section 9 that compensation should be paid for land improved by cultivation, which Section, according to the officials of the Company and the Protectorate, cannot be held to apply to my clients, for no suggestion of compensation has ever been made for the loss of the lands wrested by them from the wilderness. In 1907 the Company decided to allot the district into farms and Khama was called on to carry out his undertaking. That he did by removing his cattle posts, thereby discharging all his contractual obligations under the agreement of 1895. The significant facts that the Ababirwas were left undisturbed in 1907 and that, undoubtedly, the district was ceded to the Company not by any imaginary agreement of 1895 but by the Proclamation of 1905, in my opinion, cast the gravest doubts on the correctness of Sir Herbert's decision and on the purity of the sources from which he derived his Information...

In his decision on the suppositious agreement of 1895, Sir Herbert successfully begs the question whether the Ababirwas were Khama's to move at all.

My clients, for some reason, were not examined on the question of the chieftain to whom they owed their fealty, and the only evidence in the record on that point is to be found in Khama's address to the Court, where the Chief, who was neither sworn nor cross-examined, maintained that the Ababirwas, already in his grandfather's time, paid tribute and received the treatment of slaves. It never occurred to Sir Herbert that, in an ordinary Court of Law, such evidence would not have been deemed sufficient to decide the ownership of a dog, let alone of a thousand human beings. (Gluckmann 1922: 2)

Throughout *The Tragedy* Emanuel took care to introduce his readers to the roiling Protectorate movements, tribal and commercial, to crucial facts of popular resistance, and to the salient broad issues in law, including matters of jurisdiction for a fair trial in the cause of the Birwa. His account gives rare insights into the shifting, almost tortuous predicaments of negotiating for equity with a problematic, even divided, Administration. If legally not that of a colony but of a Protectorate within the British Dominions, it was an Administration itself on the cusp of a transition with regard to the relative advancement of tribal and settler interests. Emanuel showed how he had to escalate his appeal in a public campaign that mobilized international support and reached the Imperial Secretary, acting on behalf of Prince Arthur, the Governor-General of South Africa. His insider's account of professional ethics under colonialism documented a tortuous course. He had to tack back and forth in negotiations for a settlement or even an impartial tribunal; he had to make serious efforts to put together a whole team of experts and interpreters along with his law firm, to work out the logistics in a complex investigation, to conduct his own fieldwork with interviews of local witnesses in their home communities, displaying a sophisticated political consciousness. Emanuel's vision, which his work reveals for us as it must have for Max, perceives the interconnection of local and wider colonial forces, and it illuminates his political and legal struggle as it spread across a social field, reaching from apparently a mere tribal encounter to authorities at the heart of the British Empire. If we still have much to learn from Emanuel's story – even beyond its significance for Max's commitments and intellectual history, his grounding in actual case work reaching well beyond mere trials – it is in good measure because *The Tragedy* is not a story of success but rather of failure – the suffering subjects, the Birwa, do not overcome their obstacles, nor does their champion, Emanuel Gluckmann. By the end of the 1920s many Birwa households were impoverished; even those formerly holding herds of cattle remained too poor to sustain the social exchanges upon which they had depended before the dislocation (Molosiwa 2013: 152–4). Emanuel himself admitted to offering 'the sight of one man fighting against overwhelming odds' and it was 'not likely to gain an access in more clients to my practice' (Gluckmann 1922: 34). His is a story of being thwarted, of coming up against overpowering, inequitable forces and having to learn from defeat, without giving up hope for a better future, beyond troubled times. Addressing the wider jury of public opinion, he concluded:

> I wish to conclude with the expression of hope that you, my readers, will believe that I have drawn up this report with all honesty; I give you my assurance that I have made no attempt to suppress any fact of importance, nor to exaggerate any enormity discovered, nor did I strive after effect. The occasion is far too solemn and serious, the step I have taken too full of risk. I wish you to bear in mind that these horrors are being perpetrated at the very threshold of the Union; that the High Commissioner of South Africa is also the Governor-General of the Union; that Khama's men may be sowing a harvest which we

or our children may be called upon to reap; that it behoves us as freemen, as the dominant race of the sub-continent, in whose land the humblest can be certain to obtain a fair hearing and an impartial trial, to extend a helping hand to those dumb, helpless slaves [the dispossessed Birwa], and to insist that their case should be tried by an impartial tribunal. That is all I ask. I cannot ask less. I expect every reader who has some pride in being a South African, who can feel some pity tor those unfortunates, to write to the High Commissioner and join in my demand for a fair trial. Should the public of the Union fail to take notice of my appeal, a share of the blame must inevitably attach to them who have the remedy in their hands and refuse to exercise it. (Gluckmann 1922: 32)

Emanuel's act of putting his failure on record laid down a marker for future generations, rethinking their past and reshaping struggles in the present, as shown in recent work by Botswana's social historians on state formation and the colonial to postcolonial transformations (see Makgala 2001, 2004; Molosiwa 2013).

Reading *The Tragedy* now, with its analytic, step-by step reasoning, the cogency of an advocate's brief, brings to mind Max Gluckman's 'Bridge' essay on the social situation in modern Zululand (Gluckman 1940a). If admittedly an advocate's appeal through the press to a wider public for equity and moral conscience – his 'intent was to pillory the whole scandal in the eyes of the civilised world' (Gluckmann 1922: 17) – Emanuel's essay reads like a precursor in method, presenting an extended case: a carefully documented historical sequence of events in a whole social process, starting in the Bechuanaland Protectorate but extending well beyond it. Moreover, it was not simply a critique of chiefly despotism; Emanuel was explicit that broader imperial issues were being raised about the very nature of government under the Administration in the Protectorate – the government itself was under trial. Where the English flag flew, there the rule of law had to prevail:

I have come to the conclusion that the officials of the Administration are labouring under a great error. It is not Khama who is the autocrat of Bechuanaland, but King George V. By the Order in Council of 1891, Queen Victoria assumed for herself and her descendants the absolute rule and the responsibility for good government of the Bechuanaland Protectorate, and the chiefs of that territory were reduced to the level of petty feudatories. By retaining that principle in theory, but reversing it in practice, we run the risk of besmirching the fair fame of England and its Sovereign. (Gluckmann 1922: 33)

We might translate his anglophile, ironic argument from the imperial context into the nowadays familiar terms of 'citizen vs. subject': the system of government is toxic, inhumane, where the people are merely subjects without the rights of citizens. Even beyond that, he warned that as well as being toxic for the people of the Protectorate, it was toxic for South Africans in an imperial dominion under the Governor-General, Prince Arthur, who was also the High Commissioner for the Protectorate. In Emanuel's acceptance of imperial dominions, his commitment was to the fight for the public interest in citizens' rights against the despotic abuse of power. Seen from the twenty-first-century perspective of one of Botswana's revisionist social historians, Emanuel Gluckmann was 'a human rights lawyer' (Molosiwa 2013: 148). Frank on failure, the voice expressed in *The Tragedy*, that of the liberal, anglophile cosmopolitan, spoke to a horizon of hope and humanity in the quest for justice. If practice had won out against principle, the struggle had to go on for the rule of law and good government.

Learning with failure and the forensic disposition

But what was this lesson of failure for Max Gluckman himself? In Gordon's biography, what is most remarkable, at least in the light of Gluckman's well-known achievements by the end of his eminent career, is the biography's intimate account of his having to learn and rethink, often, from the experience of being himself vulnerable, forced into unpredictable failure and having the knowledge of success as something incomplete, almost undone. The hardest thing he had to learn from undergoing extensive psychoanalysis was how to manage his terrible rage, his sense of being frustrated. He died at work trying, unsuccessfully, to complete his path-breaking analysis from his first fieldwork on modern politics in Zululand by tracing that back to the rise of the Zulu state and the conflicted nature of its founding and complex tyrant, Shaka.

I am tempted to say that Gluckman brought to anthropology a forensic disposition, like his father's. It was distinctive in its fascination with the strange in the familiar, or perhaps the converse, the familiar in the strange. It was forensic in being motivated to examine the evidence for an argument, determined to take apart the case as already given, and to be persuasive of the real weight of the case, fairly, on balance. It was Gluckman's forensic disposition that informed his seminars, first for the Rhodes-Livingstone Institute and later for the Manchester department. At their very best, they became challengingly vital in analysis and re-analysis; if they opened in some undoing, even destructive attack, they then turned, often through Gluckman's feel for the holistic fit of key bits of ethnography, to his and other participants discovering, almost surgically, how to put the argument freshly and surprisingly together again. In my view, and I will give my grounds later in Chapter 2, this forensic disposition enabled him to practise and to theorize within a turn to interpretive anthropology, a move commonly taken to be far outside his usual definition of social anthropology as a discipline.

It is family legend that Emanuel Gluckmann used to recite Shakespeare's verse and speeches while shaving. Besides the forensic motive, he seems to have passed on to his son Max the leaning to be an anglophile, a cosmopolitan. For Max, this meant the aspiration to cross boundaries that divided people at the time of the colour bar, and, when it came to anthropology, to reach what appeared to be the greatest centre of the English academic world. In preparation for that, to win a Rhodes scholarship, he worked with great energy to make himself the kind of 'all-rounder' who excelled in highly admired sports as much as in academic brilliance.

At first intent on following in his father's footsteps, Max himself initially studied law as an undergraduate at Witwatersrand University, worked in his father's law office and attended on him at court. But then he turned to anthropology, in which his first guru was Agnes Winifred Hoernle, often praised as 'the mother of anthropology in South Africa'. Much admired and seriously acknowledged by Gluckman, Hoernle was notable for at least two things of great importance for his own thought: first, her political opposition to segregation, and second her strong academic advocacy of A. R. Radcliffe-Brown's view of the one social system in South Africa and his view of the need to study the interrelations between events, a view of process theory which I discuss in depth later, in Chapter

2.[7] A key idea of Gluckman's, about protest and the licence in ritual, he recalled, was planted in his mind by Hoernle in 1931, 'when we were trying to understand the ceremonies which Zulu women performed to their goddess Namkubulwana' (Gluckman 1956a: vii). To acknowledge this, in 1955 Gluckman dedicated to Mrs Hoernle his popular comparative essays for the BBC lectures in 'Custom and Conflict in Africa', which I discuss more fully later.

Liberal radical, student editor, team leader

Meyer Fortes has crystallized in a sketch of Radcliffe-Brown's career, for his Festschrift, a turning point as it was *perceived* in the 1920s in South African academic life, and I stress *perceived* because it was put in terms that Gluckman's work later called into question: 'a "breakdown of Bantu tribal life"'. This turning point is one that mattered greatly for the direction that Gluckman's early studies took and the long-term impact of his formative years. To contextualize this development, I quote Fortes at length:

> In 1920 an important development in South African university education, then entering a period of rapid expansion, took place. This was the establishment, at the University of Cape Town, of a Chair of Social Anthropology as the nucleus of a School of African Life and Languages. Until then there had been no provision in the young universities of South Africa for the study of the native races of the country. Yet difficult and urgent economic and social problems were arising as a result of the breakdown of Bantu tribal life and of the increasing flow of Africans into the towns and industrial areas. Leading personalities in the academic world and in political circles had been pressing for the dispassionate study of these problems, and the Chair at Cape Town was the first step in this direction. Radcliffe-Brown's appointment to this Chair in 1921 was widely acclaimed in South Africa.
>
> Five very busy years followed. First there was the task of building up the School of African Life and Languages. Radcliffe-Brown's skill as a teacher soon attracted large undergraduate audiences, and his wide scholarship and integrity quickly won him a leading position among the staff. But there was also the more formidable task of making the educated public understand the significance of anthropological studies for South Africa. This was necessary to gain the support, and more particularly, the funds for the research plans Radcliffe-Brown

had prepared. But it was also in part a personal crusade. Ever since his student days Radcliffe-Brown has held unwaveringly to the belief that the only road to the solution of the ills of human society is the long and arduous one of first building up the scientific knowledge upon which effective remedies can be based with some hope of success. This was the theme of all his extra-mural activities. He wrote for the press, gave public lectures, addressed many conferences of bodies concerned with education and social welfare, and, most successful of all, organized vacation courses in applied anthropology. (Fortes 1949b: x)

In 1926 Radcliffe-Brown left for Australia to hold a new chair of social anthropology at Sydney, when he was 'frustrated, through lack of funds, in his plans to develop extensive field research in South Africa', and eventually moved to Oxford for another new chair in social anthropology in 1937 (Fortes 1949b: xi). His influence continued to be felt in the University of Witwatersrand, 'where Mrs. A. W. Hoernle, who shared his point of view in theory and method, initiated the teaching of anthropology' (Fortes 1949b: xi).

Although Gluckman was not himself a student of Radcliffe-Brown's, he entered into an emerging social anthropology for which Radcliffe-Brown was a pioneering influence for a socially responsible discipline led by a public intellectual. In early 1934 the official mouthpiece of the National Union of South African Students, the *NUSAS*, gave a profile of Gluckman as a liberal radical which prefigures the man whom the members of the Manchester School came to know, and it also discloses the recognition he won, which must have heightened his sense of self-esteem. Perhaps it did so dangerously, later inviting not only the criticism that he was arrogant, full of himself, but also, of course, many (English) belittling efforts to 'put him in his place'.

The *NUSAS* profile says this: 'Max Gluckman came to the University of the Witwatersrand in 1928 from King Edward XII School, devoted himself chiefly to the study of primitive cultures and in 1931 graduated Bachelor of Arts with distinction in Social Anthropology and honours in Philosophy. Since then he has been engaged in an intensive study of the Bantu peoples.' During his academic career he spread his immense energy over a great variety of activities. For years he was chief editor, contributor and often chief reader of the numerous magazines, newspapers and reviews that issued from the University of the Witwatersrand. He was chairman of the Philosophical Society and of the Bantu Studies Society, and in 1933 secretary of the SRC. In addition he was an active member of the Dramatic Society, displaying an unusual aptitude for character parts in ancient Indian drama (Gordon 2018: 38, citing the *NUSAS*, 3 June 1934, 70–1).[8] A member of the Dramatic Society for life, I suggest: Max's gift for dramatizing himself and his part in events became all the more remarkable, and we will see that his capacity to project in the media – especially in broadcasts – a distinctive voice of his own did matter greatly for his growth and presence as a public intellectual concerned with human problems. Notice, also, that from the very start of his academic career, Gluckman was a tireless, hugely accomplished editor. Commentators on the history of the Manchester School have said all too little about the force of his editing in the making of the School. And I confess my own 1984 account in the *Annual Review of Anthropology* suffers from this fault.

The point is simply this. Every member of the early Manchester School, all who worked under Gluckman at the Rhodes-Livingstone Institute and then published with Manchester University Press, owed a big debt to his editing. Their grateful acknowledgements of this debt open their monographs, each in a branded series with its classy gold imprint boldly embossed on its green covers. The house style was unmistakable. Gluckman's skill in editing enabled him to raise a very substantial body of monographs to the highest standards of his discipline at the time. The Manchester School was profoundly schooled in his editing. Even more broadly, Gluckman made Manchester University Press the world leader in the publication of social science research on Central Africa. All of this gives a strong impression of the force Gluckman exercised in the social sciences through his finely cultivated orchestration of a major scholarly enterprise which yielded the timely publication of a whole body of related research.

As for other youthful characteristics, two more are perhaps most striking for his later leadership in what became a distinctive team of highly self-assertive, proudly individualistic social anthropologists. The first is his outspoken political activism, and the second is his reported team leadership and sportsmanship. According to the National Union of South African Students:

> His active association with the NUSAS began in 1933, when he was a member of the 'Cabinet' in the Durban (student) Parliament. He is now Secretary of the Bantu Studies Department and Leader of the Liberal Party in the NUSAS Parliament. (Gordon 2018: 38, citing the *NUSAS*, 3 June 1934, 70–1)

Gluckman became editor of the Witwatersrand University student newspaper *WU Views* and took over the Bantu Study Circle/Club. Gordon reports that Gluckman's often strident liberalism is obvious in many of his editorials. For example, one entitled 'Preposterous Petitions' takes aim at the numerous petitions circulating at the University of Pretoria and especially one protesting the use of black demonstrators in Bantu languages which he dismissed for 'its prejudice and intolerance as well as the foolishness', since 'a university should be unconscious of class, colour or creed: it is immanent in the word itself' (Gordon 2018: 38, quoting *WU Views*, 18 April 1932). His editorial on the report of the Native Economic Commission titled 'Mental, Moral and Physical Deserts' (*WU Views*, 3 June 1932) highlighted the appalling poverty of the Reserves and suggested that black education would allow both black and white wages to rise and thus generate economic security for all. Gluckman concluded that the situation called for tolerance, mutual understanding and education of both black and white public opinion, and intergovernmental cooperation; he ended: 'Let us set our own house in order and stop worrying about the ultimate effect on our children in hundreds of years to come; as Professor MacMillan says they will thank us more for that' (Gordon 2018: 38).

On Gluckman's team leadership and sportsmanship, the *NUSAS* profile reports:

> As a sportsman Mr Gluckman excels at golf and cricket and in both these games he has frequently represented his University. For many years, too, he has played for the University's Soccer first XI, and from 1931 has captained the team. He is also a keen yachtsman. Mr Gluckman has always taken an active interest in the Scout Movement in Johannesburg. At present he is District Pathfinder Master. (Gordon 2018: 38).

It is perhaps not surprising that as a research project head, Max continued to be something of a District Pathfinder Master, getting all the 'scouts' hiking together or enthused on an outing, say at a football match, especially Manchester United playing at home. His commitment to creating teams continually turned back-and-forth between sport and science, with a passion for promoting his own great 'stars', for whom he claimed outstanding individuality.

Notes

1 Let the reader beware, however. Gordon's biography carries a toxic Introduction. It is a travesty by the series editors, whose agenda has the unmistakable, belittling intent of turning the nuances and freshness of the biography into stale and misleading stereotypes about 'rule-bound structural functionalism', 'patriarchal authority', the 'fostering [of] sibling rivalry among his quasi-children' and demands for 'acquiescence in dogma' (Darnell and Murray 2018: ix–xi).

2 This is what Gluckman as my PhD supervisor wrote to my mother, when I was on my way to Southern Rhodesia for my first fieldwork in 1960: 'I am sending your son to my best student, Clyde Mitchell.' Clyde did become my fieldwork supervisor and remained not only my own lifelong friend but also the devoted and persistent mentor of research on networks by my wife Pnina. Clyde took much pride in his South African working-class roots and was a master chef of his home delicacy, the savoury boerwurst.

3 The everyday, which is foregrounded in current debate, was much stressed by Gluckman, using his notion of 'custom': 'therefore the first, and the most prolific source of Lozi legal rulings is *custom*, defined in the everyday sense of "usual practice", though it too has an ethical value, that it ought to be followed' (Gluckman 1955: 236).

4 Gluckman's universalist view found strong backing in Meyer Fortes's memorial tribute, which concludes: 'Gluckman's position that there are general principles that underlie all types of forensic institutions, regardless of variations in the form of political systems, is, in my opinion, by now vindicated beyond contradiction' (Fortes 1987: 144).

5 I am tempted to say that there is a twist, from Evans-Pritchard's *Witchcraft, Oracles and Magic* to Gluckman's *Judicial Process*. Whereas Evans-Pritchard *demonstrates* that, like us, Azande are not intellectuals, as intellectuals would claim to be, in their everyday lives, Gluckman *conveys* that as intellectuals, Lozi are as intellectual as we are. In 'Divination's Grasp', my account of cases of séances demonstrates with Evans-Pritchard and conveys with Gluckman (Werbner 2015).

6 For a rethinking of Gluckman's approach to the legal realists and their importance for his interest in process and the bearing of ethics and morality on legal decision-making, see P. Werbner (2014).

7 They were both critical, also, of what might be called 'culturalist' accounts which matched one culture to one society, gave culture precedence over social relations, and provided an ideology for segregation – whites with their culture, Africans with theirs. Agnes Hoernle herself acknowledged that her most important inspiration came from Durkheim and Radcliffe-Brown (see Gordon 2018: 33; Bank 2016).

8 Making the most of his 'dramatic voice', Gluckman gave radio talks, first while at the Rhodes-Livingstone Institute and later on the BBC in the 1950s, when he won the reputation of being 'the radio anthropologist'.

2

Max Gluckman's commitments, projects and legacies

For Gluckman, fame came at the height of his career from success as a sociologist of conflict, especially conflict endemic with collaboration or cooperation, and as a methodologist, most notably in publicizing the development by others of an extended case method. In my view, such fame came at a price. Too little has been said about the importance for his vision of social anthropology that at least two projects – one comparative, the other scientific and historical – had from the very beginning of his career and to which he returned throughout his academic life. I start with the comparative project, which is all the more salient given the renewed regard for alternative modes of comparison in anthropology, after a period of doubt, even dismissal, of the utility of certain modes as naively empirical or positivist (Englund and Yarrow 2013; Candea 2019).

Gluckman built his comparative project on considerable ethnographic scholarship, initially for regional comparison, then for very different modes of comparison, each to suit the problems and questions he raised. To this project he devoted huge efforts in time and energy, first to command nineteenth-century sources – travellers, missionaries, officials – then to keep his scholarship up to date through very wide-ranging, in-depth knowledge of the best ethnographies, primarily though not exclusively from Africa and on what he called 'tribal societies'.

At the start, in regional comparison, came library research on ritual: Gluckman's huge, two-volume DPhil dissertation on 'The Realm of the Supernatural among the South-Eastern Bantu' (1936). It offered many social correlations, such as for the organization of rituals at physical puberty according to the existence of age-sets. In a part, published in 1935 before the dissertation, on Zulu women in hoecultural ritual, it examined comparative issues of gender (Gluckman 1935) and took account of Gregory Bateson's early work on Sepik transvestism in Melanesia (Bateson 1935). Governance and variables linked to authority in ritual were surveyed across a culture area: 'The Bantu chief is not usually – Tshaka's excess being a mere aberration – a despot. The information we have goes to show that he acts much more as an interpreter of the general will of the people' (Gluckman 1936: 21).

Next in Gluckman's comparative project came his work on kinship and marriage over several years from the very early 1940s, including an ambitious plan for a book, 'A Comparative Study of the Instability of Lozi Marriage', which remained incomplete and unpublished (for an account from archived documents, see Gordon 2018: 253–6), but part of which did appear as 'Kinship and Marriage among the Lozi of Northern Rhodesia and the Zulu of Natal' (Gluckman 1950). In the initial plan for the book, Gluckman 'constructed a Weberian ideal-type continuum based on some fifteen points in which Lozi marriage and family rules differed from those of the Nuer and Zulu' (Gordon 2018: 252). Here his approach to comparison in modern social anthropology started from cases with substantial, up-to-date ethnography, his own and Evans-Pritchard's.

The idea that Gluckman foregrounded in his ambitious plan for the post-war Rhodes-Livingstone Institute (henceforth RLI) was itself comparative (Gluckman 1945b). It carried forward with a research method of systematic variation the interest that Godfrey Wilson, his predecessor as RLI director, had advanced to study the impact of labour migration and industrialization across South-Central Africa. In his own director's report for 1944/45/46, Gluckman assessed the RLI's achievement of these aims:

1   The systematic analysis of social problems;
2   The development of a reference library; and
3   The stimulation of general public interest in social problems in British Central Africa and in sociological research (Gluckman 1948: 64).

In the Seven-Year Plan, Gluckman argued, 'it is industrialisation with labour migration which dominates the whole trend of social development' (Gluckman 1945a: 7).[1] The areas to be examined were to be selected, primarily, according to the different ways 'they have been absorbed in our economy' in a world system, 'to enable us to gauge the general effects of modern conditions' (Gluckman 1946: 46). A comparative volume was planned, to offer systematic propositions in the light of the specific studies across the region; this plan was never fulfilled in one publication, but resonated through much RLI research.

There is a characteristic touch of irony in the article 'Human Laboratory across the Zambesi', which Gluckman wrote for the South African magazine *Libertas* to reach a popular audience with an appreciation of the RLI's forthcoming major initiative in social science research: 'to give us a general idea of social developments in the region' (1946: 39). The irony is that it was not a laboratory in the scientific sense familiar to his readers:

> Sociologists cannot work in laboratories in which they can isolate the factors they wish to observe. We have to arrive at our conclusions by comparing societies in which some factors are the same and some factors are different, so as to present relationships between them. (Gluckman 1946: 46)[2]

Aware that his readers, perhaps dazzled by the accompanying photographs of mainly exotic scenes, might fall back on their stereotypes of isolated tribes, Gluckman took care to make two things about his comparative approach clear from the very start. First, that although the plan was for research in African rural areas and among Africans in town, 'We realise full well that Europeans, Indians and Africans are all members of a single community. They affect each other's lives at every point' (Gluckman 1946: 39). Second, the comparison starts from a recognition of historic similarity, not difference: that labour migration is not a peculiarly African phenomenon: 'At the beginning of the industrial revolution in Britain a similar *process* occurred' (1946: 39, italics mine). I stress process to highlight the grounding of comparison not in society as such but in a robust regard for social process as it is transformative in integrated social relations. Finally, to drive his point home, for integrated comparative analysis, he concluded:

> For since Europeans and Africans in Central Africa form a single society, in studying the modern African we also study our fellow citizen, the European. Our studies hope to provide *all* sections of the

community with scientific analyses of social problems affecting them, and such analyses must be available for sound development. (Gluckman 1946: 49, italics mine)

I stress *all* in order to direct attention to the hope of being part of a public conversation with everyone affected by the social problems studied; all alike have to have access to scientific analyses for development to be sound. It is a democratic, inclusive premise that informs this plan for social science research. It is not a plan for the study of alterity or the Other.

This article was one of a pair of richly illustrated photographic essays – below I discuss the other, 'Zambesi River Kingdom' (1945) – in which Gluckman popularized for a South African public the findings from his own research in Barotseland, introduced social science arguments about human problems in what was then Northern Rhodesia, and offered policy suggestions for economic and political development. If an exemplary piece of, in our terms, visual anthropology, it was the work of a public intellectual sharing in a discourse about modern issues, with a feel for the past in the present and an eye to the emerging future in Africa, well beyond South Africa. Focusing attention on contemporary realities, he spoke to a promising horizon; this was all in that post-war period, which historians now characterize as the End of Empire.

The importance of following the interest in kinship, in Gluckman's planning of research, needs to be foregrounded, to get his comparative perspective right. In 1947 his intent was to have each member of the RLI:

> first write an account of kinship organization *in relation to villages and neighbourhoods*, as well as an essay on some subject in which he is especially interested. When the team returns to the field in September in 1948, I shall suggest that each officer makes a survey of kinship and local organization in an untouched area and presents a brief report on it. On the basis of detailed studies and these surveys, and other published material, I shall make an initial *comparative* analysis of this subject for Central Africa. A study of this kind has both great theoretical and practical administrative importance. (Gluckman 1948: 71, italics mine)

I stress *in relation to villages and neighbourhoods* to put into relief the analytic interest not in individual societies or 'tribes' but in the interrelation between kinship and local organization, according to a typology to emerge through the analysis. It might be argued that, initially at least, there was an underlying assumption of part-to-whole relations, but eventually the attention to mobility and fluid village membership, as in Colson's studies of Tonga, subverted such an assumption (see Chapter 3).

The next major step in his comparative project appeared in 1951, in the RLI essays that formed the core of *Seven Tribes of British Central Africa*, edited by Elizabeth Colson and Max Gluckman. It was meant to be comparative, but even in the eyes of the contributors it fell short of the intended mark. At least two things are striking. First, *Seven Tribes* had no Introduction, for which the editors apologized, on various grounds. Most importantly, it was not yet a coherent collection, and not yet the clear product of one research team or one collaborative effort in modern social anthropology. Somewhat awkwardly included were old and new articles, the work of contributors dead and alive, some not at all from Gluckman's RLI team and with very different agendas. Only in retrospect can we see the seeds of the Manchester School-to-be.

The second thing, perhaps no less noteworthy, is the pale, beyond which stood an outsider with a critical eye. This outsider was Mary Douglas, whose own research was in the Congo, beyond British Central Africa. If an outsider to the RLI and the would-be School, Douglas was an establishment figure, who married a prominent Conservative Party economist in 1951. She was the consummate insider when it came to the Oxford Institute and the immediate students of Evans-Pritchard. By contrast, the unorthodox interlopers and assertively self-positioning outsiders were in the RLI team around Gluckman. After their fieldwork, he had them brought to Oxford, given the failure of the Northern Rhodesian government to house them in Livingstone as it had hoped. Gluckman considered that they 'should be able to write their researches better at a university than in the heat and isolation of Livingstone' (Gluckman 1948: 71).

At Oxford, a war broke out, with some semblance of the acrimonious battles in the natural sciences over who published whose results first and with what permission, especially at a time of doctoral work in progress, with claims to originality. One salvo came in 1950, when the then Mary Tew, later Douglas, published her

ethnographic survey, *The Peoples of the Lake Nyasa Region*. Gluckman, as Clyde Mitchell's Oxford supervisor, complained to the
ethnographic survey editor about too much pre-publication by Tew
of Mitchell's results. In 1952 in the journal *Africa*, and with characteristically deft cut and thrust, especially on delays in scholarship,
Douglas (1952) reviewed *Seven Tribes*; and then immediately, again
in *Africa*, Elizabeth Colson and Max Gluckman (1952) counter-
attacked, blow for scholarly blow.

In following years, Douglas contributed something well needed
to the growth of the Manchester School, but as a combative critic
or counter-hero. Almost a prosecutor or unavoidable nemesis,
Douglas praised or damned in subsequent reviews monograph after
monograph of the Manchester School. What is more, one might
say with tongue in cheek that Mary Douglas was 'The Mother of
the School' because she was the first to recognize it, and 'salute' a
new school with 'a common stock of problems'. She left no doubt
that when it came to conflict studies her own sympathy lay elsewhere, though she highly praised the School's extended case studies,
and above all Clyde Mitchell's statistical analyses and his Yao ethnography. In one landmark review article, Douglas discerned Victor
Turner's shift from 'the old style cultural anthropologist':

> His special originality is to have come close enough to the field of
> action to show how meanings arise spontaneously in the minds of
> people, then are polished up and brought out to express great public
> occasions. Layer after layer of meaning accrues to each symbol as its
> application is extended. At each context a social consensus isolates a
> particular sense. (Douglas 1970: 304)

Some opinions by Douglas had Gluckman muttering, 'Mary looks
at nothing but she squints.' And you may consult Richard Fardon's
biography for her thoughts on Gluckman being 'an unattractive and
domineering personality' (1999: 51).

After taking up his chair at Manchester in 1949, Gluckman
advanced his comparisons well beyond any regional limits through
popular studies of custom and conflict, of politics, law and ritual
(1956, 1959). The voice that broadcasts so effectively through his
1955 BBC talks, *Custom and Conflict in Africa*, is that of an authoritative spokesman for a distinctive perspective in a whole field of social
anthropology. In front of me, I have my copy of *Custom and Conflict*

in Africa, and I ask the reader's indulgence to appreciate that the dedication on Max's gift moves me, even now, to be in its spirit:

Dick,
I hope that you find these ideas useful, as I am sure you will proceed far beyond them –
Affectionately,
Max 25/6/62

In *Custom and Conflict*, Gluckman the public intellectual is addressing highly topical issues; he *interprets* with a flair for literary resonance, and his approach is not merely that of the social scientist arguing for general propositions. The public intellectual is out to raise consciousness of surprising similarities, despite differences. The research is on problems studied in Africa, but of importance in societies 'all over the world' (Gluckman 1956a: 2). The listeners themselves are understood to be a broad yet sophisticated public. Gluckman speaks as at one with the Third Programme audience accustomed to T. S. Eliot, and thus open to being hooked by an introduction claiming agreement with Eliot's famous *Notes Toward a Definition of Culture*. If always the sociologist, Gluckman takes us with Eliot to foreground the poetics, or at least a critical perception of human creativity in and through conflict. Conflict, as seen by Eliot, is positive and even profitable for society. Eliot's idea is that the more the conflicting loyalties 'the better: so that everyone should be an ally of everyone else in some respects, and an opponent in several others, and no one conflict, envy or fear will predominate' (Eliot, *Notes Toward a Definition of Culture*, cited without reference in Gluckman 1956a: 2).

From the very start Gluckman put his own grasp of this idea boldly, and clarified its centrality in a coherent model of an ongoing, indeed customary, social process of conflict, while he prepared the listener for his continuous unpacking of the argument through each of his six lectures in turn. If his introduction hooks us, carrying us from the familiar English poetics to the unfamiliar problems of Africa, we are then captivated by his delight in paradoxes for his lecture titles. Sixty years later, these are still provocative, signalling open arguments: 'The Peace in the Feud', 'The Frailty in Authority', 'Estrangement in the Family', 'The Logic in Witchcraft', 'The Licence in Ritual', 'The Bonds in the Colour Bar'. These lectures are the *tour de force* that distilled the essence of recent research by Gluckman himself and his old RLI colleagues, in particular Colson, Mitchell, Barnes, Epstein and Holleman. Even more creatively, as the spokesman for this distillation, strong in ideas with ethnographic evidence, Gluckman brought that essence together in a synthesis with some of the best modern research in Africa by other social anthropologists. He was refining his concepts in the course of elucidating the ethnographic evidence.

In other words, if Gluckman, the School founder, seized the opportunity offered by the BBC lecture series to introduce his colleagues' contributions accessibly on the widest public stage, he also took care to build certain bridges. His was not a pitch for a School as such, but for an approach to a common stock of problems and to much work still in progress in the social sciences. Ongoing argument was of the essence, along with broad comparison.

Morphology, relating forms or types in a whole conceptual framework of variations, fascinated Gluckman, so much that he came back to its construction, in one way after another, throughout his comparative project. In his next popular book, partly an introductory text, *Politics, Law and Ritual in Tribal Society* (1965), he constructed a morphology of states. Some critics, such as Stanley Tambiah, took it to be an evolutionist morphology, mistakenly harking back to the evolutionary schemes of the nineteenth century, 'too diffuse to explain the particular problems that now engage anthropologists' (Tambiah 1966: 951). Against that, Gluckman defended his comparative method and its heuristic assumptions; it was not about a temporal succession. He was analysing a number of chieftaincies in Africa, and for his heuristic purposes they were represented as systematic variations, versions in a structuralist series:

> I set them out in a series, ranging from leaders with mainly symbolic functions and little secular power, to powerful kings, in order to bring out the underlying facts which affect the structures of states. Again, I do not intend to imply that the later described societies in the series have developed out of the earlier described ones, or that they have passed through each of the stages in the series. (Gluckman 1965b: 123)

Gluckman's comparative project culminated in *The Ideas in Barotse Jurisprudence* (1965), which is, of course, grounded in his own substantial fieldwork. Broadly, it extends his analysis through bold, speculative comparison to classics on ancient and feudal law and related studies in many parts of the world, not merely to Africa or on 'tribal societies'. In one of the rare assessments of the work as a peak in a comparative project, Sally Moore finds

> It is a bold attempt to relate law to society on a broad canvas, a scholarly speculation on a grand scale. He [Gluckman] plucks parallel examples from other societies here and there. His objective is to formulate generalizations from that Barotse material that will hold in other places and other times, given similar fundamental social circumstances. The extended testing of the hypotheses suggested in *The Ideas in Barotse Jurisprudence*, the detailed comparison of the legal norms, ideas and social processes of many other societies remains to be done … Gluckman's is a pioneering effort. (Moore 1978: 229–30)

The very recent return to debate about modes of comparison and their implications for reflexivity in theory is now reopening awareness of how to carry forward this pioneering effort in the light of Gluckman's approach, as Englund and Yarrow suggest (2013: 139–41). They remind us of the nub of this approach: 'Gluckman worked within a tradition of anthropology that adopted as its key interest the description of difference and specificity in human affairs, without shying away from the possibility of using universal categories in that descriptive work' (2013: 141).

The transformational project, turmoil in science and history

'Transformational' is a useful label for Gluckman's second project only if it is understood to refer to two things at once. Gluckman's transformational project was science as history, history as science; the tension between these two being creative enough to place the project at the frontiers of social anthropology as a scientific, historical discipline. His comparative project came to have this affinity with his transformational project as social *science*. Both the comparative and the transformational projects came to centre on analysed processes, movements regarded in abstractions from descriptions of complex realities. Guiding his comparisons and transformational arguments were propositions, leading to generalizations, sometimes admittedly speculative. They were meant to be open to revision and rethinking, especially in the light of fresh ethnography which the generalizations encouraged. Recognizing human problems along with the search for their resolution or betterment was fundamental; so too was the idea of scientific knowledge being cumulative, in rare moments advancing from an important breakthrough.

To understand this project of science in history, and history in science, we need to recover a sense of turmoil and disturbance in a formative moment for Gluckman's approach. We learn from a 1970s lecture at Manchester on Evans-Pritchard by Meyer Fortes that he and other young anthropologists from Malinowski's famous seminar were grappling with their awareness of openness and rethinking in contemporary science. Perhaps most important, I suggest, was the influence of disturbing controversy about quantum mechanics and field theory, about new scientific ideas on relations and events in interactive systems; they seemed to be open, dynamic and oppositional in surprising or problematic ways (see Epperson 2004: 25–60). Malinowski himself was influenced by the early modern physicist and historian of science Ernst Mach, about whom and his relational and determinist ideas on the Economy of Thought Malinowski wrote his doctoral dissertation (Thornton and Skalnik 1993: 89–116). It is doubtful that he was sympathetic or even receptive to the newly unsettled science that followed. Instead, it was Radcliffe-Brown who introduced social anthropologists, and Gluckman in particular, to the ideas on process of the mathematician and philosopher of science A. N. Whitehead.

Gordon clarifies this introduction in a richly insightful chapter on the intellectual ferment during Gluckman's period as a Rhodes Scholar at Oxford in the 1930s (Gordon 2018: 135–64). In the Whiteheadian frame, nature, or the organism, could not be thought of as simply atoms in a void, but instead was 'a structure of evolving processes ... Whitehead's work enabled both Radcliffe-Brown and Gluckman to use the organic analogy, not in the Durkheimean sense of a closed entity, but rather as a continuously emergent living process' (Gordon 2018: 138). Gluckman explicitly took up the challenge of science put by the physicist and philosopher of science Norman Campbell (1921), whose distinction between science and history highlighted *relations* between events, as in process theory. If sociology is to be scientific, Gluckman argued, it has to meet the charge Campbell put against history: 'history studies particular events ... science studies certain relations between events' (Campbell

1921: 37, cited in Gluckman 1942: 243). Taking a strong stance in line with this claim to science, Gluckman contended, 'The proof and value of my formulations must depend not only on how far they explain actual Zululand history, but also on whether scientific methods can be applied to them' (Gluckman 1942: 243).

Although much has been said about colonialism in accounts of the context for the emergence of modern social anthropology and Gluckman's contributions in particular, all too little attention has been paid to the context of its emergence in the history of science. When Gluckman began his transformational project, it was a time of troubles in science as well as in world history, facing the rise of fascism in the 1930s. There was in science at that time serious rethinking following Heisenberg's 1927 description of uncertainty relations. The disturbing problematic extended from the uncertainty in fields of relations to the objectivity or subjectivity of the observer. The phenomenon might be one; the way of knowing it demanded alternatives, more than one perspective, as Bateson's *Naven* problematized. Questions were being asked, as the philosopher-physicist Hermann Weyl put it, about how 'mathematics and physics make the world appear more and more as an open one, as a world not closed but pointing beyond itself' (Weyl 1932: [preface]). We know from Bateson's 1958 epilogue to *Naven* that before Whitehead retired from Harvard in 1937, he invited Bertrand Russell to lecture on quantum theory. Afterwards, Whitehead congratulated Russell on his brilliant exposition 'and especially on leaving ... *unobscured* ... the vast darkness of the subject' (Bateson 1958: 280, italics in original). In the philosophy of science, Whitehead's process theory had already posed radical challenges to classic views of scientific materialism; and his *Process and Reality* (1929), while widely acclaimed as pathbreaking, was arguably less understood than disturbing — it is still felt, even by metaphysicians, more as needing to be understood, than as transparent or accessible.

Process theory, the relational principle, equilibrium/disequilibrium

For his own development of process theory, Gluckman suggested terms for cultural perceptions in social change: *endoculture*, which people perceive to be their own changing custom, and *exoculture*, which they perceive to be adopted from others within the same social system (for example, converts' adoptions from missionaries) (Gluckman 1942: 246). This suggestion, intended for the analysis of a tension between interlinked processes of change but acknowledged by Gluckman to be put in awkward terms, rarely proved to be found useful or explicitly taken up.[3] Nevertheless, what is striking is the bold departure he made plain at the very start of his essay, setting forth his approach to change with process theory: 'Instead of analysing any actual changes which have occurred in Zululand, I attempt to formulate abstractly processes of social change, i.e. certain invariable relations between events in changing social systems. I illustrate these with particular examples' (Gluckman 1942: 243).

Process theory directed theoretical interest, above all, to a relational principle: *not to a single process but to the relations between processes*. I think the most highly productive, extremely influential propositions advanced by Evans-Pritchard and Fortes in their manifesto for modern social anthropology, *African Political Systems* (1940) – and much admired by Gluckman – were developments of the relational principle in process theory. To rehearse the now familiar examples: from Evans-Pritchard on processes of fission and fusion, 'The tendency of tribes and tribal sections towards fission and internal opposition between their parts is balanced by a tendency in the direction of fusion, of the combination or amalgamation of groups' (Evans-Pritchard 1940: 284); from Fortes, on the equilibrium of counter-posed dynamics, 'Every region of Tale society, from the joint family to the whole *vaguely delimited aggregate known as the Tallensi*, exhibits a dynamic equilibrium of like units balanced against one another, of counterpoised ties and cleavages, of complementary institutions and ideological notions...' (Fortes 1940: 271, italics mine).[4] Equilibrium is problematized in these propositions, which offered a way of comprehending dynamics and tendencies towards disequilibrium; and it is worth saying that they were advanced at a time when challenges were being put to equilibrium perspectives, questioning, for example, in 1930s economics, ideas of temporality in stationary models of the economy (Zappia 2001: 56).

Young pioneers: Bateson, Fortes, Evans-Pritchard

Following the clue from Fortes's lecture in the 1970s, we may see the seeds, in the 1930s turmoil about relations and process theory in contemporary science and the philosophy of science, of a good number of ideas eventually fostered in and through fieldwork by the leading young social anthropologists, members of Malinowski's seminar, pioneering contemporaries with whom Gluckman identified and began his transformational project: Bateson on schismogenesis and even on equilibrium; Fortes on social fields of clanship and kinship as a web of processes; Evans-Pritchard on fission in relation to fusion and, perhaps more for the understanding of the troubled times in world history, his idea of the secondary elaboration of belief in closed systems of thought.

In the following, I want to consider how, in developing his transformational project, Gluckman was inspired by and responded to the pioneering contributions of his contemporary young anthropologists in turn, starting with a dialogue with Bateson. In *Naven* Bateson conceptualized 'a dynamic equilibrium in which changes are continually taking place' (1958: 175); and he sought to comprehend 'processes of differentiation' and other processes 'which continually counteract this tendency towards differentiation', the latter illuminated in his broad concept of schismogenesis. Here, to get right its inspiring significance for Gluckman's contemporary turn to process theory, we need to take care to see the concept in its open, interactive context. It might now be thought, mistakenly, that schismogenesis was a concept developed, from the start, to treat Melanesian life in the way that Sally Moore has argued 'was a dominant mode of anthropology of the time, which was to treat African life as a separate, closed system' (Moore 2006: 296). Contrary to this misreading of contemporary anthropology, Bateson made it plain that he first presented the concept in his article on 'Culture Contact and Schismogenesis' (1935) with hardly any reference to New Guinea (Bateson 1958: 175). His sociological problems were about an emerging conjuncture, not about a 'closed system'. Inspired by reading *Naven*, Gluckman looked at the opposition between Commissioner or white magistrate and chief in modern Zululand as exemplifying a process of schismogenesis (see Gluckman 1963a: 44).[5] His analysis of their positions highlighted powerful dominance along with strong opposition to create an unsettled balance in cooperation that shifted from situation to situation, and that was perceived in varying, conflicted ways (Gluckman 1940a: 46–51; 1963b: 171–7). Lest Gluckman's view of powerful dominance be misunderstood, I must stress that he saw alien rule as backed up by the force of the colonial state. In Gluckman's view, also, Bateson was the one who made the big step in a new treatment of ritual, beyond Durkheim's and Radcliffe-Brown's theories: it was the step in process theory that discovered ritual as a process 'exaggerating conflicts of social rules and affirming that there was unity despite these conflicts' (Gluckman 1963b: 18).

What Gluckman also acknowledged (1963b: 18) is that he came to grasp, most fully, this insight into ritual as process through much conversation and close reading of Fortes's early essays (1936, 1937) and then his first monograph (1945). In Gluckman's collected essays, *Order and Rebellion in Tribal Africa* (1963), he placed first 'An Advance in African Sociology' (originally published in 1945), his tribute to Fortes's seminal work. Gluckman was attempting to get the reader of his essays on 'Tribal Africa' to reflect by comparison, first, not on a 'tribe' but on a social system of ritual collaboration transcending hostilities across an unbounded region marked by clusters around shrines at a central place. The people Fortes called Tallensi stretch across an area of Upper Volta 'without political unity across the land' and without being marked off as a bounded, distinct unit (Gluckman 1963b: 53; see my discussion of Voltaic regional cults, Werbner 1989: 223–44; 2009: 49–58).

Fortes paid much attention to flows across boundaries. I want to stress this point here, as I have elsewhere (2009: 50–2), because it has come to be a matter of conventional wisdom, or intergenerational fable, to dismiss Fortes and other colonial anthropologists for structural functional myopia – as if they had such a narrow view of the local that they put the translocal out of sight. Few fables of anthropology are told more often than the one about the colonial anthropologist as the inventor of the closed society (for a recent refabulation of this, see Lebner 2017). Appreciated in terms of process theory, Taleland is a conceptual fiction, an as-if, for purposes of analysis in *The Dynamics of Clanship* (1945). Rather than being a bounded entity, it was merely an extension of ties across overlapping regions, or in Fortes's terms, *socio-geographic zones*, none of which was a precisely defined territory.

Building on certain corporate relations in zones, Fortes's later treatment in *The Web of Kinship* (1949) foregrounded the interpersonal network much more. His analysis disclosed the expected stages through which a man passed in his everyday participation in the public sphere. From one stage to the next, a man engaged with different things and people and accessed different spaces. Objects of ritual were the tangible souvenirs that traced a man's public life course across Taleland. Fortes showed how a man's public life course, culminating in elderhood, was expected to realize the public ethics of endurance in amity while giving the public service that affirms, through ritual and ritual objects, the unboundedness of network relations.

Turning to Gluckman's response to Evans-Pritchard's early contributions, I want to focus specifically on his idea of a social process for explaining away failure: the secondary elaboration of belief in closed systems of thought (Evans-Pritchard 1937). This idea has become possibly the most familiar one in his masterpiece, *Witchcraft, Oracles and Magic among the Azande* (1937), which I examine more fully in the first chapter of my own book, *Divination's Grasp* (Werbner 2015: 27–51). Over decades, Gluckman showed how this idea spoke to his times, not merely in Africa but rather across the world; very broadly, he brought it to the interest of social scientists, historians and philosophers of science and, through a BBC talk, to a very wide public. Already in 1937, Gluckman applied this idea to labour relations on South African farms, when he gave evidence to a government commission (1944a: 33 n.1). Extending the argument further beyond witchcraft, Gluckman later compared Azande ideology and Nazi ideology in his earliest published discussion of Evans-Pritchard's contribution (Gluckman 1944a: 31, 34; 1944b: 71–2).

There is a related idea, also very familiar from Evans-Pritchard's masterpiece, which became critical for later perspectives on situations and for what has come to be known as 'situational selection'. Famous as this passage on the practice is, it bears being recalled, having been omitted from the abridged edition of Evans-Pritchard's masterpiece:

> Each situation demands the particular pattern of thought appropriate to it. Hence an individual in one situation will employ a notion he excludes in a different situation. The many beliefs I have recorded are so many different tools of thought and he selects the ones that are chiefly to his advantage…

> A man uses for his individual needs in certain situations those
> notions that most favour his desires. Azande cannot go beyond the
> limits set by their culture and invent notions, but within these limits
> human behaviour is not rigidly determined by custom and a man has
> some freedom of action and thought. (1937: 351)

Rereading this now, we recover a missing aspect of 'the moulding
of British social anthropology as it was when [Evans-Pritchard] took
over the chair at Oxford in 1952' (Singer 1981: vii). This aspect
– and its regard for self-interest and rational choice – was later
heralded in the transactionalist perspectives of the 1960s and 1970s
(Barth 1966; Kapferer 1976). Admittedly, in these now dated perspectives, the over-concentration on tactical transactions exaggerated individualist tendencies far beyond Evans-Pritchard's own
views. Nevertheless, Evans-Pritchard's elucidation of advantage-
seeking in different situations anticipated approaches by members of
the Manchester School to 'situational analysis' with 'situational
selection' and interest-driven manipulation of 'norms in conflict'
(see van Velsen 1964, 1967); I say more about situational analysis,
and in particular Clyde Mitchell's approach to it, in Chapter 4.

From Evans-Pritchard to ecology and political economy

Following Evans-Pritchard's *The Nuer* (1940), and pursuing his
commitment to the cumulative project in science, Gluckman continued to build, in *The Economy of the Central Barotse Plain* (1941),
on Evans-Pritchard's major work by relating it to his own early
fieldwork, on ecology, political economy and historical sociology.[6]
Of these, outstanding for his transformational project was his bringing history to bear on the general arguments and broad formulations
that Evans-Pritchard advanced. From an ecological perspective, there
was, of course, the obvious interest in comparing very different
peoples, both having economies involving transhumance in flood-
plains: the Nuer and the Lozi; and Gluckman highlighted the fact
that the Lozi 'had a land basis for social inequality of power, as the
egalitarian Nuer did not' (Gluckman 1941: 104). There was also a
shared tradition in fieldwork, influenced by Malinowski; he stressed,
as Fortes recalled, 'the first priority in fieldwork must be the study
of a people's modes of livelihood, their economy, their technology

of production and organization of consumption and exchange, their systems of land tenure, their responses to modern economic incentives and opportunities like the labour market' (Fortes 1983: 20).

Gluckman set out to evaluate 'the structural principles which operated in the old [pre-colonial] system … and to show how the weight of various principles changed with innovations' (1941: 2). But rather than claiming a breakthrough of his own, he credited his mentor with the exemplary treatment of change and innovation: 'Evans-Pritchard has succeeded admirably on the Nuer and Anuak; and in his account of the structural principles underlying mystical beliefs' (1941: 2 n.2). Nevertheless, Gluckman also made the point that his own methodology 'has previously been used by some historians' (1941: 3 n.1).

In Gluckman's view, each system, the pre-colonial and the colonial, developed through change; neither was static. One challenge for a sociological analysis was to work out the relative balance over time of certain principles enduring in one form or another from the old to the new system. Another challenge was to understand that the changes which came with British political sovereignty, mining, European farming, a cash economy and labour migration meant that 'an entirely different social system has to be studied [in the colonial period]' (Gluckman 1941: 3).

Taking the long view, to start with Gluckman was willing to speculate on earlier state formation through the pre-colonial accomplishments of immigrants to the Plain from grasslands beyond it, who expanded their tribe into a tributary state. It became a centralized kingdom of many tribes, in command of the floodplain as the heartland of a whole region with internal and external trade based on a differentiated economy. 'A land of milk and honey', Loziland appeared to be in the eyes of early travellers, missionaries and traders, upon whose nineteenth-century observations Gluckman drew for his reconstruction of the past system and its mode of production and distribution. In this past system, he argued, the growth of inequality in power along with centralized hierarchy had its basis in the ways that physical resources, such as mounds, the scarce sites above the floods, were turned into social resources. As such, they were deployed, with reciprocity and without marked exploitation, in widely extended productive cooperation, barter and economic exchange of surpluses. Even tribute-taking proceeded with a return to the giver. Increasing the labour supply, bringing in dependants and more children from subject communities, was critical to meet and generate new needs, especially in the development of irrigation canals: only the Lozi kings 'had the labour force to dig the big canals which made communication easier, and which were later used to drain wide tracts of marsh in the outer-plain, and even some of the damboes [*sic*, now dambos, seasonally waterlogged depressions] in the bush' (Gluckman 1941: 92).

If not timeless, then each system was shown to be not isolated from wider intervention, such as, in the pre-colonial period, from foreign invaders who, during a time of civil war in about 1840, took over the kingdom under their own kings until 1864, and from the penetration from the coast of long-distance commercial trade in guns, cloth, ivory and slaves; in the colonial period, from involvement in trade for many new commodities and a cash economy within a modern world system. The impact of external trade was relatively small until late in the pre-colonial period. Towards the end of the nineteenth century, 'What the new trade effected was to give these commodities (cattle, beeswax, ivory, skins, etc.) and slaves high exchange value where previously they had little, and to make far more profitable such enterprises as hunting and beekeeping' (Gluckman 1941: 80–1). Some preliminary threats to the existing commitments to 'kinship-labour assistance and political tribute-labour' had begun to be felt due to the introduction of money by European travellers and traders in payment for short-time service, with no other obligations and responsibilities.

Underlying the analysis is the question of capitalism and the factors for and against its emergence in Loziland from pre-capitalism (something Gluckman delineated but did not label as such). For his answer, he looked to the early limits on the accumulation and storage of wealth, on exchange value and consumption of goods, on the making of profit; and to scarcities in labour, to kinship and tributary obligations, and poor communications. These limits were already being somewhat or slightly overcome in late nineteenth-century pre-capitalism, with significant economic and social consequences. Beyond that, Gluckman's account of modern change showed how innovations, including salaries for leading Lozi – the king, royals and influential elites around the king – enabled these royals to push even further beyond their limits; to control of the means of production, primarily still on the land, and wealth of their own, not strongly subject to redistributive obligations. These made 'these big Lozi into capitalist employers, while the commoners work as wage-labourers for them, as for Whites' (Gluckman 1941: 111).[7]

At a time of post-war hope for betterment in African colonies, Gluckman made his academic work accessible to a wider South African readership, and published 'Zambesi River Kingdom' (1945), his first popular photographic essay. He reflected on increased poverty, pressing hardships and polarization between rich and poor since his first fieldwork, and expressed the need for political change in the face of exploitation. He concluded: 'New conflicts and demands require the creation of a new political system: the "democracy of tribal life" was rooted in a simple economy which lacked variation in standards of living. Into it have been thrown the riches of our machines' (Gluckman 1945b: 39)

At this point, although it is something of an aside, I want to address the question of the changing influence of Marx's ideas in Gluckman's approach. It was an influence that was perhaps most strongly evident in this study of the economy. This was at a time when Gluckman's wife Mary had inspired his reading and interest in Marxism, and when her own intellectual influence had most drawn him to dialectical and materialist thought. By the 1950s, however, what appeared, somehow, at least as strong, if not stronger, was the influence of ideas from Durkheim, as Epstein observed:

> In a word, if Marx – or perhaps Engels – appeared to occupy less of the foreground of Gluckman's mind, it is because Durkheim was no less a powerful intellectual influence ... while I was in the Department Gluckman neither lectured nor gave courses on Marx or Marxism, whereas he did teach a regular course on Durkheim's *Rules of Sociological Method*. (Epstein 1992b: xxi)

Although I basically agree with Epstein, and remember that course and Gluckman's close textual reading of Durkheim's work, spiced with references to classics in social anthropology, I want to add this evidence of the continued attraction of Marx's ideas. Marx's *18th Brumaire* was the text Gluckman had me read in 1959, during my first year of graduate study, in order to learn from it as the best example of the extended case method. How do sequences of events – *relations between events* not the events as such – and relationships matter and make it possible for a central, would-be heroic figure to play his part? It was a question of documenting and analysing a highly significant *social process*, Marx's method being exemplary for that.

In terms of methodology for the whole study of *The Economy of the Central Barotse Plain*, Gluckman acknowledged the basis in his first major series of essays – mainly from his fieldwork on Zululand, its past and modern present – of which one essay, 'Analysis of a Social Situation in Modern Zululand' (1940), was and is an outstanding watershed. Here I comment on it briefly.[8] The reason is that a whole body of commentaries, reinterpreting it, rethinking its importance, repositioning it within old and new debates, now flows from this essay, the most recent and perhaps most insightful being Robert Gordon's chapter 3, 'How the Guinea Pig Burnt his own Bridge' (Gordon 2018: 95–134).[9] Now known in our literature as 'The Bridge', it tells of a unique occasion, a bridge-opening ceremony involving Zulu and whites. The essay came to be seen as opening a whole line of analysis fostered in some RLI studies, and as exemplary for approaches to the uncertain, haphazard and untidy in social life. Rather than only showing the systematically interdependent, it is still promising through the study of an actual occasion or, in extended cases, a whole sequence of events as interrelated. Nevertheless, it was totalizing, the systematic bent to which Gluckman appealed initially, in 1941: 'the analysis reveals the underlying system of relationships between the social structure of the community, the parts of the social structure, the physical environment and the physiological life of the community's members' (Gluckman 1940a: 9).

After decades of research by members of the Manchester School and others, and to convey an anticipation of theoretical developments, he reformulated his stance to foreground counter-processes: 'I showed there [in the 1940 essay] how individuals in certain key positions could create and exploit social situations in terms of their power and their culture, and yet how certain other processes, arising from the larger society, led to standardised but unplanned relationships and associations' (1967: xx).[10] In my own early review of the Manchester School and of this essay in particular, I found, 'No attempt was made [in 'The Bridge'] to account for a micro-history of events involving the individuals prior to that day. Nor were the actors' own definitions of the situation taken to be problematic' (Werbner 1984b: 162)

'The Bridge', along with its sequel, 'Some Processes of Social Change Illustrated from Zululand' (1942), verged on being a manifesto, not for dogma but for points of departure, for generations of anthropologists around Gluckman, from the early RLI research fellows to their students at Manchester. Being around Gluckman, they had to read it – he made sure of that. 'The Bridge, the Bridge, all the time the first few years', Ian Cunnison remarked about Gluckman's training during the early RLI years (Schumaker 2001: 78). I think that when Clyde Mitchell told the historian Lyn Schumaker that in the early RLI period, 'Gluckman rammed history down our throats' (Schumaker 2001: 299 n.150), he had in mind Gluckman's pushing the arguments in 'The Bridge' as fundamental for RLI research, and for a modern version of social anthropology. Colson found that, later, a change took place in the RLI which shifted it from the direction Gluckman and Wilson had planned towards 'pure research and away from applied work. The research officers became each other's primary reference group and began to write for this audience and for other anthropologists and sociologists rather than the general public' (Colson 1977: 293).

The enduring problematic of equilibrium/disequilibrium dynamics

My view of Gluckman's development of structuralism in conflict studies was, and still is, this, as I argued in my early review of the Manchester School:

> Gluckman's solution [to revise structuralism and take account of modern social problems] introduced a historical perspective with an emphasis upon process and a distinction between structures or systems according to their relative stability. At its starkest, the distinction obscured gradual and limited change in favour of an extreme contrast between repetitive and changing systems. In the former, changes follow an established pattern, in the latter, they do not, with the possibilities of catastrophes and radical breaks from the pattern. The difference depends on how or whether conflicts, which are always present in any system, can be and are resolved ... Thus, in a version of Fortes' and Evans-Pritchard's binary model of fission and fusion,

each structure or system was a synthesis of alternative aspects, conflict *and* the overcoming of conflict, antagonism and co-operation: Gluckman's was a dialectical view. (Werbner 1990: 157)

For Gluckman, accepting the early comprehension by Fortes and Evans-Pritchard of equilibrium/disequilibrium dynamics did not put an end to the problematic of equilibrium. Rather, even late in the 1960s he found he had to re-enter debate about it. He elaborated his views on types of change: radical, repetitive, situational, with continuity on one level being radical change on another, rather than the same mode being true throughout a whole social system. He argued for rethinking: to overcome ambiguities in earlier schemes; to defend against the term 'structuralist' serving as a new generation's label of abuse of a past generation; to fight the gross dismissal, as static, of analyses of change and continuity which he knew to be dynamic; and the better to work out issues of duration and temporality, especially the distinct timescales of different institutions (Gluckman 1968a). His argument, initially presented to a 1966 plenary session of the American Anthropological Association, was for an 'as-if' suspension for heuristic purposes; as-if in analysis to disregard external interventions: 'In an analysis of this kind, the emphasis is on the manner in which the institution would operate through time if internal contradictions or external intruding events did not interfere with its passage through its structural duration' (Gluckman 1968a: 219). The times in the 1960s were not welcoming for such 'as-if' thinking, for the heuristic suspension of actual history, in defence of the utility of an equilibrium model; as Bruce Kapferer noted:

> It was the period of the Vietnam War and radical attack by academics and intellectuals upon the ideas and institutions which were conceived as instrumental in Western destructiveness and oppression. Gluckman's championing of equilibrium in this context of the sixties was easily open to the charge of being a conservative defence of the *status quo*. (Kapferer 1987: 19 n.7)

A further charge, I think, in good measure inspired by Gluckman's return to equilibrium analysis, was the one raised by Elizabeth Colson: 'Gluckman himself moved further away from Central

African realities and became immersed in the theoretical issues of academic social anthropology' (Colson 1977: 293).

Gluckman's own understanding was that he was arguing in the face of current caricatures of ideas and orientations which, if from early modern social anthropology and no longer novel but open to revision, were arguably still useful for the analysis of continuity in relation to change. At this time, late in his career, the social scientific credo he rehearsed is the one to which he had long subscribed: 'I believe firmly that anthropology is a science and therefore progressive and accumulating in that, speaking for myself, I feel we pass the test that the fool of the later generation outdoes the genius of the previous generation' (Gluckman 1968a: 235).

The unfinished analysis of state formation

But was Gluckman, after all, a 'fool' in the prison-house of his own generation? When it came to pre-colonial African political systems, Gluckman's vision, Sally Moore argued mistakenly, was 'inherently conservative' and limited by the structural-functionalism of his times to a static view of mutually isolated entities (Moore 1994: 15–16). In line with Gluckman's distinction between rebellion and revolution – between the mere 'replacement of personnel in key positions of power' and actual change in 'the structure of the political economy' – his view of pre-colonial political struggles allegedly saw mere perpetuation, rather than transformation, as in the colonial period (Moore 1994: 16). It is ironic that the work that most calls this now widely received yet wrong judgement into question is Gluckman's study which was longest in gestation, from his fieldwork in the 1930s, through his early essay mainly on the modern Zulu kingdom (Gluckman 1940b), to his last essays on the rise of King Shaka (1960a, 1974b), and to 'The Rise of the Zulu Nation', the unpublished manuscript he was revising at the time of his death. It is worth saying that in developing his approach from the mid-1960s onwards, he clearly had in mind countering the current anthropological trend to transactionalism led by Frederik Barth. Gluckman regarded it as a turn to misreading the nature of change merely in terms of interaction between persons; that is, in terms of exchange and, at worst, of competition, with choices free of the constraints of the environment on individuals (for his brief explicit criticism of Barth, see Gluckman 1974b: 135 n.25).

Admittedly, historians have come to raise doubts about the historicity of Shaka's life story or to reinterpret it as heroic myth, now a charter for a turn to modernity, black power and nationalism, rather than an account of actual events (Golan 1990). Of course, Gluckman was himself well aware of entering a controversial terrain around a great hero:

> Shaka has become a hero for very many Africans in South Africa, and at least one tragedy has been written about him by a West African. Among American Blacks, he and his Zulu are also esteemed as heroic (*as indeed they were and are*): in Minneapolis ... there is a Black group which calls itself 'Shaka's Zulu Warriors' and in Philadelphia the dominant Black 'gang' calls itself 'the Zulu Nation' ... Adulation of Shaka has led some South African Africans to affirm that accounts of Shaka's atrocities were exaggerated propaganda, promoted by Dingane, his brother who murdered and succeeded him, to justify his own actions, and by contemporary and later Europeans, in order perhaps to make a tale of the terrors they had faced. (Gluckman 1974b: 118, italics mine)

As my italics indicate, Gluckman's stance towards the terror was not that of disenchantment, which obviates a close appreciation of the heroic. Gluckman claimed that while drawing on contemporary records and oral traditions for Shaka's reign as well as earlier descriptions from mariners for pre-Shakan society, he did what historians could demand in source criticism: 'This problem is dealt with in detail in my full account of "The Rise of the Zulu Nation"; here I can only assure readers that I have scrutinized the sources very carefully, and the evidence makes clear that Shaka did act cruelly and tyrannously' (Gluckman 1974b: 118).

In terms of historiography, also, he upheld the historian's craft by reviewing other scholars' debates, their hypotheses and interpretations, and by defending his own. What is important for our understanding of Gluckman's vision is not the final word on the true facts of the pre-colonial rise of the Zulu nation but the nature of his approach to pre-colonial state formation. Was he trying to explain stability or change? Was he weighing up the importance of the Great Man or the constraints of technology and the environment?

The answer is not 'either or' but 'both and'; that is, stability in relation to change, which he saw as 'substantial' but in a certain sense, not radical; and the creative effectiveness of the Great Man as it was dependent upon limiting conditions, according to facts of economy and technology and a certain pressure in the environment. His relational approach was double-barrelled; it comprehended a movement from one period to another, and the distinctiveness of continuity or discontinuity in each period. There was first a highly stable period, perhaps from the late fifteenth century until well into the eighteenth century, with pre-Shakan polities, many small tribes, varying in size from about 300 to about 2,500 or exceptionally 5,000 persons, dispersed in small villages and under chiefs who faced constant conflicts over power, including civil wars led by their relatives, but who who rarely fought with each other to conquer territory. The tribes, including the Nguni tribe that was precursor to Shaka's Zulu nation, were relatively peaceful. In what Gluckman reconstructed as a 'state of stasis' there was:

> much strife, many quarrels and wars, efforts by men to improve or defend their power, and so forth. New tribes were formed, either after rebellion or after peaceful separation. But there was no change in the pattern of tribal organization or the institutions of chieftainship, and the technology remained the same, new tribes and new chiefs duplicated the pattern in space and repeated it in time. (Gluckman 1974b: 126)

In brief, Nguni stability was all on the side of the fault line which Moore took to be, in Gluckman's view, the whole pre-colonial story: the rebellion, repetitive or static side. On the contrary, that was not the whole story, in Gluckman's view.

Rapid as was the shift to the conquest state under Shaka, with much innovation to his credit – a new great standing army newly quartered in military barracks for men newly required to be celibate and thus more dedicated warriors, with new military tactics and a new weapon of war, the short stabbing spear (like Shaka's small penis, Gluckman discerned), with a new quick consolidation of many tribes along with the Nguni – it was, nevertheless, a sudden development that had its primary cause in a major crisis already in progress. Above all, it was arguably a crisis in production, from pressure on the land; and Gluckman had to admit that he was speculating in the absence of 'conclusive evidence': 'there are strong indications that the critical point of population density had been reached for the Nguni production system. The early political system could persist in stasis with only local serious disturbances as long as the ratio of population to land did not exceed a certain point' (Gluckman 1974b: 137). By about the beginning of the nineteenth century, a long-term process reached that excess, and climaxed in campaigns of territorial conquest, culminating in Shaka's own campaign from 1816 onwards until he turned also to raids for cattle and tribute, but not more territory. 'He and groups fleeing from him, solved the land population problem, as tens of thousands of people must have died' (Gluckman 1974b: 139). Summing up his assessment of the transformation brought Gluckman to the point of systemic change in this second period. He called it 'substantial' rather than 'radical', in part because of the limited structural change Shaka could and did achieve: 'he duplicated in his great new nation early Nguni tribal organization, though on a much larger scale and with a deeper hierarchy of officials' (Gluckman 1974b: 134). In part, also, the change was 'substantial' not 'radical' because what mattered most was not the character or exceptional ability of the Great Man – and Gluckman felt that Shaka was a 'near psychotic and had a very disturbed psychosexuality' (Gluckman 1974b: 140) – but the simple determinants in certain real and enduring conditions: 'Simple tools, simple consumable goods, limited trade, simple means of communication, and simple weapons held by all warriors determined the form of political organization much more than Shaka's character, with all his striking ability, or than did his tyrannical and capricious power' (Gluckman 1974b: 135). The unfinished nature of Gluckman's study of state formation leaves us as much with promises and clues as with substantial analysis and overarching theory. Yet as a long enduring work-in-progress, it affords an illuminating perspective on the realities that continued to be fundamental in Gluckman's 'sticking to his last' as a social anthropologist.

Such realities discerned in this last work in his transformational project are still challenging for twenty-first-century social anthropology. Among them I find his commitment not only to fieldwork in the present but also to the historian's craft in the archives for the past, his care for 'the big picture' and the analysis of broad issues of continuing and emerging structural constraints on power and the

Great Man, his curiosity about motivation that might be subconscious rather than practical as rational calculation.

That said, I think it is reasonable to conclude that throughout the whole of this project, Gluckman proceeded with deep yet wide-ranging ethnographic scholarship, with *interdisciplinary* arguments, with the social scientist's interest in open questions, in general propositions and broader comparisons of social processes and, above all, with a search for deeper understanding of likeness, the realities of our shared humanity; that is, the kind of social anthropology that we now need urgently so as to study our contemporaries, as Adam Kuper rightly argues: 'So if we want to understand those realistic, pragmatic and cosmopolitan people, our contemporaries, we need a realistic, pragmatic, cosmopolitan anthropology' (Kuper 2019: 20).

Gluckman, collegiality and the intellectual ferment in the RLI

If we turn now from Gluckman's own major projects, comparative and transformational, to his formative impact on the RLI, and the Manchester School and even its loose-knit network, there is an obvious question. A good part of the answer lies in what Clyde Mitchell told me in 1983, when I was preparing my early account of the Manchester School: 'Seen from the outside, the Manchester School was a school. But seen from the inside, it was a seething contradiction. And perhaps the only thing we had in common was that Max was our teacher, and that meant we wrote ethnography rich in actual cases.'[11]

I want to quote at length from Mitchell's 1956 preface to his monograph, *The Yao Village*. My reason is that this preface, published at a peak in Manchester School publications, put forward an understanding of collegiality, or schoolness, now widely shared regarding the emergence of the Manchester School from its source in the Rhodes-Livingstone Institute:

> Throughout my study of the Yao, in the field and in analysis. I have been supported in every way by the Rhodes-Livingstone Institute and its staff. Not only did the Institute provide the finance for academic and disinterested research, but it also created the framework in which a group of sociologists of divergent interests and backgrounds, could work out common problems. (1956b: x)

Mitchell went on to acknowledge the considered and in-depth responses by his Institute colleagues to his papers and book drafts. From this, we learn that they developed mutual interest and collaboration as a continuing strength of what became the Manchester School. Mitchell expressed his special gratitude to Max Gluckman who was not only his director in the Institute but also his DPhil supervisor at Oxford. 'To him', he says, 'I owe more than any other of my colleagues' (1956b: ix). With a characteristically generous further acknowledgement, Clyde concludes, 'I would like to say in appreciation that both Max Gluckman and Elizabeth Colson, as successive Directors of the Rhodes-Livingstone Institute, have always given me complete freedom in the conduct of my research and have only given me "direction" when I asked for it' (1956b: ix).

'In February 1947', Colson recalled,

> all the officers came to Livingstone for the first conference of the Institute … The conference had no particular theme beyond the stress upon the collection of demographic data and the emphasis upon how economic factors structured life in rural areas. Nevertheless, the free, and sometimes fiery, discussions helped to create an *esprit de corps* among the officers who continued their arguments via the post. (Colson 1977: 292)

What is now well known, of course, is the outstanding part Gluckman played in these discussions, and indeed it anticipated his later role in many Manchester seminars.[12] Gordon documents this closely, in part from material Raymond Firth collected for a British Academy tributary memoir. According to Gordon:

> What stood out in Mitchell's memory was Gluckman's creativity in handling field data at the RLI seminars. They had to present their data while still very much groping in the dark, and Max would ask what appeared to be irrelevant questions and then 'slowly a pattern would begin to emerge and soon we were all agog with excitement as he showed us how it all fitted together in a meaningful way.' The purpose of the seminar, Mitchell felt, was to examine the problems that each fieldworker saw in their material and to get inside the problem and to make sense of it (JCM [J. Clyde Mitchell] to RF [Raymond Firth] October 22, 1975, LSERF [London School of Economics, Raymond Firth]. (Gordon 2018: 337)

If we are to view the RLI's collegiality in a conflict perspective, we need to appreciate something problematic, endemic and perhaps paradoxically creative in the RLI, at least under Gluckman. There was, on the one hand, an ethos of non-hierarchy, an unmistakably known and commonly spoken of ethos. The directors who only gave direction when asked were matched by the mature fellows, who were proud of their independence, and who included war heroes, men who 'had had a good war', such as the legendary RAF navigator Clyde Mitchell. On the other hand, and problematic for this ethos of non-hierarchy, was a rule of hierarchy in administration. This rule is less uttered in RLI or Manchester public pronouncements or writings. But the director was, after all, a director, and the head of department was a head. Gordon's evidence, and my own understanding, is that Gluckman as the director was a strong boss, who nevertheless was sometimes tolerant of open disobedience, and that around him tension was endemic; if often expressed in jokes about 'the Chief', it simmered in the conflict between the rule of hierarchy and the ethos of non-hierarchy. Most likely, to Gluckman himself, it was clear in which situations or events one or the other, hierarchy or non-hierarchy, had to prevail. Clarity on his side, yes. As for agreement, on the other side, among the team, so to speak, about that we may well wonder, or rather doubt. 'I won't have that man telling me what to do again' is what I heard Mitchell say when I was still a young fieldworker in Zimbabwe in 1961; he said it, almost involuntarily and to my innocent ears, on suddenly opening a letter from Gluckman with too many plans for his proposed professorship in sociology at Manchester. Later in Chapter 3 I say more about the problematic tensions that Gluckman and Mitchell's relations exemplify. Was it one of those ironies of history for Max that as the exponent of a theory of rebellion in cycles, he repeatedly had to have rebels and rebelliousness around him?

Oxford encounters

Between 1947 and 1949, while Gluckman was a lecturer at Oxford, he gathered around him his team of early stars of the Manchester School from the RLI staff, namely Elizabeth Colson, John Barnes and Clyde Mitchell. If not quite simply 'a group of eclectic and left-leaning marginals in an upper middle-class academic discipline' (Mills 2006: 166),[13] nevertheless, Max's team made a collective stir at Oxford when all gave lectures on their research. After an initial writing-up they returned to the RLI in Livingstone. Oxford then served as a foil, against which the RLI stars won the game, so to speak, according to their moves in opposition along with collaboration, which the following letter, from Gluckman at Oxford to Mitchell in Zambia, reflects. I cite it at some length from the report by David Mills, who points out that it reveals 'a growing difference of intellectual opinion between Gluckman and Evans-Pritchard over just what it meant to be a social anthropologist':

> We've been having rather a battle this term in seminars with an idealistic wave – it started with Mrs Bohannan in a discussion of Malinowski's Argonauts saying that sociological theories were just attempts of the mind to bring order, and there is no way of testing between theories. Then EP, Lienhardt and others said there were no facts about a people, only what the observer wrote in his notebooks. Meyer and I are fighting hard for our scientific attitude: the facts are public, DCs and Barotse read what I write about the Lozi and it has meaning for them, the facts are checkable in the subject so that I told Lienhardt that even if he wanted to lie about the Dinka he couldn't get away with it. That we have a series of propositions which are being tested all the time etc. And more and more I feel I am a social anthropologist, and I must stick to my last [Gluckman to Mitchell 12 February 1949]. (Mills 2008: 102–3)

This difference culminated in the intellectual parting of the ways in which Evans-Pritchard became a new advocate of history in his Marrett Lecture, and Gluckman still pushed forward, through the rest of his life, his view of social anthropology as, at once, testable science *and* history. There is a further difference, of course. Evans-Pritchard's exemplary ethnographies, general propositions, theoretical arguments and influential paradigms generated rich streams of social anthropology, including comparative works by others, and in particular by Gluckman. But whereas Gluckman throughout his career sustained his comparative work with re-analyses of others' ethnographic data, Evans-Pritchard did not, and seemed even to gain no boost from accounts other than his own: becoming the historian, he was no longer, if ever, the explicit comparativist.

Interdisciplinarity at Manchester and beyond

Stimulated by Gluckman, his Manchester colleagues from other disciplines recognized the novel and surprising relevance, in the 1950s and early 1960s, of Evans-Pritchard's ideas about explaining away failure and the use of secondary elaborations to keep a system of thought closed. With this in mind, the economist Ely Devons illuminated 'the magic of statistics' in economic analysis and policy (1961: 134–5; see also Gluckman and Devons 1964: 259). Bringing the idea to bear in a pioneering study of Lancashire work groups, the sociologist Tom Lupton opened out a whole field of micro-management research through a radical departure from a dominant trend in American sociology (Lupton 1963).[14] Even further, and in perhaps the most outstanding development at Manchester of Evans-Pritchard's idea, came the controversial work on personal knowledge by the physical chemist and philosopher of science Michael Polanyi.[15] He was the father of 'the rationality debate' in its engagement with 'a system of not explicitly asserted beliefs' (Polanyi 1952: 221).[16] Going beyond his seminal articles (Polanyi 1950, 1952), he wrote of 'incommensurability' and opened a major debate over how or whether scientists as protagonists of incommensurable conceptual frameworks 'think differently, use different languages and occupy different worlds' (Polanyi 1958: 174).

Where Polanyi made his breakthrough and opened out a mainstream of philosophical interest in Evans-Pritchard's interpretive account was in *comparison*. Polanyi took the arguments about the stability of belief and extended them from insight into exotic mystical thought to insight into more familiar modes and systems of belief. In doing so, he shook up much established opinion or at least conventional wisdom about the limits of doubt and scientific rationality in the face of contradictions to current scientific conceptions.

Gluckman's role in brokering this and other key ideas of Evans-Pritchard's was fundamental. It advanced not only Gluckman's own transformational project, but also the development of the Manchester School in an interdisciplinary context that was highly productive. Commitment to collaboration across the social sciences was, of course, long-standing and basic to Gluckman's initiatives for his kind of social anthropology from his early plans for the RLI onwards: his intent was to have his RLI team of sociologists cooperate with and include specialists in other social sciences – an economist, a demographer, a lawyer, an industrial psychologist. Under Gluckman's leadership, the Manchester Seminar in Social Anthropology, which became widely known for its critical, sometimes abrasive arguments, entered into an open exchange of ideas in the social sciences. Along with Gluckman, Polanyi, Devons and others, including the political scientist William Mackenzie, these Manchester professors shared a view of the unity of the social sciences and regularly attended seminars in each others' departments.

Here a word on their care for academic freedom along with academic merit is illuminating. An example shows the inclusive academic practice which meant that a Marxist and liberation activist such as the communist political scientist and lawyer Jack Simons could get a full and welcome hearing in the anthropology department at Manchester and, indeed, in the university itself. At the request of the African National Congress leader Oliver Tambo, in the late 1970s Simons gave lectures to the armed wing of the ANC in their Tanzanian camps. Simons was part of a circle of left-wing academics from South Africa with whom Max Gluckman kept in close contact, and some of whom he brought to Manchester on research fellowships attached to Anthropology. In 1965–66, Simons wrote *African Women: Their Legal Status in South Africa* (1968) during his fellowship, the award of which posed a hurdle because of the risk that Simons might not be able to get a passport. Gluckman reported the overcoming of this hurdle to Clyde Mitchell, who was about to come to Manchester:

> You and Hilary [Mitchell's second wife, herself a South African radical activist] will be pleased to hear about Manchester that when I gave his political record and his banning and the possibility that he might not get a passport, the Committee decided that these were not its business – that they would consider him for his intellectual merits ... He has been appointed. (MG to CM, 17 March 1965, MBPL)

Having won support for his view that theoretical insights from Africa were illuminating in Britain for the sociology of management, of medicine and of community studies (see Frankenberg 1957, 1966), Gluckman further widened the relevance of his arguments to Israel through a big project by the last generation of his students, under the fieldwork direction of Emanuel Marx, who himself founded the anthropology department at the University of Tel Aviv. The outcome in books and articles on Israel represents one of the very first major studies of a nation-state by social anthropologists.

Case method, processual analysis: recent Manchester studies

I want to conclude with a brief overview of some of the recent work at Manchester, which builds on classic Manchester School studies. Following Mitchell, who was my fieldwork supervisor, and Gluckman and Turner, my other teachers at Manchester, I took two steps in case method and processual analysis in *Tears of the Dead* (1991), a social biography of one family over several generations, from the colonial to the postcolonial period, based on fieldwork in Zimbabwe over a thirty-year period. First, while examining the relations between events in the life histories that family members gave me, I analysed their narration in its diversity and many voices; my aim was to disclose the artfulness in the personal narrative genres – nostalgia, matter-of-fact witnessing, romantic idealization, heroic self-fulfilment against ordeals – by which they told their stories and recounted their memories in more or less rapport with me, and mutually positioned themselves in the development of a big and prominent extended family. Of course, I also position myself reflexively in my growth from raw novice fieldworker to being an elder, many years later, welcomed on my safe return to the family. The fact that as resources for an extended case, the foundational works of Mitchell and Turner relied quite simply on memory stories and after-the-fact re-presentations has received all too little critical attention; the need was, my monograph illustrated, for critical reflexivity, rather than reliance on retrospection at face-value (Werbner 1991).[17] As a narrative study of the moral imagination, *Tears of the Dead* showed how shifting contexts were perceived by family members who, having endured dislocation and dispossession by white settlers, had become, during a long period of resettlement and reconstruction, inward-looking, much concerned with internal rivalries and quarrels; but then, as events unfolded, they had to face the trauma of guerrilla warfare, and after it, state terror at the hands of special forces sent by their own government, to which they had looked for liberation. I found their post-war narratives heavy in painful disillusionment; they commented bitterly on President Robert Mugabe, inflation, trends and changes in the wider sense; and they foregrounded their ordeals with outsiders primarily, rather than internal quarrel stories. They felt compelled to bring the wider scene into perspective (Werbner 1995: 110).

My second step was moved by disruption and uncertainty, by the people's sense and not only my own that the times were out of joint, that we were in times of crisis so troublesome as to be almost beyond comprehension in any familiar ways. Yet I was being required to be a witness, even to be a whistle-blower and critic of power, to let the world know of the state terror. Crisis in the classic village studies, while intensely a breach of community, appeared to be not unprecedented but rather predictable, at least in analysis. And yet, committed to an approach within process theory, and to bringing to bear, from archives, government documents and casual observations, knowledge of the state and an official world the people could not and were not intended to see clearly, I tried to illuminate the rise of what I called quasi-nationalism in the formation of the nation-state in the twentieth century.

Most recently, I have turned to the resources of the Granada Centre for Visual Anthropology in order to make a film to accompany my text for *Divination's Grasp* (Werbner 2015). In Chapter 9 I present an extended case study of consultation in seances. The account draws on my film-making over more than a decade with two friends, Martha and Njebe. In my analysis, I argue:

> The advantages in an extended case study involving intimates are well known. Because it documents their micro-history in fine detail, the extended case study unfolds certain changes they know, interpret, and to some extent direct over a significant period in their lives. Carrying that documentation forward through filmmaking now offers important opportunities to enhance the method. Applied to divination, and with filmmaking (Werbner 2005, 2007, 2008, 2011), the method focuses on the re-creative process in and around the séance: on the situational expression of the moral imagination, on the disclosure of emerging difference in felt experience, and on the conscious, somewhat shifting comprehension people reach of the accepted truths in everyday life. On this basis, documented in rare depth, emerges the force of a social and cultural account that is rich in experience, and thus fitting for a

phenomenological approach; that records the fleeting moments and their understood significance in retrospect; that brings together the ethnographic understanding of micro-historical process and its theoretical analysis. (Werbner 2015: 22)

Among my own students, four – Isaac Mazonde, Harri Englund, Anthony Simpson and Mattia Fumanti – pursued further steps in their ethnographies, for relevant understanding of our contemporary realities, with some depth in time, the present in relation to the past, and with an eye to a horizon, a possible future. I discuss their monographs in order of publication.

Isaac Mazonde, who is himself a pioneer as Botswana's first social anthropologist, has written the first in-depth account, using the extended case method focused on a relatively small number of persons, of a major transformation in progress in southern Africa, with the transfer to Africans of freehold farms formerly owned by European settlers.[18] Mazonde built his analysis, for the settlers, on personal profiles and micro-histories of change in family firms over at least three generations in south-eastern Botswana's Tuli Block. On this basis, he argued for the emergence and variable entrepreneurship of extreme types of development. Part of his argument, like Harri Englund's, addressed issues of bordermanship, here the strategic actions and social networks by which settler entrepreneurs straddled two countries, South Africa and Botswana. For the Africans, Mazonde examined 'the transformations which have been, and still are, occurring, as former tribesmen become large-scale capitalists, holding land as a commodity, along with livestock as commercial assets. The transformations epitomise many of the major social changes within a wider field in the nation as a whole' (Mazonde 1994: ix).

Englund's first monograph brought the extended case method to bear on problems of borders and borderlands through multi-sited ethnography. Regarding war, displacement and repatriation on the Mozambique–Malawi borderland, it drew 'attention to refugees and their local hosts as persons whose relationships had histories beyond the immediate challenges of an unprecedented crisis' (Englund 2002a: 164). In his account Englund reworked the very notion of the refugee in the light of the variable negotiations of sociality before and after the displacements of civil war and political violence. He deployed the extended case method to illuminate the actual agency that specific personal relationships afforded border-land people in their rebuilding of trust, moral value and legitimate authority.[19]

Anthony Simpson's ethnography, focused on life in the 1990s in a Zambian boys' Catholic mission boarding school, but grounded in his knowledge of the school as a teacher in the 1970s and 1980s, balanced considerable participant observation with a life-history approach to make many voices speak in his innovative use of the extended case method (Simpson 2003; see also his sequel, Simpson 2009). In a perceptive commentary on Simpson's monograph, Henrietta Moore remarked:

> Drawing critically on Foucault's aesthetics of the self, Simpson argues that the students engage in performances and productions of self that seek through comportment, dress, language and orientation both to accept the regime of the Catholic mission school and to hold up that regime to ridicule, even to critique and transcend it (2003: 44, 82) … Simpson resists the easy elision of Foucauldian discipline and forms of subjectification, arguing contra the Comaroffs and, by implication, much of the literature on historical transformation of subjectivities in Africa, that the architecture of the school, and its forms of regimentation do not generate a 'cogent vision of subject and society' (Comaroff and Comaroff, 1991: 33; Simpson, 2003: 82). His subtle analysis emphasizes the multiplicity and plurality of discourses and processes of self-fashioning and subjectification. (Moore 2011: 56–7)

It is a special strength of Moore's understanding of the original advance in Simpson's work that she highlighted its implications for theories of othering, abjection and alienation:

> it seems worthwhile exploring the contentious mutuality of identification and desire at play in this context, which cannot, as Simpson so brilliantly demonstrates, be captured by an analysis which proceeds from the assumption that the categories 'African' and 'wasungu' [white] are already self-evident or suspended in a particular relation of hierarchy and exclusion. (Moore 2011: 58)

Simpson's ethnography, like my own, attends to the importance of dialogic relations; but by making bridges explicitly between insights from Bakhtin and the late Foucault, his analysis enters more widely into critical debate about how strangers negotiate dislocation and disjunction in everyday life within institutional settings.

At the core of Mattia Fumanti's monograph, *The Politics of Distinction* (2016), is an extended case study of old and new elites, which illuminates the changing politics of the public sphere in urban Namibia. What is the creative moral force of everyday political rhetoric and practice is a central question, closely addressed on the basis of nuanced evidence from a middle-range frontier town, Rundu. Fumanti shows how elites rework their moral agency and subjectivity from generation to generation. In particular, these generational relations are revealed as they shape and are reshaped during the critical juncture of transition from apartheid and civil war to independence and post-independence.

Located on the border between Namibia and Angola, Rundu is one of countless such towns across Africa, whose study has largely been neglected by Africanists preoccupied with the 'problem of Africa', while being apparently blind to much urban change in everyday public life on the continent, especially in small towns. Without losing sight of the importance of personal relationships, most of all among the youth he came to know intimately – and their mocking wit and flair resonate evocatively in his text – Fumanti enables us to comprehend relevant post-apartheid issues in southern Africa as they have come to be reflected in public debates about education, the state, citizenship, governance and the role of ethnic and settler minorities. As Robert Gordon suggests on the book's cover, 'The book is a vibrant antidote to Afro-pessimism and views that emphasize the spectacle of disaster, kleptomania and corruption of the weak state.'

These monographs have no single house style, no hidden hand for orchestration. Each is unmistakably the product of the author's personal venture into his own ethnographic discovery at the frontiers of debate in social anthropology. Nevertheless, taken together, these monographs reflect the interest at Manchester, sustained from the early RLI research to this day, in documenting and analysing the contemporary realities of change in south-central Africa in ways that are suggestive for broader theoretical arguments.

Notes

1 For the published version, Gluckman was awarded the Wellcome Medal of the Royal Anthropological Institute, 'as the best submitted essay of the year on the problems of culture contact' (Gluckman 1948: 71).

2 For a useful but somewhat different gloss on 'the human laboratory', see Schumaker 2001: 75–116.

3 See Gordon 2018: 148 for an alternative reading of the suggestion in current terms of emic and etic. For an exceptional response to this suggestion, see Abner Cohen's analysis of continuity and change in Arab border villages (1965).

4 The italicized phrase, *vaguely delimited aggregate known as the Tallensi*, captures Fortes's regard, in his heuristic purposes, for something problematic that he knows or calls 'the Tallensi', but that is, he admits also, not a bounded unit or a 'society'. I note that recent work on relationality, arguing against a theoretical overdetermination by the idea of 'society' in 'classic' social anthropology, suffers from a failure to appreciate this problematic and Fortes's heuristic approach to it (see Lebner 2017: 8–11).

5 Gluckman also conceptualized his understanding of schismogenesis in terms of 'social inertia', meaning 'continual development in the same straight line or direction, unless acted upon by some external force' (1940a: 64). He applied this understanding to a view of the impact of a dominant cleavage in a changing system on structural developments expressed in interrelated cooperation and opposition.

6 For a bold and challenging 'thought experiment' which looks at the Manchester School from what is seen as the perspective in Evans-Pritchard's *Nuer*, see van Binsbergen 2007.

7 For a Marxist reading of Gluckman's study and an account of the later history of 'big Lozi' seen as a ruling class, see Frankenberg 1978.

8 I return to its influence on RLI urban studies in Chapter 4, in my discussion of Clyde Mitchell's development of situational analysis in his *Kalela Dance* (1956).

9 See also Garbett 1970; Macmillan 1995; Schumaker 2001: 42–3; Mitchell 2006: 28–9; Englund 2018: 122; and the collection of essays in Evens and Handelman 2006, especially, Frankenberg 2006; Handelman 2006: 96–8; Kapferer 2006; Mills 2006: 167–8; Moore 2006: 292–3.

10 In the 1940 essay, Gluckman did make plain his method of proceeding from description of events to analysis of their interrelationships to abstractions about social structure: 'As a starting point for my analysis I describe a series of events as I recorded them on a single day. Social situations are a large part of the raw material of the anthropologist. They are the events he observes and from them and their interrelationships in a particular society he abstracts the social structure, relationships, institutions etc., of that society. By them, and by new situations, he must check the validity of his generalizations' (1940a: 2).

11 Gordon reports that Barnes held a similar view: 'He felt that it was the shared experience of apprenticeship, as well as the sharing of social and intellectual networks in the field and later in the pubs of Oxford, that generated their cohesion rather than any overarching paradigm' (Gordon 2018: 335).

12 For an acute description, see Kapferer 2006: 121–2.

13 The description does not apply to Elizabeth Colson; see Chapter 3.

14 Lupton carried out his fieldwork in 1955–56 as a sociologist in Manchester's then joint department of Social Anthropology and Sociology and later became head of the Manchester Business School in 1966.

15 At the University of Manchester, Polanyi was a physical chemist turned philosopher, who took his chair in social sciences at the time in the 1950s when Manchester's Social Anthropology Seminar was at its interdisciplinary best.

16 Among philosophers, the debate intensified in the 1960s, with works reprinted in the 1970s (Winch 1972 [1964]; MacIntyre 1981 [1967]). As Stanley Tambiah wryly remarks, 'it was an occasion when modern philosophers dipped into exotic anthropological ethnography to argue their philosophical positions' (1990: 117).

17 I argued that their approach blocked out phenomenological questions of selective perception and the present reconstruction of the past. For example, in the Yao village, 'In the total village genealogy which the ethnographer was able to piece together as a whole, even for a quite large village, a simple representation of "us" vs. "them" was given repeatedly. Yet Mitchell did not recognize that the Yao regularly simplified the demographic binary scheme; descent was a construction after the fact' (Werbner 1991: 161).

18 Mazonde carried out his fieldwork in the Tuli Block, the same area about which Gluckmann wrote *The Tragedy*.

19 Englund's second monograph, 2006, won the Amaury Talbot Prize of the Royal Anthropological Institute. For his more recent use of the extended case method in his third monograph, see Englund 2011, and 2018, for a comparative overview.

3

Elizabeth Colson: home town anthropologist, systems sceptic

The pioneers of modern social anthropology made their ethnographic and comparative breakthroughs in times of remarkable crisis: from pre-war to post-war times, from the colonial to the postcolonial periods. Much of their legacy is now underestimated or even neglected as if it were hopelessly out of date. Yet because this legacy speaks to troubled times, it is vital for understanding intractable realities in the present. Aware of that significant presence of the past, and addressing the Diamond Jubilee Conference of the Association of Social Anthropologists of the UK and Commonwealth, Elizabeth Colson reflected, as a founding member of the association, on its history (2008b).[1] Colson called her fellow social anthropologists to be conscious of a paradox: proud of our capacity for empathy, we suffer from a constitutional – almost necessary – lack of it when it comes to the 'others' who are our predecessors and ancestors. She reopened the question of continuity within apparently radical change: how very far we ourselves had moved from our association's founding moment, immediately after the Second World War, and yet how near we still circle back to past predicaments and old dilemmas in new guises, given our unwitting custom of actively dismissing the past or merely forgetting it.

Resolving Colson's paradox demands rediscovery. In response, this chapter reviews the work and life of Elizabeth Colson through an intellectual history focused on her social biography. The central argument is that her legacy matters for coming generations of anthropologists, and for very good reasons. Of these, three are offered by way of introduction, to be followed by a good number of others, and much substantial evidence. Along with that argument, and also substantiated below, my contention is that coming from a Midwestern town in Minnesota, distinguished by the uneasy coexistence of displaced Ojibwa Indians and white settler farmers, predisposed Colson towards concerns with discrimination, emplacement and displacement, egalitarianism and participatory democracy, and towards being a systems sceptic. By this, I mean a sceptic who casts doubt on the utility of any model of a system as if it were something consistently well integrated as a totality, whether a social system or a cultural system. My account of Colson's legacy views it in relation to the approaches of other pioneering social anthropologists, primarily Max Gluckman and his respected seniors, Edward Evans-Pritchard and Meyer Fortes.[2]

The first reason for turning to her work and life now, shortly after her death at the age of 99 in June 2016, is her transatlantic role. Early in her long career, mediating in one direction, she introduced to British social anthropology approaches from American sociology. Remarkably, she also made a breakthrough regarding cross-cutting ties in conflict resolution, which called into question, at least in Britain, the utility of the mainstream structuralist model of segmentary opposition. Later, her efforts mediated in the other direction, to American anthropology. In particular, she advanced the reception of work by members of what came to be labelled the Manchester School as it emerged in Britain, under Max Gluckman's leadership, from its origin in the Rhodes-Livingstone Institute.[3] Important as recalling Colson's impact itself is, no less valuable is knowledge of the intense networking, the broad critical reviewing, and the sustained collaboration that she accomplished.

The second reason is the question of classic ethnography. Is its day done? The answer may still be 'no' if coming generations can be attracted to reading her exemplary ethnographies (1953, 1958, 1960, 1971b, 2006; Colson and Scudder 1988). Colson wrote all these books in a spare, accessible, jargon-free style. Her priorities were empirical – the analysis was primarily about her own findings; those of others did figure explicitly but usually for comparison in the background. The closest she came to a label for her approach was, perhaps teasingly, 'eclectic'. Her aim was not to create simple models, nor to make a detachable part of her texts wholly abstract

and theoretical. There were no extensive references in her monographs to general theorists or philosophers and their works; contrary to much present-day anthropology, no Great Thinker worried
Colson or her readers, at least not as an obsession in the monograph. Instead, she positioned herself and her own basic intellectual
stance, often implicitly, in deft sketches of significant others, mostly
in a considerable stream of reviews, obituaries and encyclopedia
entries, which reflect her continuously wide reading in the social
sciences.[4]

As an essayist and, on a good number of occasions, a distinguished lecturer, Colson was witty and direct, pithy and cogent,
yet not abrasive in argument. She was given to making a bold,
striking case, free of dated labels and once-fashionable conceptual
schemes. She did so without being confrontational. Her remarkable
tour de force of essays from her 1973 Lewis Henry Morgan Lectures,
Tradition and Contract: The Problem of Order (1974) belongs on the
same anthropological shelf of slim classics as Malinowski's *Crime and
Custom in Savage Society* (1926) and Gluckman's *Custom and Conflict
in Africa* (1955) – all open texts for each generation's reimagining
of where our lasting heritage in anthropology could and possibly
should still lead us.

Despite claims to the contrary, the questions anthropologists are
now asking – about moral virtue, choice and the limits on freedom
in the apparently new departures of a rapidly growing sub-field
called 'The Anthropology of Ethics' (Lambek 2010; Faubion 2011;
Laidlaw 2014a, 2014b; Fassin 2015; Werbner 2015, 2017) – are, in
fact, not novel. They are Colson's questions. She, too, had to ask
them in troubling times, as she recognized at the very start of her
Morgan Lectures. Admittedly, she considered that her answers
belonged to arguments about governance and social control in
political anthropology. The arguments reached back, she showed,
to opposed positions held by the founders of social anthropology:
Lewis Henry Morgan on contract and Sir Henry Maine on custom
(1974b: 5).

If the second reason (the present need to revitalize ethnography)
is new, the third reason is an old problem, now acutely renewed.
It is the problem anthropologists have in their attempt to make
sense of flux and perilous uncertainties in changing and increasingly
more complex social fields. It is the very problem that Colson

foregrounded in 'Culture and Progress', her 1975 AAA Distinguished Lecture:

> For me, at least, fieldwork in the United States at the end of the 1930's and in the early 1940's put in question current theories about holistic cultures and societies as bounded social units. It made it difficult for me to be comfortable with any theoretical scheme that did not view social phenomena as in flux, never reaching an equilibrium, adaptive to such forces as played upon them, including purposive human beings, but given continuity and order by the human desire to predict the future and make sense of the past by the creation both of normative rules and a conceptual model of a stable world. (1976: 264)

In my view, here and elsewhere Colson positions herself even more fully as a system sceptic. Colson's basic points – questioning current holistic models or systemic theories – are part of a dialogue with and against the ideas and arguments (especially on closed systems and on the utility of equilibrium models) of Max Gluckman, her great friend and old colleague (Gluckman 1965b: 279–301; 1968a).

On his side, of course, Gluckman was a devoted broker of her work, reinterpreted for the widest possible public. For an appreciation of the force of Colson's influential and basic contribution to the development of theory in the Manchester School, one must turn, first, to Gluckman's remarks in his introduction to *The Craft of Social Anthropology*, the School's methods book:

> As we appreciate more fully that customs and values are to some extent independent of one another, discrepant, conflicting, contradictory, we shall have to evolve concepts to deal with social life which are less rigid and which can cope with the lack of interdependence as well as the existence of interdependence, and with the haphazard as well as the systematic. (1967: xix)

If somewhat of a confession, in my view, these remarks seem to register the powerful systems-builder in the act of rethinking the systematic along with the anti-systematic and on the brink of 'an advance' – the future might lie all the more with the systems sceptic, Colson herself. The stronger thrust in theory came to be the one that she advocated more fully in her 1975 distinguished lecture – based on a view of social phenomena as in flux, never reaching an equilibrium (Colson 1976). Gluckman's idea, from natural science, that equilibrium 'is the tendency of a system to return after disturbance to its previous state' (1965b: 279) was, for Colson, not at all a good starting point for social theory or ethnographic analysis.

In perhaps her most reflexive overview of her own approach, Colson argued in 1989 that consistent assumptions had informed her contributions to anthropology over fifty years. Assumptions about flux and freedom were basic. 'I have assumed', said Colson, 'the transience of social forms and a higher degree of freedom of action than many anthropologists appear to grant to whatever it is that they define as "others"' (1989: 1). Even further, in one of her last articles, she drew lessons from certain refugee studies, which appraised the 'powerful forces that destabilize societies and transform citizens into outcasts' (2007c: 332). The need, she saw, is for an engaged anthropology that grapples through fine-grained ethnography with flux and the specially heightened uncertainty of freedom in the troubled times of the twenty-first century.

Colson's fame as one of the foremost anthropologists engaged in the critical understanding of human problems owes much to her late career research, from the mid-1950s onwards, on forced change among Gwembe Valley Tonga in Zambia. She asked, first, questions of emplacement: how Gwembe Valley Tonga had consciously adapted to change in their environment and ecology in the past and what were their established survival strategies in a highly flexible social field (1960). Then, in sustained collaboration with a former student, Thayer Scudder, she turned to the ways Gwembe Valley Tonga endured massive displacement and resettlement. The construction of the Kariba Dam brought high social, economic and political costs. It was a project, Colson argued, driven foolishly by technological considerations in disregard of their social consequences (1971b; Colson and Scudder 1988; Scudder 2005). Nevertheless, her aim was not to pursue or discredit the developers but to understand the ingenuity and even the folly of the people coping with development.

The home town social anthropologist: emplacement, displacement, mobility

A small, relatively egalitarian farming community around Wadena, near Hewitt, might seem an unlikely place for one of the greatest ethnographers in her generation to grow up, but Colson was deeply attached to the town. 'In my generation', she told an interviewer, 'the hometown was something that rooted you, even though you never lived there as an adult' (Colson 2002: 80). The town itself was named Wadena after an Ojibwa Indian chief. Her mother was a high school principal, her college-educated father a superintendent of schools. Her father's father, a Swedish immigrant, had a farm, which remained in the family until the Great Depression (Colson 2002: 1–6). Colson was devoted to her mother, who lived at their home in Minnesota until her death in her nineties.

Wadena was a place of uneasy displacement: for some people, not at all a stable world. Ojibwa Indians, who had lost their lands to white settlers, were still living nearby, many in reservations. It was also a place of comfortable – perhaps too cosy – emplacement, at least for the settlers. In their small community, most farmers might well have claimed Scandinavian or German origins; they could have taken pride in being Midwesterners, believed in individualism, and assumed they enjoyed a good measure of freedom of action and were free to make choices in a participatory democracy.

The moral vision underlying Colson's extended ethnography for more than sixty years of research among Tonga of Zambia is that of 'a participatory democracy' (2006: 28). She perceived that Tonga, too, had 'a basic egalitarianism' (2002: 86). Perhaps even more than Wadena people, both Ojibwa and white Americans, Tonga had to cope with predicaments of restraining violence, protecting their freedom yet deliberately limiting it, and having to be 'on the move'. They were consciously adapting as more encroachments and interventions threatened their small-scale communities.

In holding her home town moral vision, Colson was also already disposed to be a systems sceptic, even before her fieldwork. Growing up in Wadena, she could be highly conscious of conflicted co-presence. On one side were the Indigenous people, redefined as dispossessed strangers in their own land; on the opposite side were the farmer-settlers, who had become homebodies in the land of the others. Colson was not simply one or the other, if perhaps somebody somehow aware of being in-between, or even with a memory of uneasy inclusion – her German grandmother had to conceal her identity during the First World War and was fearful of peaceful Ojibwa trespassing on the family farm. Hence, Colson's curiosity about assimilation (1945) and strangers, which she followed in numerous studies (1966a, 1967, 1968, 1970, 1971b, 1976, 1986, 1996, 2007a). Remarkably, even the very earliest of Colson's studies was motivated by the quest for truths about both displacement and emplacement – indeed, the tensions between them. Her early teachers encouraged this motive. Her first fieldwork in 1939 and 1940 was supervised as part of a long-term study of intercultural relations by Bernard and Ethel Aginsky at the Field Laboratory for Research in the Social Sciences (Aginsky and Aginsky 1947; Colson 1989: 7).

The idea of long-term anthropological research, attentive to the immediate moment and yet seeing it in history, was with Colson from the start with the Aginskys. Based on that fieldwork, she wrote her University of Minnesota master's thesis on acculturation among Pomo women of San Francisco Bay (1940).[5] In a published revision of that thesis, Colson remarked, 'All three [Pomo] women have lived in a world shattered by the impact of white settlement and have shared a compromise culture which lies between that of their Pomo ancestors and that of their white neighbors' (1974a: 1). For her Radcliffe MA in 1941 and PhD in social anthropology (1945), she undertook fieldwork on assimilation and resistance among Makah of Neah Bay, Washington. Colson reached one striking revelation from observing Makah in contrast to the Pomo. Makah had confidence among themselves, despite their experience of white American efforts to dominate them. Still living on their own land and with a 'semblance of economic independence', they 'were prepared to use the courts to fight off efforts to displace them' (1989: 8).

In 1942 Colson interrupted her Makah fieldwork for a year to work on the impact on Japanese Americans of internment in the Poston War Relocation Center in Arizona (Colson 1943; Pritchett 2007: 136). For her later development as a social anthropologist, it was a watershed, largely because of working with Edward Spicer.[6] Through Spicer, recalled Colson, 'getting ideas coming out of Radcliffe-Brown's tradition, [meant] that one could start by trying to see what the organization was, what were the institutions, that was solid ground under one's feet' (Colson 2002: 97). With characteristic frankness, Colson reflected, also, on the questionable ethics of that war relocation research:

> Recently anthropologists like myself who carried out research on 'war-relocation' camps have been criticised on the grounds that we

provided legitimation for the internment and the losses suffered by those interned. I can only say that we regarded the internment as a gross violation of civil rights. But I thought then as I think now that witnesses were needed and that anthropologists had skills needed to that task. (1989: 9)

Also significant, I suggest, is that she came to her research with the gifts of a natural fieldworker. At ease in role reversal – an apparently dominant other (the white American) becoming an inferior and having as her superior anybody who would teach her in her research – she was unafraid of stumbling in ignorance or partial knowledge or in the awkwardness of a language not quite mastered (eventually, she did become very fluent in Tonga).[7] It appealed to her sense of humour to continue, even in old age, to be called 'Kamwale' by Tonga, 'a word used for a young woman between puberty and the birth of her first child' (Colson 2002: 83). In fieldwork – as in birdwatching, her precious hobby – she enjoyed knowing in and through great patience. We still have much to learn from her frankness, telling in *The Makah Indians* about the limitations of her own early fieldwork, during the early 1940s in America, despite its yield in a substantial monograph (1953).

To carry out fieldwork in the late 1940s and early 1950s as an American woman in a British colony, Northern Rhodesia, was particularly challenging. Had Colson ever experienced any discrimination as a woman anthropologist? 'No', she replied to a young female American scholar, who was so surprised that she was eager to explain Colson's answer away (Schumaker 2001: 120). In truth, Colson's answer reflected how deftly and firmly she negotiated her way past the pitfalls of the gender biases of her time. Usually in slacks and jeans – and even in her brother-in-law's cast-offs, khaki army trousers – she had the fun of what people around her in the field, administrators and Tonga alike, took to be ambiguous or even improper cross-dressing (Colson 2002: 76; Schumaker 2001: 134). Tonga had to be reassured that she was 'really a woman and not the man her clothing indicated' (Colson 1958: 266).

'A quiet unassuming sort of person' – that was the self-image Colson said she managed to present, even to the white settlers on the farm near her base among Plateau Tonga (Schumaker 2001: 134). Characteristically, she struck up a lifelong friendship with the mother of the family, and later with the children, which lasted until the end of her life when, birdwatching on the veranda at her home on their farm, she died at the age of 99 of a stroke. Characteristically also, what she greatly esteemed in her long-term field assistant Benjamin Shipopa was that he was 'a man of integrity who could make friends and win respect' (Schumaker 2001: 204).

To be clear, in no way am I suggesting that Colson was meek or risk averse. If, for Mary Douglas, Max Gluckman was 'an unattractive and domineering personality' (Fardon 1999: 51), around and towards Colson he was more the gentle giant. In good measure, this was because Colson was not really a 'serious person'. She was known for being very funny, yet wise and kind in her own thoughtful way.

Her playful touch can be seen in her ethics essay on 'Heroism, Martyrdom, Courage' (1971). Esteemed by Tonga, a true man of virtue turned out to be readier to resist domineering or intimidation not by standing up to it but by running away – danger past, he would astutely come home. Presented in a Festschrift for Evans-Pritchard, such masculinity was ironic, even mischievous, if understood by contrast to his romantic picture of proud, heroic men – Nuer and himself also. Colson knew Evans-Pritchard was renowned for spellbinding tales of his Second World War exploits as a bush irregular or *bimbashi* sergeant in the Sudan (Geertz 1988: 51–7).

My own understanding is that being confrontational did not come easily to Colson. It was more a last resort, something one did if really pushed; being playful was better, if possible.[8] Hence, Manchester legend has it that in the departmental seminar, Colson would knit. When Gluckman had reached and seemed to be going beyond his peak in argument, laying down the law, Colson would let loose her ball of wool. As the caring gentleman (at least at that moment), Gluckman would roll it up and let others have their say.

Individual mobility, which always remained a great topic of her research, became a personal hallmark. After her RLI research and administrative posts in Zambia, she held a good number of academic posts, first in Britain (at Oxford and Manchester, as the first Simon Fellow and the first senior lecturer in social anthropology), back in the United States (at Goucher College, Boston University, Brandeis University, Northwestern University, University of California, California Institute of Technology and Palo Alto's Center for Advanced

Study in the Behavioral Sciences) and, after her retirement in 1984 from the University of California, again in both Britain (Oxford's Refugee Studies Centre) and Zambia (Institute of African Studies, formerly the RLI, University of Zambia).

Pioneering career: from breakthrough to bridge building

The stir caused by Colson's notable lectures to the Royal Anthropological Institute, first on 'Rain Shrines' in 1948, then in 1951 on 'Social Control and Vengeance', was only in part due to ethnographic discovery. Colson's findings on small-scale interactions among Tonga did disclose a 'new type of society'. Tonga were 'have-nots' in the past, not merely stateless and without a hierarchy of authority but also without segmentary lineages, age grades, secret societies and social stratification of any kind. They had been severely hammered in the nineteenth century by the predatory states around them (see Colson 1969; Colson and Gluckman 1951). It was not always clear to whom the name Tonga should be applied. In all directions they included peoples possessing similar cultures but called by other names, and the boundaries at which people called themselves by other tribal names and were called by them varied considerably (Gluckman 1965b: 92).

It was against a powerful structuralist mainstream in British social anthropology during the 1940s and 1950s that Colson's ethnographic contributions first took on their broader significance. 'She was the only anthropologist in the late 1940's and early 1950's who was making a distinctive theoretical breakaway in social anthropology', according to Emrys Peters, himself an outstanding critic of segmentary lineage theory (Peters, letter to the Chair, Anthropology, University of California, Berkeley, 2 April 1967, GPJRUML). Most important for her breakthrough were the political anthropology waves in the wake of *African Political Systems* (Fortes and Evans-Pritchard 1940) and *The Nuer* (Evans-Pritchard 1940). Oxford was the dominant centre of the new waves and, as is well known, the teachings of Radcliffe-Brown informed many shared assumptions for these.

Seen to be under attack was the dominant paradigm of segmentary lineage systems, which predicated a balanced opposition between bounded political units, whereas Colson's analysis opened the interest in alliance, in the spread of disparate bonds, in cross-cutting ties and, eventually, in diffuse units or networks. Some of the implications of Colson's discovery for political anthropology and social theory, however, only became more clearly recognized over the following decades. Against the contemporary theories of inter-dependent institutions, she argued that

> the cross-cutting of ties also operates in the same fashion in societies organized on the lineage principle, and that a further analysis of the data would show that these societies obtain their stability not because their local groups are unilineally organized, but because of the presence within each local group of people with a diverse set of ties linking them to others in other areas. (1962: 120)

One paradoxical suggestion, by Gluckman, was that 'in its very formlessness Tonga society has a structure which exerts some control over its individualistic members' (1962: vi). Gluckman made a valiant effort in his foreword to Colson's Tonga social and religious essays to push the argument beyond her systems scepticism and further in the direction of structuralist analysis.[9] He used Radcliffe-Brown's ideas on joking relationships to pursue a Durkheimian view of society as a whole moral system: 'Hence the clans stand for an ultimate social morality, through the system which interlinks many clans as clan-jokers, and the set of values of social life are embodied in the only enduring groups, as other values are represented through rain-shrines' (1962: xi).

Against that, Colson felt uncomfortable with Durkheimian thought on the moral system. Even more, throughout her career as a social anthropologist, especially when teaching in the United States, Colson had difficulty coming to positive terms with Durkheim's influence (Colson 1974b; 1989: 7). More congenial, and more important in her own intellectual history, was the influence of Locke, Hume, Ferguson and other moral philosophers of the seventeenth and eighteenth centuries, and their ideas on the 'freedom to create displayed by human inventiveness' (1989: 7).[10]

In accord with her systems scepticism, moreover, Colson was averse to totalizing disparate parts into a nice, whole structure, even one in flux, not in equilibrium. Despite appeals for more holistic integration from Gluckman, the influential systems builder, she avoided making her early social and religious essays into the usual unitary monograph. For this reason, these essays still richly repay close attention by anthropologists interested in what Marilyn Strathern (2005), with an eye to perspectives on scale and proportion, would call partial connections on scale and diversity (see also Colson 1980).

Responding to Fortes: kinship and mainstream structuralism

In the late 1940s and early 1950s there was a further challenge for Colson in that the contemporary structuralist mainstream was profoundly forceful not merely in political anthropology but also in the innovative study of kinship. Radcliffe-Brown's teachings had also inspired Fortes in his masterpiece (Fortes 1949a). Colson held it in the highest respect. Her review of it concludes: 'Any anthropologist engaged in fieldwork would do well to take a copy with him as he will find it a stimulus to new investigation as well as a source of illumination for the problems that his particular tribe or group pose in the fields of kinship and social organization' (1950a: 205).

It is not certain whether she followed her own good advice. But one can see in her substantial monograph the richness of observed practice in her response to Fortes's masterpiece. Of course, there was no room for his preoccupation with a balance between polar social principles. Never at ease with Fortes's assumptions from Radcliffe-Brown about the essential importance of basic moral axioms, Colson shifted the kinship focus 'to the way in which changing economic and general social conditions are impinging upon the Tonga family and the regulation of marriage' (1958: 119).

Colson's contemporaries gave the marriage book mixed reviews. Malinowski's student, Hortense Powdermaker, generously recognized its 'excellent and detailed description' but faulted it for having 'no theory of social change' (1959: 1121). Evans-Pritchard's student, Mary Douglas, noted that the book well documented a familiar trend in familial change, but she called into question the value of the focus of the book, even because of its being comprehensive: 'the subject of domestic relations tends to make an unrewarding theme for a major book. If it is to be comprehensive, it is inevitably discursive; and it affords little in the way of theoretical framework' (1960: 197).

Colson's influence on kinship studies and the relation between the family and more extended groups or clans has not matched her influence on contemporary political anthropology. Similarly limited was her impact on power and gender studies, despite her fine analysis of the grounds for interpersonal equality among Tonga men and women.

Problems of order: the two Morgans, Colson's ethnography

There is a very significant difference between the Morgan in Colson's Morgan Lectures of 1973 and the Morgan in the lectures of 1963 by Fortes. I take it that Colson was well aware of her departure from her predecessor's lectures. If somewhat implicitly by contrast to his as a backdrop – and I want to read between the lines – she shaped hers to argue for her approach as a fresh alternative for a very different decade. Even a brief rehearsal of the two approaches to Morgan and his ethnography is thus essential for our understanding of where Colson wanted to take us in her own lecture.

To start with Fortes: not surprisingly, with the apparent passing of the heyday of structuralist studies, Fortes was at pains, in his big and weighty, monumental, long and deeply considered 1970 book of the 1963 lectures, to claim Morgan for his own intellectual lineage from Radcliffe-Brown and for this view of the kinship system: 'System, for Morgan, means therefore a self-balancing, internally coherent, and harmonious arrangement of recognised relationships, centered on Ego and based upon fundamental conceptions common to all humanity' (1970: 34). Even further, Morgan was the father of that Radcliffe-Brownian lineage because he appreciated the corporate nature of the *gens* or descent group (1970: 39). But of little or almost no interest, perhaps given Fortes's tight focus on kinship relations, was Morgan as the ethnographer, who learned from the Iroquois the lessons for participatory democracy with deliberation in decision making that his fellow Americans needed, and indeed now need to know even more than ever.

Reintroduced by Colson, Morgan's ethnography foregrounded the decisive moral and political agency of women. Holding their own offices, Iroquois women had the authority to appoint men to be their council spokesmen in public deliberation. Women were living at home at peace, while men away at war were absent, sometimes for a whole year at a time. Not men but women were in control of the basic social exchange in which they circulated men in marriage between exogamous matrilineal clans and, at their discretion, rescued war captives from gruesome torture to marry them as aliens, assimilated yet ever subject to the approval of women. Thus, networking, so important in the making of moral and political decisions, was primarily women's work.

All of this recovered ethnography was brought to bear by Colson to interrogate a model of corporate groups in a segmentary system that Fortes could well derive from Morgan. This classic model underplayed the dispersal of ties between corporate groups and thus also underplayed strategy in networking – how actors might deliberately realign, promote order and reorganize themselves to meet contingencies. Colson was not directing us to dismiss that model out of hand, however. Instead, she stood on its head the Morgan-derived model in order to make a key point of her own, which she unpacked throughout much of her lectures.

Colson drew on her ethnography of Tonga clanship to disclose the very work of social modelling as it lends a reassuring appearance of stability to the changing flow of social relations. She showed how a twelve-clan version of that classic model was used conceptually, and even rigidly maintained in practice, as what might now be called a folk model. Without ever adding new clans, it was held for peaceful purposes to absorb newcomers or aliens, like Colson herself, within a moral order of shared humanity. Tonga clans were not corporate groups or groups fixed forever by descent, but open categories that could be equated with others outside Tonga areas. Hence, with clanship came the possibility of finding one's place over great distances across cultural and social boundaries, even from one Central African country to another. The resonance of Colson's understanding of clanship can be considered to echo Lévi-Strauss on totemism as 'a vision of humanity without frontiers' (Colson 1966a: 166). At its broadest, Colson's own argument was about categorization as a social accomplishment that people create and, within limits they set for themselves, sometimes recreate.

Colson began her lectures by throwing down a gauntlet for herself. She found herself challenged by her awareness that members of 'a generation disillusioned with the old order' were struggling to work out moral alternatives, sometimes with an idealized vision of the virtues of life in small-scale communities (1974b: 1–2). They were too often deluded, she discerned, and the task that followed for anthropologists like herself was to engage deeply with the questions of 'the advantages and disadvantages of living under authority' (1974b: 4). If a society of equals was sought, then a good number of problems of order – moral as well as political – had to be addressed. These were the problems she went on to illuminate from chapter to chapter in her classic book, from achieving consensus and knowing rules to establishing the limits of authority and appreciating critically the current search for utopia in a New World Order.

The 'eclectic', the modern and the postmodern

On this basis, I want to consider the long-term development of Colson's thought by looking backward from the lectures to *The Makah Indians*, her first monograph. The monograph cited only two anthropologists: Ralph Linton and Clyde Kluckhohn. Moreover, the only explicit conceptual debate with the ideas of her fellow anthropologists is a brief (almost perfunctory) bit in the conclusion (1953: 280 n.1, 284). If now dated, it hardly matters for the brilliance of the ethnography itself.

As a Radcliffe student, she was introduced by Talcott Parsons to Max Weber's work on social action (Colson 1989: 7). If an influence, his hand is well hidden in her monographs. Only in her last book was she seriously tempted, with mixed results, to test against her ethnography of Tonga highly abstract models (Mary Douglas's about grid and group) and to elaborate her own comparative method, mainly by reference to the varied practices of peoples near Tonga (2006: 19–34).

If we seek to grasp what made, and still makes, even her very first monograph a recognized classic, we find it in her ability to get us to share her fascination with actual practice – the love of gossip, for example – and to get us to recognize, perhaps in a convex mirror, a human comedy in which we too can be intimately placed. She thanked the Makah themselves for 'their outrageous humour' (1953: xii). Her chapter 7, 'The Makah and Their Traditions', can hardly be matched in our literature for its record of what later came to be called the 'invention of tradition' and for its analytic insights into what people are doing to themselves and their way of life, both intentionally and unintentionally, through their bickering and personal sniping. The nub of much of Colson's analysis is this:

> The Makah criticize others in terms of a set of values which operate within the group to govern the behaviour of members of the group. The constant criticism, gossip, and back-biting is a re-assessment of these values, which today can be expressed in no other way. If they repressed the gossip and back-biting, the values would disappear, and with them much of the feeling that the Makah are a distinct people. To some extent, the back-biting itself has become an end in itself, a system of behaviour into which the Makah have thrown themselves with a zest and a determination, which have brought the art of verbal denigration to a high peak. Certainly the malicious statements of their fellows give rise to hatred and unhappiness and to a retreat from public view, but from the zest with which they recount their experiences in the field of slander, it is apparent that they have developed this type of behaviour into a game with its own rules and behaviour. (1953: 229)

It is possible to read *The Makah Indians* in the way that Gluckman so persuasively did and so generously publicized in his famous lectures around the world, to Australia and back home, first published in an article as 'Gossip and Scandal' (Gluckman 1963a). This reading revealed a modernist work, and Gluckman made it out as giving strong support for the one theory of his, equilibrium theory (1965b: 296–9), that Colson, as we have seen, found most unsympathetic, so much so that she publicly rejected it in her 1975 lecture.

I want to offer an alternative reading. In good measure, I read her work as a narrative study paving the way for my own regard in *Tears of the Dead* (Werbner 1991) for the Rashomon effect – the ways an event is told in contradictory stories by individual witnesses from different viewpoints. I am tempted to claim that *The Makah Indians* is a postmodernist work, or at least that in its turn to the Rashomon effect it is more postmodern than modern. It is, of course, an admittedly incomplete work, as perhaps a postmodern text should be, a part still seeking something more if ever it is to be a whole. Colson 'knew the interaction of the Makah with the [American] whites chiefly from the Makah side' (1953: x), and, among Makah, knew women best and young and middle-aged men almost entirely from village gossip. Her narrative accomplishment was to capture the contradictory stories of individuals – importantly, the flux in the very storytelling – and to present their interwoven significance (as it were, the morals of the stories) in a gripping account that is historic.

It is a tribute to the accompanying sociological analysis that even readers unsympathetic to a postmodernist turn have seen the strength of the Makah book. Its reception in British social anthropology ranked it among the best monographs of its time. Maurice Freedman of the London School of Economics called it 'the best book in anthropology in several years' (Peters, letter to the Chair, Anthropology, University of California, Berkeley, 2 April 1967, GPJRUML); 'I consider your book on them [the Makah] one of the greatest books in anthropology', wrote Gluckman to Colson in 1964 (MG to EC, 21 February 1964, GPJRUML).

Bridge building from American sociology and among social anthropologists

If her Makah book, like much of Colson's work, turned on qualitative research, it is striking, nevertheless, that she was a strong advocate of quantitative method of a kind much favoured in American sociology. Originally, Colson's intent, which Gluckman encouraged, was to start her Plateau Tonga book with her essay on small-sample communities (Colson 1961). It would have pitched her tent, so to speak, in a world of variables and hypotheses – the entry into a mass of quantitative data in preparation for the qualitative material to follow. Plans changed, in part due to publishers' demands, and the small-sample article was excluded. Colson and Gluckman corresponded about a default position – the idea of an RLI methods book (MG to EC, 28 February 1961, GPJRUML), which eventually started with a revised version of Colson's methods article (1967, original 1954). Colson concluded, characteristically, with some temperance:

> The result of the intensive study of small units may not make for the best description in the style of a standard ethnography, but it is likely to provide us with the type of information we need for testing hypotheses and for formulating new research into the relation between various social factors. (1967: 15)

During the late 1940s and early 1950s, Colson was the natural bridge builder across the Atlantic between newly self-defining social anthropologists based in post-war Britain and the social scientists back home in the United States. Even among British social anthropologists, as rivals and competitors – some in London, others mainly in Oxford, Cambridge and Manchester – hers was a triumph of cross-cutting ties.[11] Eventually, Colson accomplished something of a balancing act between two of that time's rival Great Men: Raymond Firth in the lead at the LSE and Max Gluckman at Manchester. In her 1975 distinguished lecture, she praised the pragmatic actor orientation in each of their opposed yet complementary approaches.

There are two apparently nice bits of conventional wisdom about the Manchester School in the making, neither of which suited Colson and her gift for bridge building. The first is a method myth that finds a genetic relationship between Chicago sociologists led by Robert Park and Manchester anthropologists, simply on the grounds that case studies were first developed at Chicago, then at Manchester. Against that, in a 2008 critical review of *The Manchester School* (Evens and Handelman 2006), Colson clarified an actual transatlantic relationship that meant that 'Manchester owed more to American sociology than to American anthropology' (2008a: 336). She traced the deliberate connecting efforts that she made along with John Barnes and Clyde Mitchell during the beginnings of the Manchester School. Together, they turned more to Gestalt psychology and Kurt Lewin's field theory, to Jacob Moreno's approach to sociometry, leading to network analysis, and to 'work on social dynamics underway in the United States'. Colson herself got Gluckman to invite the American sociologist George Homans, whose *The Human Group* became 'a key text' for the Manchester School.

From her training for her MA and PhD at Radcliffe in the 1940s, Colson knew how much Lewin was influenced by being a refugee – that is, being unable to rely on custom and habit as 'sufficient guides to conduct' (Colson 1989: 6, citing Coser 1984: 15). She found that Lewin's 'approach was appealing to a Midwesterner who shared the typical American belief in the importance of the individual and the possibility of exercising choice in a world that was not predetermined' (Colson 1989: 6).

Another Manchester myth verged on a mix between *machismo* and political ideology. Supposedly, anthropologists at Manchester were 'viewing themselves as a group of eclectic and left-leaning marginals in an upper-middle class academic discipline' (Mills 2006: 166). This myth left no place for Colson. The truth is that if Gluckman was ever something of a Marxist and a leftist, then Colson was not, and from the start she let him know that she 'was not prepared to take on any political ideology'. Her story is that she won him over, playfully:

> I quoted him an Ogden Nash poem, something about being liberal and being able to see both ends of something or another, and you didn't know whether or not it meant you were this or that or had a wobbly spine. And he laughed, and from then on it was understood we each had our own way of handling what we thought. (Colson 2002: 78)

Exhausted after a demanding trip to Australia in 1960, and offering an apology for not being able to keep his promise to lecture and join Colson, then at Brandeis University, Gluckman expressed his lasting admiration:

> You know Elizabeth that there is no one whom I hold in greater affection than you, and there is no colleague whose opinion I value more. I only write to you in this way because I see no alternative. I really am desperately exhausted.
> Most affectionate regards,
> Yours ever,
> Max (MG to EC, 14 November 1960, GPJRUML)

With the same fond respect, Colson sent Gluckman a copy of her Morgan Lectures. 'Dear Max', she wrote on the flyleaf, 'I wish you had had a chance to read this in manuscript. It needed your fine finishing touch.'

A lifelong and deep friendship was something that Colson shared not only with Gluckman but also with Barnes and Mitchell, who both worked with her as early RLI anthropologists (then sociologists). I have suggested, in a review of the Manchester School, that it developed from a close-knit group into a loose-knit network linking widely dispersed scholars (Werbner 1984b, 1991). The core of this network was anything but loose-knit, however. Colson continued to devote much time and energy in keeping her RLI friends, prominently Gluckman, in close contact with her and each other. She did this by sharing work in progress and after publication; by letters, visits and invitations; and by passing news of them and their students, whom she met warmly and helped – and I include myself.

As usual in her transatlantic bridge building, at Berkeley from 1964 she introduced Gluckman's work, hot off the press, to Nader for Gluckman's law studies, and to many of her own students interested in conflict, ritual and social control. Colson intended to join Barnes in Australia to collaborate on an urban project on Darwin as a small colonial town transformed into a modern city. She wanted to refresh her curiosity, and perhaps her zest for life, in fresh fieldwork. Although in 1965 and July–September 1966 she did brief initial fieldwork, the project fell through when Barnes went to Cambridge for a professorship.

Fighting against academic discrimination, negotiating amity

Besides bridge building, Colson brought to academic life a fine sense of others' vulnerability to aggression. She took bold risks, well aware of the cost to herself, in standing up publicly against bullying of others and discrimination in academic life. One example was her signal resignation from Brandeis University in 1963. At the time of the Cuban Missile Crisis, the president of Brandeis University humiliated her colleague Kathleen Gough. The abuse followed Gough's encouraging her students to make a political protest. If she had been in Grosvenor Square at the time, Gough would have shouted 'Viva Fidel, Kennedy to hell.' At a meeting, the president bullied her for a public apology.

Informed of the situation in April 1963 while in the field in Zambia, Colson cabled her resignation in protest. She had no job in sight. 'No job was better than a Brandeis job', she then wrote to Gluckman. Though she was not wholly in sympathy with her colleagues' political case, she had to stand by them. Having been head of the department, she had to fight the administration's aggression, their toxic backbiting, their shouting-down and intimidation, their unwillingness to hear the other side (EC to MG, April 1963, GPJRUML). It was especially painful for Colson, who wrote so brilliantly in *The Makah Indians* (1953) on the consequences for a community when gossip passes into scandal (see below).

Against that painful lesson, the haven Colson found at Berkeley brought out her gift for persuasion, for hearing the other side while negotiating collegial amity. Though wide-eyed, knowing the dark arts in the world of academic committees – and she came to serve influentially on a good number, including the budget committee – she tried to make her way with the care for the common good in negotiation that her experience of societies originally 'without a developed executive' had taught her (Colson 1974b: 5). Laura Nader recalled:

> When Colson came to Berkeley, her impact on the department was noticeable first in faculty meetings. She listened, she commented in a forthright and crisp manner if she felt like it, and she was short about it, sometimes inspiring the same in others. Furthermore, her manner, both professional and collegial, made disagreements acceptable while not personal. Indeed, having been there first, I noticed that pettiness and personal animosities were reduced. (2002: iii)

In 1984, controversial but not aggressive in the push for equality at Berkeley, Colson wrote an influential report on the status of women on campus (Starr 1984). Over many years, she continued her fight against sex discrimination in academia. She carried her strong concern for fairness and equality even further. The cause of vulnerable young colleagues mattered greatly to her, particularly in an environment where they might be exploited as cheap, early-career staff, all-too-easily dismissed without tenure. In 1966 this concern led her to reject, after first accepting, an honorary doctorate from Smith, a world-class college for women (Colson 1966b). She could not accept the award for excellence, where excellence was being hurt by a denial of tenure on dubious grounds that blackened the reputation of an excellent, promising young anthropologist.

Thus, too, in her 1975 distinguished lecture, Colson brought to bear a memorable sensitivity to the interests of younger anthropologists. She held her notoriously critical audience captive. As Nader recalled:

> I remember how well aware she was of the young in her audience, the concerns they had about jobs, the dilemma in our field after

colonialism and with independence, as anthropology in the midst of biting ethical and intellectual critiques was trying to recover and uncover new directions. Her talk allowed for optimism amidst all the pessimism. She stirred her audience and there followed a standing ovation, an appreciation and recognition that Colson had used her intellectual skills to examine how our field progresses and how we find new paths and interesting questions. It was part of her generosity towards younger colleagues. (2002: vii)

Changing spiralists, cultivating gardener

Colson recognized, in her 1975 lecture, a trend among her senior colleagues. They were changing into spiralists, going here and there, and were no longer gardeners, cultivating the old sites. Such a shift had served ethnography extremely well when ethnographers moved away from familiar people and places for the sake of refreshing insights. Colson, by doing so, had actually carried forward – and sharpened rather than shifted – her own basic stance. But for a punchline, she left to the very end of her lecture her own current choice: long-term fieldwork. Having her Gwembe Valley research already well in hand, she was, in fact, taking the lead in opening major debate about long-term field research in social anthropology (Colson 1976).

The outcome was somewhat contrary, even to some of Colson's own expectations. She became, in her terms, an exemplary gardener, all the more true to Mary Douglas's early appreciation of Colson's ethnography of Plateau Tonga: 'this people may be added to the small number of African tribes whose ethnographic record has been made as complete as humanly possible' (Douglas 1960: 197). Colson's intimate, tireless and immensely productive observation of Tonga and their social and cultural problems over the last forty years of her long life culminated with her final monograph in a wealth of insights on a whole century of change in religious pluralism (Colson 2006).

Nevertheless, she had no time for My People-ism, the ethnographer's folly in the delusion that she alone could tell the whole truth, and from one perspective. Honoured in a Festschrift as the 'foremost student' of the Tonga-speaking peoples (Lancaster and Vickery 2007: i), she seized the opportunity, as a self-caricatured naive empiricist (Colson 1976: 274), for a perspectival moment, somewhat of a postmodernist kind. In the afterword of the Festschrift, from her own perspective, she shed light on the disparate perspectives of the other students, the shifts in scale in their accounts, and the surprising complexity of Tonga lives from the pre-colonial period – in a buffer zone between predatory states – to the unanticipated transformations in the colonial and postcolonial periods (2007a).

To reach from this an apparently obvious conclusion – that she held herself to be, above all, an Africanist – would be mistaken, and not merely because she sustained her lifelong fascination with American Indians, even in her teaching at Berkeley. When Berkeley wanted her as a 'first-rate Africanist', she made sure to be hired in the anthropology post. In it, by comparison to even the most distinguished of her colleagues, she proved to be more widely read, more open to diversity and, never an imperialist, less given to demanding her own line from students. This generous strength attracted to her students with wide interests in research across the world, 'as far afield as Indonesia, Morocco, Tunisia, Kenya, Japan, Canada, Sweden, Scotland, the U.S., and, of course, Zambia' (Pritchett 2007: 137).

In retrospect, with prospects

The traces of her past, rather than fading, have recently become all the more brilliantly clear. Though perhaps still incomplete, 'A New Bibliography of Elizabeth Colson' now contains hundreds of citations (Bachignani 2016). Her voice, too, can be heard, still crisp and warmly evocative, in recorded interviews (Colson 2007b); one of the longest is available in a full and indexed transcript (Colson 2002). What is revealed is a major body of her work, yet to be published together, that still speaks not so much in cross-cutting ties but in the undercutting arguments we always need in social science research.[12]

Notes

1 In 1947 Colson became the only American to be a founding member of the ASA. Exceptionally, she had never been a student in Bronislaw

Malinowski's seminar, or even seen him (Colson 2008b). Her Commonwealth job and her social anthropology PhD qualified her (Colson 2002: 90).

2 See Colson's obituary of Gluckman, which reviews his main contributions (Colson 1979).

3 As Gluckman's successor at the RLI, she took the lead in developing and implementing a New Five-Year Plan (Colson 1950b; 1977; 2002: 81–8; Schumaker 2001: 119–30). While she was at Oxford in 1947, writing up and with John Barnes and Clyde Mitchell, she was involved in making new RLI appointments, seeing people at the colonial office, and meeting the secretary of the Colonial Social Science and Research Council.

4 For a full list, see Bachignani 2016.

5 Among her early teachers at the University of Minnesota were Wilson Wallis, with his interest in moral philosophy (Colson 1968), and David Mandelbaum, who was 'a breath of fresh air' with an emphasis on 'the need to study cultures in the process of change' (Colson 1988: 412).

6 Spicer had a University of Chicago PhD and some training there by Radcliffe-Brown.

7 For the revealing otherness in her perception of the big-city anthropologist from London, her friend Lucy Mair, see Colson 1986.

8 When asked to comment on the cross-cultural meaning of 'happiness', she remarked on her perception of Tonga and other Zambians, from whom she learned so much: 'In Zambia, under most circumstances it is appropriate to appear as though all is well with one's world, to smile and joke even under adversity, and to conceal pain and anger, but at funerals women should wail and shed tears' (Colson 2012: 8).

9 For his further interpretation of Colson's Tonga material, see Gluckman 1956a: 8–9; 1965b: 91–103.

10 She owed this interest in moral philosophy, stressing inventiveness, in good measure originally from her MA training at Minnesota, to the impact of her old teacher and friend Wilson Wallis. In homage to him, she borrowed his book title, *Culture and Progress* (1931), for her 1975 distinguished lecture (1976).

11 For her memory of being an outsider in the anthropologists' academic factionalism in the late 1940s to early 1950s, see Colson 2008b. Like the other early RLI researchers Clyde Mitchell and John Barnes, she also attended Raymond Firth's and Darryl Forde's combined University College and LSE seminar, and she later remembered meeting most of the social anthropologists of that time in Britain (Colson 2002: 90).

12 When I first met Elizabeth Colson at Boston University in 1959 she not only advised me about her old colleagues at Manchester, but she took an interest in hearing about my own early research under the direction of Paul Radin among Winnebago Indians. We kept in contact intermittently for much of the rest of her life, including during some of the year of my sabbatical at Berkeley in 1981.

4

Clyde Mitchell and A. L.
Epstein: urban perspectives

J. Clyde Mitchell reflected on the course of his life, on 19 July
1990, some five years before his death, during a long interview with
Russell Bernard, the American cultural anthropologist and research
methods expert (Bernard 1990). One turning point after another
was, said Mitchell, with characteristically ironic self-effacement, an
accident, a matter of a lucky encounter. For example, there was his
brother noticing Max Gluckman's advertisement for a job, which,
somewhat on the off-chance, Mitchell got. His yarn was that he
somehow hypnotized Gluckman with the magic of Chi-square
values. He became, as an RAF veteran in 1945, an early, post-war
recruit for the Rhodes-Livingstone Institute where, until 1955, he
spent the first ten years of his professional life, rising from assistant
anthropologist to become the director in 1952.

Where the actor attributes accident, there the analyst discovers
pattern – so might Mitchell have himself proposed and then proved.
In his spirit of inquiry, curious about regularity and structure in
apparent chaos, I want, in this chapter, to trace, document and
analyse certain patterns in Mitchell's intellectual history and life
course.

Origins and finding a way in the world

Born in Pietermaritzburg, Natal in 1918, Mitchell had no home
town with which he could have identified from having grown up
in the place. Instead, because his Scottish father worked on the
railway, he moved in Natal from place to place and had to learn
from early on to navigate his way along routes and the railway

line. When he turned his attention as a mature scholar to urban growth in South Central Africa, he was tempted to speculate on the changing importance of line-of-rail towns in the life cycle of migrants (1987: 80–2). His home language, along with English, was Zulu – it was a time when servants were spoken to in their own language, according to Mitchell. A middle son, the fourth among seven, he recalled being aware throughout his childhood and youth that his family was always short of money. I believe their support for him made him all the more proud of his working-class origin and his upward mobility.[1] But along with the concern for finding his own way in the world, there is a returning question of confidence, given this early experience of being footloose and relatively poor.

If being wryly diffident about his actual accomplishments was something he cultivated and enjoyed, his letters to close friends, such as Gluckman, John Barnes and Bill Epstein often expressed moments of depression, self-doubt, unease about being able to complete work and meet the challenge at hand. 'I think your difficulty', remarked Gluckman, 'is that you have lost confidence in your own work and that this makes you constipated about writing. And I only tell you this, about reviews you have been getting of the Yao book, all here who are in the forefront of the subject, think it is brilliant' (MG to CM, 24 January 1957, MPBL). 'Mitchell was not drawn to scholarly combat', notes Susan Smith, 'quite the opposite, as he wrote to Max Gluckman in the late 1950s: "one wants to seek happiness and contentment and peace with life and fly in the face of ambition doing it"' (CM to MG, 7 July 1959, cited in Smith 2019: 119 n.34.).

What Mitchell did realize early in his life, with a good measure of upwardly mobile ambition as well as intense intellectual curiosity, was that his best way forward was through education and an entry into research. As Smith reports:

> Initially struggling both to afford, and to win, access to a University education, Clyde settled into life as a civil servant, as a hospital clerk monitoring the cost of treating infectious diseases. To break out of this, which he felt he must, he pursued a part time degree in social science (by evening class) mounted in 1938 by the University of Natal, then a College of the University of South Africa.
>
> Apparently he had social work in mind as a new career. However, he excelled in sociology and psychology, and this opened up a whole

new world. Intellectually, he found his niche as an anthropologist, though he was ambivalent about the label and eschewed the disciplinism it implied. (Smith 2019: 95)

Later, while training to be a pilot in the air force in the 1940s, he spent some of his spare time calculating Chi-square values for illegitimacy and religion among the Zulu on a slide rule. Although he did become a pilot with many successful and, indeed, daring sorties to his credit, he soon discovered that his outstanding ability was in navigation, for which he got specialist training in Cairo and then pursued, safely, for the rest of his missions.

Departures and breakthroughs: towards sociology

Although perhaps best known as an urban sociologist, we must appreciate the importance of Mitchell's early village study to understand rightly his pioneering contributions to basic approaches in social anthropology. Based on his RLI fieldwork, his seminal monograph, *The Yao Village* (1956), established for the Manchester School the use of micro-histories of sequences of village events in the analysis of local crises and factional politics.[2]

This use was, of course, taken a significant stage further in *Schism and Continuity in an African Society* (1957), Victor Turner's work on Ndembu and socio-drama, which I discuss in Chapters 8 and 9. In the collegiate and cumulative way of the Manchester School at its very best, Turner was able to build his version of an extended case method on the path-breaking example that Mitchell gave. Gluckman himself acknowledged that he found it a shortcoming in his own study among Barotse that he never managed to follow Mitchell's example and publish an extended case for the Barotse. It is worth saying also that, according to Gluckman, when Mitchell made his original advance in his Oxford doctoral thesis, his external examiner tried to persuade him to cut out or pare away the micro-histories. His examiner warned that no publisher would want them. Again, it is a tribute to Gluckman as editor that Manchester University Press was more than proud to publish these micro-histories. Through them, Mitchell pioneered a distinctive approach for the village studies sequels in the Manchester School series. It was, of course, Gluckman who did the needed work of promotion, making it known as a Manchester School advance: the extended case method. Mitchell claimed to have been drawn, as an undergraduate and before Gluckman's influence, to appreciate the social theories of the German sociologists Georg Simmel on conflict and Leopold von Wiese on social relations as social process.[3]

There is a second exemplary contribution of Mitchell's, which was pace-setting for Manchester School monographs. This contribution appears unmistakable in the 29 tables of *The Yao Village*. Not only is the monograph intimately qualitative in its actual cases, but it is also richly quantitative. As shown in the tables and their analysis, the methodology is meticulous and systematic, rigorous and intentionally scientific; in brief, a *tour de force* for an anthropologist who joined the RLI as a professionally trained social worker with a strong interest in statistics.

Such quantitative study accompanying the qualitative was a methodology Gluckman much admired, and he sought to have a demographer participate in the RLI research; his own genealogies and censuses for Barotseland were destroyed in a fire so that he never analysed them in relation to his other evidence on kinship and family relations. At his insistence, all of his students working in Africa took an obligatory highly detailed census in the field, often on punch cards after the model of the RLI census card which Mitchell designed.

Prestige, ranking and social perception

Proud as Mitchell was of his working-class origin and upward mobility in a largely middle-class academic environment, his intellectual curiosity drove him elsewhere. The comparative puzzle that held his interest was not class. Nor was it social mobility as such. Class was boring, he once told me. His curiosity was about stratification as a hierarchical phenomenon. How do people place each other in terms of prestige and rank, rather than class? How do they mark or signify that placement, and how responsive are their rankings and ratings to changing circumstances? These became enduring problems which captured Mitchell's interest over the whole of his career, culminating in his last published article, 'The Marks of Prestige of Yao Village Headmen' (1994). In *The Yao Village* when

Mitchell made his pioneering contribution to the development of the extended case method, he introduced another departure in method, at first for village studies and then for urban research by social anthropologists. It was the turn with a substantial body of numerical data to a thoroughly quantitative analysis. He put that first, before he presented in the extended case method the micro-histories for the making of social distance among village sections and for the politics of reputation among headmen and would-be headmen. Like the good navigator, as he explored the regularities in claims and competition among village headmen, he located his reader in a socially recognized framework of indicators of prestige and rank.

Carrying this interest in prestige forward, from his rural to his urban research (Mitchell 1964), and initially in collaboration with his fellow RLI researcher Epstein – and Epstein and Mitchell continued to be close collaborators over many years – Mitchell turned to questions of how occupations are valued during social change in urban Africa. The key, at least for 1950s Zambia, could not be a 'Western model' of class; on the basis of even preliminary research, the evidence in the 1950s according to Mitchell and Epstein was that a class structure on 'Western lines', if a possibility for the future, had not yet developed. But despite that, might there already be across industrialized societies similar valuations for the ranking of occupations by their social prestige?

Mitchell and Epstein's method of data collection for occupational ranking was through questionnaires, for which in 1954 some 653 boys from schools and a teacher training college filled out written answers. Such data, from student subjects unfamiliar with the very tests, now seems dubious to say the least, and the fact that Mitchell felt, even in 1987, that he had to continue to rely on ever more elaborate computing of this 1954 data is something I cannot explain.[4] It was clearly not a sample in any sense representative or typical, as Mitchell and Epstein admitted; compared to many urban Africans, the subjects were 'obviously younger, better educated, and probably more accustomed to town life' (Mitchell and Epstein 1959: 23). Nevertheless, Mitchell and Epstein went ahead; they applied very sophisticated statistical procedures to the data, and yielded correlations, indexes and tables for a prestige scale. On it, the rank order of occupations appeared 'familiar to us from similar studies in European communities. At the head of the list are the "brain" workers, followed by the skilled workers and the supervisors, while the unskilled manual workers are at the bottom' (Mitchell and Epstein 1959: 30).

Mitchell was a manual or skilled worker's son who crossed the railway tracks and himself became a 'brain' worker. Yet nowhere in this article with Epstein or in a series of later contributions (Mitchell 1964; 1966; 1987: 134–79) does he give any serious attention to social mobility relative to the prestige scale and ratings. The well-known fact that education was believed to be a gateway to more prestigious occupations is mentioned, but not adequately weighted in the analysis (Mitchell and Epstein 1959: 33). Given Mitchell's substantial overview of the literature on occupational prestige in comparative sociology (1964), it is a puzzling blind spot, for which I have no explanation.

The circulation of labour: relations between country and town

If Mitchell's view of the social standing that people have because of their work was remarkably short on social mobility, his pioneering work on urbanization pushed arguments on colonial social change to the frontiers of RLI transformational research. From the start of the RLI, the study of major transformations, primarily industrialization and with it the circulation of labour across a whole region of Central Africa, was a very high priority. What had to be problematized came to be called 'circulatory migration'. In this, many workers came from their rural homes to town and went home again, intermittently for periods of varying length, in their active lives as labourers; they usually finally returned back home in old age or when no longer able or willing to work. The countryside had to bear the social costs of reproducing the labour; there was no social security or system of industrial welfare payments. It was all part of that exploitative form of colonial capitalism which Gluckman analysed in his influential essay on 'Anthropological Problems arising from the African Industrial Revolution' (1961). But how much and which costs should industry and the state meet and for whom? The underlying issues of conflict and political economy were addressed in RLI urban research, importantly fostered by

Mitchell and carried out, from 1953, in a seminal study by Epstein (1958) while Mitchell was RLI director.

As I showed in Chapter 2 in my account of Gluckman's transformational project, he recognized that it called for fundamental research on the changing interrelations between town and country; and he planned in his RLI Seven-Year Plan, with a framework of variables, for a whole body of related studies; but although he made a beginning in this study among Barotse, with their rapid loss of youth to towns, he himself raised more questions than he was able to answer with substantial evidence. The person at the RLI who most systematically addressed the regional problems of social change by managing the collection and statistical analysis of a huge amount of demographic data, including social surveys from the line-of-rail towns, and who then advanced fresh general propositions, was Mitchell. Not surprisingly, mapping loomed large in Mitchell's pioneering work, from an early paper on 'The Distribution of African Labour by Area of Origin in the Copper Mines of Northern Rhodesia' (1954), to one of his last Central African articles, 'Distance, Transportation and Urban Involvement in Zambia' (1974).[5] The Copperbelt survey he directed afforded the opportunity to provide evidence from divorce rates which indicated that there was relative stability, with continuing high rates of divorce for migrants from matrilineal communities, and relatively lower rates for other migrants (1957). From his schoolboy survey he derived another scale, besides the one for prestige, to show how respondents in town ranked tribes or ethnic groups by reputation and placed them according to social distance (1956).

Mitchell's finding was that people in town sorted each other into categories, for urban purposes of interaction, according to simple principles: one was familiarity and the other, cultural similarity. Using these principles, people known in the countryside to be from different tribes could overcome difference in the town and label themselves according to cultural similarity. For example, in town they used the label Bemba for different countryside tribes, including Bemba but also neighbouring tribes such as Bisa, Lala, Lamba etc. All these were included in town in the single super-tribe, *a category, not a group*, that emerged in town. I stress *not a group* or political unit to highlight that the analysis was of interpersonal relations in what we would now call interethnic encounters; tribes as organized groups appeared in the countryside, and not in town, Mitchell found. Because of the multiplicity of tribes in the countryside, the town had to have a way of simplifying or reducing the differences for purposes of interpersonal interaction, especially between strangers. Even further, using such principles and tribal categories, Africans generated relationships where there had been none in the countryside. Besides such cultural perception of common identity, people also sorted themselves according to lack of familiarity or social distance.

Of course, Mitchell and Epstein did not stop merely by recognizing the general similarity in prestige scales. For their interest in prestige under conditions of major social change, they considered colonial domination by Europeans to be fundamental. Coming to be subordinate to Europeans had meant that Africans reached new perceptions of occupational prestige; some Africans constructed or appropriated an image of the 'European way of life' perceived as 'civilized'. They spoke of *shiviliseseni* in the town lingua franca, *chicopperbelti*, and used that image to make significant differences among *themselves*:

> Our own point of view is that the social grading of occupations among town Africans in Northern Rhodesia [now Zambia], as in other parts of Africa, is related to the degree to which the occupation calls for the qualifications which would enable the incumbents to follow what they consider to be a 'civilized' way of life. In other words, the social grading of occupations reflects the more generalized prestige system which manifests itself as the emulation of the way of life of the socially dominant Europeans. (Mitchell and Epstein 1959: 32)

Clarifying this point of emulation more carefully with regard to the unskilled workers who performed dances in town, Mitchell made it plain that for them and other townsmen, the emulation was immediately not of Europeans but of prestigious Africans, such as white-collar workers. Images of 'civilization' or 'the European way of life' were brought into play, and so labelled by the people themselves in their lingua franca:

> The European way-of-life has now become so much a part and parcel of life in the urban areas that the Europeans themselves have faded from the foreground. *Kalela* dancers do not seek vicarious participation in European society but vicarious participation in the upper levels of African society, from which, by their lack of qualification, they are

excluded. The prestige system in urban areas thus uses 'civilization' or 'the European way-of-life as a standard or scale of prestige'. (Mitchell 1956a: 15)

It is worth noting that before Mitchell published *The Kalela Dance*, Gluckman commented, 'I think you need to bring out much more explicitly the extent to which the dance is related to developing class differences in the African population, as against the European population as an ideal' (MG to CM, 17 January 1956, MBPL).

Against a likely criticism,[6] Mitchell came to argue that there was a political component to the prestige scale in that if political opposition to Europeans became violent, the value of certain occupations would change or become more marked by ambivalence (Mitchell 1964: 84). Mitchell and Epstein concluded that,

> while there is a fairly clear-cut system of prestige based on the outward marks of Western civilization, and this clearly affects inter-personal relationships among Africans in towns, this prestige scale does not yet provide a basis for the recruitment of corporately acting groups [such as classes]. (1959: 36)

When Mitchell did consider the question of middle-class Africans in 1955, his view was that

> however much they have taken over European values and modes of behaviour, Africans are not fully accepted by the European group. This means that middle class Africans must be subjected to intense frustrations. The ideology they have absorbed is that of a society in which there is mobility among the social classes, but in spite of their anticipatory socialization they are not accepted by the class to which they aspire. They are thus foredoomed in frustration. This frustration must lead, and has led, to organizations which challenge the existing social order. The precursor of the present African National Congress which challenges the dominant position of the Europeans came into being in the early thirties [in the form of African welfare societies]. (Mitchell 1956a: 6)

The Kalela Dance

Fascinated as Mitchell was by what he could learn from quantitative evidence, he was also the fieldworker who could be drawn by the sound of African drums, accompanied by the play of ribald humour in songs (they much appealed to his own hearty sense of humour), by the sight of convivial crowds of people having fun, and by their greater enthusiasm in bigger crowds for new performances of popular culture than for the traditional masquerades still performed in town. All of that conviviality resonated in *The Kalela Dance* (1956), Mitchell's pioneering account of the invention of ethnic difference and personhood in a modern plural city of colonial Africa.[7] Also remarkable is its contemporary resonance with what Francis Nyamnjoh expresses in his perception of paradoxes and conviviality in present-day urban life, 'the prickly paradoxes of intimacy and mutuality, representative of contestations with belonging taking place in urban African crucibles of becoming' (Nyamnjoh 2016: 256). In my view, *The Kalela Dance* needs to be read as a forerunner answering the urgent call for an analytic focus on urban conviviality that Nyamnjoh makes in his intervention in the debate on decolonization, #Rhodes Must Fall (2016).

I want to make it clear, also, that in *The Kalela Dance* there is a fieldworker's sensibility towards appreciating new popular culture that Epstein shared with Mitchell. The same resonance was strongly expressed in the argot *chicopperbelti*, when described by Epstein as the distinctive language of the towns:

> it mirrors vividly much that is characteristic of the new way of life of the towns: its humour and patience in the face of poverty and squalor; its uncertainties, ambivalence, and frequent intolerance; but, above all, its tremendous zest and gusto, its crude vigour and general restlessness. (Epstein 1959: 251)

In the foreground of *kalela* we find satire and social commentary, personal display and creativity: the innovative performance of popular culture. The performers of the dance were nearly all young unmarried men, unskilled workers who lived alongside others from different parts of the country, in bachelor hostels. There was one female member, in the role of 'nurse'. One might say that during their performances the young men came over like cocks of the walk after hens. They swanked in smart clothes, made themselves attractive and desirable for the women in their audience, sang boastfully about their own tribe and origins, while providing a running commentary on the moral realities of the town; they made the most of their licence to be playful jokers. They indulged in mockery and teasing insults of different tribes which usually evoked not hostility but laughter and immense enjoyment, especially among the mocked spectators. As in a joking relationship, when accepted on both sides, hostility was expressed without incurring animosity.

Mitchell introduced his account by acknowledging that he was trying to follow the method Gluckman used in 1940 in his 'Analysis of a Social Situation in Modern Zululand'. It was, of course, the method of situational analysis that started from description of a single, one-off event, the ceremony in Zululand at the opening of a bridge by the Chief Native Commissioner. From that came the analysis of the significance in the ceremony of elements important in 'the larger society'. As Mitchell understood Gluckman's method of situational analysis, it was by following out the leads in the ceremony that Gluckman was 'led to a historical and sociological analysis of the total structure of modern Zululand' (Mitchell 1956a: 1).

Carrying forward Gluckman's method of situational analysis, Mitchell framed his approach in this way:

> I start with a description of the *kalela* dance and then relate the dominant features of the dance to the system of relationships among Africans on the Copperbelt. In order to do this I must take into account, to some extent, the general system of Black–White relationships in Northern Rhodesia. By working outwards from a specific social situation on the Copperbelt the whole social fabric of the Territory is therefore taken in. It is only when this process has been followed to a conclusion that we can return to the dance and fully appreciate its significance. (Mitchell 1956a: 1)

In Mitchell's time *kalela* songs and dances were not overtly political; they did not sing protest songs, lambast the colonial state or bureaucracy, or call for party political solidarity – all of which became features of some popular performance, including those of *kalela*, at the end of the colonial period, especially during the intense party politics around independence, and now in the postcolonial period (Matongo 1992). In the colonial *kalela*, the recreation was personal recreation, it was display in which the performers celebrated themselves and their appearance as if they were really members of the modern elite. They put themselves in their tribal identities on top of an imagined order of statuses. In Mitchell's study, *kalela* was taken as a kind of allegory of what tribalism in town was. This is because it seemed to dramatize in song and dance certain aspects of tribalism in a single popular form, what we might call a popular drama. This dramatic action unified what are seemingly disparate and possibly contradictory elements.

Mitchell was struck by a paradox in the dance. In some tribal dances, people dressed up in all their tribal paraphernalia and danced traditional dances, while chanting traditional songs. By contrast, the *kalela* dance included no tribal elements or insignia. The dancers were immaculately dressed in smart, modern clothes, and the main roles performed were modern – the king, the leader (blowing a football referee's whistle), a doctor and a nurse. They performed before a popular audience distinctive of town, drawn from a wider public than any tribe or ethnic group. The language of the dance was the town argot, *chicopperbelti*, a mix of Bemba, English and a Creole of Zulu called *Fanikolo*.[8] Yet in an apparent paradox, the composition of the performing team was tribal – they were nearly all Bisa – in the team best known to Mitchell; they came from the same tribal group under chief Matipa and were almost all Roman Catholics, with one Muslim. And in a tribal tradition of praise singing, 'they set out to praise the Bisa in general, and their chief Matipa in particular' (Mitchell 1956a: 42). To put the point in other words, rather than being rootless in town, what they celebrated was being double-rooted, rooted in the countryside and the town also, and, accordingly, they had, we may say, a double consciousness.

The Kalela Dance is not so much a study of the dance, as a study which takes the leisure situation as a platform for understanding casual social interaction in town. A central point was that tribalism was not about the tribe as such: 'except in these dancing teams, tribalism does not form the basis for the organization of corporate groups' (Mitchell 1956a: 42). Mitchell focused most of his analysis on issues of the people's construction of their cultural and ethnic identities, their use of social categories, and their making of a modern subjectivity for themselves. He made it clear that in his view, ethnicity or tribalism was not one thing or even about one thing, but was actually open to recreation, play and fun also.

If Mitchell's analysis was primarily oriented towards innovation in town, it did not assume a *tabula rasa*. He recognized what we know to be double rootedness, expressed in the popular performance of *kalela* both in praise-singing for a chief in the countryside, and also in the ostentatious display of smart, modern clothes, like those of an urban elite. He was well aware that new as certain social categories were, they were used in the light of a past history with some established traditions.[9] He applied this view to the practice of joking, primarily between strangers. It was cast in categories in the image of past hostility between tribes, before colonization put an end to tribal wars. A key argument of Mitchell's was that tribal joking relationships in town were highly situational. He contended that they did not operate between co-workers in industry or between officials of a trade union; and he made a similar point for the wider urban framework of tribal categories beyond the joking relationship.

I quote at length from *The Kalela Dance* to document his basic view of tribalism, political divisiveness and the expression of hostility:

> It is significant that nowhere in *kalela* are any anti-white sentiments expressed. In urban areas, in particular, Black and White are brought together by the nexus of productive activity and it is in urban areas that hostility is most freely expressed. But these expressions of hostility take place largely in political and quasi-political situations, through organizations and institutions such as the Urban Advisory Boards, African Representative Councils, the African Mine Workers' Union, and the African National Congress.
>
> The better-educated Africans appreciate that tribalism is divisive and make pleas for 'unity' but such pleas are made in a context of Black–White relationships: they seek African unity against Europeans. From the evidence we have at present, tribalism on the Copperbelt is still the dominant category of interaction in social fields in which *Africans alone* are involved. But it is not a relevant category in the field of Black-White relations. (Mitchell 1956a: 35, my italics)

Mitchell appreciated that while not significant or important in the context of management–worker relationships, tribalism did become significant in tribal fights. In the struggle for power within a trade union, 'home boys' might turn to each other for trust and mutual support, and could make up factions and label and identify themselves by tribe, for example Bemba vs. Lozi.

Tribalism and categorical relations, situations and social change

Strangerhood loomed large in Mitchell's and other RLI urban research. Mitchell contextualized urban strangerhood within the specifically colonial conditions of contemporary Zambia. Colonial practice in Central Africa made the most of strangerhood; stranger-hood became a distinctive product of town life under alien rule, and not a natural reality of town life, as a universal town condition.

In Zambia, married townsmen and townswomen could not and did not live in ethnic neighbourhoods, homogeneous by tribal origin or language. They had to live with their neighbours, who were strangers from different ethnic or linguistic backgrounds, including a good number of different languages. Houses were tied to jobs. Much housing was in the hands of the mining company or municipality. African townsmen and townswomen usually had to get houses, other than shacks, from employers, some of whom as a matter of deliberate policy mixed together people of different ethnic origins. In the bachelor hostels on the Copperbelt there was some tendency for rooms to be occupied by from four to six men from the same ethnic group. But beyond that there was great heterogene-ity in residence. Tribes were scattered across townships. Hence, as RLI research showed, the modern forms and practices of stranger-hood were distinctive to towns colonially organized around het-erogeneity and diversity. The plural African city in South Central Africa was in part a product of deliberate colonial policy. The argu-ment of the RLI research was that just as the towns and colonialism could change, so too could tribalism as social and cultural practice.

To the question, 'In which situations do urban Africans classify and categorise strangers on tribal lines?', Mitchell's answer was, pri-marily in 'unstructured situations', that is, apart from the structure of industrial and other work organizations: 'Interaction in a work situation, for example, is likely to be highly structured' (1966: 59). It was, Mitchell contended, above all in non-work situations that urban Africans resorted to tribalism as a cultural practice, when they created and generated social relations where there were none before. Using tribal categories innovatively, they did so not in the way they used them in village or 'tribal' contexts at home. This view was put by Mitchell in opposition to the 'detribalization' view common among white settlers, colonial government officials and mine or company managers. They assumed that tribe was a primary identity, somehow primordial, something essential and given to the person as if it were natural; and that in urban social change this was thrown into disarray, into 'detribalization'.

One version of the 'detribalization' view was simply a stereo-type of an individual adrift in a place of fleeting encounters, as it were an urban jungle, unlike the stable, customary place of home; as Mitchell put it, 'The "urbanized" African was in fact viewed as a "detribalized" person, whose sheet anchor of traditional customs and values had slipped and who was in consequence a disorganized and dissociated person' (Mitchell 1987: 99). In a somewhat more sophisticated version, the idea was that the move of migrants to towns and mines from their rural homes put them at risk of demor-alization, a breakdown in their personal relationships and commit-ments to each other, and related aspects of social disorganization.[10]

It had become common by the 1930s for some white settlers and colonial administrators to talk of 'detribalization', as if it were an obvious truth. Hence for members of the RLI, 'detribalization' was recognized to be a view of urban change that was extremely important for colonial policies and for the management of colonial industrial capitalism. It and its assumptions had to be taken apart critically, and with substantial evidence.

'Detribalization' was also, of course, taken up in academic approaches, of which Mitchell was highly critical, perhaps most trenchantly in the most influential of his early theoretical essays on urbanization in Africa, 'Theoretical Orientations in African Urban Studies'.[11] He objected to 'urban studies which formulate their problems in terms of "detribalization" or "westernization" or simply acculturation in general' (1966: 45). Part of his objection was simply to the framing of social change in terms of 'culture' and culture contact, with consequences for the individual. The part he himself considered to be more important, more innovative theoretically, was in his conceptualization of two distinct kinds of social change: the 'processive' and the 'situational'. The 'processive' referred to 'overall changes in the social system', such as cumulative or his-toric shifts, sometimes developments over a longer period than a fieldworker could directly observe. The 'situational', by contrast, was a concept for observable alternations, even momentary and ephemeral, in which people behave differently according to their interaction in different contexts, for example, domestic, leisure and work contexts and, indeed, the rural tribal context. Mitchell drove home the point that both types of change were ongoing at the same time, and the challenge for analysis and theory was to comprehend their relative autonomy and interrelation. Implicit as the distinction was in earlier arguments by Gluckman on the impact of the industrial revolution in Africa (Gluckman 1961a), it was a distinction that too many urban studies obscured, and thus they failed to get their descriptions of specifically urban change right.

In pushing Gluckman's arguments a stage further, Mitchell took certain further steps. One was bold and agenda-setting. It not only declared that urban institutions are specifically urban, developed in town to meet urban needs and not adaptations of rural ways turned into urban modes. It also problematized the modernity of the town – it had to be studied as an emergent phenomenon but on the assumption of something common in urban Africa: that the towns and cities discussed actually were modern; they all started, as it were, from scratch, under colonialism. If this modernist assumption was relatively sound for the cities Mitchell knew in south-central and southern Africa, we can now see that it needs rethinking to qualify the generalization where long-term historical difference matters. Of course, Mitchell was aware of a distinction between 'broad types of African town … for example, those towns which have grown up on the basis of a non-industrial and non-Western economy, as against those which have come into being through the activities of colonial powers and foreign entrepreneurs' (Mitchell 1966: 50). Urban studies have yet to comprehend comparatively, at one extreme, the West African cities which encompass and reconstitute the ancient capitals of pre-colonial kingdoms – their sacred central places attract exchange, investment and moments of great public significance for contemporary urban life, and tribal unions and tribal associations have an importance not found in much of south-central Africa, at least during the colonial period. Problematic at another extreme are the cities where the colonial power deliberately sought to design and engineer modern, cosmopolitan spaces which would regenerate cultural difference, for example in the French colonial Moroccan city spaces that recreated Arab, and not merely Western, civilization (Rabinow 1995).

A second step that Mitchell took, following Gluckman (1961b), opened out even further the application of field theory to the city. If it was formerly safe or at least useful for what Mitchell called 'the classical anthropological study' to work with an assumption of closure and total interconnectedness of 'interlocking institutions, structures, norms and values' (Mitchell 1966: 56), that assumption, which was no longer valid even for 'tribal' studies in modern Africa, was profoundly misleading for urban studies. The old view of a single social system had to go: 'there is no heuristic value in assuming that the town is a single social system in which all social activities and relationships are necessarily interconnected with one another' (Mitchell 1966: 59). Relative autonomy, with possible uncertainty, had to be conceptualized and explored in empirical research on partial connections and disparate social fields. Here a point needs to be suggested about an alternative, not Gluckman's influence on Mitchell, but Mitchell's impact on Gluckman's thought: I think that along with Colson's arguments, discussed in Chapter 3, it was Mitchell's conceptualization of urban relative autonomy that led Gluckman to see in his later views more complexity within an analytic framework, more of an appreciation of sub-systems that are semi-independent, to some extent even isolated.

It was in the analysis of personal networks, coupled with the study of the same people in many different social situations, that Mitchell discerned and promoted, already in the 1960s, what he felt was a very promising way forward for urban research (1966: 58). I want to say more, later in Chapter 5, about this and about major contributions by Mitchell and Epstein to the international development of network analysis. First, let me turn to the most challenging reception of Mitchell's work on urbanization in Africa.

Critical debate, personal passion and professional risk

Mitchell's arguments about prestige, emulation of elites, tribalism, interpersonal relations, circulatory labour migration and, indeed, Mitchell and Epstein's whole approach to urban social change in the late colonial period evoked intense debate in *Current Anthropology* (1971). As a wider debate about social stratification in colonial society, the debate was fierce, aggressive and politically passionate, even by the standards of the journal's well-earned reputation for sharp controversy. On the polemical and deliberately provocative attack, fighting apparently false consciousness from a Marxist perspective on class, was the South African sociologist Bernard Magubane. I have to say that I found rereading Magubane's attack and the whole debate in *Current Anthropology* painful.[12]

Magubane inveighed against social scientists who more or less unconsciously tended to 'vindicate the cultural supremacy of whites over Africans' (Magubane 1971: 423) and who failed to face and explain the truth about what was the basic cause of a host of phenomena – 'migrant labour, patterns of rural urban migration, settlement in towns, secularization, and the diversification in the form of social stratification' (1971: 443). Perhaps his strongest support came from 'one of the foremost writers in the Yoruba language' (Barber 2006: 28), Oladejo Okediji. He extended the debate beyond Mitchell and Epstein's work to a wholesale criticism of 'many other well-known British social anthropologists' (Magubane 1971: 436). They were 'trapped between the competing claims of academic objectivity and pro-colonial leanings' (1971: 437).

For the political passion in the *Current Anthropology* debate, the immediate postcolonial moment was important. It followed the independence of most new African states, but it was still a transitional moment for liberation movements in the early postcolonial period: the South African liberation movement was reaching out to overseas activists for the anti-apartheid campaign of disinvestment in South Africa, and it was about to establish its ANC mission at the United Nations in New York. At this moment, Magubane became a prominent spokesman in exile for the ANC and the South African liberation struggle as well as a leading campaigner in the USA for disinvestment in South Africa. He fought for the idea that 'African nationalism combines the dynamics of national liberation and class struggle' (Magubane 1971: 441). It is an idea that has become ever more challenged with the passage of postcolonial time, in particular in South Africa (on the critique of class analysis with nationalism as liberation of the masses, see Mbembe 2002; Adebanwi 2014).

Among the good reasons for still taking Magubane's 1971 attack very seriously – and I want to position it historically at some length – is Magubane's reputation for leading scholarly critique as a progressive activist in exile. According to the sociologist and freelance journalist William Minter, 'Influenced particularly by ANC colleagues in Zambia such as Jack Simons, he was among the leading progressive African scholars critical of the assumptions and biases of mainstream Western scholarship about Africa' (Magubane and Minter 2004: 1). For some twenty-seven years a professor of anthropology at the University of Connecticut from 1970 onwards (perhaps first drafting his 1971 critique while teaching in Zambia from 1967 to 1970), Magubane positioned himself with a deliberately provocative voice, denouncing anthropology as a reactionary force of imperialism, counter to national liberation and decolonization (Magubane and Faris 1985). As the anti-anthropology professor of anthropology, his mantra could be, I think: do unto anthropologists as they do unto Others. As he saw it, anthropology was guilty in the present as in the past of exoticizing its objects of study and thus Othering them; now it was the anthropologists' turn to be Othered.

In a long and reflective life-history interview with Minter, Magubane has significantly presented himself and his thought in ways that afford a better understanding of his fierce objections (Magubane and Minter 2004). Of his early life in racist South Africa, he recalled poverty, the hardships of living in Durban in an informal settlement (where, unlike most Zambian townsmen, he was himself never rooted in the countryside),[13] and his struggle for education, culminating in his winning a scholarship as a way out of South Africa. Having completed his UCLA PhD in sociology in the United States, where he then felt alienated, he had taken up a post at the University of Zambia. There he experienced what he strongly advocated in his critical attack on the work of Epstein and Mitchell: *unlearning*. This was in conversations with the South African lawyer and political activist Jack Simons, about Marxism and the political economy: 'In fact, almost everything that I had learned for my PhD I had to unlearn from the lectures he gave [as professor of political science and sociology]' (Magubane and Minter 2004: 20). Later, reading and reviewing Frantz Fanon's *The Wretched of the Earth* took Magubane further in his view of 'the dialectic of oppression and resistance' in South Africa; and revising his PhD thesis, he published an award-winning version of it on African-American consciousness of Africa (1979). In it, he turned his gift for scathing critique into an attack on much American sociology. Other targets were American campaigners in the interracial Civil Rights movement, 'traditional civil groups with their white liberal friends [who] have helped the black petty bourgeoisie to establish a middle-class hegemony over the black masses' (Magubane 1979: 185). Drawing on Fanon in a way that resonates with his earlier attack on Mitchell's interpretation of *kalela*, with its appreciation of creativity in popular culture, Magubane perceived a twist of white oppression. His perception was that the past of oppressed people gets rediscovered by white oppressors not in its misery, but in a beautiful image that is therapeutic for the whites themselves (1979: 85).

Magubane himself did not merely attack Mitchell and Epstein's methods and supposedly superficial findings, or their arguments and theoretical orientations that allegedly disregarded conflict, protest and political struggle. He called into question also their motives and reputation. And he started from his own diasporic sensibility in the USA towards a deformed, sick society in Africa, for which, he objected, Mitchell and Epstein saw no cause in a historical perspective, and offered neither remedy nor needed explanation. Why had they made so much of the warped obsession of the urban individual with conspicuous consumption, especially dressing up in European clothes? While blinded by their own colonial ideology to the social structure of alien capitalism, had they not unwittingly disclosed not creativity and resilience but alienation and a situation in which 'personalities are warped and their values distorted' (Magubane 1971: 442). Was he himself unwittingly offering a mirror image of the 'detribalized' person? His postcolonial ideology, he proclaimed, was for national liberation, with the raised 'self-consciousness of the African people', and against a current neocolonial hangover for 'the critical appraisal of the past "formed" for us by studies done during the colonial era' (1971: 442). Magubane felt that he knew from his own experience the need for 'unlearning'. Coming to self-consciousness himself gave him what comes over as an unchallengeable sense of holding to a fundamental truth, with certainty, about what is progressive and liberating and what is not, that is, colonial social science without Marxist political economy.

In response to Magubane,[14] Mitchell himself asked a difficult and critical question about his own approach, situational analysis, in urban studies. It is the question of 'cities and society'. Are so-called urban problems merely 'aspects of the wider society', which must be studied with regard, above all, to relationships established throughout the society as a whole? The proof of how important this question was to Mitchell is in the fact that he took it up to set a framework at the beginning of his last book (1987), which he meant to be his final *tour de force* on urbanization.

Not surprisingly, his answer to this basic question was 'No', in part because he felt it meant too little 'concern with the day-to-day activities of town dwellers' (Mitchell 1987: 5). Even further, and here he located Magubane's criticisms in the context of similar objections by a good number of other Marxist writers,

> In effect Magubane was saying that instead of trying to interpret the interactional data relating to ethnicity or social status as located as they are in urban conditions constituted by the wider colonial order (which we took as given in our analyses), we ought to have been conducting a Marxist analysis of the colonial social system itself. (1987: 6)

Against this, Mitchell went on to argue that if there was a weakness in his earlier analysis, it was actually a weakness pointed out by Kingsley Garbett (1970), in conceptualizing not the total social system but different aspects of the social situation; on the one hand, as it is defined in practice by the actors themselves with their own symbolic and meaningful understandings, and on the other, as it is defined by the analyst – 'a limited set of events which the analyst has reason to assume may be linked together in some way and be capable of being interpreted *logically* in terms of *general* understanding of the way in which social actions take place' (Mitchell 1987: 8, italics mine). Analysis entails, on this view, thinking through both aspects, the actors' and the analyst's perceptions, and moving in argument with a theory to guide the logic and the generality.

Mitchell's admission is that his own turn to the social situation is, in the end, a matter of personal preference: 'I am personally more interested in social behaviour in interpersonal situations (including, of course, the meanings actors attribute to their actions) than in more abstract aspects of social structure, but this does not deny the validity of other kinds of analysis, [which are not mutually exclusive]' (1987: 8). As against Magubane's fundamentalism, Mitchell's position is that of a *relativist*, allowing for the possibility of other, very different concerns with 'large-scale structural phenomena'.

If Magubane may now be considered as anticipating the call for 'decolonization' through an anthropology moving towards liberation (Harrison 1991; Allen and Jobson 2016), his general stance can itself be viewed as being surpassed historically. It was situated in a first phase of postcolonial studies of stratification and the history of labour in newly industrialized societies, a phase overtaken in its turn, as Pnina Werbner argues:

> During the 1960s to 1980s, early research on the African 'working class' was heavily influenced ... by economistic Marxist and especially Fanonian perspectives. This body of scholarship was later challenged, especially by social historians of Africa inspired by the work of E. P. Thompson. Most recently, the move has been towards theories of African stratification based on lifestyle and consumption, influenced by Pierre Bourdieu's arguments on the interaction of habitus, cultural capital and 'distinction'. (P. Werbner 2018: 8)

At this point, given this historical perspective on Magubane's critique, and rather than rehearse the accusations and counter-accusations of misreadings and false statements in *Current Anthropology* and elsewhere, I want to deal with two issues, of reputation and motive. The first is that of class bias, and the other of blindness to colonial struggles and the critique of power. Driving Mitchell and Epstein's approach, according to Magubane, was 'the arrogance typical of middle-class social scientists who, having been accustomed to "good standards" since infancy, profess to see in working-class ambitions a conscious imitation of upper-class attributes' (Magubane 1971: 425–6).[15] From his own experience from childhood onwards, growing up in a poor informal settlement, Magubane himself knew what a harsh struggle it was to rise from an underclass, living hand-to-mouth under racist conditions in South Africa. But clearly unaware of Mitchell's working-class origins and his personal experience of relative poverty, Magubane relied here as elsewhere on projecting his own stereotypes on to others.

Worse still was Magubane's claim that 'Mitchell and Epstein assume that no conflict existed between Africans and their white overlords' (1971: 425). In fact, in his award-winning *Politics in an Urban African Community* (1958), Epstein devoted chapter after chapter to the continuous struggle for power and improved positions within the new industrial society. One part of his historical account of politics over twenty-five years in a mining company town, Luanshya, showed different pressures, some within trade unionism and others brought to bear by unions against the mining company; another part of his account documented and analysed the growth of the African National Congress; and each part weighed up issues of political consciousness in specific moments, for example, the moment when certain African leaders on the Copperbelt 'saw their problem as the need to mobilize African opinion and organize themselves on a territorial basis' (Epstein 1958: 159). The trade union had to counteract the mining company policy that assumed the danger of 'detribalization' and the need to control workers with tribal or rural origins through some contrived tribal organization under tribal elders. In his perceptive and substantial account of the RLI Copperbelt research, Ulf Hannerz remarked that Epstein's findings showed that

> As Africans began to get their bearings in the urban-industrial milieu, they had realized that their internal tribal divisions were irrelevant in their confrontation with European miners and management, and so they had organized on a class basis instead, with lines clearly drawn, instead of confounded by the ambiguities of tribal elders. (Hannerz 1980: 141)

As Epstein himself saw his approach to change, it was informed, 'Hegel-like', by contradiction and conflict; it was a dialectic approach:

> This [his article title, 'Tribal Elders to Trade Unions'] refers to the way in which, as part of an unfolding historical process, one mode of political organisation, with its associated pattern of leadership gradually comes to be replaced by another ... For, to take but one aspect of the problem, while the African Mine Workers Trade Union had indeed secured the passing of the system of tribal representation on the mines, it was also plain that developing cleavages within the union were apt to be explained by Africans themselves in tribal terms. (Epstein 1992b: xiii)

In response to Magubane's imputing of motive, we need to know more than the simple facts of Epstein's published work and his approach to 'conflict as providing the dynamics of change' (Epstein 1992b: xiii). We need to be aware of the risks and difficulties of politically sensitive anthropological research, whether colonial or postcolonial, and in particular the troubling consequences for Epstein himself of being branded 'a subversive' during his research. Like the Rhodes-Livingstone's first director, Godfrey Wilson, who was banned by the Chamber of Mines at the very start of Copperbelt research in the colonial period, Epstein was labelled by the Chamber as a 'subversive', a *persona non grata*, and banned from continuing his fieldwork in the mining township (Epstein 1992b: 5–6, 17–19; Gray 2019). He had after all, in the authorities' suspicions, mixed with mine workers' leaders and other agitators, who would supposedly have learned their political tactics from him, the white man; and the authorities claimed to have reports that Epstein had addressed a meeting and offered to help the union in its disputes. Epstein has reported Mitchell's fight on his behalf with the authorities; Mitchell tried but failed to get the governor, Sir Gilbert Rennie, the chairman of the RLI governing body, to hold a meeting to review and defend Epstein's research (Epstein 1992b: 10–11). Although Epstein was never a prohibited immigrant, his colonial 'security' record followed him from Africa to Australia, where his application for a visa to the Australian Territory of New Guinea, his new fieldwork site, was at first turned down in 1959. Gluckman wanted to make this a *cause célèbre* and fight it with a public campaign. Instead, only after much quiet, sensitive and behind-the-scenes diplomacy by another Manchester man, John Barnes, then professor at the Australian National University, was Epstein given permission to go for his research to the island of Matupit, near Rabaul in New Britain, New Guinea.[16] The threats to academic freedom posed by colonial security assessments of anthropologists are well documented in Geoffrey Gray's recent and full account of Epstein's difficulties, as well as the attempt to ban Gluckman from Papua New Guinea (Gray 2019).

Carrying out fieldwork in politically sensitive conditions and crisis times often means for the fieldworker a high personal cost – it means becoming, under 'cross-fire', an object of suspicion from people on opposite sides, as Epstein felt driven to explain:

> I have come to the conclusion that urban research in Central Africa is not really my cup of tea. It seems to me that urban field investigations of an intensive kind where one can really get among the people cannot be undertaken without getting oneself involved in a situation such as I

found myself in on my last trip. The whole protracted process of tight-rope walking is conducive neither to good work nor to one's mental balance. This does not mean that I wish to sever my ties with the Institute, or to cease working in Northern Rhodesia. What I should like to do is a rural study. (ALE to CM, 30 March 1955, MPBL)

Responding much later, from the university in Harare, Mitchell wrote, 'I much appreciate very keenly, of course, your feelings about staying in Africa. Who with any conscience has not had them? I am afraid this is something you will have to sort out for yourself' (CM to ALE, 28 February 1956, MPBL).

Engaged and contested social science in the eye of the storm

In our present postcolonial moment, the resurgence of critical debate about anthropology's colonial past and its significance for our future – a resurgence moved by present demands for anti-racist decolonization of knowledge, symbols and institutions (Nyamnjoh 2016) – has made it all the more important for us to understand the *contested* and *vulnerable* nature of the social science which Mitchell directed, following Wilson, Gluckman and Colson, the other early RLI directors.

The predicament faced by an anthropologist like Epstein, carrying out political research in troubled times, has often been even more entangled than we have seen so far (Epstein 1992b: 7). It is as if studying factionalism, such as in struggles over union leadership, almost inevitably means that the anthropologist is suspected of being on one side or the other, or both, in turns; and surviving the swings in suspicion, as Epstein did, without becoming embittered is one of the most formidable challenges of the fieldwork.

Much of the RLI research was engaged and controversial social science, anti-racist and anti-colonial; and it had to be fought for, often at personal risk, even high personal cost in the face of failure.[17] Even further, under Mitchell, 'the RLI had, far from acting as an agent of colonial rule, become thoroughly Africanized' (Smith 2019: 30). In urban studies, it showed how Africans came to be locked in political struggles to change the colonial inequalities that gave benefits to whites as real townsmen at the expense of blacks as tribesmen, and thus mere sojourners in towns. It also showed that the struggles were for the benefits of recreation, equal pay, better working conditions, and that they were carried out through open strikes and more informal pressures. As Mitchell pointed out, early welfare societies, which drew their members regardless of tribal origin, 'were formed to improve the conditions of all Africans living in towns ... It was inevitable that they should take up a political point of view. In due course they amalgamated to form the African National Congress which draws its members from all levels and all tribes' (1956: 17).

For Mitchell himself, it became inevitable that, having struggled to defend the integrity of the RLI, he had to leave it, after a short, three-year tenure as director from 1952 to 1955. Towards the end he was stressed and frustrated by 'running a liberal research institute in an illiberal atmosphere' (CM to MG, 9 February 1955, cited by Smith 2019: 124). This is the turning point, documented by Smith:

> By June that year [1955], Mitchell was ready to leave. He and Gluck-man were increasingly disaffected with the Institute, its governance and its productivity as an academic centre. Before long, their doubts about its direction, independence and critical edge were leading them to sever all remaining ties. 'The R.L.I as we knew it' wrote Mitchell (17.6.57), 'no longer exists'; 'it seems quite clear to me' replied Gluck-man two months later, 'that the RLI is going to become an adjunct to government' (8.8.57). (cited in Smith 2019: 124)

In 1955 Mitchell moved to Salisbury and took up his professorship at the University College of Rhodesia and Nyasaland (UCRN). Here he again took up the challenge of institution building against white settler privilege and racial discrimination:

> with the help of grants from the Ford Foundation, he transformed a dominantly white degree programme into one with more balanced (50/50) participation. As an academic administrator his work was, nevertheless, compromised. His attempts to recruit Epstein to UCRN were, for example, blocked. When Epstein wrote on 10 February 1956 declaring that anyway he felt himself shrinking increasingly away from the field situation ... Mitchell replied (28.2.56) 'I appreciate very keenly, of course, your concerns about staying in Africa. Who with any conscience has not had them?' These concerns quickly increased, and as the 1960s gathered pace, the pressures became intolerable. (Smith 2019: 125)

It was early in this period, in 1960–61, that I myself witnessed Mitchell's strong commitment to critical and engaged anthropology, when at a time of emergency and heightened police surveillance I carried out my fieldwork among Kalanga in western Zimbabwe under his supervision. This is how, in *Tears of the Dead*, my social biography of an African family in the colonial and postcolonial periods, I acknowledged my lasting debt to him:

> Clyde Mitchell, my fieldwork supervisor at the University College of Rhodesia and Nyasaland, did his best to get me to appreciate the impact of state intervention in the people's lives – he urged me to study current social problems, most importantly the attack on African agriculture and the social consequences of measures under the Land Husbandry Act. (Werbner 1991: vii)

Along with this personal truth, I want to make it very clear that for Mitchell, engaged anthropology was *public* anthropology. While he was vice-principal of UNCR from 1961–62, and indeed throughout his time at UNCR, he carried on the struggle for academic freedom in the hostile colonial context. That meant he had to confront Ian Smith's white settler regime head on. He did so, for example, when Smith attempted 'to hijack professional anthropology to legitimize his decision to disenfranchise black Africans' (Smith 2019: 126). Against that:

> Within a week [of Ian Smith's announced claim to support from 'people who have made a lifetime study of African Custom and African law'], Mitchell had assembled a group of scholars to argue publicly for the democratic rights of Africans. Their position, set out on page 1 of the September 22 1964 edition of the *Guardian* was that 'No other method [than the right to vote] can give valid results'. 'We are' the group is quoted as saying 'utterly opposed to the idea that there is something peculiar to Africans that makes it impossible to test their opinions by normal procedures.' For this they were roundly attacked by the government, with several signatories to the *Guardian* letter (including Mitchell's then-wife Hilary Flegg-Mitchell) apparently banned from re-entering the country. (Smith 2019: 126)

In December 1965, shortly after the settler regime's declaration of UDI, Mitchell tried unsuccessfully to get the principal of the University College to support a declaration of the principles upon which it could maintain its academic independence; and realizing his own position had become intolerable, he finally agreed to accept Gluckman's offer of a chair at Manchester. There Mitchell remained engaged in post-UDI politics, and 'raised funds to meet the defence costs of African political detainees and prisoners' (Smith 2019: 127).

It is remarkable that hardly any of this history has been taken into account and appreciated from the perspective of a leading Zimbabwean anthropologist such as Victor Muzvidziwa. When Muzvidziwa recently traced trends in anthropological research and teaching in his country, his finding was that in the early 1960s, Manchester School anthropologists 'could still be critical of the colonial-settler regime without predicting fundamental shifts ... The early years [in the 1960s] were characterized by an eclectic theoretical approach that avoided asking questions that would lead to the restructuring of social relations. Issues of class, race and gender were conveniently ignored' (Muzvidziwa 2006: 105). Neither in terms of theory or praxis and activism against racial discrimination and the white settler regime does that contention fit my own experience of being a fieldworker and graduate student in Mitchell's department in 1960–61, and in eventually becoming a prohibited immigrant under the Smith regime, shortly before its declaration of 'Independence'. Even further, Muzvidziwa's account, in my view, is too depoliticized to meet the pressing concerns of decolonization. It has to be made clear that under the white settler regime of his country, and very commonly in colonial states, anthropologists were regarded with considerable suspicion, because they were held to be taking the side of the people against the state.[18] It was a threat that was dealt with by stopping the fieldworker's research and banning the fieldworker, who was then declared a prohibited immigrant.

In my own experience, as in the case of other fieldworkers, there were costly personal consequences in postcolonial Africa for my engaged anthropology. My hope is that in our present times of turmoil in Zimbabwe, the country's anthropologists will look back the better to look forward in confronting the serious problematics of carrying out engaged anthropology in the eye of political storms, such as those at the End of Empire and in postcolonial Africa in times of state terror and, unmistakably again in present-day Zimbabwe under President Munagagwa, of tyranny and the brutal suppression of civil rights.[19]

Beyond anthropology

At the end of Mitchell's career, while a research fellow at Nuffield College from 1966 to 1974, it was not anthropologists – and he was himself the only anthropologist to be then a Nuffield fellow – but the young geographers, graduate students he supervised, who 'kept me intellectually alive', as he remarked (Bernard 1990). Mitchell capped his academic career by immersing himself as much, if not more, in the data of the young geographers as in his own anthropological research. He habitually worked the quantitative analysis through for them. He taught himself to write computer programs for their problems, proving as much to himself as to them that he could find the way through complexity to simplicity. With remarkably laborious and fascinated devotion, he computed their fine bits of survey research until he could reach significant results, at best a surprising determination or structure, with up-to-date techniques and a sophisticated statistical model. Examples are in the articles he co-authored with his students (Mitchell and Critchley 1994; Peach and Mitchell 1988; Kelly, Mitchell and Smith 1990). As his former student, the geographer Susan Smith, acutely perceives, in her very substantial British Academy memoir for Mitchell, he had 'an insatiable appetite for using formal descriptive tools to illuminate the substance of social life' (Smith 2019: 104).[20] 'I am more interested in handling data than in ideas', remarked Mitchell to Gluckman. 'Hence if I have a choice I will pore over some statistical table rather than try to phrase ideas' (CM to MG, 17 February 1965, GPJRUML).

His fascination with mapping, social geography and big numerical data informed his plans well before coming to Nuffield College, of course. When he was about to leave Africa and take up his chair in sociology at Manchester in 1965, he let Gluckman know that he intended

> to exploit the census data for Manchester ... Perhaps one of the first things I will do is prepare a social base map of the Manchester conurbation ... We will work out some sort of index of social class, ethnicity etc. and run the data for the enumeration areas of Manchester and plot the social profile of the city. On the basis of this I hope we can get some research going of the sort which Bruce Kapferer [then Mitchell's graduate student at UCRN] is doing in Broken Hill:

studies of the social networks in factories and then follow these out into the communities. (CM to MG, 28 March 1965, GPJRUML)

Surveys useful for testing hypotheses with socio-geographic variables were methodologically valued and promoted by Mitchell from the beginning of his urban research. In 1951–54 he had a big team of interviewers carry out a survey of a total of 8,787 adults (men and women) living in five Copperbelt towns. With this survey data, he found the required empirical support for a hypothesis that Philip Mayer had advanced in his study of migrants in the South African town of East London. Mitchell concluded that his own statistical findings from the relatively large survey were

> consistent with Mayer's suggestion that the degree to which an individual is able to become caught up in urban life depends upon the extent to which he is able to sustain his participation in events and affairs in his rural home without finding it necessary to absent himself completely from the town for long periods. (Mitchell 1973: 311)

Even further, the statistical analysis, while it confirmed the importance of geographical distance, also disclosed departures from that regularity. Measurement was considered by Mitchell to be essential for the scientific study of the relations between distance, transportation and urban involvement in Zambia.

Notes

1 Mitchell wrote of the joy that the sight of his Yao book gave his father: 'coming from lower middle class stock in Scotland the achievement of a son in the literary world meant a good deal to him' (CM to MG, 4 October 1956, MPBL).
2 Gordon suggests that Gluckman's 'use of the case method derived *much* from his encounters with psychoanalysis' (Gordon 2018: 261, italics mine). The actual history of the development of the case method, particularly under Mitchell's influence, for the extended case method and by Gluckman for legal cases runs counter to this suggestion, at least as a major derivation. Gluckman himself acknowledged his debt to Malinowski and *Crime and Custom*, which influenced his turn to situations and cases (Gluckman 1973a: 612).
3 The claim is briefly put in Mitchell's 1956 preface to *The Yao Village* (1956b: viii).
4 After raising critical doubts about Mitchell's survey data as well as the unmet challenge of recent studies which his arguments neglect,

Margaret Peil concludes her review of his last book (Mitchell 1987) with this fair judgement: 'This book is mainly recommended for those who want a very readable and theoretically-based summary of the early Central African Urban studies, by someone who was there' (Peil 1988: 264). Smith draws attention to the fact that Mitchell's 'Northern Rhodesia Survey' was 'innovative for its time'; 'A carefully stratified sample of around 12,000 people, interviewed over five years in all the major Copperbelt towns, answered a range of questions that went far beyond a simple census to create a rounded "social profile of the people"' (Smith 2019: 98).

5 That is, apart from his final social network studies.

6 I note that Mitchell qualified his argument by reference to the mining industry for which a study with S. Irvine showed that perceptions of prestige by respondents varied situationally with their location in the industry (Mitchell 1987: 178; see also Mitchell and Irvine 1965).

7 For a critique of Mitchell's view of innovation in *kalela* and an argument for the contrary, the tenacious resilience of rural forms, and indeed expressions of encapsulation, see Argyle 1991.

8 For the account of this argot on the Copperbelt, which highlights the importance and, indeed, complexity of notions of prestige in linguistic innovation with the argot, and thus sustains Mitchell's appreciation of the Copperbelt workers' stress on prestige, see Epstein 1959.

9 In his study of East African dance associations with military brass bands, the historian Terence Ranger reconsiders the modernity of the associations. He found significant continuities as well as responsive innovations in the sixty-year development of the associations from competitions in pre-colonial coastal towns to their apparent end in the early postcolonial period (Ranger 1975). Against Magubane's critique of the dance study as a trivializing of Africans' lives, Ranger also defends the interest in popular culture for the analysis of social change (1975: 8)

10 This is the idea that Mitchell argued was a basic weakness in much of the work of the Chicago School, led by Robert Park, writing in the 1920s on immigrants and their problems of adjustment to urban life. Mitchell allowed, also, that these urban sociologists did attend to voluntary associations and the intimate, intensely supportive personal relationships of individuals in town; the point was that such relationships were less important to the urbanite than to the person who lives in a rural society (Mitchell 1987: 301).

11 For more of Mitchell's broad argument on urbanization and detribalization, see Mitchell 1969; and for his contrast of African and American migration and urbanization as well as his full critique of work by the Chicago School on migrants to urban America, see Mitchell 1987: 296–310.

12 For a sensitive appreciation of Bernard Magubane's 'massive attack on Rhodes-Livingstone anthropology', see Hannerz 1980: 158–60.

13 For an argument on the contrast in the significance of the colonial imaginary of 'detribalization' where the settler regime introduced social

engineering for family life in domestic housing, rather than bachelor quarters, as in the Copperbelt, see Hickel 2015. See Epstein 1981 for his analysis of how African migrants to town from the countryside upheld the importance of kinship and affinal ties, when they coped in domestic relationships with problems arising in a strange environment.

14 For Mitchell's immediate response, see Mitchell 1971.

15 For an alternative view of the making of an African working class that recognizes an assertive self-consciousness marked by 'the fusing of cosmopolitan and local culture', see P. Werbner 2014.

16 In an obituary for Epstein, Michael Young recalled, 'Bill's happiest years of fieldwork were spent among the Tolai of Matupit, a people whom he loved and admired, though at first he found it difficult to overcome their suspicion that he was an agent of government (the colonial situation in Rabaul was becoming as tense as it had been on the Copperbelt). Following his initial work in Matupit (resulting in his 1968 monograph on land, politics and social change) "ToBill" re-visited his field site three times. His last visit was in August 1994, just before Rabaul was devastated by volcanic eruptions. On this occasion he was initiated into the highest grade of the men's *tubuan* cult, an honour which, although immensely gratifying, placed him in a professional predicament. For the next few years he wrestled with the dilemma of whether or not to publish what he had been taught about the cult's esoteric lore. By the end of 1997 he had drafted a 200- page account of the *tubuan* entitled *A Melanesian masquerade*, but after consulting fellow Tolai initiates he decided to commit it to the obscurity of an archive' (Young 2000: 122).

17 For an appreciation of how RLI directors fought against racism for the political independence of the RLI and fostered collaboration with African researchers and their careers, see Smith 2019: 123.

18 For white settler stereotypes of anthropologists, see Hannerz 1980: 160.

19 President Mnangagwa has now admitted responsibility for recent army brutality against civilians involved in non-violent protests against his regime: 'After previous denials, *The Standard*, on 1 February 2019, reported that President Mnangagwa told a Zanu PF "thank you" rally in Mwenezi district he deployed the army to carry out a brutal crackdown against opposition and civil society activists, and he was ready to deploy the soldiers again to quell further protests against his rule' (Brickhill 2019: 2).

20 I want to acknowledge the fine insights and careful scholarship in Smith's memoir, which I have found very stimulating for this chapter.

5

Relational thought, networks, circles

The turn by Mitchell and Epstein to relational thought applied to stratification and personal ties of friendship and kinship – in brief, to the idea of 'the network' – came in the early 1950s following Manchester seminars convened by Max Gluckman and subsequent publications by John Barnes (1954) and Elizabeth Bott (1957). In the Introduction, I stressed the importance in the seminars and in the work arising from them of interdisciplinary collaboration. An example is in the link to relational thought through the American sociologist George Homans. In this early 1950s period, Homans took part in the Manchester seminars as a visitor. John Scott has illuminated the impressive pioneering of network analysis by Homans.[1] In one example, decoded by Scott, Homans arrived by a trial-and-error process, without any formal mathematical methods, at a matrix for discerning the patterns of cliques in work groups observed by Warner's colleagues in Old City, Mississippi. The re-analysis by Homans effectively anticipated or was analogous to a much later departure in social network analysis, suggests Scott. It was something of a forerunner for what with the radical develop-ment of algorithms and computer power came to be called 'block modelling'. The contributions by Homans were in the study of small-scale social interaction, in his aims, in his general propositions and in his development of methods, such as in the use of matrices.

If in the 1930s an earlier generation had turned to the philoso-phy of science and physics for the development of 'process theory', as I argued in Chapter 2, Mitchell sought to give greater precision and more conceptual 'rigour' to the analysis of the formal properties of networks through mathematics, especially recent developments in graph theory (Harary and Norman 1953; Harary, Norman and Cartwright 1965). This turn to mathematics was anticipated in structuralist theory, if not in practice, by Radcliffe-Brown, Gluckman's mentor:

Relational analysis, even if not metrical, may be mathematical, in the sense

> that it will apply non-quantitative, relational mathematics. The kind of mathematics which will be required ultimately for a full development of the science of society will not be metrical, but will be that hitherto comparatively neglected branch of mathematics, the calculus of relations, which, I think, is on the whole more fundamental than quantitative mathematics. (Radcliffe-Brown 1957: 69)[2]

Mitchell saw the relational turn as a theoretical move away from a form of structural functionalism, and towards an approach which apparently 'provided a coherent and systematic framework into which all the daily activities of people and their relationships with one another could be fitted' (1969: 9). Even further, in empirical terms, he saw it to be a turn driven by the problematics of moving from the study of 'classical tribal society', highly localized on the small scale, to studies of 'more complex societies', especially urban, large-scale ones. Barnes himself saw the making of the turn somewhat differently: it was located within a longer tradition of thought in social anthropology, responsive to the complex phenomenon of kinship in 'classical tribal society', and to the problematics of disparate or overlapping relations in the social fields of such a society, as in Meyer Fortes's seminal accounts of clanship and kinship among Tallensi.[3] The idea of the network, remarked Barnes, was 'an idea I had picked up from my elders, principally from Fortes' book, *The Web of Kinship* (1949). I used it to describe how notions of class equality were applied, and how individuals made use of personal ties of kinship and friendship in Bremnes, a community in Norway' (Barnes 1969a: 52). Barnes cautioned about the need for care in adopting terminology and concepts from topology and graph theory, and he tried to sort out ideas of connectedness and connectivity in an early article (1969b). One of his concerns was the approach to subsets, and the analysis of how insiders are more closely in touch with one another than they are with outsiders (1969b: 227). Later, in the early 1980s, with the aim of making the mathematical and structural analysis of networks more accessible to anthropologists, Barnes, while professor of sociology at Cambridge, gave his critical support to a study by Per Hage and Frank Harary. In the book from this study, remarked Barnes, 'they demonstrate with admirable clarity and with an impressive range of illustrations, how the concepts and, more importantly, the theorems and techniques of graph theory can be applied to ordinary ethnographic evidence' (Barnes 1983: x).

Notice that in Barnes's reading of his early descriptive use of the network idea, he attached it both to a division in social stratification, to class, and also to individual choice in practice. In his usage, according to Barnes, 'we can never speak of an ego–centric network' (Barnes 1969b: 57). Instead, he found it preferable to use the term 'network' 'only when some kind of social field is intended'; and he gave examples of what he called 'partial networks', such as the cognatic web of kinship, and various networks of marriage or politics.

Against that, both Mitchell and Epstein did speak of the network as ego-centric, but they differed among themselves, more or less implicitly, and with unlike regard for relational thought about sociocentric, and not only ego-centric, constructs, as I will explain more fully later. What Mitchell and Epstein shared, in their turn to what came to be known as social network analysis, was a heightened concern for certain specifically innovative aspects of modern life in urban Africa. This was their awareness of choice-making: that in the face of urban complexity and uncertainties, *individuals* often felt the need to manoeuvre, negotiate and even manipulate others, especially friends, acquaintances and often kin or conjugal partners. I stress *individuals* because of the importance that recognition of individuals as *particular* persons had in the Mitchell and Epstein turn to social network analysis. Initially, at least, they had in mind the new urban dwellers of Zambia, finding their town ways in recently created new towns, rather than Africa's ancient communities, such as the Swahili towns on the Indian Ocean coast, and not towns with a profusion of voluntary associations and clubs, as in many West African cities. Writing to John Barnes in 1958, this is the description Mitchell gave of his early network interest at the start of his Harare survey, while at the University College of Rhodesia and Nyasaland:

> I am trying to get a picture of the way in which a migrant builds up a network of social relationships around himself as he comes into

town. The sort of hypothesis I am working on at the moment is that he moves initially on kinship and quasi-kinship (funeral societies) and then builds up other relationships on work associations. Hence the high turnover of membership of burial associations. But we have just started and this is nothing more than a direction along which I hope to collect material. (CM to JB, 2 February 1958, MPBL)

To a fieldworker like Epstein, in the Zambian towns much of the individual's behaviour appeared, *at least at the start*, to be, as he put it, 'random or haphazard', allowing for the gross impression that 'the haphazard is more conspicuous than the regular, and all is in a state of flux' (Epstein 1992b: 49). Given the concern for casual social encounters with strangers and for the problem of fitting strangers into personal categories reconstituted in town, it is remarkable that, as Hannerz notes, 'Network analysts ... hardly ever include strangers in networks' (Hannerz 1980: 336 n.9). We might now find such network analysis remarkably dated, given our own deluge of experience of connectivity, willy-nilly, with strangers through social media or through the unauthorized dissemination of contacts and personal information to unknown others; even the recognition of one's face has come to be a matter for intrusive datasets under the command of remote anonymous others. How to regulate this, how to impose social control or privacy against covert manipulation, has become one of the pressing questions of twenty-first-century networks.

When Epstein informed Mitchell of his interest in network analysis, at the time when he began to develop it in 1958, in order to understand momentary linkages and situational clustering, he highlighted a distinctive challenge for relational thought. It was not by contrast to 'classical tribal society', as Mitchell would have it, but in the study of different towns: one 'disorderly', Ndola, the line-of-rail and administrative boom town; the other, by contrast, 'highly structured', Luanshya, the mining town:

One of the reasons I have been so tardy about getting on with Ndola was that I really didn't see any way of ordering the material. Ndola is not so 'orderly' as Luanshya where to some extent I had a formal structure to hang myself on, so to speak. And in any case I was questing after a different approach. Now at last I think I have made the breakthrough. By that I don't mean that I have solved all the problems but I've got some sort of framework within which I can

begin battering at them. The idea – the central idea – came to me
in Ndola itself, and I introduced it in a paper I gave to the Dept. It
was a feeler, and not very satisfactory! I started talking about 'gossip'
groups and the importance of gossip. I took a case of adultery as my
starting point, and traced out the various gossip ramifications as far as
my material led. More recently, I re-worked this and this led me to
formulate the concept of a network (similar to Liz Bott's who got it
from John); the network is built up of a number of different principles – neighbourhood and locality, kinship, church affiliation, and so
on. The network is activated in given social situations, a number of
individuals are linked momentarily by a common interest, a case of
adultery. The nature of this common interest is revealed in the gossip
about the case, and the gossip brings out the prestige system – the
main organizing principle in the town and overriding or rather the
one that embraces the other principles. This is expressed rather crudely
here, but if you are interested I can send you the paper where I make
the first tentative attempt to work out the idea. (ALE to CM, 24
January 1958, MPBL)

In Epstein's first notion of the network, four aspects are salient: 1)
it is centred not on an individual but on a common interest, shared
among individuals, namely an adultery case; 2) it is temporary or
momentary; 3) the network is situational in that it is activated
in 'given social situations'; and 4) it is built up on distinct social
principles.

By the time Epstein published his analysis he had recast his
notion, although traces of the earlier one remained. The two essays
he published in the 1960s (1961, 1969) brought a network perspective to bear on fine, detailed evidence. In the first essay this
was the casual and informal interactions of one man, a research
assistant, and a series of his own and his household guests' visits, as
he himself recorded them over a few days. The method of investigation was thus ego-centric, but in Epstein's published analysis
the approach was still in some respects more socio-centric and
situational than the one Mitchell later came to advance. Epstein
foregrounded fields of relationships, such as that of neighbours
in a set, and that of kinship, a field, very importantly, of widespread ties, some recreated or some even 'de-structured', according to different situations, for town purposes of equality in casual
encounters. In accord with the contextualizing of kinship ties,

not merely the ties of a specific individual, Epstein concluded, 'The wide extent and range of kinship recognized in the towns thus introduces an important element of stability into what is an extremely fluid situation' (1969: 99). Epstein carried forward from Barnes the interest in inequality and the question of how network analysis illuminated stratification. Hence he probed where in the network people do or do not recognize each other as social equals.

In the second essay, on flows of gossip and information between individuals, Epstein fulfilled more of the plan for his idea of the network to which he had alerted Mitchell. According to the second essay, Epstein heard about the involvement of a number of persons in an actual incident, and the stories about it that Epstein tracked down as they were passed between a number of individuals, first of all in an inner set of prestigious intimates, all knowing each other, and from them to others, known to some but not to all of the intimates and including less prestigious persons. The opinions formed among the prestigious 'percolated' down and influenced the less prestigious. In both his essays, Epstein carried forward a key interest which Barnes raised in his seminal analysis: inequality and the importance of ties criss-crossing social divisions.

If we turn back to Epstein's first network letter to Mitchell, what is striking is the absence of any orientation to one person; there is no reference to a single individual at the centre of the network. Social principles of equality and inequality and social situations are explicitly considered. Although in his published essays Epstein does follow that single-person orientation in part – in one sense, a specific network 'exists only and is defined with reference to a particular individual' (Epstein 1969: 109) – in part, also, he follows Barnes in his socio-centric view of the network and its clusters within a differentiated social field which, as such, is not oriented to a particular individual or reference point but exists in certain social situations and is constituted in its own terms. The consensus about gossip among the prestigious cluster in Epstein's case, for example, is not an ego-centric phenomenon; it does not arise through centrality in connectedness, nor is it to be understood by reference to a particular individual. To cope with empirical complexity, Epstein pursued his own direction in relational thought by introducing a distinction between the *effective* and the *extended* network, which covered over the shift from only the ego-centric view:

> The *effective* network then consists of clusters of persons fairly closely knitted together. The limits of such clusters – to use Barnes' term – are vague, but in some situations they show an exclusiveness so marked as to suggest the existence of groups in the strict sense, and to point to recognizable divisions within the community. The *extended* network, on the other hand, which makes greater allowance for the gradations of social status, tends to cut across such divisions. (Epstein 1969: 111)

Epstein's analysis anticipated later work, even though it was not acknowledged in it, on a very widespread phenomenon of clustering – in structures of links (not ego-centric networks) there were found to be *thick spots*, 'relatively unchanging clusters or collections of individuals who are linked by frequent interaction and often by sentimental ties', and '*thin areas* where interaction does occur, but tends to be less frequent and to involve very little if any sentiment' (Freeman and Webster 1994: 225).

At this point, I want to draw attention to Gluckman's offer of support in 1962 for quantitative network research by Mitchell. The facts are important for a clearer perspective on the intellectual and personal exchanges between Mitchell and Gluckman. At seminars that Gluckman had convened at Manchester in the 1950s, he had already expressed early and positive interest in problems of network analysis, particularly in Elizabeth Bott's network hypothesis (Bott 1957), and he kept hoping to persuade Mitchell to come to Manchester, take up a chair in sociology, and direct a major research project on networks, using big data:

> This is the sort of problem which we ought to follow up. [Gluckman then mentions his aim to raise funds] ... We will need a wide-scale survey to check a hypothesis, if we can draft suitable questions. I wrote to EB [Elizabeth Bott] and she is interested. But it is no good my trying to follow this up unless I have somebody with your class of mind to oversee the whole enterprise. Beyond that I think we now need to hunt out and study the networks of people in the middle and professional class; and again the kind of work that you are doing in Salisbury gives a theoretical lead for this. [4](MG to CM, 12 June 1962, GPJRUML)

What Epstein did not attempt was the use of diagrams of linkages or the abstract representation of patterns in figures, graphs or matrices. Such usage and the elaboration of a whole box of 'conceptual tools' – anchorage, reachability, density, content, durability, intensity, frequency – distinguished Mitchell's approach to social network analysis. Even further, and supported by the strong interest of his colleague Kingsley Garbett, Mitchell turned from sociology to mathematics for his relational thought and his interest in the morphology of personal linkages. He advanced his basic network concepts in the 1960s, first in the introduction to a collection of essays (Mitchell 1969)[5] arising from seminars he conducted at the University College of Rhodesia and Nyasaland in 1964 and 1965, and next at the 1969 symposium of the Afrika-Studiecentrum at Leiden (Mitchell 1973).

Notably, although there was in this decade a sense of a stir in studies said to be about 'the network', with high expectations of a major turn in theory, by the end of the decade these expectations had 'largely not been realised … few interesting hypotheses or statements containing useful sociological insights have emerged which were dependent on the application of a network analysis' (Kapferer 1972: 6). This was remarked by Kapferer from the viewpoint of the first of Mitchell's students to carry out a very substantial and sophisticated study of personal relations in a factory.

Like other fieldworkers, and as in my own experience, Kapferer found that Mitchell's caring and generous guidance led to very methodical and systematic research, but 'the network' represented no more than a descriptive device. It needed a theory to be explanatory and fruitful in general propositions. In accord with the then current impact of American individualist sociology, Kapferer and others, such as Jeremy Boissevain (1974), turned to advocate two approaches: transactionalism and 'exchange theory', derived, primarily, from Peter Blau (1964). By the time both approaches had had their day, subject to much disquiet among anthropologists and abandoned by their past advocates, further criticism came from Pnina Werbner, another student of Mitchell's – she was informally supervised by him for her PhD fieldwork in 1975. In her first monograph, she argued:

> The explicit application of exchange theory to network analysis has hitherto been based on neo-classical economic models, with an

associated stress on maximisation and individual strategy. The most thorough application has been by Kapferer (1972, 1973) who provides a meticulous detailed network analysis of individual strategies and transaction in a restricted context. A less rigorous application has been that of Boissevain (1974) who discusses networks of friends in Malta ... The most problematic feature of both Kapferer and Boissevain's accounts relates to the assumption that all transactions are, by definition, equivalent and interchangeable. This obscures the cultural basis of friendship, grounded in agreed definitions of exchangeable goods, ranked *values*, and the resulting flows of goods through a social network. We lack the basis for an analysis of the 'cultures of exchange' observed by the two authors, seen as historically evolving systems within the context of friendship and work relations. (P. Werbner 1990: 205–6, italics mine).[6]

Her analysis of networks thus reflected the gift economy of Pakistanis as it evolved in Manchester. Later I will say more about how Pnina Werbner brought such a culturally and historically informed analysis to bear in her own network studies while applying advanced computer programs to the comparison of elite and factory worker networks among Pakistanis in Manchester.

If, perhaps indirectly, through Gluckman, Radcliffe-Brown might have influenced Mitchell towards mathematical sociology, Mitchell himself seems to have aimed to introduce numerical measurements for connectivity. He was very aware, however, of formidable hurdles that anthropologists faced during fieldwork in the collection of data in the range and detail needed for the mathematical operationalizing. This required, as he saw in his early work, 'not only a clear idea of what characteristics of networks need to be observed and recorded but also an intensity of fieldwork few research workers are able to achieve' (Mitchell 1969: 30). Even a decade later, after network studies by anthropologists, he still observed: 'Very few have been able to, or perhaps felt it necessary to present their material systematically, such as in the form of adjacency matrices, which would permit application of standard graph theoretical procedures' (Mitchell 1979: 428). It was a paradox, remarked Mitchell, that the 'fieldworker is best placed to initiate the study after he has completed it' (Mitchell 1974a: 296).

Somehow, Mitchell got Pnina Werbner to stick to it, so that for the Pakistani migrant elite and factory worker networks, she collected the very detailed, comprehensive and systematic data his computer programs, matrices and mathematical model required. From the data, he helped her to calculate such network variables as the index of compactness, overall density and maximum finite distance; and certain matrices showed the approximate boundaries of blocks of acquaintances and cliques in successive phases in a kind of developmental cycle (P. Werbner 1990: 186–97). As for generalization from the evident regularities, at least one point was clear from the start. Size mattered. The comparison of variables, such as density, had to be of like-to-like: small networks to small, large to large; the immediate and still present difficulty being the absence in the literature of networks of comparable data with variables similarly computed.

Impressive as the computer analysis is, it has to be seen and evaluated alongside the ethnographer's qualitative statements and the observations she has had to make to interpret the data for the variables. The question of redundancy, as against ethnographic discovery, is troubling at the heart of the matter. Has all the enumeration and mathematical operation merely confirmed, perhaps somewhat more precisely, or with an appearance of greater precision, what the ethnographer had come to understand already? That is to ask, where in the relational thought of social anthropology does the immediate advance in network analysis come?

In my view, at least in Werbner's study, it came far less from the turn to mathematics than during the sheer labour of highly methodical, systematic data collection, followed of course by institutional analysis in the light of comparative perspectives on such things as class, lifestyles and social differentiation, friendship expectations and the efflorescence of the Punjabi Muslim gift economy in the British urban context. For all that, the ethnographer had to go well beyond the mathematical model with its abstract simplifications to address anthropological studies of both South Asia and Britain.

This ethnographic and historical turn enabled Werbner to illuminate power struggles and issues of resistance in class and gender relations. Some of these seemed to result in revivals of traditional South Asian kinship and familial roles, especially for women. Yet what they actually extended was an innovative process: the assertion by women of their capacity to create, largely through cultural performances and personal exchanges, intimacy and sociality in a domain of inter-household relations, which Werbner conceptualised as 'the interdomestic domain'. Clarifying the nub of her argument for network analysis, she suggested that 'It is in the interdomestic networks that we can seek the infrastructure of urban relations. It is in this domain that equality and inequality, friendship, *zat*, *biraderi*, or class find their daily expression' (P. Werbner 1990: 121). She also showed how circles of male friends are 'drawn from the dense acquaintance network of overlapping pools generated in specific associations' (1990: 208). It follows from this account that for relational thought to be fruitful for social anthropology in particular, even apart from mathematical sociology, social network analysis needs social institutional analysis – it has to be informed by the observation and interpretation of cultural performance, by the recognition of kinship structures, and by the processual analysis of social situations.

As against that, the major growth in mathematical sociology for social network analysis has prominently relied on questionnaires, big surveys and remote data, such as the electronic traces captured from the internet. The data is taken to be objective, which, of course, by its very nature of being remote from the subject sets it apart from the ethnographic interest of many anthropologists. Here the best positioned link in Mitchell's own personal network is Martin Everett. Mitchell and the mathematician Aubrey Ingleton co-supervised Everett's Oxford DPhil thesis, 'A Graph Theoretic Blocking Procedure for Social Networks', submitted in 1980. Currently co-editor of *Social Networks* (a journal co-founded by Mitchell, as associate editor), professor of social networks at the University of Manchester and co-director of the university's Centre for Social Network Analysis, named after Mitchell, Everett has carried forward Mitchell's torch, notably in being the co-author of one of the most highly popular software programs, UCINET, which originally had its origin in an earlier program of Mitchell's and which developed in work Everett carried out at the University of California, Irvine, at Mitchell's recommendation. Everett is also the author of a considerable number of quantitative analyses of social networks, methodological studies and guides to the application of software. On his website, he credits Mitchell with being, at least in the UK, the founder of the discipline, that is, the social network.

What has to be said, despite the handing on of the torch, is that Mitchell's own work, as is so often true of pioneers, has been overshadowed and is now all too little cited, other than as a tribute to an untroubling ancestor. In his 1990 interview with Russell Bernard, Mitchell was so doubtful, or perhaps merely diffident, about his continuing influence that he spoke of network analysis – perhaps primarily with studies in anthropology in mind – as being dead in the UK, though not in Europe.

Mistaken and harsh as this death notice was, it is telling of a difficulty, but not one that proved fatal, as I explain below. The difficulty was this: in Mitchell's pioneering contributions, he protected the simple coherence of his approach; he predicated it upon the known centrality in the network (Mitchell 1969: 49). As an unintended consequence, Mitchell seems to have separated his main object of study, at least primarily, from a wider interest in relational thought; that is, in structural patterns of long linkage and in cohesive cliques or emergent subsets not fully visible to the actors themselves, some arising in, through and between various social institutions, such as the directorates of international corporations and their interlocking relations. This separation and the restriction to ego-centric networks closed his early work off from many later developments in social network analysis, especially for so-called 'global' or whole networks and the broader examination of nodal structures or social linkages, not necessarily binary or dyadic, and their implications. It meant also that the pioneering importance of his early work, although often piously noticed, was taken to be now far surpassed. It appeared to be ancient history even in the leading journal, *Social Networks*, that Mitchell helped to found.[7]

The fact is, however, that Mitchell himself recognized the major limitation of his own earlier approach to the network, and he responded with very timely innovation at a crucial moment in the surge of a newly emerging mainstream, later known as 'the renaissance of social network analysis' (Freeman 2004: 12–129). This was 'block modelling', the approach Harrison White was developing at Harvard. I understand from John Scott, who was working with Mitchell at the time, that for Mitchell the appeal of block modelling along with its CONCOR algorithm was that 'it specifically went beyond ego-centric measures to the global properties of networks' (Scott to Werbner, personal communication, 22 April 2019). In response, Mitchell took up block modelling in a program of his own, but based on CONCOR. For whole or global networks, he thus enabled the computing of maximum similarities in patterns of connections and the discovery of subsets or blocks of relations not otherwise visible or perhaps perceived as such by the people themselves. White and his colleagues seemed, at least at first in 1976, to be unaware of Mitchell's innovative departure and connection to their own work. Hence they claimed that 'block modelling', their own mathematical approach to role structures and positions in small populations, was intended to be a radical break from and not a development of Mitchell's and Barnes's notions of the network:

> Insightful expositions of recent work on network interrelations are those by Mitchell (1969, chap. 1) and Barnes (1972). While we use them as central references, we want to state one fundamental disagreement. Both see network analysis to date as, at best, an eclectic bag of techniques (Barnes 1972, p. 3) for studying the details of individuals' variability around some basic ordering by categories and concrete organizations (Mitchell 1969, p. 10). We would like the reader to entertain instead the idea that the presently existing, largely categorical descriptions of social structure have no solid theoretical grounding; furthermore, network concepts may provide the only way to construct a theory of social structure. (White, Boorman and Breiger 1976: 732)

Freeman has clarified the actual efflorescence in the 1970s of social network programming, an efflorescence which Mitchell and his colleagues at Oxford strove to advance:

> These early [computer] programs varied widely. They were concerned with groups, positions, centrality, kinship structure and distribution of structural properties ... But at the beginning of the 1980s various attempts were made to tie all of these separate approaches together by producing a general-purpose network analysis program. (Freeman 2004: 140)

Freeman goes on to recognize that Mitchell was then among those who were trying 'to produce an integrated set of network analysis tools'. 'Unfortunately', remarks Freeman, 'none of these efforts panned out; none produced a program of general use' (Freeman 2004: 140). Eventually, by the 1990s programs such as UCINET 'were explicitly designed to include all the procedures that network

analysts – regardless of their backgrounds – might want to use'
(Freeman 2004: 140).

Towards the end of his life, Mitchell did write several papers
on networks in the UK;[8] even as late as 1993 he delivered the
keynote address to the European Network Association in Munich;
and with the sociologist John Scott he founded a networks group
at the British Sociological Association. In reply to my request for
his memory of Mitchell himself and his interests, Scott recalled a
major shift in his interest, from 1974 onwards, in good measure
stimulated by his understanding of the turn to block modelling:

> We got into correspondence in 1974 when Clyde responded to a note
> that I wrote in the BSA Quantitative Sociology Newsletter asking for
> help with computer programs for analysing networks of interlocking
> directors. Clyde had attended the BSA conference earlier that year
> and heard a paper by Harrison White and he had then started work
> on writing a Fortran program that would implement the technique
> described by White (block modelling). Our correspondence concerned
> the fine-tuning of this program. Clyde sent me a deck of cards [optical
> cards were then used] and I then learned Fortran in order to read the
> print out and work out what the program was doing. This allowed
> us to get a working version that would handle large data sets. We
> were both very excited when it analysed a substantial matrix in 40
> seconds, but then found that a slightly larger matrix took almost 20
> minutes. (The version running on the UCINET package developed
> by Steve Borgatti, Martin Everett and Lin Freeman now takes a frac-
> tion of a second). I had to run this program on the Manchester super
> computer, the only one in the UK capable of handling it. Every run
> – even debugs – consumed a quarter of the total weekly computer
> time that Leicester University rented on the computer – much to the
> annoyance of the physicists. The results of using the program were
> reported mainly in my book *Capitalist Property and Financial Power*
> [1986, see also 1979]. (Scott to Werbner, 21 April 2019, personal
> communication)

Scott makes the critical point that Mitchell's own work tended to
restrict social network analysis too much to the analysis of interpersonal relations, apart from structures of institutional relations; that
is, only 'to the interpersonal sphere that is left behind after formal
economic, political roles are extracted' (Scott 2017: 34). It is due
to this restriction that, according to Scott, social network analysis

'largely failed to attract adherents from outside the area of community studies' (2017: 34).

It was thus mainly through the work of other social network analysts to which Mitchell contributed or with whom he cooperated – and his fellow network analysts prided themselves on a collaborative ethos[9] – that his late innovations turned out to be part of a rapid growth, since the 1970s, of a huge industry around social network analysis for big datasets and for 'small worlds'. This has become mainstream mathematical sociology for the study of interlocking directorates between corporations, for chains of decision-making in organizational behaviour, for long chains of opportunity in large-scale societies, for patterns of social influence and acquaintance, and most recently for research on the World Wide Web (Watts 2003; Freeman 2004; Wasserman 2005; Scott 2017). Mitchell's work, along with that of Barnes and Epstein, was thus foundational for opening out problems of how the structure of networks constrains the spread of ideas and influences in social relations.

It is worth asking about the spread of their own ideas and influence beyond Central Africa and among anthropologists working more recently on relationality, especially with insights from research in Melanesia. A special issue of *Social Analysis* focuses on the intellectual exchange that might have been involved. Knut Myhre, as editor, introduces the issue with a strong thesis of debt, as if the Melanesian research on relations owed much to the Central African, from which concepts and approaches were imported. The outcome was, supposedly, a hybrid, 'Afronesian' perspective on networks, rationality and exchange (Myhre 2013). There is an obvious difficulty with this thesis. If the Central Africanists and the Melanesianists had sustained a productive conversation, or if the earlier arguments had been rethought when recontextualized in Melanesia, we would have found a trail of citations, or signs of attempts to rework contributions afresh. No such trail exists. Admittedly, some points made in the later research, such as about network limits or stops, might now well be seen as anticipated in the earlier studies by Barnes, Mitchell and Epstein; and here it would be too much of an aside for me to spell this out in detail. The fact is that there has been a striking disjuncture between social network analysis as it developed internationally and the Melanesianists' studies of relationality. It is the autonomy in the development of their thinking about relationality that calls for analysis and explanation. Perhaps most problematic is the way that the interest in mathematical modelling, so important for the growth of a whole field well beyond Manchester School studies, has passed Melanesianist perspectives by so completely as to be beyond any consideration at all.

Now for some anthropologists, the time has come to question the significance of relationality. Is it a greedy shape-shifter, like the term 'culture', as Marilyn Strathern once wryly remarked, while noting that it is limited only by another shape-shifter, 'nature' (Strathern 1992)? What can and should be the limits of relationality? Do we have to rediscover the significance of an alternative or counterpart idea, 'detachment' (Candea et al. 2015; Strathern 2015; see also Strathern 1996). The anthropological questioning, still at an early, tentative stage, is somewhat compartmentalized or 'detached' from any attention to the recent surge in social network analysis and mainstream mathematical sociology. Hence there is still an outstanding challenge for anthropology fully to come to terms with the foundational work by Barnes, Mitchell and Epstein on the coordination of relations and the structuralist mainstream of relational thought in which that work endures.

Notes

1 On the power of Homans's synthesis of sociometric and anthropological research, see Scott 2017: 28–9.
2 In the light of this passage and other contributions, especially in teaching across the world, Linton Freeman argues that Radclife-Brown's influence was huge and foundational for network analysis, especially for the later development of formal mathematical models (Freeman 2004: 103).
3 Scott argues that later in what came to be called the Harvard Renaissance, a key element in the 1980s breakthrough towards the study of the global properties of networks 'was the development of algebraic models of groups using set theory to model kinship and other relations in the spirit of Levi-Strauss' (Scott 2017: 34).
4 By the time of his last interview, in 1990, Mitchell had a different memory of Gluckman's interest in networks: 'The idea began to spread into the Department in Manchester. But Max was always somewhat opposed to it. I don't know why it was, he thought this. I don't know why, he was never terribly enthusiastic about it' (Bernard 1990: 2). Mitchell also recalled Gluckman's story of the awakening impact of the Manchester seminar on Elizabeth Bott when she presented a paper on family and class. 'And Max's story – I wasn't there I was in Africa – is

that in the seminar the whole possibility of the use of networks was raised and she went back and re-wrote what she was doing in terms of it' (Bernard 1990: 2). Barnes had presented his initial ideas in 1953 at seminars in Manchester and Oxford, and Bott learned of Barnes's work in 1954 (Scott 2017: 31). For his turn to graph theory, perhaps following Barnes, Mitchell seems to have relied on the 1953 version of Frank Harary and Robert Norman's *Graph Theory as a Mathematical Model in Social Science*, but he would almost certainly have followed, also, the later version (Harary, Norman and Cartwright 1965).

5 Mitchell dedicated this collection 'To Max Gluckman, point source of our network' (Mitchell 1969: ii).

6 I note that Bruce Kapferer was an editor of the series 'Explorations in Anthropology' in which Pnina Werbner published her ethnography.

7 For an early review, see Wolfe 1978; and for a careful acknowledgement that alongside Gluckman, Mitchell was a founding contributor among British social anthropologists, see Linton Freeman's major historical review of the development of social network analysis (2004).

8 An example of Mitchell's application of a program he wrote himself for the formal analysis of blocks is in his analysis of the networks of two homeless families in Manchester (1986).

9 Freeman claims this hallmark for the development of social network analysis: 'Social network analysis is one of the few social science endeavors in which people influence one another in such a way that they all work together to build a cumulative body of knowledge' (Freeman 2004: 6).

6

Friendship, interlocking directorates, cosmopolitanism

My own analysis of friendship as a social process among urban elites carries forward three of the interests in Epstein and Mitchell's studies.[1] The first is the broad interest that foregrounds the moral in the social, because it is not reducible to power and its many guises or disguises. An alternative approach, relentlessly rehearsing the social as no more than instrumental or tactical transactions over resources, has become virtually a spent force, after its decades of intellectual dominance, especially in political anthropology. Against that stands the exploration of how actual practice creates and responds to moral *passion*, to a distinctive *ethos*, to highly situated *values*.

A second and related interest, arising from Mitchell and Epstein's work, is in their central concern with the meanings that persons in a network contribute to their relationships, and how these meanings circulate or become realized in gossip. Even further, this interest extends to the importance in networks of both density and multiplexity, density being the mutual implication of network members independently with each other, such that they know and meet each other directly and are not merely linked through one person as the focus of the network, and multiplexity being the many-strandedness and diversity of their interconnection.

The third interest, linked to but going beyond Mitchell and Epstein's interest in prestige and stratification, is in the recent problematizing of elites, distinction and the making of civic virtue (see Lentz 1994; Fumanti 2007, 2016; Werbner 2004a, 2008, 2012b, 2014b; Savage and Williams 2008). For this third interest, Epstein's work is perhaps the most relevant of the Manchester network studies. As we have seen, Epstein (1969) points a way forward in his analysis of the flows of gossip, of their openness and closure among urban elites themselves, and their impact on norms and values of non-elites.

Elites of the first postcolonial generation as friends

Members of the first postcolonial generation to rise to the decision-making echelon of the civil service in an African state sometimes form urban-based friendships within very distinctive friendship circles, the elite cliques being mainly generated from shared occupation. Over the course of their upwardly mobile careers – from youth to elderhood, from student to top civil servant, and beyond that, upon leaving the civil service, from civil servant to elite politician or government minister, leading professional, corporate executive or company director – they look primarily to one another for the friendships they value and invest in the most. Being few in number, they are aware of being very much the vanguard for an expanding salariat. It is usually such a small world for insiders joining or belonging to the top echelon of an emerging postcolonial civil service that they are able to keep close track of their fellows; they make it their business to know each other's movements, successes and failures. A great deal of political and professional gossip circulates among them: it is finely detailed and entails highly coloured knowledge of personal conduct, which they use in defining their friendship circles more or less exclusively.

Some elites in the first postcolonial generation become what I would call 'boon-companions'. Postcolonial elite boon-companions are both highly convivial, often sharing their leisure time with one another, and also mutually supportive in business partnerships, joint entrepreneurship and the risk-taking ventures of their lives. Like many friendships in Africa and elsewhere, boon-companionship tends to be a relation of homophily, of like with like in many respects, and above all same sex, roughly same generation and professional history (e.g., the civil service). Unlike friendships in isolated dyadic relations, however, these elite boon-companionships thrive or fail in tandem with friendship circles.

In such friendship circles, the ethos, values and purposes come to be heavily influenced by experiences that are formative for the rise of first-generation postcolonial elites. Of course, much depends on the stability and legitimacy of the postcolonial regime itself. Given peaceful, negotiated transfers of power from one administration to the next, the formative experiences occur, nevertheless, in unprecedented moments, for it is a matter not merely of rising, often very rapidly, in a new civil service, but of having to inherit, yet reform or somewhat disengage from, the ways of the old colonial regime. There are also the fresh dilemmas that a professional or technocrat faces when, as a 'been-to', he or she comes from the shared ordeals of student life, often in the metropolitan academies of former colonial powers, and goes on to deal with strangers in the public, while negotiating ways through the inner corridors of government. Looking back, perhaps after leaving the civil service, and especially when confronted by changes introduced by a second or even third generation of elite successors, first-generation elites readily turn their formative experiences into a highly significant imaginary past of shared beginnings. For all their present differences, there was a time, they now recall, when they went through so much together, projecting an image of being alike, even equal, in some deeper or perhaps merely sentimentally felt sense. All of that – the formative experiences accompanied by fresh dilemmas, the remembered beginnings – is productive of a shared consciousness of special accomplishment and, indeed, of a sense of distinction, setting first-generation elite friendship circles apart.

How far such elite friendship circles reach across ethnic differences varies considerably, from postcolony to postcolony, and over time, even within the same postcolony. Usually, however, being urban based and with a diaspora beyond a rural home area, the elite friendship circles reflect and contribute to ethnic processes that emerge in urban settings, such as the formation of super-tribes or the use of old rural-derived labels for more inclusive ethnic categories.[2] If a first-generation elite friendship circle appears to be dominantly or even exclusively from one ethnic group, this tends to be one that draws together strangers with distinct origins perhaps in distant rural areas, but whose ethnicity has been redefined in various ways by their elite positioning. In no simple way is the first-generation elite friendship circle merely an after-effect of ethnicity. Indeed, perceptions to the contrary – the sense of an opening out to include others as friends across old ethnic boundaries – are often important for first-generation elites in their formation of a circle.

That said, a brief comment is needed about kinship and about straddling town and country. Most first-generation elites from the national decision-making echelon tend, at least in Botswana, to be urban villagers based in the city who straddle town and country by also keeping homes in their villages of origin. It is now well known that in Africa such urban villagers usually take care not to cut themselves off from their kin in the countryside and that they have to exercise much social skill to meet their translocal commitments to kin. How friendship circles affect and respond to straddling is an open question, the answers to which continue to be renegotiated throughout the course of the lives of members of first-generation postcolonial elites.

Elite friends in Botswana's capital

In this discussion, I want to explore first-generation elite friendship through an account of an elders' friendship circle formed mainly by Kalanga urban villagers, almost all men, in Botswana's capital city, Gaborone. Elsewhere, I have discussed the cosmopolitan ethnicity and politics of recognition among Kalanga (Werbner 2002b, 2002c, 2004a, 2008, 2014b), and here I mention their ethnic relations only briefly. One might conceptualize the friendship circle as having a core of Kalanga and a periphery of non-Kalanga who, like Kalanga, are elites long established in Gaborone. But for convenience here, I regard the friendship circle primarily in terms of its core. The men who are closest to one another within the circle correspond to those I refer to as boon-companions. Boon-companionship is not ethnically restricted, and some Kalanga do have Tswana boon-companions, but the density of links that these Tswana boon-companions have with inner circle Kalanga elders is considerable, and thus they, too, like Kalanga, are effectively embedded within the same friendship circle.

Included in this circle of leading members of the state and commercial elites are the most prominent of the self-identifying Kalanga in the capital. Kalanga are now regarded as the largest and most assertive of the country's minorities, Tswana being the recognized majority. Friends belonging to this minority elite circle all know each other well, and most are or have been more or less close friends for decades. Among them – and the list is not complete[3] – are the late chief justice, the former attorney general and later foreign minister, the late minister of finance, the late minister of mines, former high commissioners, the former managing director of British Petroleum, the long-term chairman of Barclays Bank, directors of this and other financial or investment institutions, the retired head of one of the biggest retail chains who was an assessor on the Industrial Tribunal until his recent death, and the managing directors and important shareholders in some of the capital's largest private enterprises under citizen direction or ownership. All of them have been top civil servants from the decision-making echelon: they all own real estate in the capital. Moreover, holding portfolios of company shares, perhaps most importantly in companies they founded, each has become, in their phrase, 'a man of substance', 'a substantial person', without first becoming a successful or top politician, such as a minister, until very recently (except for the one woman among the friends, herself a very prominent and early minister of education, and the late minister of finance, a brilliant economist and technocrat somewhat above party politics).

Pioneer graduates and the egalitarian ethos

Beginning my Botswana research among Kalanga in 1964, before independence, I easily came to meet and know most of the friends in the capital's elite circle of Kalanga elders early in their careers and mine, largely through the density of their own network, through the accidents of fieldwork for very different purposes in several parts of the country, and through their early study visits to Britain. Before them, at the end of the colonial protectorate, there were less than a couple of dozen graduates. Even that first postcolonial graduate cadre was quite small. It included a select few from the Lesotho-based predecessor of the University of Botswana and others, such as the founders of the Botswana Student Association in the United Kingdom, whose particularly close bonds with each other continued to be highly significant for the inner circle of friends. The friendship circle was thus mainly founded upon the shared egalitarian experience of peers in their youth. As a consequence of my early and long engagement, I was able to enjoy, during my fieldwork, the convivial fellowship of being associated not only with what they poignantly call 'the hard times', but also with the 'times of truly being', in another much-loved and often used phrase, 'down-to-earth and accessible'.

'Down-to-earth and accessible' – in the friends' ethos, the beginning of elite wisdom is knowing oneself to be a man or woman of the people, not removed from the shared earth by rank, position, wealth or power. Nevertheless, when not addressing me by one of my Kalanga nicknames or my clan honorific, *Nkumbudzi* (Remembrancer), some of the friends took pleasure in calling me 'Professor', to which I responded, as expected, in a mutual recognition of honour and distinction: 'CJ' for the chief justice, 'AG' for the attorney general, and so forth. So, too, when my wife Pnina and I accompanied them or other dignitaries on civic occasions, we were always given rosettes, clearly marked 'VIP' It is no paradox, therefore, to say that along with the admiration for leadership skills in being 'down-to-earth and accessible', the elite friends, like most of their countrymen and countrywomen, also have a fine sense of prestige, hierarchy and status; having an office does matter, though one has to wear it with modesty and, if possible, wit.

If you go on a Saturday night to an extreme corner of the capital's Notwane Club, in front of the glass cases full of winners' glittering trophies, inscribed sports shields and silver loving cups, you might find many of the inner circle of friends, drinking and mainly talking about business and politics, besides sports. Their favourite spot was known somewhat jokingly as the 'Top Table', perhaps after a place in the first president's old college, Balliol. But the Notwane Club was not posh, snobbish or expensive, unlike its neighbour immediately up the road, the Golf Club, which attracted expatriates along with a city smart set, including jet-setting academics. Instead, the Notwane Club was popular, with cheap beer, and despite the 'members only' sign it attracted mixed crowds, members and non-members, rich and poor, and many civil servants of different grades. It also had an unwritten rule of free speech.

Open critical argument about issues of the day was, above all, the pride of the 'Top Table'. Members of this inner circle of friends have carried this engagement well beyond the 'Top Table', I should stress. They have helped found and lead a good number of public forums and other racially and ethnically integrated institutions for good governance, civic interests and the critique of public policy (Werbner 2004a, 2008). They have counteracted the tendency within government to operate from an inner circle by giving considerable backing to the tendency to strengthen open and informed debate. Such cultural and political work reflects the civic importance of the elite friendship circle, and its contribution to the expansion of the public sphere.

That contribution is advanced, along with other contributions, to elite communication across party lines and personal influence on public policy, an influence linked to a long history of personal relations among the first-generation postcolonial elites. I was told that for a former president, himself a member of that generation and once a friend and frequent member of the 'Top Table', a going away party was held as he was about to take up his new office, and the farewell speech for him was full of banter about his banishment from the club to prison, the State House. The phrase 'Kitchen Cabinet' was used, however, for the casual consultations and substantial arguments about politics and policy issues that the president was well known to continue having with members of the inner circle of friends, on publicly visible visits, when he would drink at their homes. Indeed, since this president made no secret of it, rumours would fly about the inclusion in the 'Kitchen Cabinet' of a senior and very eminent adviser to the main opposition party, himself a retired permanent secretary, sometime managing director and substantial investor. Against pressure from each of their parties, both refused to give up their long and very close friendship, starting from many years of working together in the civil service, or their pleasure in drinking and talking freely with each other.

Postcolonial urban transitions and the friendship circle

Two urban transitions have been most important for the central placement and then growth of the friendship circle: first, the founding of the city itself as Botswana's capital, and second, decades later, the diamond boom and the rapid expansion of the city along with vast increases in the value of real estate. The friendship circle was created in the capital in the south by Kalanga originally from very different chiefdoms in the north, where they continue to keep homes. Some of the circle's members had already become friends during their schooldays at a boarding school near Gaborone, but it was in the capital as a small town that the circle began to take its present form. As a country, Botswana itself is small, in population if not in territory. The capital Gaborone, the country's one city, has very recently grown at an unprecedented rate. However, immediately after independence in 1966 and in the city's first decades, during the early careers of the present elders, it was a very small town, in every respect. Most of its middle- and upper-echelon civil servants knew one another; spotting people and their origins simply by their car licence plates (which in the past indicated home district and thus, to some extent, tribal origin) was something of a Gaborone guessing game, and its car parks were open books of calling cards for other residents. The circle and its boon-companionships thus formed in a context of smalltown familiarity and intimacy among people who were especially drawn to know each other well as civil servants, participating in the same round of formal and informal public occasions and identified by their ethnicity as among the upwardly mobile achievers.

As for the second transition, the diamond-led boom and its impact, we need to recognize the unstable, perhaps footloose nature of the special positioning which put some Kalanga in the vanguard of an emerging commercial elite. In the 1980s top businessmen and eventually businesswomen came from the ranks of the most senior civil servants. Leading the way in this enterprising transfer and thus gaining a valuable head start were Kalanga, some of whom felt not only pulled by their anticipation of the coming diamond-led boom, but also pushed by their sense of a glass ceiling in the civil service, of being blocked from full advancement by majoritarian discrimination. Members of this enterprising minority saw others from the majority safely cocooned within 'the system', but not themselves. In the classical discontented style of minorities 'of uneasy feet', to follow Veblen's characterization (1950), they went further afield, took command of fresh opportunities and got ahead with the next phase of competition and cooperation. They also founded a series of real estate companies, some of which won state allocations of land for skyscrapers and now provide both rents and continuing occasions for their participation in joint affairs.

The inner circle elites have become closely linked in big business. They are the directors or shareholders of a recognizable set of companies, which they formed mainly during the boom of the 1980s. Some have origins in local elites of the past, being the children or close relatives of school teachers and headmasters, minor chiefs or storekeepers, but they are very much aware of themselves as first-generation elites in their own contexts. As they have advanced in their careers, most have shared in making, from the state salariat, the core of what I call the national directorate.

Primarily based in the capital, the national directorate is an interlocking establishment of company directors who wear many hats, sit on many boards and meet regularly on one occasion after another, again and again. There are now some outstanding directors who have made their way only through business, or only through having been politicians, but even as less active elders the one-time top civil servants command many of the posts and still are influential in the national directorate. One might speak of the growth of a directorate-technocrat complex to convey the mutual interpenetration of establishments.

By this directorate-technocrat complex I do not mean to convey a cosy monolith. On the contrary, members usually do know their rivals and competitors very well, often from their schooldays, and, if anything, it sharpens their formation and reformation of political factions and related blocs or sides in business. My attention, though, was repeatedly drawn to the exceptional individual who was often much welcomed for being on both sides. 'Business is politics, and politics is business', one of the most influential directors told me in spelling out the connections between state and commercial elites and between political factions and business blocs. Between 2008 and 2011 a dispute over investments linked to the Botswana Stock Exchange brought considerable public attention and media reports on the interlocking business interests of a former president, a former chief justice, former permanent secretaries, former ambassadors and other public figures (Morewagae 2011a, 2011b).

Enduring boon-companionship, trust and interethnicity

Within this context of network density and the interlocking relations of the directorate-technocrat complex, it is not surprising that certain boon-companionships are long-lasting and expansive, although vulnerable to major struggles within the directorate-technocrat

complex.[4] Given present limits, two examples, a pair of Tswana
and Kalanga friends and another of Kalanga only, must suffice to
illustrate this. The Tswana and Kalanga friends reached the top of
the civil service through highly successful postcolonial careers in
local posts, and without treading in one another's footsteps. The
Kalanga friend recently died. They built their friendship in the
capital Gaborone, which remained their base for about fifty years;
and they and a third friend, now deceased also, formed the third
president's 'Kitchen Cabinet' of trusted intimates. The Tswana
friend came to the civil service as a professional; as the son of a
headteacher and prominent activist in South Africa, originally from
the south of Botswana, he grew up and was educated in South
Africa, taking his degree in chemistry at Fort Hare. At the peak
of his career, he became director of personnel for the civil service,
then founder of the Botswana Power Corporation and eventually
manager of a number of other parastatals. Coming from the other
end of Botswana with barely a primary school education and learning very much on the job, the Kalanga friend rose through the ranks
in one ministry after another, starting as a clerk and interpreter and
eventually serving as permanent secretary in the Ministry of Home
Affairs. It was the Kalanga friend who retired from public service
and ventured into the private sector first, becoming a corporate
manager for a major company with huge construction projects at
the beginning of Botswana's great building boom. But together,
and working as business partners, the two friends became substantial investors in real estate and other companies, some of which
they themselves founded along with prominent Kalanga and others.
As an elder, the Kalanga friend became partially sighted, and the
Tswana, as his constant companion, became his driver, putting his
own Mercedes at his Kalanga friend's ready disposal. They became
a familiar sight together, especially at their favourite drinking place,
the Notwane sports club, where the Tswana friend continued to
be an accomplished tennis player even in his old age. Although
the Tswana friend took no part in the public debate over minority
rights, which recently became increasingly intense, he remained
steadfast in his friendship as his Kalanga boon-companion pursued a
lifelong campaign in support of the Kalanga language, ethnic equality and diversity in public life. As younger men, they were the vocal
leaders, first of the Bechuanaland African Civil Service Association

and then of its postcolonial successor, the Botswana Civil Service Association. Over the decades of their very close friendship, they both sustained a strong commitment to interethnic voluntary associations, from the Botswana Society to Botswana's branch of Transparency International, and including their favourite sports club. In good measure, their interethnic boon-companionship thrived on the fact that they contributed to causes in the wider public and civic interest, and won distinction in their efforts to expand critical deliberation in the public sphere.

Comparison to a case of ethnic boon-companionship among Kalanga is illuminating. In this case, the links between the two Kalanga boon-companions were extremely close, from years of one being the civil service deputy of the other, of granting high-level foreign service and local posts to one another in turn, and having lived nearby in great amity for very many years before a troubling quarrel. In business, they tended to concentrate more on one company's board than another, as it were dividing the labour between them. Thus, one was a director of Barclays and Stockbrokers Botswana and the other of the Standard Bank and Botswana Power Corporation. In addition, they jointly planned and invested in a number of projects, from the manufacture of PVC pipes (a somewhat unsuccessful venture) to catering for airlines at Sir Seretse Khama Airport, then very busy due to sanctions against apartheid in South Africa.

I want to stress how important their experience at the highest levels of the foreign service has been for their sensitivity to prospects in global markets and international trade, and thus for the long-term success of their partnership with each other and with their non-Kalanga partners who were very prominent and wealthy Indians. Their Indian partners started from opposite ends of the country, and based their major growth in different sectors, one being wholesale supplies and the other the motor trade with exclusive import franchises, such as for Toyota and Mercedes. Hence their partnerships, although independent, developed from one another, and differentiated in ways that were complementary rather than involving competition or rivalry. Although a major struggle over control of a leading investment firm, with 30 per cent ownership of the Botswana Stock Exchange, drew them into what the media called 'a bitter fight over money and shares' (Morewagae 2011b), they were able to reach an agreed out-of-court settlement and continued their cooperation in a major venture known as '21st Century Holdings'. Their families, especially their wives, sustained mutual goodwill among themselves, so that with the settlement of their troubles, they came together with an appropriate measure of conviviality at weddings and other public occasions.

This example reveals a positive dynamic between intraethnic friendship and interethnic trust: one is not advanced at the expense or to the exclusion of the other, as is sometimes assumed. Trust among Kalanga themselves was the well-spring for extending trust to potentially trustworthy others beyond their own ethnic group. In other words, for these elites, the beneficial and supportive strength of their intraethnic relations was crucial for opening out the same potential in interethnic relations and thus for enhancing their friendship as a cosmopolitan accomplishment. Of course, all of these partnerships thrive within a broader context, immediately in the public sphere sustained by a state that stands out in Africa for being capable, stable and financially creditworthy. Taking that as given, my argument addresses the problem of trust and the selective dynamics in friendship, ethnicity and entrepreneurship (for more analysis in depth, see Werbner 2004a, 2008).

Kinship and friendship

So far, I have said rather little about kinship. It is beyond my present scope fully to consider elite kinship in its urban and translocal meanings. But getting even a brief perspective on friendship in relation to kinship is essential. Although some elders of the friendship circle are related, one being the mother's brother of another, they are, on the whole, not close kin or affines. Their friendships have not been steps on the way to becoming relatives. None of the children or grandchildren of the friends have married each other, and relatively few of these offspring have become close friends. What is reproduced from generation to generation is not the specific friendship circle, but the capacity to constitute circles appropriate to each generation. The friendship circle and the relations of boon-companionship, while primarily for a founding generation, have nevertheless been embedded in dense networks and multiplex relations: they have thus been enduring, highly stable and not fragile or volatile. The same, it is worth saying, is true of the marriages of the elite friends: none has divorced, and all were married to non-Kalanga, as I have explained elsewhere (Werbner 2002b, 2004a, 2008).

The most striking march of kinship together with friendship is in mobilization sets for the public occasions of rites of passage, such as weddings and funerals.[5] For such occasions, along with the relatives, the boon-companions are always prominently mobilized, and usually also many of the inner circle. It is a matter of obligation for them all, friends along with kin, and during the period of AIDS in Botswana, it has been a heavy, time-consuming obligation which makes for a great deal of public sociability and intensified social circulation, connecting friends and kin informally. Friends also join kin and family members in domestic space, being entertained and fed at each other's homes, often on weekend *braais* or barbecues, with abundant meat and drink.

By contrast, where friendship most distinctively comes into its own space is in the club and pub. Although some women, including players of club sports, do come to both, the inner circle friends' wives almost never join their husbands at either; nor do fathers and sons usually drink together. If family matters come up in casual gossip, they are usually marginal to the general flow of conversation. Hence the divide between kinship and friendship is most realized in convivial leisure, which is, however, not divorced from matters of business, politics and sport as favourite topics.

I would argue that in Gaborone for minority elites of the first postcolonial generation, both the urban friendship circle and boon-companionship mesh durably with kinship, and do not displace it nor take any load or emotional charge from it. Compared to kinship, both are more narrowly defined, being specific to the same generation, gender and class, unlike kinship, which is reproduced from generation to generation and extends across gender and class. The friendship circle and boon-companionship formed a personal sphere which complemented that of kinship, while overlapping and in part interpenetrating it. This postcolonial formation was not a response to some supposedly typical transition in urbanization, such as a move from a universe of personal relations in the countryside to impersonal ones in town. The early urban transition in the friendship circle's formative years at the beginning of the postcolonial era was more a move from one universe of personal relations to another, which if somewhat mixed, was still dominated by personal relations, and even more closely linked to the countryside and the affairs of kin. While the later urban transition during the diamond-led boom came with a vast expansion in the postcolonial state bureaucracy, in impersonal relations, ethnic heterogeneity and host–stranger relations, it also locked the elite friends even more closely into interdependence between their leisure, business, financial and even political affairs. The outcome was a strengthening of their standing as one of the capital's power elites and, I would argue, an enhancement of their capacity to meet their highly valued commitments and obligations of kinship.

It is evident, from my arguments, that the dynamics of elite friendships during postcolonial transformations have to be studied over the long term and from generation to generation (see also Fumanti 2016). In the next stage of analysis, we will require a much richer understanding of how elite friendships affect and, in turn, are affected by the making not merely of kinship but of elite dynasties (see Pina-Cabral and de Lima 2000). For Botswana, my own account stands at a threshold before a major field that is emerging in the anthropology of social mobility, elite sociality and friendship.

The funeral of a rooted public cosmopolitan

I want to carry my account of elite friendship a stage further by documenting how an elite funeral became, among other realities, an occasion for the mobilization of a considerable, diverse public, for an assertion of public cosmopolitanism, and for recreating personal relations among a friendship circle along with significant others at a sensitive postcolonial moment.[6] The occasion was the funeral of Richard Ngwabe Mannathoko, who came from a long-stigmatized though now powerful ethnic minority, the Kalanga, and was a leading member of the first postcolonial generation to be senior civil servants in the highest decision-making echelon. He was also a founding and leading member of the civil servants' association (the precursor of a union), an NGO head, ambassador and multinational director, real estate investor, lawyer and large-scale farmer. Mannathoko died at the age of 79, and was buried early in December 2005 in his home city, Francistown.

Mannathoko belonged to that inner circle, mainly Kalanga and drawn from the first postcolonial generation of top-echelon civil servants who built up Botswana's interlocking big business directorates. The establishment of Botswana's postcolonial technocrat-directorate complex is, in good measure, their accomplishment, though not exclusively theirs (Werbner 2004a). Members of this inner circle have also been influential in making public cosmopolitanism meaningful in Botswana by both constructing difference and transcending it.

In assertion of minority rights and ethnic dignity, they founded cultural associations, for example the Society for the Promotion and Advancement of the Ikalanga Language (SPIL). But they also took leading roles in the development of public forums and other racially and ethnically integrated institutions concerned with good governance or critical of current public policy (Werbner 2004a: 187). Not that they ignored the hot arenas of party politics – and Mannathoko himself was identified with a faction, at least in the media – but it was in these forums and institutions, above all, that Mannathoko and other public cosmopolitans sought, recognized and sustained allies in the realization of their cosmopolitan potential. Their attention to their changing problem of alliance contributed significantly to the remarkable growth of voluntary associations as NGOs in Botswana, admittedly, as elsewhere across Africa, a growth much driven at its peak by foreign donor funding.

Where to create alliances was the open question from one postcolonial moment to another, a question, of course, relative to the life course and repositioning of the public cosmopolitans themselves. In Mannathoko's case, the move in responsive alliance was from one extreme of founding leadership to another, from his service in the 1960s as secretary general of the Botswana Civil Servants' Association to his establishment of the umbrella council, the Botswana Confederation of Commerce, Industry and Manpower (BOCCIM), which for a decade under his presidency in the 1990s brought together state officials and business executives and had a major impact on public policy (on BOCCIM, see Maundeni 2004: 77). Mannathoko's contribution as a bridge-builder was acknowledged by BOCCIM's representative, who spoke before me at the funeral.

Mannathoko's cosmopolitanism continued to be known and effectively carried forward by the women closest to him, his wife, the former mayor of Botswana's capital and a leading philanthropist who herself died in April 2017,[7] and his daughters. One daughter was, at the time of his funeral, regional director of a UNICEF programme for Eastern and Southern Africa; a second, the assistant director general of the World Health Organization in Geneva (she later became a vice-president for development in the World Bank in Washington DC); and a third daughter, a senior economist formerly with USAID, and later with the World Bank. These women are in the forefront of Botswana's new generation of international public servants, a signficantly growing number. True to a public cosmopolitan ethic, they take upon themselves a more inclusive responsibility for bettering the quality of life, not merely for people in their own country but reaching well beyond that to a wider, shared world. Elegant women in black, they came, living proof of the realization of their father's public cosmopolitan vision, from across the world to mourn at his funeral.

Civic culture: biography and documentary practice

Hundreds of mourners, people from all walks of life, including many of the great and the good in the country, came to Mannathoko's funeral. This very public event was hosted, in between a requiem Mass and the other solemn last rites, with a generous excess of feasting on much-loved local foods, from juicy, fresh-killed goat meat to thick porridge and rich stews, with abundant greens and other tasty relishes. Grand and lavish as Mannathoko's funeral was, it was nevertheless a moment common and true to the civic culture, now widely shared throughout much of Botswana, in remote villages no less than in the towns and cities (see Durham and Klaits 2002; Werbner 2014a, 2014b, 2018a, 2018b).

This civic culture fosters very careful regard for social biography. The individuation of the subject matters a great deal. Not individualism or the cult of the heroic individual, I stress, but that individuation that strains to do justice to the problem of the member as a special and vital part of a greater whole. Careful individuation calls, in death and faithful to life, for a highly ceremonious relating of the subject to significant others: first, through their recognized presence and solemn procession at the last rites, normally wearing their respectful best; second, through illuminating biography in oratory;

and, third, through the reading of personal, written messages, along with the display of their floral wreaths.

Funerals proceed, accordingly, with an announced, meticulously detailed programme. It is often printed to list the schedule of times and places, the main participants, their immediate roles and usually their relationships to the deceased. The deceased's personal profile, briefly given in the programme, usually with a characteristic photograph, is always rehearsed in the round.

From their distinct perspectives, significant others trace the special moments of a life course, individual and highly specific, through to the fine particulars of death. The details matter; an honest, or at least credible, account is expected; the life, at death, must be put on the public record as a meaningful chain of events for a known and now memorable character. No one, not even a young woman or teenage boy, dies without a bare trace and without some public oratory of personal dignity.

There is a cherishing in memory of the life that was, including quirks, jokes and moments comic enough to make everyone laugh, unchecked by the solemn presence of the coffin and its corpse, before whose exposed face, composed in death, mourners bend their heads in reflection – that is the carefully observed and respected truth of this civic culture in Botswana.

Civic culture: the predicament of public cosmopolitanism

Endemic in all this is a predicament of civic culture which can be highly problematic for the public cosmopolitan in particular. In Botswana people value highly the smooth surface of social life, indeed, civility itself. Yet the documentary practice in funerals puts that value at risk, making it precarious and vulnerable to tensions, even open quarrels and the exposure of personal grievances. Even beyond that, the predicament takes on a special sensitivity when the occasion responds to the life of a public cosmopolitan well known to be a controversial maverick, never branded someone else's own or fully domesticated.

It hardly needs saying that such a maverick is not likely merely to serve social life's smooth surface, even when his time comes to rest in peace. But what does need saying for the public cosmopolitan, more generally, goes to the horizon above the surface. The force of public cosmopolitanism is uncontained and uncontainable, for it comes from looking beyond, seeing a horizon as open, perhaps barely glimpsed yet with potential somehow to be realized in the public sphere. If restless in life, and given to seeking beyond the horizon, the public cosmopolitan makes an uneasy subject for the documentary practice of funerals to command.

The partial measure of the public man: funeral programmes

So too in Mannathoko's funeral: a partial measure of the public man was made visible in each of two programmes, one for the requiem Mass on 9 December at St James's parish church, ending with the 'Profile of a Gifted Son of Botswana', and the other for 10 December, the day of his burial. This second programme, folio size with computer-generated personal graphics on each of its twelve pages, is a remarkable representation of public distinction in an exemplary life. The first page reprints the profile on the requiem programme. Next appears the Mannathoko family tree, with the couple's 1962 photograph from Leeds and law student days above a diagram spread across the whole page. It is as if to remind all, including the social anthropologist, that genealogy lives on; it is not passé.

The third and fourth pages are devoted to the order of service. Listed, among others, and in English and Kalanga, but not Tswana, are the two masters of ceremonies, the three traffic masters, the thirty-two pall bearers (turn-takers along the way from house to grave), the ten speakers at the hall (each identified by relationship, for example in-law, BOCCIM representative, BP representative), the thirteen readers of messages, the wreath bearers and the several speakers, including Members of Parliament, at the graveside. The whole list registers the richness of personal and public association over a lifetime. Considerable as the list is, nearly seventy participants in all, it conveys but a bare hint of the funeral's substantial logistics in mobilizing so many kin, friends and the general public, very quickly, from across the country and beyond.

Pages 5 to 8 portray Mannathoko's professional life, illustrated by photographs of him with the country's first president, with his colleagues at the Ministry of Local Government, with fellow trainees for the foreign service in 1966, with fellow ambassadors at the Organization for African Unity in Addis Ababa in 1968, as High

Commissioner with the Zambian vice-president in 1967, and with other Barclays Bank of Botswana board members. The narrative of family life on page 10 follows him from birth to marriage, his own and his wife Rosinah's early education and practice as teachers both in Botswana and Southern Rhodesia, the birth and upbringing of the surviving four of his six children and eight grandchildren, and his retirement and active advisory role as senior uncle to the current Chief Masunga, some time head of Botswana's House of Chiefs. (Among all his public distinctions, Mannathoko much prized his claim to chiefly descent. 'I am always a headman, wherever I go', he would boast to me, with a characteristic chuckle.)

The accompanying illustrations are brim-full of family, children and grandchildren, with their glowing smiles, around Mannathoko and his wife. 'Dick', the physical giant, the champion athlete, footballer and tennis player, emerges in the account and photos for social life on page 11; all this is above the final section for the proudest of his lifelong passions, breeding and accumulating cattle. He was president of the Nata Farmers Association at the time of his death, and this section's illustration, 'Breeding at the Farm', shows stock from his highly valuable prize herd, from his remarkable accomplishment in cross-breeding Brahman, Charolais and Simmertals. Finally comes his full-page portrait, with the caption 'Rest in Peace', and in Kalanga, 'Ezelani Nge Dothodzo Ntombo'.

If not Cosmopolitan, *worldly cosmopolitan?*

If not a candidate for the glossy cover of *Cosmopolitan* magazine, Mannathoko could easily have passed for the most familiar appearance of the worldly cosmopolitan. Widely travelled as an ambassador on behalf of his country, he had shaken hands with the sheikhs of this world, taken their oil and his seat on the international board of BP, the first ever for an African, yielded hugely increased corporate profit, and drunk copiously from the best of the British Empire's legacy in Scotch and from the rest of the world's good red wines.

A trained lawyer, who helped write his country's constitution, he had the advocate's skill in making the best of a case, of getting sharply to the rights and principles in conflict. It was a skill he brought to bear in the civil service, diplomacy, corporate enterprise, in the designing and leading of NGOs and on presidential commissions, but not in legal practice as such.

Of the worldly cosmopolitan's competence in languages he again had a broad grasp, being fluent in at least three African languages and two European. He made close and strong friendships across national, racial and ethnic differences. As a host, he had the rare gift of putting his guest at ease. A charming *bon vivant*, he apparently never felt himself a stranger, however strange the place he was in – or at least, his stream of jokes and spontaneous banter made people laugh, whether they were San herders on his huge farm or 1960s with-it Oxford dons (when I saw him at Oxford on his diplomatic training).

That said, I must add a significant qualification to the word 'never'. There came a time in retirement when he felt he had had enough of life in the capital, Gaborone, a city of which he was not very fond, and he and his southern-born wife moved their home back north to Francistown, the city near the chiefdom of his birth. It was to be, as he told me, 'near my roots'.

Rooted public cosmopolitanism: biography and ethnography

The story of Mannathoko's professional life in the larger programme represents him as 'a free thinker', 'never constrained by tradition, rules or conformist approaches'. He was regarded as a charismatic, strong leader already as a head boy at St Joseph's College. At the time the protectorate's leading southern boarding school, St Joseph's became a major crucible for postcolonial elite formation, its powerful old-boys' and old-girls' network including at least one vice-president of Botswana and numerous other politicians, very senior civil servants and big entrepreneurs in the country's interlocking directorates.

While still a schoolboy, Mannathoko wrote and spoke fearlessly, even recklessly, at a high moment of deference to alien rule. Among other things, ahead of revisionist postcolonial historians, he dismissed the founding myth of the protectorate: that Queen Victoria gave her protection as grace and favour to Tswana chiefs petitioning her through missionaries in the Christian civilizing mission.

The point is that his debunking was not taken lightly by the authorities as mere schoolboy posturing. At heavy personal cost, he gained a lifelong reputation for daring to stand his ground against the powers that be. 'His scholarship at college was withdrawn when he insisted that British Colonial Rule had been imposed on the country', the programme reports, 'when what our Botswana Chiefs had sought was an alliance. This led to him being perceived as a threat and troublemaker, and he was forced to teach in Southern Rhodesia rather than Bechuanaland.' The programme goes on to tell of his 'sentencing a white man to imprisonment while he was a [protectorate] District Officer, because it was the right thing to do: an act which was considered unthinkable at the time'. In explaining this daring to think the unthinkable and act upon it, the programme does not use the word cosmopolitan, but it represents his motivation in cosmopolitan terms, in terms of moral principles, rights and universals of humanity, beyond race or nation: 'He respected all men and believed in equality before the law.'

This representation catches the nub of the legend that surrounded Mannathoko in his lifetime, for being anti-imperialist and anti-racist. When, before independence neared in 1966, he studied to become one of the country's first handful of university graduates, he was the only one whose radical politics ruled him out of the protectorate government's largesse for overseas courses. Nor did his legend and tactically sharp tongue endear him to the old guard of senior former protectorate officials who at first dominated the President's Office and most of the ministries, in the very early years of the postcolony.[8] He was watched with more than suspicion.

As a radical activist, he was a founding member of the Bechuanaland African Civil Service Association and later secretary general of the Botswana Civil Servants Association. He helped draft and present the Protectorate Association's thoroughgoing critique of the colonial government's discrimination in favour of expatriates at the expense of locals.[9] This is still regarded as an opening salvo in a continuing controversy over localization.

The old guard consensus was that Mannathoko was a dangerous tribalist; that his talk of rights, justice, principle was no more than a cover for self-interest; that he was always on the make to look after his own Kalanga people, above all. In the cocktail parties of the small world of the capital in those days, his wife told me, one or another senior expatriate official would come up to him and say, whatever the merits of the case, 'I see you got another job for one of your people', or, 'Not yours this time, eh!' If not deliberate divide and rule, after the celebrated caricature of perfidious Albion's imperial policy, it was nevertheless more than a casual response to the expanding horizons of local elites, to their rooted cosmopolitanism in the making. There was a late imperial mind-set, with a long self-congratulatory wisdom of its own, that reserved the moral high ground for the old guard themselves. They left, among the likes of Mannathoko, little or no room for what the British call 'a safe pair of hands'.

It is worth saying that the vicissitudes of his career never made Mannathoko bitter against the British, or for that matter, bitter at all. After all, human beings would get up to their antics, and that for him was a source of endless jokes and shared humour.[10] However, characteristically, in 1964, when Mannathoko and I first sat drinking together in a Francistown bar, then usually segregated by race, on an informal basis he warned me that being seen with him would cause me trouble with some people, and then laughed heartily. Or, rather, we both laughed heartily.

Not surprisingly, the programme passes silently over one consequence for Mannathoko of being such a maverick: conspiracy theories, defamation and rumour, even about plotting a *coup d'état* with other top Kalanga civil servants. 'Guns under the Bed' ran the headline in a 1969 pre-election issue of the *Bulawayo Chronicle*, then the main source of gossip and news in the absence of any local newspaper in Botswana. The story had leading Kalanga, including Mannathoko and a future cabinet minister, plotting a takeover and arming themselves at night, in the capital. At the time, however, they were actually President Khama's guests for Easter in his Serowe home. The president traced the rumour to expatriate police officers in the CID and sacked them. But the rumour never quite died; it has become one of those 'truths', often whispered in the capital, about the 'hidden agenda' of Kalanga elites as a minority about to take over from the majority (see Werbner 2004a: 71–4). A Tswana cabinet minister told me frankly, but only on the basis of anonymity, that in his view Mannathoko, who was regarded as a potential head of the civil service, never attained his potential in the civil service, nor became a minister, in part because the accusation of being a tribalist plotter gave him a reputation that stuck.

Family friend: Richard Werbner

I took up some of these issues in my own speech at the funeral, which follows in italics. Speaking first in Kalanga, I made the customary opening address to the funeral, announced that I would speak in English and Kalanga, and then took the liberty of asking the interpreter to rest. Otherwise, he offered a clean but hurried translation in Tswana between each Kalanga or English speaker's sentence or two. And rest he did, after translating my request into Tswana.

I felt I had to concentrate, myself, and be aided in that by a close hearing from my fellow mourners. If a liberty, then perhaps a wise one, or so the interpreter himself conveyed later, when he somewhat jokingly told me, after the speeches, that he would have been bound to edit some of my remarks:

The passing of a great man leaves lasting inspiration for generation after generation. Some great men get riches for themselves, their families, even their country. Other great men give public service of the highest value. Still other great men build the institutions and the organizations upon which daily life depends. But the true mark of the great man is always powerful vision. To see beyond, to open out the horizon of hope, of trust and of promise, to dare to be ahead of the times, all that marks out the great man.

Richard Ngwabe Mannathoko was such a great man. Here we can only begin to tell of his remarkable life. He did not have to wait for us to eulogize him in endless stories and in his fund of jokes. He was already a legend living in our midst. But I have a confession to make to put the record straight. We carried on our conversation over more than forty years, from the time when he was a young law student and I, a novice anthropologist. During that time, I sometimes referred to him and his ideas in my published work; the references are a dozen in my latest book. What I want to confess is – and I know he forgave me for this – I ought to have made dozens and dozens more acknowledgements to his contributions. He was such a good talker, so cogent, so sharp and persuasive in his analysis of the issues, that I often came away thinking I had got the point by myself even before he had driven it home.

This confession takes me to the heart of the matter, which in this country cannot be distant from diamonds and the public good. Every

Motswana now knows the answer to the question: Who owns Botswana's diamonds? The people of Botswana, of course. Obvious and to be taken for granted? Perhaps! But the fact is for it to be effectively true took, and still does take, much deliberate effort by this country's leading decision-makers. Here Richard was in the vanguard.

Early on, he saw that the many tribes of the Bechuanaland Protectorate had to give way to the one nation-state in the Republic of Botswana, when it came to mineral rights. To realise his republican vision, he set about as Principal Secretary to the Prime Minister and as Permanent Secretary of the Ministry of Lands and Local Government, campaigning very successfully to get the chiefs on board. No longer, as a result, did tribes claim mineral rights. Of course, I am not saying that Richard was single-handed in the founding of this basis for a stable, viable Republic. Obviously, Sir Seretse Khama took the lead. But I am saying that Richard's republican contribution was outstanding.

Richard had a well-deserved reputation for being bold, outspoken, fearless and ready to speak truth to power. I will say more about that, shortly. But first I want you to have in mind his virtue as a gentle giant, the diplomatic virtue which made his republican contribution possible. In this, Richard brought to bear his skill as a consummate negotiator; he did so much to convince chiefs, men proud of their dignity and honour, that they would be respected all the more by agreeing to put the national interest first, before the tribal.

Many of you may immediately wonder whether Richard the republican was also Richard the tribalist. For you will well recall Richard's much publicized blast at the height of the recent Balopi Commission. Then he called the late Ngwato regent Tshekedi Khama 'a terrorist'. It was for Tshekedi's part during the 1940s in unleashing violent regiments leading to the imprisonment and exile of the prominent Kalanga chief Nswazi and his subjects. Many were Richard's relatives. As a youth, he visited them doing hard labour in prison. The injustice rankled with Richard. It made him determined to fight against what he saw as oppression of the many by the few. The immediate lesson he drew was about wrongs against Kalanga, his own people, and it led him to be a proud founding member of the first Kalanga student cultural association. But he also looked beyond that immediate lesson to the wider moral horizon in his vision of public respect and dignity for all minorities on an equal basis with the majority. Richard was a strong advocate of the universal rights of the citizen, every citizen without discrimination.

Let me quote from one of those places in my most recent book where I did acknowledge his ideas. This quotation, explaining the remarkable importance of Kalanga as lawyers, is actually about a perception Richard had from his own experience:

> Mannathoko notices that facing stigma and inequality often makes minorities great supporters of universal rights. Minorities turn to law as a profession, he suggests, because the experience of discrimination by a majority gives them a passion for justice, and even more the determination to know how to get it. (Werbner 2004a: 108)

A passion for justice, yes, Richard was moved by that. While serving on a highly sensitive Presidential Commission of Enquiry, he felt he had to expose a trail of scandal and corruption no matter where or to whom it led. If this made him unforgiving enemies, well, so be it and, indeed, so it was. He had taken an oath as a Commissioner and could not go back on that, he told me.

Richard was a passionate, determined man who enjoyed being a politically controversial figure. A good number of leading civil servants felt he had the potential to be the head of the civil service or, at least, a minister. In his prime, some talked of a glass ceiling against Kalanga, especially to keep them from certain sensitive areas of public security.

I had the gall to ask Richard why that potential of his was never fully realized. He was philosophical about it. With a twinkle in his eye and a characteristic grin, he told me he was by nature better suited to being a general.

As I have said, he was ahead of his time – nowadays in Botswana, a Kalanga can be Minister of State in the President's Office and not merely Attorney General or Chief Justice, and like anyone else, a general, too, can hold high office, perhaps the highest.

If something of a general, Richard was at his very best in crisis, when, so to speak, the war was on. Take the oil crisis, for example. In the 1970s when sanctions were hitting apartheid South Africa, and thus the refineries for Botswana's oil, the Cabinet and permanent secretaries, including Richard, suddenly faced the emergency of oil supplies running out almost immediately. So critical and outspoken was Richard on the folly of those responsible, I am told, that by general consensus, he was given the brief to get the oil somehow, somewhere, and very quickly. But where?

You will appreciate that at that time to give the answer, Botswana had no central intelligence agency of its own. Or rather, the agency was so undercover in a library that only Richard knew that the one who could come to the rescue was the librarian, the beautiful woman he loved from his youth at their boarding school, his wife Rosinah. Rosinah did the library research; she identified the oil sources, and off Richard went on his successful, if hair-raising, hunt, eventually finding an old friend from his student days who turned out to be a most highly placed Saudi, eager to help a poor country like Botswana.

The rest of the story is familiar history to many of you who will recall often seeing Richard's face in the Botswana Telephone Directory ad for BP. Having reached his peak in the civil service and as a top diplomat and ambassador, Richard became, of course, the first African to be a member of the international board of BP. Not that this was his only achievement in the world of corporate capital and wise invest- ment. It is enough to say here that he managed often to beat the manager of Barclays at his own game, tennis.

My last memory of Richard brings to mind the biblical verse from Exodus (13: 21) about the Israelites on their trek in the Wilderness. What the Israelites followed by the day was a pillar of cloud sent by God. So too did my wife and I follow a great pillar of dust, just a few months ago, when enjoying the freedom to speed at the wheel of his old yet still fast-moving van, Richard led us like an angel to his Nata farm, to his promised land. I savour still the liver he roasted so skilfully, on an open fire outside, from the goat he slaughtered in our honour. And very nearby, I recall too, was the sound of the prize bull, eager to be on the job, a bellow which was always music to Richard's ears. Richard's farm was a Spartan place, without luxuries, and with hardly any creature comforts from the city. It spoke of a highly produc- tive man, caring for his capital investment in his herd, but who rather disdained the world of consumer goods; a brave old man who was determined, above all, to die as he lived, rooted and still nourished by the countryside.

Finally, in Richard Mannathoko's honour, I recited the praises of his clan, which are partly in Pedi and partly in Kalanga:

Bo Mannathoko, Zwitetembo zwenyu zwiapo zwinodha mo ludzi gwa ba Pedi. Ndoti Ntombo, Mperi, Bamagwasa, Bamagadagadang

*majwana, matlhari aana magwasa. Bantswi la tswiritswiri. Bari tjin-
digwi kiya. Hakilagwi nyama mbisi, kiya ndambala. Bari Mannathoko tiya. Baka sebona atama, atsena semokopela. Moswazi o tlhabile
pologolo. Boelela motlhaba tlou, osekare maabane ke tlhabile. Nswazvi
gogola kwano, shango haina bathu.*

Ezelani nde dothodzo, Ntombo.

Public cosmopolitanism, patriotic divide: the senior statesman's speech

The next to speak was the most honoured mourner, Sir Ketumile
Masire, Botswana's second president. For our understanding of Mannathoko's public cosmopolitanism, we need to appreciate a remarkable divide, both in sensibility and in cultural politics, because that
divide set Mannathoko and Masire apart. Patriotism united them, of
course, but patriotism also divided them. If apparently a paradox, it
is important, because it is revealing for patriotism and public cosmopolitanism more generally, and because it reaches the respect for
constitutional order, which citizens of a republic, like Botswana or
the United States for that matter, must owe (on the general issues,
see Appiah 1998: 101). I want to unpack the paradox and then say
more about the divide in sensibility and cultural politics.

At the heart of the matter is the debate about difference and
variety. This debate we know, in Botswana as elsewhere, is about
that many splendoured chameleon, multiculturalism.[11] As Kwame
Appiah, above all, has made us recognize, one can be a patriot of
some sort without valuing difference and variety highly, but not a
cosmopolitan patriot (Appiah 1998). I have to rehearse the point for
the multiculturalism debate, even at the risk of labouring over the
now perhaps all too familiar. The point is this: public cosmopolitans,
finding discrimination in their country's laws or constitution, have
to press for legal and constitutional change because they are patriots
who respect constitutional order and because they are also cosmopolitans who value difference. Not being cosmopolitans, opponents
of such change can still take their stance as patriots. On both sides
of the divide lies actual or claimed motivation by patriotism.

In Botswana, and for Mannathoko and Masire in particular, the
opposition between the sides came to a head at the height of a

Presidential Commission on tribal and other discrimination in Botswana's constitution. Earlier, in nationalist speeches about the danger of 'letting the tiger loose', the spectre of ethnic violence on the horizon, Sir Ketumile, while president, repeatedly gave dire warnings. In 2000, during a Presidential Commission hearing at the capital, at a moment which I, too, felt to be electric, the former president raised the full weight of his reputation as a founding father and one of the authors of the Constitution, and he brought that weight to bear forcefully in defence of the status quo. He spoke very movingly of his fears for the danger to unity and public order if minority cultural and language politics went unchecked (see Werbner 2004a: 44). Against that view, Mannathoko, himself also responsible for the drafting of the Constitution, fought for change; the time had come to end tribal clauses. Speaking before the Commission in his home city but capturing much publicity in the national media, Mannathoko made his battle cry heard, by calling the late Ngwato regent Tshekedi Khama 'a terrorist', as I recalled at his funeral. The two national leaders thus stood, with outspoken passion, on opposite sides of what is still a great and sensitive debate about minorities and multiculturalism in Botswana.

That said, I turn to illuminate more of the contrast in sensibility as it relates to cultural politics and cosmopolitanism. Of the two men, only Mannathoko spoke the other's home language, Masire being renowned in his prime as one of the most gifted popular orators in Setswana, the national language, the official one being English. Where Mannathoko was a pluralist – the cosmopolitan who celebrated the variety of culture and the patriot who insisted on public recognition and support for his language along with others – Masire was more the unitarian, the one-nation advocate of homogeneity. Masire's government carried forward an assimilationist policy, a policy that virtually reserved the public cultural space for a perceived majority, the Tswana, including Masire himself. In Botswana's first postcolonial period, building one state was building one nation – the Tswana nation.[12]

At the funeral, former President Masire came to praise Mannathoko, and not merely to bury him along with the still simmering factional disputes of the ruling party, the BDP. Mannathoko had been a founding BDP member, one of the most prominent, and of unwavering party loyalty. Being myself something of a relic of fieldwork BDBP – Before Diamonds in the Bechuanaland Protectorate – I was nevertheless bemused to hear the octogenarian Sir Ketumile apologize in his eulogy for not being an anthropologist.

Unlike the anthropologist who spoke immediately before him, this surviving father of his country could not recite Mannathoko's clan praises in Mannathoko's own languages – Kalanga and Pedi. He also joked about the way two of the speakers before him (colleague and friend Gobe Matenge, and family friend Richard Werbner) appeared to have got together to talk up Kalanga issues, which left other things for him. Significantly, even if no one had addressed Mannathoko's sense of outrage at Tswana cultural dominance over Kalanga, that would still have been documented at the funeral, because the programme records that 'Throughout his adult life he [Mannathoko] promoted the use and development of the Ikalanga language, because he considered it a *crime* to let part of Botswana's rich, diverse culture and tradition die' (my italics). Later gossip with well-informed others, off the record, confirmed my feeling that the former president was defusing a politically charged moment very deftly, for his concern might well have been that he had come to be regarded, even by some Kalanga once close to him, as being too suspicious of minorities such as Kalanga, and perhaps an enemy or at least somewhat hostile to their advancement.[13]

Sir Ketumile rose gracefully to the occasion. His eulogy, given spontaneously with much personal affection, was a seamless fusion of languages. It resounded with a richness of Tswana drawn from the common poetry of the people. But it was a richness commanded in the service of development-speak, that official rhetoric without which no great civic occasion in Botswana can proceed.

In the government's own newspaper, the *Daily News*, Sir Ketumile was later quoted as saying,

> Richard Mannathoko was a man whose development ideology was rooted in his confidence in the ability of Batswana. Mannathoko was driven by an urgent desire to see Botswana recognised as a valuable global player because of the capacity of its citizens. He used every window of opportunity to enable the full realisation of Batswanas' potential. (12 December 2005)

In fact, this is a quotation from the last paragraph of the profile of a gifted son of Botswana, on both funeral programmes. Sir Ketumile spoke without notes and did not say this. I was too overcome by my own participation, sitting among the other speakers, and too long preoccupied later to make even mental notes of my own. Nevertheless, I believe the Botswana *Daily News* rightly reported what Sir Ketumile should have said and what, at least in sentiment and sensibility, he actually did express.

'Botswana is recognised as a valuable global player, because of the potential of its citizens'; the vision is unmistakably patriotic. And the former president's presence in itself spoke in honour of Mannathoko's patriotism; after all, they came together in the state-building vanguard, creating Botswana as a new nation-state. But how plain was or is it, for all the words *valuable global player*, that equally this public vision is cosmopolitan?

The quest for the horizon: the promise in the people

That it is an optimistic vision no one at the funeral could have doubted, of course. After all, well known in the background, the unspoken stereotype, against which Mannathoko himself fought tenaciously, was this: the country, as the Bechuanaland Protectorate, was held to be a remote, relatively unimportant outpost of Empire. It was, overwhelmingly, more a backward, custodial burden – in a word, a desert – than anything else in imperial eyes, which for long saw rather little potential in most of the people themselves – tribesmen at home with cattle when not mine workers. 'The British were poor', remarked Mannathoko, 'when it came to investing in our human capital.'

But the cosmopolitan optimism may have seemed less bold in this present, second postcolonial era than it was in the first, when Mannathoko, as a young diplomat at the OAU and elsewhere, began his quest for wider recognition for Botswana and its citizens. For, now, more to the foreground rings the acclaim for 'Botswana, the Cinderella of Africa', 'an African miracle', even in the face of the AIDS pandemic, rising unemployment and dire poverty for far too many Batswana.

Admittedly, the acclaim for accomplishment pleased Manna-thoko, given his rightful patriotic pride in his own national contri-butions. But the stress, in the programme as in the sometimes explosive assertions of Mannathoko's will to change, is on his trust in human potential. Not diamonds, not more yet-to-be-discovered natural resources for international exploitation, but here it is the world-reaching promise in the people themselves that opens the horizon, as befits a distinctively public cosmopolitan vision.

Who could have expected, at the end of the Bechuanaland Protectorate, that one man's wife would become the mayor of Botswana's booming capital and that three of his daughters would be 'global players' in our cosmopoliticum, in the United Nations and international agencies? But this, as I record earlier, came to be true for Mannathoko and his wife and daughters. These daughters were the last to speak in the hall. They gave me an immediate sense of déjà vu, responding to their fun in the memory of their father's own playful humour. I saw them once again as the mischievous children they were, when I first knew their father as a young law student, and he was given to teasing their interest in the wonders of English. H-I-P-P-O-P-O-T-A-M-U-S, they chanted gleefully for the assembled mourners, spells hippopotamus. 'The rhinoceros', the programme records him reading them from wildlife books, 'is found in Africa comma but comma is not as common as the elephant full stop!'

Afterthought

It is striking in African postcolonies, such as Botswana and Ghana, how dramatically revealing a rooted public cosmopolitan's funeral becomes (see Appiah 1998). There are several reasons for this. Most importantly, for our purposes, we are made aware of the cultivated appeals for moral passion – tolerance, patience, reconciliation, compassion – and yet, also, the changing tensions that characterize rooted cosmopolitanism.

The second reason is historical: we see how people respond to rooted cosmopolitanism, when a great civic occasion remarkably carries forward a perceived transition from one postcolonial moment to the next. In Richard Ngwabe Mannathoko's case for Botswana, it is forward to Africa's emerging second liberation struggle, this time an emancipatory moment perceived, hopefully, to promise good governance and deliberative democracy and, hopefully also, development.

A third reason is that the occasion, like so many postcolonial funerals in Africa, calls for richly significant biography; not a monologue, but a number of characteristic stories in a dialogue as various as the speakers themselves. For public cosmopolitanism, such occasions give us what Victor Turner called 'a limited area of transparency on the otherwise opaque surface of regular, uneventful social life' (Turner 1957: 93).

Here some might say that I should stick to the surer ground around my late friend Richard Mannathoko, and only address the immediate postcolonial horizon that I study in the safety of informed biography and ethnography. Admittedly, much remains to be said about that, spelling out the distinctively postcolonial significance of the creative force a maverick has as a rooted public cosmopolitan. But the more I reflect on that, the more I am convinced that by its very unsettling nature, such force leads to reflection at the most open horizons of the patriotic, the imperial and the cosmopolitan; that is, for us, too, about powerfully uncertain issues of our changing world order.

If compelling over centuries of world history, the imperial question looked curiously dated, even antiquarian, when the twentieth century gave a moment's notice: the End of Empire. But now we wonder anew about empire: is it about us again, though in a fresh guise? The world's dominant and, currently, its only global power, my native USA, denies officially that it wants its own American Empire. The old self-proclaiming empires reached for sovereignty and subjects to the possible limits of territorial expansion. America as an empire in denial actively avoids that; it is not a return of the Romans, the Turks or the British. But it does adhere to the proposition that all men, being created equal, are entitled to be treated, for the sake of democracy, world peace and security, to a pre-emptive strike when their country, or rather its atrocious regime, deserves it. And in applying this proposition arrogantly and without recourse to the judgement of the United Nations or any other major body of world opinion, America has already turned out to be the judge and executioner in its own devastating case against atrocity.

The darkness on the horizon threatens to be vast, and it may now be in vain to try to learn lessons to go beyond that darkness. But if cosmopolitanism has any deeper value for us, it must be in opening out the urge to think the unthinkable about, in Lévi-Strauss's phrase for totemism, 'humanity without frontiers'. Our focus in this chapter has, of course, been more specific, but perhaps for that very reason it has meant a more critical understanding of the political struggles and culturally creative tensions in and around cosmopolitanism and the roles of elites. We have seen how through such struggles and tensions, rooted public cosmopolitanism continues to be socially viable in postcolonial Africa.

Message of condolence at the death of Rosinah Mannathoko

This is the message of condolence we sent to Rosinah Mannathoko's family:

Dear Changu, Joy, Ita, Ndapiwa, and all our dear Mannathoko Family,

My wife Pnina joins me, mourning with you and sharing the loss of our precious Rosinah. Young and strikingly beautiful, when I first met her in Francistown in 1964, she grew old always ever so feminine, gracious, and wise. It was easy to understand how even as a school-girl, and a star of her class at St. Joseph's College, she won the heart of a man whose ego was big, and all the bigger because he got her to marry him and yet to remain free, true to her own, profoundly independent spirit.

Over the many decades of my cultural and social studies in Botswana, I drew much inspiration from them both *— and I say both because each of them, Rosinah and Richard, talked of things and people in their own outspoken ways. They both agreed on the deep issues of equality, to the point that Richard himself seems to have wondered whether any man could be the equal of a daughter of his and Rosinah's. But, if I have to say what the difference was I would have to say that only Rosinah made and kept the friends who turned to foes in Richard's battles for an accountable government.*

To know her was to know the importance of fellow feeling that being engaged and very practical made a generous difference in our lives. Hers was the caring kind of feminism — she saw to it that she fulfilled herself in great devotion to family and home life; and she also made sure to lead in public service. I am aware of how hard it must be for young women and whole generations in Botswana to imagine the hurdles Rosinah overcame in her personal career. Her victories for generations of women are now all too readily taken for granted.

The fact is she pioneered the way forward from the back-room female positions of the Bechuanaland Protectorate to today's rightful places in the public sphere, within Botswana and internationally on the global stage. She was the first woman to become mayor of Gaborone, re-elected twice, first in 1974 and again in 1978, an accomplishment all the more extraordinary in that it took decades for another woman to take on the mayorship of the capital. She was a founding member of the Botswana Council of Churches. She made the Red Cross in Francistown one of the city's fine welfare institutions. Throughout her life, she kept her support for the Roman Catholic Church strong and faithful.

As I offer this message of condolence to you, I have in front of me her picture, making her presence still close and well in mind; and I share it with you as I share our lasting affection and love for Rosinah.

May she rest in peace.

With love,

Richard

Notes

1 I carried out urban research on elites in Gaborone in 1999 with support from the Nuffield Foundation, and in 2000–02 and 2007 with partial support from the Economic and Social Research Council (grants R00239145, RES-000-22-2483), the International Centre for Contemporary Cultural Research and the University of Manchester. For parts of this discussion, I draw on Werbner 2002b and 2004a.

2 For my view of 'permeable ethnicity', which continues in overlapping, multiple loyalties from pre-colonial to postcolonial times in contexts of migration, mixing and interchange between variable ethnic groups, see Werbner 2004a: 68–9.

3 At the time of my writing of the first draft of this chapter, one of the elite friends was standing for parliament, and was viewed as a possible minister in the future. He won his seat, held one prominent ministry, then became a backbencher and eventually deputy minister of finance. The attorney general at the time of my early fieldwork later became the foreign minister.

4 See Solway 2002 for a full and illuminating analysis of the importance of public trust and state-backed institutions for the development of interethnic relations and the debate about multiculturalism.

5 For an account of the funeral of a leading member of the elite friendship circle, see Werbner 2008; for a film of a controversial funeral in a railway town, see Werbner 2014a.

6 For an illuminating analysis of an elite postcolonial funeral in Namibia, see Fumanti 2007; 2016: 91–6.

7 When Rosinah Mannathoko died, I sent a message of condolence to her family. This message, which was read at her funeral, is at the end of this chapter.

8 On the opposition between the old guard and the Young Turks, see Werbner 2004a: 174–6.

9 See *Report on Localisation and Training* (1966), cited in Werbner 2004a: 161.

10 Of course, as an American, I am myself perhaps a poor judge of the anti-British, although I am told by a Fellow of the British Academy, 'You have become truly English.'

11 For an insightful analysis on Botswana, see Solway 2002; also Werbner 2002a, 2002b, 2004a; Nyamnjoh 2006.

12 On the one-nation consensus and its fate from the first to the second postcolonial period, see Werbner 2004a: 38–9, 79–83.

13 On perceived discrimination in his President's Office and the Leno Affair, see Werbner 2004a: 74, 79–80.

7

A. L. Epstein's enduring argument: the reasonable man and emotion

A personal portrait

Arnold Leonard 'Bill' Epstein, like his fellow pioneers in the Manchester School, was no stranger to controversy, but his abiding interest in argument and argumentation was remarkably distinctive. It led him to make enduring contributions in the anthropology of law. He had a strong sense of justice, and his friends came to know he was aroused to fight for it when his accent turned most to the Irish sound of his youth and his rearing in Belfast.[1] It is fair to say, though, that in balanced temperament he could hardly have been more unlike his teacher Max Gluckman. Having come to know Epstein well in Australia and as a fellow Melanesianist, the anthropologist Michael Young wrote the following in Epstein's obituary: 'Bill was notoriously modest and apt to minimise his own achievements ... He was shy as well as modest ... Of placid temperament, Bill was the mildest mannered man imaginable' (Young 2000: 123). The following is an abbreviated list of Epstein's distinctions in academic posts and professional roles, later in his career after he gave up research in Africa and, at John Barnes's invitation, joined him and began research in Australia: professorial fellow, Australian National University, 1966–70; professor and head of department, ANU, 1970–72; professor and head of department, University of Sussex, 1972–82; chairman of the Association of Social Anthropologists, 1977–81; vice-president, Royal Anthropological Society, 1982–84.

This was Epstein's early background, according to Young:

> Arnold Leonard Epstein was born in Liverpool on 13 September 1924 into a Jewish family whose roots lay in Austrian Poland. He spent

most of his youth in Belfast and studied law at Queen's University. It was there that a chance reading of Malinowski's *Crime and custom in savage society* pointed him towards anthropology. (Young 2000: 119; see also Yelvington 1997)

Epstein was one of Gluckman's first two PhD students, starting in 1951, the other supervisee being Victor Turner, and both graduated in 1955. It is helpful to understand, from the start, the figure that Epstein presented, according to Gluckman, and how he himself as a teacher was seen and represented by his students.

In 1958, when Epstein applied for a professorship at the University of Sydney in New South Wales, Gluckman offered this opinion in a supporting reference to the Registrar:

> The quality of his work is very high indeed; and the quality improves from book to book. He has that capacity to develop his analysis from one study to another and to absorb what he can learn from others which is so important in an anthropological research. As a research worker and write[r] he would therefore undoubtedly be a distinguished occupant of your Chair...
>
> He is a very likeable and co-operative person, well-read in general anthropology, with a cultivated mind...
>
> Epstein is particularly strong in absorbing and developing ideas, and in taking in the comments of others on his own ideas; he produces original ideas, but is only now beginning to develop a strong line of his own in general theorising. (Gluckman to the Registrar, University of Sydney, 5 February 1958, RAI Archive [D105])

It took Gluckman little more than a week to have second thoughts. What he had misjudged, he realized, was not his old student's capacity to learn from others, in deliberate steps, on the way to his own originality. Instead, with better evidence, after hearing Epstein's latest course on problems of urbanization, Gluckman reconsidered his judgement of how far Epstein had already got on his own line:

> it is now clear to me that he is developing a strong line in the general theory of this subject, and shows a most remarkable development since I heard him lecture on this last year. I am confident that the only Social Anthropologist in the British Commonwealth with equivalent understanding of these general problems is Professor Mitchell of the University College of the Rhodesias and Nyasaland. (Gluckman to

the Registrar, University of Sydney, 13 February 1958, RAI Archive [D105])

The Israeli anthropologist Moshe Shokeid, reflecting in another obituary, offers this telling perception of Epstein's character, as it appeared to Shokeid when he was a PhD student at Manchester in 1965, and Epstein a senior lecturer:

> Coming from a place where people are impatient, it took me some time to get used to Bill's slow manner of speaking, which seemed, at first, somewhat hesitant. But I came to realize he spoke with great care, as if dictating an article intended to be published without copyediting. He measured his words, avoiding waste and redundancy. You felt you could observe his thought process. (Shokeid 2000: 858)

Alan Rew, another former student of Epstein's, recalled:

> He was no firebrand. He was approachable and known for his even-handedness in seminar debates and for stressing the importance of ethnographic context. Postgraduate students attending his 'Manchester School', and then Sussex, seminars in the 1960s and 1970s greatly appreciated the detailed accounts of central African urban life and marvelled that his many insights were ever achieved given the restrictions placed on him. (Rew 1999; for a short biography, see Grillo 2004)

The beginnings in urban court research

Epstein began his lifelong contributions to the anthropology of law with a short article (1951) about African urban courts on the Copperbelt of what was then Northern Rhodesia, now Zambia. A Colonial Office Social Science Research Council Fellowship for 1950–51 funded his early fieldwork and a year at the London School of Economics, and in accordance with a requirement of his fellowship, Epstein turned his short article into a longer report to the Colonial Office. Before publication, Epstein passed the report on to Max Gluckman. Much later, Epstein recalled:

> That was one of the most embarrassing experiences of my life, because I don't think there was a page that escaped his red pencil and the marginal comment 'bad sentence' 'bloody awful sentence.' You know, I didn't regard myself as completely illiterate, but it was very embarrassing. (Yelvington 1997: 292)

The whole report was substantial and acutely critical of the colonial administration of justice, for it appreciated certain problematic tensions between politics and law under the prevailing form of alien or indirect rule. Basic in the research was a question not of the invention or even reinvention of law, but of adaptation. 'The terms of reference for that study', Epstein later recalled, 'were to investigate the problems of the adaptation of African customary law to the very different conditions prevailing in the new urban centres' (Epstein 1973: 653). In his report, Epstein criticized the way the urban courts, established in 1938, were run on the basis of tribal representation and tribal leadership. Each court had four or five judges appointed by chiefs or Native Authorities, from rural areas. In town as in the countryside, the colonial administration buttressed tribal rule, despite the emergence of a new African leadership, and against its fresh aspirations and its drive not to hark back primarily to tribal elders and chiefs for decision-making.

There was a leadership struggle going on, and by the end of his first year of fieldwork in 1951, Epstein became increasingly aware that the urban courts had become 'the focus of a struggle for political power within the urban community' (Epstein 1992b: 42). The Copperbelt community was urban; it called for urban leaders; it was not to have its disputes handled under customary law as if they were merely disputes among temporary sojourners in town, ever about to return home.

Nevertheless, the emerging power struggle had to be seen in the light of the facts of an already understood morality and common sense. That is the argument Epstein was to develop later, on thinking his urban evidence through more profoundly. In spite of increased social diversity and economic differentiation, there was 'still a broad consensus amongst urban Africans on the applicability of tribal norms in regulating many of their social relationships in town' (1958: 199). Insofar as justice was widely held to be afforded through customary courts in town, it was in good measure, Epstein's argument suggested, because still very generally shared along with these tribal norms were certain related, well-established moral ideas, presuppositions about fairness and equity, and indeed, a consensus on basic principles and premises of common sense. If new unprecedented cases were emerging, if old rules of law were often no longer applicable, tribal morality had yet to break down. And perhaps it might never quite do so, he seemed to guess.

Much of Epstein's report depends upon his having probed cases, from court records or his own observation, to unpack the recent adaptation of customary law. 'Procedure is best studied through the cases themselves', he asserted (1954: 25). It was not Epstein's intent to work out an encompassing code. He was not interested in setting out rules: 'to produce a digest of Urban Native Law ... would have been formal and sterile' (Epstein 1953: 1). Instead, his early legal training predisposed him towards the direction now taken to be a hallmark of the Manchester School: some form of a case method. He completed his LLB at Queen's University in Belfast in 1944, and there he learned from enthusiastic visiting Harvard Law School professors about their case method (Yelvington 1997: 291). Looking back on the origins of his own use of a case method, he remarked:

> One of the few books I had read at that time [during his undergradu-ate study in the early 1940s] was Llewellyn and Hoebel's '*The Chey-enne Way*' [1941], but I had come across a short article in the *Yale Law Journal* that stressed 'cases, cases, cases' and that stuck in my mind. (Yelvington 1997: 291)

Epstein's recommendations in his report foregrounded a number of professionalizing provisions. They were to be non-tribal and inclusive, irrespective of the rural or urban origins of court members and litigants: provisions for legal training, for reliable court records, for a new Court of Appeal with binding authority over all the African urban courts, for the development of a system of case law, for the recruitment of court members primarily on the basis of judicial fitness. The Colonial Office passed Epstein's report on to the Northern Rhodesia government. The former was, Epstein remarks wryly,

> seeking the latter's approval for publication of the report. The North-ern Rhodesian Government did agree to publication – but on the condition that the recommendations were not included in the pub-lished version. In this way presumably it avoided commitment to taking any action in the matter. (Epstein 1992b: 269 n.5)

Under the grand imprint of Her Majesty's Stationery Office, a somewhat revised and abridged version of the report appeared as a mimeographed publication, like any piece of grey policy literature, in the Colonial Office Research Series as *The Administration of Justice and the Urban African*. It says something about changing currents or fads in the social sciences that even in the library of the University of Manchester, after 1975, the volume remained in storage, apparently not borrowed for more than forty years.

With characteristic patience and care, having completed the required policy document for the Colonial Office, Epstein then produced another methodical yet more academic account: *Judicial Techniques and the Judicial Process – A Study in African Customary Law* (1954). It was to meet the challenge of carrying forward to fairly recently established courts in a fresh field of social relations the original analysis of judicial decision-making by his teacher Gluckman. The challenge was all the greater, in comparative terms, because the impetus was from Gluckman's considerable Barotse research, between 1942 and 1947, in a highly stratified kingdom with a hierarchy of courts endowed with claims to archaic standing for its significantly and historically titled judges, themselves often eminent men of much distinction – indeed, great judges. They were judges who had to learn from each other, in effect getting training and gaining skill and gravity in the court by hearing each other out, according to seniority, from the most junior to the most senior. One might say, very loosely, they were more like career or professional judges, if not a specialized class, by comparison to the more or less skilled and sometimes relatively inexperienced recruits to the urban courts who often had to resort to a new lingua franca, the Copperbelt version of Bemba (Lozi was the old lingua franca in Barotseland).

It is evident that for both teacher and student, the immediate task at hand was demanding, so much such so that the priority was not to situate the different courts in their unlike places within Northern Rhodesia's colonial political economy (for a sharp critique of this priority and its consequences, see the discussion of 'Historical Time and the Model of the Tribal Society' in Moore 1978: 58–63). Instead, the focus was on trials and the actual judicial practice in the courts in the present. As Gluckman described it in his study,

> From these trials, checked against earlier records and informants' texts, I have in this volume extracted the way in which judges approach their task, how they assess evidence, what sources they draw on for

judicial decision, the logic of their arguments, and how they apply
legal rules to the varied and changing circumstances of life. (1955: 33)

Epstein, like Gluckman, focused primarily on 'Law in Action'
in the front-stage, observable setting of hearings and records of litigation, but Epstein pursued the interest further, to legal pluralism,
by covering cases of appeal to the District Commissioner's court.
Epstein took care to clarify one important aspect of the semi-
autonomy of the urban and rural courts: 'The prohibition of ordeals
apart, and the exclusion of certain categories of case from their
jurisdiction, there have been no attempts by means of legislation to
alter the modes of hearing and settling cases in Native courts'
(Epstein 1954: 23). This clarification complements Gluckman's contention, asserting the indigenous nature of basic aspects of the Lozi
judicial process:

> The modes of reasoning involved in this complex process are so deeply
> imbedded in Lozi institutions and thought, that I consider my whole
> analysis emphasizes their indigenous existence. There is no evidence
> that in these respects the Lozi have been influenced by the work of
> British courts, whose procedures are alien and often incomprehensible
> to them. (Gluckman 1955: 33)

To turn to Epstein's *Judicial Techniques and the Judicial Process* is,
admittedly, not to find any strong critique of Gluckman's concepts
and problems in *The Judicial Process*. It is, instead, to see their fruitful
rehearsal by a faithful disciple who, as a trained lawyer, was beginning to open out further the issues of change and certainty, flexibility and ambiguity in law, by enquiring into legal systematics.

Two extremes were in question, for Epstein. First, which novel
types of offences were recognized and penalized because they were
'capable of restatement in terms of indigenous law and ethics'
(Epstein 1954: 31)? His tentative answer, on the basis of available
cases, was that 'in the fields of crime, of tort and delict, and of
contract, the customary law is extremely malleable' (1954: 31)
Hence judges were able to develop 'judicial legislation' and justify
it 'as being in line with tribal *mores* and customary notions of right-
doing and wrongdoing' (1954: 35).

Second, by contrast, in which situations and disputed social
relations were judgments often stifled, to the point that a court

might be reduced 'to a state of near impotence' (Epstein 1954: 34)? Epstein gave his answer by considering a case, heard at Ndola, the commercial and industrial centre of the Copperbelt. It appeared as 'The Case of the Third Wife' in a chapter on 'Norms in Conflict' (1954: 22–35). Earlier chapters spelled out the usual procedure and basic judicial techniques in the court. Very briefly, and I risk over-simplifying much of Epstein's analysis, each side in a case made their statements in turn, and only after that, usually, did judges 'break into' the statements, cast doubt on the story of one or another of the litigants in the light of 'customary patterns of behaviour, values and attitudes', and try to make them recognize where their conduct was wrong.

Lest this overly brief statement obscure a basic consideration in Epstein's treatment, I must stress this point. Here, in these chapters, and in his chapter on 'Court and Community' in his later work, *Politics in an Urban African Community* (1958), Epstein foregrounded 'the moral element in the Urban Court procedure' (1958: 202). Indeed, Epstein went so far as to argue that 'the Urban Court emerges as a repository of moral, as well as legal norms' (1958: 202).

By quoting from 'The Case of the Third Wife' at some length, though I abbreviate it, I want to document Epstein's method of exposition, because how he tells the trial story – his narrative art in the case method – is significant, perhaps no less than his conclusion from it:

> The plaintiffs were two co-wives and the defendant their husband, who had recently taken a third wife. The complaint was that when their husband had received his pay he had come to them saying that he intended to use ten shillings to pay his tax, another forty shillings to pay off some debts, and to give thirty shillings to his new wife. The senior wives at once protested that they needed the money to feed themselves and their children: when he had done that he could go and clothe his third wife. The husband then gave them each half-a-crown, and told them they would have to go and stay with their brothers elsewhere on the Copperbelt. When he got some more money he would send for them. But the two women again protested, arguing that if they went elsewhere other men were bound to approach them and then he, the husband, would come troubling them with cases. In any case, why should they who were his senior wives be sent away?

The husband explained to the court the arrangement he wanted to make. On the previous pay day he had given his two senior wives one pound each, and nothing to the third wife. There was no question of his chasing them away. He has just lost his job, and they wanted to crucify him. They were just like Judas, he added.

When the court turned to the examination of the two co-wives they at once pointed out that it was not just on account of the half-a-crown apiece they had been given that they were annoyed. Their husband did not feed them properly, and even in the past had not given them enough. They were agreeable to continue living with him, but they besought the court to instruct him so that he should care for them properly. 'We have no dresses, and here on the railway line we have to look smart'.

At this point the President of the court referred to the minutes of a Conference of Court Members of the Urban Courts held some years previously, when it was resolved that polygamous unions should be prohibited in the towns. Then he turned to the husband and began to question him. The husband agreed that a woman still capable of child-bearing could have her womb spoiled by disease if her husband kept 'marrying' other women. He admitted too the value and impor-tance of having children. 'If one had a barren wife, and then one returned to the village who would there be to greet one if there were no children?' he asked. But he had not given his wives any disease. His senior wife had just complained that he did not feed her properly? Yet what woman could stay with a man for ten years if she was not cared for in that time? No, when he married a third wife his two senior wives said he was doing ill in 'playing' with another woman. One of them said he was killing the unborn child she was carrying by committing adultery while she was pregnant (a common belief in Central Africa), and told him he would have to marry. He had not intended to do so, and they had said these things, and he had no choice but to marry.

The court rounded on the husband, 'If somebody says something against you, must you at once proceed to do the very thing of which you are accused? ... Listen, a man who marries in the village has certain duties to perform for his wife. He has to feed and clothe her, he has to cultivate gardens and build her a house. Now at home if a man does marry three wives he can give them all separate huts, but here in the towns all of them have to be crowded into one small space where they have to live like goats. These women have come here to court because they want a proper way of living. Now it was decided at a meeting of the court members that where a man living in town has married more than one wife one of them should be sent home. It would have been better if you had not introduced the third woman into the house. What kind of lives can these women lead? What they say is quite true. How can they be expected to live and feed their children on half-a-crown?'

The parties were dismissed from the court, and returned shortly to hear the judgment.

'You, the husband, have brought all of these difficulties upon yourself. We don't want to hear any more of this nonsense. You must go and look after your wives. As for the women, we have heard their words, and we thank them for what they said about going to live with their brothers on the Copperbelt, for they have warned their husband. But now you must go and try and live harmoniously together. There will be no compensation. But if the matter is brought before the court again there will be a serious case.' (Epstein 1954: 31–3)

The starting point for Epstein's commentary was his perception of a shortcoming in the process of decision-making. The court offered rebukes, even made a final threat, but in judgment it appeared not to have made a definite finding against either the plaintiff or the complainants. Epstein's analysis disclosed a matrimonial dilemma and contradictions. The court president tried to get round the dilemma by invoking the Minutes of the Conference Members of the Urban Courts. But against that, the Conference was merely an advisory body, its recommendations or norms had no legal force. Even further, against its norms was the fact that what was recognized in the law of the colonial state of Northern Rhodesia was marriage according to Native Law and Custom, which permits polygamy. But the domestic situation of most urban workers made it almost impossible for men to maintain polygamous unions, given the type of housing available, usually from a European employer, and given the current wage rates, usually inadequate for the higher standard of living which wives were coming to demand. Here the dilemma of the court that Epstein discerned was this: 'it is called upon to evaluate the behaviour of a man which is objectionable in terms of those tribal *mores* the judges are enjoined upon to uphold, but which must appear as dubious, to say the least, when it requires people to live together "like goats"' (Epstein 1954: 33). Epstein went on to spell out the contradictions in greater detail than we need to examine here. The most glaring contradiction came at the end of the judgment, in his view: 'Addressing the husband, the court declared, "What the wives say is true. How can they be expected to live together under these circumstances?" And yet by the very terms of the judgment, it is to such a way that the court condemns them' (1954: 34).

And as for the president's final words of warning – it would be a serious case if the matter came before the court again – these, Epstein contends, 'were empty threats by which the court sought to conceal its powerlessness to handle the problem confronting it' (1954: 34). Epstein's conclusion – and it answers our second question, above, about the limits on the developmental process through 'judicial legislation' – is that it is in disputes involving domestic relations when norms come to be challenged that 'the court *may be* reduced, as in the Case of the Third Wife, to a state of near impotence' (1954: 34, italics mine). I stress 'may be' because, finally, Epstein had no absolute conclusion. In the way of a pragmatic lawyer, he allowed that if not in all cases, especially marginal cases, then in some domestic disputes, given the generality of the standard of what is reasonable and customary, the judicial reasoning might be able to accommodate 'the changing *mores* of the urban areas'.

The timing of Epstein's next contribution on reasonableness is significant. Epstein's explicit critique came at a moment when Gluckman himself was once more revisiting the reasonable man. Earlier, there had been a considerable tide of reviews and critical debate about the whole of Gluckman's seminal work (1955). For its second edition in 1966, he offered a 'Reappraisal' as chapter 9, in which he entered trenchantly into dispute with his critics, but also frankly reviewed telling criticisms, gaps in his fieldwork and what he considered the shortcomings of his contributions.

Critique and response

Although it is something of an aside, I want to stress at this point a key insight in Sally Moore's evaluation of Gluckman's *Judicial Process among the Barotse* (Moore 1973). It is the importance of the innovative case approach. Moore was aware that Gluckman came from a family of lawyers, having constant dinner chat about actual cases. She gave Gluckman the highest praise for being the first anthropologist to document and analyse a major body of cases that were actually observed by the ethnographer himself. What has somewhat obscured the force of this evaluation is, perhaps paradoxically, a tendency to canonize Gluckman's earlier study, 'Analysis of a Social Situation in Modern Zululand' (1940). Nicknamed 'The Bridge', it has appeared to be foundational for mainstream contributions of the Manchester School (Englund 2018). Rehearsing this view, Bruce Kapferer contended that 'Situational analysis and the extended case method saw their beginnings in Gluckman's analysis of a bridge opening – in the study of a particular event or case' (Kapferer 2006: 320). More critically, Emanuel Marx has recently called for rethinking what has now been too readily received as conventional wisdom. Bringing into better perspective Gluckman's wealth of case material in *The Judicial Process*, Marx illuminated that this study 'probably influenced the development of the Manchester School more than Gluckman's *The Analysis of a Social Situation in Modern Zululand* (1958), as the contributors to Evens and Handelman 2006 want us to believe' (Marx 2014).

Gluckman's masterpiece made grounded ethnography, rich in actual cases, the standard of excellence in the Manchester School.[2] Although some refer to 'The Bridge' as if it were a case or even a forerunner of the extended case method, in my view it exemplifies the study of one event, not a series, in relation to a wider social context of conflict and cooperation. It is, of course, not to be confused with the waging of a dispute and its forensic hearing – a case in and outside court – upon which Epstein focuses (1967). Admittedly, Gluckman came to see a limitation: his own contribution in seeing each case, primarily, 'as an isolated incident coming before a court' called for a further step 'in deepening our understanding of law and morality – the intensive study of the processes of social control in a limited area of social life viewed over a period of time' (Gluckman 1967: xvi).

Later, I consider more of the implications of Gluckman's contention about indigenous judicial process, when I discuss what I call the 'Western jurisprudence controversy' and Epstein's part in that. Epstein was stimulated in the direction of his early research on courts by reading a manuscript draft of what became Gluckman's great work, *The Judicial Process among the Barotse* (1955). The most important of the ideas in the core of Gluckman's study of the judicial process were about the reasonable man and reasonableness.

They were outstanding in what Gluckman himself took to be his ethnographic and theoretical advance in the anthropology of law. Gluckman famously asserted that 'The reasonable man is regarded as the central figure in all developed systems of law, but his presence in simpler legal systems has not been noticed' (1955: 83). Gluckman left no doubt about his broadly general, comparative and universalist stance: 'my study of the Lozi judicial process, which is akin to our own judicial process, faithfully depicts modes of reasoning which are probably found wherever men apply norms in varied disputes' (1955: 33). It was the American sociologist George Homans who, according to the story Gluckman himself enjoyed retelling, heard Gluckman's BBC talk on 'The Reasonable Man in Barotse Law' and quipped, 'You have reached the top now. All that is left is a long, slow coast downhill' (Gluckman 1963b: 178).

Epstein went ahead, sometimes rehearsing in agreement, but sometimes restating or revising that core of Gluckman's approach. Their early agreement turned on Gluckman's view of continuity and change in law, of the apparent certainty in law and the utility of ambiguous or uncertain concepts and general standards in sustaining that appearance through change. Throughout his career, and until Gluckman died, Epstein sustained a running conversation with Gluckman in many letters and for joint ventures from the conference meetings to the conference book.[3] What is the concept of the reasonable man? Is it either a 'folk' concept or an analytic concept? And if in some sense the former, is it something explicit, in vernacular terms, or is it implicit and unformulated, something that an analyst infers from the reasoning and argument of judges? They might have no words for it, like the Tiv (Bohannon 1957; Gluckman 1973b: xxix). The contrast is with the Barotse, who explicitly speak of *mutu yangana* – *mutu*, the person, *yangana*, of mind, wisdom, intelligence, intellect, reason, sense, common sense (Gluckman 1973b: 125, 386). Similarly, Bemba on the Copperbelt speak of *umuntu wa mano*, the person of 'intelligence, brains, wit, commonsense' (Epstein 1973: 652). But might the concept be something slippery, sometimes either 'folk' or analytic, and sometimes both? In comparative terms, might the very profile of the reasonable figure vary? Might it loom large in certain types of society and hardly at all in others, or perhaps only in specific domains of the law, being in the same domain more central or more marginal, according to the society? And is reasonableness simply a matter of what is fair and equitable, or does it imply having sufficient common sense and moral sensibility to foresee the probable consequences of one's actions?

These are among the questions to which Epstein was able to turn most critically when, no longer the young disciple, he became the mature scholar. Having reached the high point of his Manchester professional career – he was Simon Research Fellow from 1957 to 1958, lecturer from 1961 to 1964, senior lecturer from 1964 to 1966[4] – he became a professorial fellow in 1966 at the Australian National University and in 1970 chair of anthropology at the Research School in Pacific Studies. In 1972 he returned to Britain as professor at the University of Sussex. It was in the summer of the following year that he published 'The Reasonable Man Revisited: Some Problems in the Anthropology of Law' (Epstein 1973). In it he deepened his dialogue with Gluckman and advanced a critique which was in part a defence of their earlier contributions and in part a revisionist attack.

The Western jurisprudence controversy

Most acute, and continuing unresolved in later years, was what I would call the 'Western jurisprudence controversy': whether using Western jurisprudence, concepts and legal theory, as Gluckman did, was to fall into distortions, even into 'backwards translation' from our own legal system into those of others. In his 1966 'Reappraisal', he was candid: 'I realise now that it would have been better had I merely stated the similarities and the differences [between the Lozi and the Western judicial processes], without coming to the overall assessment that similarities outweighed differences' (1966a: 375). In further response in April 1973, Gluckman took the opportunity of presenting a Wilson Memorial Lecture in the School of Scots Law at the University of Edinburgh not merely to stand by his arguments but to apply them even more generally (1973a).

Returning to an early source in the long-standing controversy, Paul Bohannan's *Justice and Judgment among the Tiv* (1957), Gluckman positioned him as 'the main protagonist of the argument that each "folk-system" of law has its central dominant conceptions, and that the study of these should correspondingly dominate the

analyst's study' (Gluckman 1973b: xxvii). Against that, and with
an eye to broader similarity, in the Memorial Lecture and later in
an abbreviated version in the 1973 edition of *The Judicial Process
among the Barotse* (1973b: xxvii–xxxii), he re-analysed actual cases to
prove, among other things, the importance of the reasonable man
in Tiv judicial reasoning and decision-making (see also Gluckman
1966a). 'Bohannon authorized me to say', Gluckman reported, '
he accepts all but the final part of my argument. He says that Tiv
clearly work, in cross-examination and coming to judgment, with
a general conception of a reasonable man, but it is not explicitly
formulated. Hence he does not regard it as a Tiv "folk concept"'
(Gluckman 1973b: xxix).[5] If Gluckman's re-analysis did not put an
end to the broader controversy, it did move the immediate debate
a step forward.

Epstein was clearly on Gluckman's side in this Western jurisprudence controversy. Indeed, he sought to push much further than
Gluckman the use of our own legal distinctions, such as between
rules and standards, to clarify the analysis of the judicial process in
different societies. Even more, concerned about the need to dis-
criminate analytic categories, Epstein recognized inconsistencies in
his urban study; he had taken reasonableness, ambiguously, to mean
fair and equitable and, also, to mean plausible in common sense.
That was unwitting, and it drove home to Epstein this pitfall. Critics
were right to find too much ambiguity in Gluckman's core arguments. It was as if the reasonable man were a figure for all seasons,
sometimes appearing to be a 'folk concept', sometimes an analytic
one. Epstein wanted to reserve the term 'the reasonable man' for
the 'folk' usage, and for the analytic concept he introduced a new
term, 'standard of normative expectation', which actually never
caught on in the literature. 'By importing the flexibility of the
"folk" conception into his analytic usage', asserted Epstein, 'Gluckman confuses a number of distinct procedures by lumping them
together under a single rubric defined in terms of reasonableness'
(1973: 646–7). One gets the sense that Epstein could not resist
patting himself on the back for being, even in his earlier work,
more rigorous than his mentor:

> I followed Gluckman in seeking to show how the African judges of
> the urban courts there [in the Copperbelt] made use of the standard

of reasonable expectations, but I was also careful to point out the limits of the operation, for, when the device had been pushed as far as it would go, other techniques and procedures had to be invoked. (1973: 646)

If Gluckman appeared, after all, in hindsight to be something of a lumper, Epstein was determined to be the splitter. Taking up the comparative challenge, Epstein deployed the mode of critique that sharpened contrasts; that cast doubt on assertions about broad similarities; that introduced even more distinctions or refinements into the general arguments. Much of his fine, highly scholastic reasoning turns on the premise that things have to be 'either or' – that is, one thing or another, such as rules or standards – but not 'both and'. It is an awkward, even subversive premise, especially when applied to the study of complex cases, as I show below.

Earlier, Gluckman had complained, in the 'Reappraisal' chapter of his great book's second edition, that 'None of those who have criticized my use of the conception of the reasonable man on general grounds have attempted to re-analyse the cases I reported without any conception or some similar conceptions' (1966a: 390). Aware of this complaint, Epstein made such an attempt, in the first part of his critique; and here he came up against the greater strength of his mentor on his own ethnographic grounds. It is remarkable that, contrary to Epstein's cultivation of the case method, the re-analysis of another ethnographer's cases turned out not to be his forte; his re-analysis of Gluckman's cases is not very cogent.

In my view, Epstein stumbled repeatedly, especially in his splitter's effort to cut the complexity of certain Lozi cases to fit his conventional, juridical distinctions, such as between 'standards and rules'. The difficulty is that in a complex case the judges may have to take considerable trouble dealing with both rules and standards. They do so, according to Gluckman's account, because a large part of the social personalities of the parties may be involved. If it were a simple matter only, no more, say, than a complaint of assault by one stranger on another, the judges might be able to rush to judgment when satisfied that a rule had been breached. But even a simple matter, a breach clear to everyone, may be entangled with worrisome implications, moral and legal, for the parties involved, implications which the judges might not want or be able to ignore.

A central point in Gluckman's own argument was that of social positioning. He observed that in Barotseland most important disputes arose between individuals in multiplex enduring relationships. 'Hence', he concluded, 'the reasonable man of Lozi law might be more accurately described as the reasonable and customary occupier of a specific position' (Gluckman 1955: 155).

Using a case method

Epstein's undoing is perhaps most striking in his oversimplification of 'The Case of the Violent Councillor', easily the most famous of Gluckman's sixty cases (Gluckman 1955: 83–94). Let me tell some of the story, and then come back to Epstein's difficulty with it. 'The Case of the Violent Councillor' was the case for Gluckman's great ethnographic discovery, of which he was deeply proud, and about which, in his notably well-received and, as he himself said, highly popular 1954 BBC talks, he boasted: it drove him to inscribe 'in huge letters on the blank page opposite my notebook's record of the process of cross examination, "Hullo, the reasonable man!"' (Gluckman 1963b: 179).

But what was that moment for the Lozi themselves? It was a moment of scandalous high drama, during an appeal in one of the highest courts of the land, in the Barotse flood-season capital, and it went on in a remarkable hearing over two days. The suit, at its simplest, was about compensation or a fine for assault – the complaint by the plaintiff being that when the children of his village headman, the councillor Saywa, attacked him, the councillor joined in to support them. It is significant that the child in the forefront of the fight was the councillor's *crippled* son. I stress this fact and return later to its importance for Epstein's reading of the case. If on the face of it a personal matter, the occasion was nevertheless a grave one for the Barotse kingdom. Remarkably, there was the gentlest of the kingdom's great judges uncharacteristically outraged in the cross-examination of one of his most eminent peers, the accused in the suit. Remarkably also, there was the accused himself, who was, so to speak, having to eat humble pie, because he had not run his village affairs properly. Being shamed, he had to listen to the rehearsal of the breaches of the village peace in fighting and in his children's rude threats: 'You will defecate', that is, be choked until you defecate when we fight.

Saywa had to endure being caught out in defensive, self-interested lying to prove he was not unreasonable but fit to be a high court councillor. In jeopardy was his very grand position as the head of the royal village destined to be the burial village of the then reigning chief. His whole family could be expelled and lose their places in the village, if he were discharged. It was a moment of such intense suspense that overnight much gossip, even rumour about courtly intrigue among Saywa's important allies, about who was and was not lying, spread among the Lozi, camped with Gluckman as his entourage on the flood plain. Many of them, being loyal to the councillor, could only guess, somewhat fearfully, about the outcome and the councillor's chances of not being discharged.

Here I need to qualify a point I made earlier in general terms about how Gluckman, followed by Epstein, focused mainly on the front-stage in their early use of the case method for analysis of the judicial process. In particular, to illustrate his prime case of ethnographic discovery in fieldwork – his Eureka moment – Gluckman brought forward the back-stage also. He found out that evening and reported 'precedents of the kind that were in everyone's minds', though not cited in the court itself. Summarized in Gluckman's account, these precedents were five cases 'in which councillors had been punished for themselves using violence' (1955: 88). The fact that the cases were not cited in court was not surprising. It was rare in Barotse courts, and indeed, in many tribal courts in Africa, for judges to cite cases as precedents; there was not an elaborate body of case law.

Further from the back-stage, Gluckman reported the rumour that Saywa's allies, including some judges, were contending that Saywa was being trapped with lies, remarkably lies not uttered. The very fact that no witnesses had changed their evidence to back Saywa by lying themselves was a twist. They could be expected to lie, and not lying implied a bad motive: they all hated him. Gluckman developed the point in his insight into common sense in the reasonable expectation about lying.

Extending his case method took Gluckman further beyond cross-examination and the norms and standards brought to bear during the trial itself. After Saywa was judged in the wrong, had to pay compensation, and was threatened with discharge as a councillor if he was ever violent again, Gluckman tried to find out whether Sawya was convicted, in the fullest sense. That is, did the judges actually manage to bring home to him the enormity of his offence? And after all their lengthy efforts to expose him in cross-examination, did he accept his guilt? Saywa did not; or rather, when eventually asked by Gluckman, he refused to acknowledge that he was guilty. Gluckman did intend to follow the case up in a later visit to Barotseland in order to find out if the royal villagers ever settled down again 'in bearable, if aloof, relationships', but he was unable to do so (Gluckman 1973b: 436).

It is worth recording that Gluckman's account itself had an after-life. It did live on in the memory of Saywa's family. This I discovered in 1965, when we met in Zambia, and I arranged for Gluckman to talk with a young Lozi historian, Matumba Mainga. Before Gluckman arrived, I tried with some difficulty to get her opinion about his work. 'You are his student', she told me, 'and I do not like to say.' She feared I would take his side, and not want to hear criticism.[6] Persuaded to speak freely, she complained that Gluckman gave the names of people when he told their stories, and in the case of her uncle, he reported him saying, 'You will shit in your pants.' Gluckman arrived, and they spoke in Lozi, fluently and with unmistakable delight on both sides. When he left, and she was still beaming, I asked her what was so good about their chat. 'He knows my whole family', she answered, 'and all their names.' Charmed as she was by Gluckman himself, she no longer seemed worried by his old tale of her uncle's shaming in court. As a matter of care in Gluckman's case method, I want to mention a simple fact, although it may now be merely ironic and no comfort to Saywa's family. In Gluckman's account and on his genealogy the children are identified merely by letter, and the councillor is named, not personally or by a family title, but only by his venerable and national title, Saywa.

The reasonable man, feelings and rationality

But what, in the end, was Epstein's conclusion about this notable case? It was, in brief, that rules were decisive, not the bearing of the figure of the reasonable man. According to Epstein (1973: 548), Gluckman slipped, as he allegedly did frequently in other cases, where he equated 'what is reasonable with what is right and lawful'. Gluckman had argued that Saywa was convicted 'because the kuta [court] was able to show that when his actions as he described them were measured against the ways in which a reasonable man would have behaved in the situations in question, they were the actions of an unreasonable man' (1955: 93). Epstein objected that Gluckman's formulation on Saywa's conviction obscured the issue and in doing so deprived the concept of reasonableness of much of its cutting edge: 'For Saywa was convicted not because the kuta was able to show that his actions were those of an unreasonable man but because on all the evidence before it, including Saywa's own, it was satisfied that he had breached the rules that govern the behaviour of a headman' (Epstein 1973: 549).

This conclusion about rules is surprising. Of course, the issue in question is not rule-uncertainty as such – both Gluckman and Epstein held to the view that most disputes are concerned not so much with what the rules are, but how they should be applied (see MG to ALE, 1968, UCSD). Epstein's conclusion on Saywa's case appears to be something of a *volte face* away from his earlier stance with Gluckman on the reasonable man. After all, the conviction from the judges' point of view, if not for the defendant himself, arose from their success in undermining his credibility through cross-examination which proved that a reasonable man would not have behaved as the defendant did. What Epstein seemed to miss, also, is Gluckman's account of mitigation, or even clemency: the significant fact that the councillor intervened on behalf of a son who was *crippled*: 'the judges forgave the violent councilor because they considered he was enraged when he saw his *crippled* son involved in a fight' (Gluckman 1973a: 636). In such a case, the reasonable man is a figure whose parental feelings are taken into consideration by the judges in reaching a conviction – it is tempered by clemency for the headman being in the wrong as a headman, but behaving, as a father, as might be expected. It is worth mentioning that in Epstein's seminal work on law and affect, he took up this point about reason and rage and much illuminated its significance. Later and more fully, I return to this in my discussion of his Melanesian contributions.

An exchange of letters between Colson and Epstein reveals a remarkable perception about rationality.

> When I try to think what has been the consistent line of Max's [Gluckman's] thought, it seems to be linked to a belief in rationality, tied to a respect for law – judgement, reputation (its bases and assessment), situational analysis interest him because they allow him to work out this basic premise. I could be wrong. (EC to ALE, 28 September 1973, ALEPSD)

In reply, Epstein added his understanding that for Gluckman the figure of the reasonable man was not merely a tool of analysis but even more an expression of a deep sympathy between the ethnographer and his subjects.

> Yes, I think you are right about the belief in rationality as a consistent theme in Max's thought. The concept of the reasonable man as Max developed it is not just an analytical tool, it is rather something that he saw in the Lozi because it represents something very profound in himself. (ALE to EC, 9 October 1973, ALEPSD)

Epstein's conclusion about rules and the reasonable man needs to be considered further in terms of at least two issues. One is its impact in the related literature; and the other is what it might mean in the light of an ongoing critique of the importance of rules in Gluckman's work on law.

To my knowledge, the impact has been relatively little. For example, in a memorial Festschrift for Gluckman on *Cross-Examinations* (Gulliver 1978), Epstein's critique is not taken up, and is merely mentioned in one footnote rehearsing his quote from Lord Devlin that the reasonable man is not to be confused with the rational man (Yngvesson 1978: 134 n.3). The rules issue, however, is discussed in the Festschrift at some length, in particular by Sally Moore, when she weighs up the influence that Gluckman's early, if limited, legal training in formal Roman-Dutch law had. How important was it in his effort to prove that a tribal society, in particular one remarkable kingdom, had an authentic legal tradition of its own – true law and justice?

If not always a blessing, in some ways because of the stress on rules, early legal training was a heavy burden to bear. It weighed

down all the more, Moore considers, because Gluckman was under
the baleful influence of Radcliffe-Brown and the contemporary
anthropology that sought norms, not cases. The concept of the
reasonable man came to the rescue:

> In this concept, Gluckman had an analytic device that enabled him
> to acknowledge the high degree of negotiability that existed in the
> particularities of actual long-term relations. It also enabled him to
> decently paper-over a great deal of the indeterminacy he observed in
> Barotse judicial behaviour with something that at least had the look
> of an authentic legal standard. Since he was trained in an anthropo-
> logical tradition that sought norms, not case histories, this attention to
> episodes and cases, not just to statements about custom and rules,
> presaged deep changes in social anthropology itself, many of which
> he was instrumental in generating. The case approach was a central
> methodological contribution which became a standard addition to
> previous techniques. (Moore 1978: 65)

'The look of an authentic legal standard' – keeping that look in
sight clearly mattered a great deal in Gluckman's comparative
view, for the purpose of revealing universals in law, or at least
very widespread similarities in the judicial process, whether African
or Western. For Epstein, as for Gluckman, it mattered a great deal,
too, not to make Malinowski's mistake in *Crime and Custom in
Savage Society* (1926): 'by defining law so that it became coexten-
sive with the whole of social process, he distracted attention from
other questions of more immediate jurisprudential interest' (Epstein
1973: 4).

But especially with regard to rules and cases, was the significance
of early legal training the same for Epstein as arguably, at least
according to Moore, it might have been for Gluckman? After all,
Epstein had no tribe of his own, unlike nearly all his contemporary
anthropologists; he had no quest for archaic law on the Zambezi
that would exemplify things over the *longue durée* and yet catch the
ethnographic present. I have already given Epstein's memory that
while an undergraduate in Belfast, he learned, from enthusiastic
teachers, about the Harvard case method. Looking back in 1973,
he evidently rethought his legal training. It appeared to have led
him into naive expectations, not expectations of reasonableness. I
quote at length his perhaps more self-critical recall of a shift in his

legal consciousness, an awakening during his fieldwork in the urban courts:

> After spending some considerable time attending regularly the hearings in these courts I found myself increasingly puzzled by a number of features. Probably because of my own earlier training in law, I had expected – perhaps naively – that cases would mostly be argued in terms of rules of law, particularly as the litigants often came from different tribes and presumably acknowledged different 'personal' laws. Thus I found myself asking time and time again at the conclusion of a case: What rule of law has been stated or exemplified in the dispute? It gradually dawned on me that a more profitable approach was to ask what was the nature of the process I was observing, and how did the judges arrive at decisions that were apparently satisfactory to most of the litigants? Once the focus shifted to procedure, the matter began to appear in quite a different light. As Gluckman and I were to argue subsequently, the whole system rested on the central premise that litigants and judges alike were operating with the same norms and standards of behavior. (Epstein 1973: 643–4)

The Eureka moment of discovery in fieldwork, of the kind that Gluckman so proudly boasted regarding the reasonable man, was not for Epstein in his deliberations. Instead came discovery that 'gradually dawned on me'.

Given this evidence of agreement between Epstein and Gluckman on a central premise, a related problem of rules needs to be raised. In the comparative efforts of his Wilson Lecture, Gluckman offered close and very substantial re-analyses not only of Paul Bohannon's Tiv cases but also of Philip Gulliver's Arusha cases (Gluckman 1974a: 239–42). This is the general conclusion that Gluckman reached in his objection to Gulliver's analysis of his cases:

> Gulliver argues either as if any body of law consists of single isolated rules or of logically consistent rules, instead of seeing it as sets of rules many of which are independent of one another, and sometimes even inconsistent with one another. From these, judges and conciliators, if they can, select the most appropriate principle to give a just, or the tolerable determination. (1974a: 242)

My reading of Epstein's early work leads me to suggest that in his basic agreement with Gluckman, he shared this argument about fuzzy sets of rules.

From revisionism to radical departure

So far, our appreciation of Epstein's deliberate dialogue with Gluck-man has kept to relatively narrow revisionism. To understand how Epstein came to make a more radical departure from the core of Gluckman's arguments, we need to look beyond Central Africa to Melanesia, beyond courts to moots, beyond legal training to some instruction about psychoanalysis (which Epstein felt he got all too briefly, and not a personal analysis, in 1971 on a visit to Anna Freud's Hampstead clinic), and beyond reasonableness to passion, to assertiveness and will, to competition for power and prestige. It is as if Epstein was working through a basic premise of his own in contradistinction to that of his mentor and perhaps representing something as profound in himself as was rationality for Gluckman. All of these alternatives matter a great deal for the distinctive devel-opment of Epstein's intellectual history and his still challenging con-tributions to legal anthropology.

Before Epstein could make even small steps to follow these alternatives, however, he had to overcome the political record he had to bear from his fieldwork under colonial rule in Zambia. Branded a subversive, he suffered being kicked out and left with a damning official record, as I describe in Chapter 4. Later, among Tolai and based upon fieldwork mainly in 1959–60 and 1961, and on a very brief visit in 1968, Epstein made his most substantial and distinctive contributions to the anthropology of law.

Not long after Epstein arrived among Tolai, he wrote very happily to Gluckman that he had found a community to study: 'At last, therefore, I can say I am engaged in an "orthodox" anthropo-logical study, except that "orthodoxy" has little meaning where there has been so much social and cultural change' (ALE to MG, 7 April 1960, GPJRUML). Happy, too, in reply, Gluckman expressed the approval of an old teacher: 'I am delighted that you are doing a more orthodox study, because I think it would be good for your development' (MG to ALE, 22 May 1960, GPJRUML).

Lest I give the impression that in Epstein's New Guinea field-work, by contrast to his African hazards, things went smoothly, I must report what he told Gluckman:

> I always seem to pick areas for fieldwork that are political dynamite. Now, at last, as I had long anticipated, the balloon, or more aptly

perhaps the volcano, seems to be going up around Rambaul. A new political association called Mataungan has emerged and some very unpleasant incidents have recently been reported. Need I say that the Matupi are in it up to their necks? (ALE to MG, 17 February 1960, GPJRUML)

In an article on 'Autonomy and Identity', Epstein later published his analysis of the emergence of Mataungan and the 'heightening tensions between the demands of dependency on the one hand and the drive for autonomy on the other' (Epstein 1970: 427). Young makes the point on identity in Epstein's work, as reflected in this article:

> As the leitmotif of much of his work, the problem of identity preoccupied him long before it became a fashionable topic of anthropological discourse. There was a subjective dimension to this intellectual concern. It went back to his youthful experience of being an 'outsider' in sectarian Belfast, where to say that you were neither a 'Mick' nor a 'Prod' but a 'Jew' was simply to invite the question 'A Catholic Jew or a Protestant Jew?' (Young 2000: 122)

For a study of law, the timing of Epstein's main fieldwork in Matupit was particularly opportune. It was a late colonial moment when, in New Guinea by contrast to Africa, law stood out as one of the most neglected fields of anthropological interest. It was also a moment when, during roughly the following decade from the early 1960s through at least the early 1970s, a mainstream surged, which explored, as Yngveson suggests, 'the political significance of disputes, focusing in particular on the ways in which distribution of scarce resources (e.g., power, land, cattle) is challenged and defended within the considerable arena of a particular dispute or series of disputes' (1978: 134).[7]

One part of Epstein's Matupit research focused on this. What he recalled later was recognizing much in common in the procedure for hearing cases without judges in Matupit and in the Copperbelt courts. But in the light of that, in certain cases an important politicized difference stood out, and it was problematic in comparative terms:

> I was at first puzzled to find that many village meetings at which disputes over land were submitted for public arbitration had to break

up without arriving at any satisfactory resolution of the issues. The fact was that what I was observing was less a judicial hearing than part of an ongoing political process. The disputants might point to the wrongs they had been done, and couch their arguments in terms of an appeal to jural norms and precedents, but it was apparent that they were rival leaders canvassing support and recognition of their authority; such hearings provided a forum for a trial of political strength as between opposed groups and not merely for the adjudication of legal issues and a claim for redress as between individual litigants. (Epstein 1967b: 224)

In pursuing this observation through his account of land litigation and the political process in modern Matupit, Epstein was at the forefront of the exploration of what might now be called legal warfare in an arena where politics and law unmistakably meet (Epstein 1969: esp. ch. 6). Going beyond that took Epstein to problems of artful mediation. His interest was in showing how the mediator, who is neutral to a dispute and has a keen sense of the appropriate moment to intervene, seeks to exert moral pressure; and, in their turn, how and when the parties might be ready to make concessions for the sake of reconciliation (Epstein 1984: 112).

Each of these steps in Epstein's developing approach are significant in themselves. But to appreciate his most radical departure we need to raise our own perspective. We need to consider in more theoretical terms the full breadth of what Epstein calls into question in his Matupit monograph and also in *Gunantuna*, his last collection of essays on the person, the self and the individual, published in 1999. There is an obvious part, which carries forward his dialogue with Gluckman but which in doing so reaches, even more importantly, to the past frontiers between social anthropology and psychology. The well-known fact is that Gluckman long and often projected the substantial and theoretical line dividing, on the one side, the interest in the social, whether system, structure or situation, from, on the other side, the psychological, as in the study of affect or cognition. Gluckman himself never completed the one long manuscript he was tempted to write in a psychoanalytic vein, about the Zulu king Shaka, notorious in legend no less for his small penis than for his violent terror with the short stabbing spear. My memory does not serve me well enough to recall which puns, if any, Epstein characteristically made about that.

However, perhaps energized by the fun of rebellion, if that was his actual drive, as I believe, perhaps following his psychoanalysis with Anna Freud, Epstein did cross his mentor's line. He did so by publishing, first, *Ethos and Identity* in 1978, his comparative exploration of ethnicity and subjectivity, then in 1984 his comparative study in the anthropology of affect, *The Experience of Shame in Melanesia*, reprinted in his collection of essays which appeared under the title *Gunantuna* (literally, 'real place', but metaphorically 'person'), and finally his last monograph, *In the Midst of Life*, subtitled *Affect and Ideation in the World of the Tolai* (1992).

Let me get closer to the nub of the matter by quoting from the frontispiece for Epstein's last monograph. The citation comes from the American psychologist Silvan Tomkins. 'Massive in scope and originality' runs Epstein's own estimation of Tomkins's masterly two-volume *Affect, Imagery, Consciousness* (1963–64). Tomkins says,

> The human being['s] ... superiority over other animals is as much a consequence of his more complex affect system as it is of his more complex analytical capacities. Out of the marriage of reason with affect there issues clarity with passion ... The combination of affect and reason guarantees man's high degree of freedom. (1963: I, 112, cited in Epstein 1992a: vi)

With this epigraph in mind, Epstein's habitual questioning in his monograph can be seen, as it were, as a wake-up call, extended by a man well aware that he is standing on a giant's shoulders and thus seeing more clearly than the rest of us. On his horizon is the still hardly explored interest in the marriage of reason with affect. Given felt imbalances in this marriage, what do people do? How and why? Can such questions about the dynamics of reason and affect be significantly put in comparative terms, with an eye to similarities or even universals across social and cultural differences? On a somewhat different track, within an alternative intellectual tradition, other social scientists, including cultural anthropologists, had much to say about distinct worlds of emotional talk, or at least the culturally specific words and clusters of lexical terms for affect.

Following this lead, an early part of Epstein's last monograph reveals the fruits of his command of an adopted lexical approach. By applying it to the Tolai language of emotions, such as pride, envy or anger, Epstein works out sets of categories, including alternative states and moods of the self, then discloses the importance of Tolai notions of self and other for the study of the emotions. Here, however, as a Manchester man, confronting new trends in ethnopsychology, Epstein was, I guess, not himself feeling the emotion of satisfaction in his guts, *a balana*, as Tolai would put it, for, as Epstein tells us, 'many of the Tolai words relating to the emotions are in fact no more than attempts to express in language the feeling experienced in the *balana*' (1992a: 64).

The Manchester man's gut feeling seems to get better the more he turns to actual everyday practice in social situations and, eventually, to the evidence from dispute cases. Well within the Manchester School tradition of conflict studies is his perception that among Tolai there is 'an unremitting tension between envy on the one hand and the desire for achievement on the other; each pulled in a different direction' (1992a: 115). As Epstein says, it is a deeprooted conflict, which has not had the dampening effect on development or innovation familiar elsewhere; hence it raises 'a number of interesting questions about envy for which at present we have no adequate explanation' (1992a: 115).

This leads me to the heart of the matter, to the *balana* as Tolai express it, to my own gut feeling. Quite simply it is about caring and compassion. Here the Tolai word is *Varmari*, compassion, concern, human fellowship and, indeed, love. *Varmari* means love, not in a sexual sense but as concern. To put it in terms more familiar perhaps to Christians commemorating the Last Supper, we may speak of *agape*, human fellowship, as distinct from *eros*, sexual desire. Here we have to consider not only what Epstein tells us about *Varmari* but how he tells it as an ethnographic discovery relevant for the anthropology of law, and with broad implications for the social sciences as well as for anthropology as a comparative discipline.

The fieldwork setting for Epstein's account is a village assembly for dispute settlement. This local forum largely reaches towards reconciliation led by the local councillor and his committee. With evidence from the Tolai disputes, Epstein returns to his longstanding argument with his teacher Gluckman in order to open our eyes to the comparative issues. Of all his ethnographic discoveries, as I have stressed, Gluckman was most proud of finding a basic figure of our own jurisprudence, the 'reasonable man', among the

Barotse. Revealed in the exotic was the familiar. Gluckman's contribution illuminated judicial reasoning along with the efforts of
litigants to present themselves in a reasonable light. But what did
this tell us about the emotional roots of disputes?

With this question in mind, Epstein observed among Tolai
something missing from Gluckman's framework, namely the force
of emotion or emotional dynamics, such as from rage to compassion. On the way to reconciliation, the village forum often has to
deal with outbursts of anger, even in the forum itself, for the man
of honour, asserting himself as a man of anger, is admired by Tolai.
But that admiration is within limits. Thus no less often in this forum
come emotive appeals to *Varmari*. Pressure is brought to bear to get
people to acknowledge that, however justified, anger or even violence has to be tempered by compassion, by fellow feeling. In
particular, relatives, who are the usual parties to a quarrel, must be
seen to be caring; caring befits their closeness, and without caring
kinship withers. Participation in this forum constantly reminds Tolai
of the risk of becoming, as Epstein remarks, 'the moral leper, one
who because he is incapable of feeling concern for others threatens
the very basis of community itself' (1992a: 149). Here Epstein's
account probes the depths of fellow feeling demanded, ironically
enough, by people who are notorious for their egalitarian, competi-
tive assertiveness.

Notes

1 Ralph Grillo, personal communication, April 2018.
2 For Epstein's argument that the use of the case method should take
  priority over rule discourse with informants, see Epstein 1967b: 210–17.
3 See the A. L. Epstein and T. Scarlett Epstein collection at the University
  of California, San Diego, Special Collections and Archives.
4 During an interval from 1958 to 1961, he held a research fellowship at
  the Australian National University.
5 Bohannon made this remark in the discussion of a paper that Gluckman
  read in 1963 to the Law School of Northwestern University (see Gluckman 1966b: 388), and Gluckman first cites the remark and the Tiv case
  re-analysis in Gluckman 1966a.
6 In my experience, criticism by one of his students was, for Gluckman,
  water off a duck's back, so to speak. He relished dissent, if not disobedience or rebellion against his authority. Having engaged with my
  criticism in Manchester lectures in the early 1960s, when I reviewed his
  work *Order and Rebellion*, primarily with reference to Bemba (Gluckman

1963b: 84–109), he saw to it that I was invited to a Wenner-Gren conference on law. It was held in August 1966, and this led to my publication of two critical articles (Werbner 1967, 1969). In the same spirit of positive intellectual exchange, Gluckman responded generously in his Reappraisal chapter to points I raised about the appeal process (Gluckman 1966a: 372–4).

7 I note further that, in comparison with Africa, anthropological attention to official and unofficial courts in New Guinea also came late. See the pioneering contribution by Marilyn Strathern (1972).

8

Victor Turner's
'voyage of discovery'

The continuities in Victor Turner's vision ran deep: a British-trained social anthropologist, a pupil of Max Gluckman, a member of the Manchester School and a celebrated ethnographer.[1] Turner deliberately identified, throughout his career, with one people, the Ndembu hunter-hoe cultivators and labour migrants, living in the tiny, scattered, highly mobile villages of the woodlands in north-western Zambia. At the height of his career, having moved from Britain to America, Turner delighted in the histrionic guise of a legendary figure. He enjoyed a personal fable. It seems, from his telling and retelling of a life story, that he had to free himself, in the words of his favourite poet, Blake, from 'mind-forged mana-cles', and in doing so became a born-again man. Turner was a playful man, even when most serious in the sustained rehearsal, over some thirty years, of his ethnography from his early fieldwork among Ndembu in Zambia. But it was as if, on an odyssey even in his own eyes – 'on a personal voyage of discovery' (Turner 1982a: 7) – he became a nomadic celebrity. He was the one who not only travelled widely from place to place, sometimes on pil-grimage, sometimes as visiting professor or research fellow in insti-tutions around the world, but who also felt that he had to keep on toiling, almost Sisyphus-like, restlessly striving to move away from his early intellectual roots in social anthropology and yet over-whelmingly retreading the original insights he presented in roughly his first post-PhD decade.

Yet Turner's 'voyage of discovery' did reach a hard place, during the 1970s, when debate turned fierce, arguing over what part British social anthropologists played, wittingly or unwittingly, in the colonial period. The arguments are, of course, still acutely with us, if now rephrased in polarized contention about decolonization. What has to be better understood in the light of contemporary correspondence and archival evidence is not only how Turner became caught up in this fierce debate, but also how it unravelled his personal fable of restless, rebellious striving and tested, almost to the breaking point, his close and deep friendship with his much-admired mentor Gluckman.

My impression is that, as a teacher, Turner avoided the burdens of undergraduate teaching as much as possible. And so, too, as a professor he resisted as best he could the bearing of bureaucratic responsibilities in administration: 'the Cornell department expected him [Turner]', reports Engelke,

> to pull his weight on administrative duties, which Vic found increasingly difficult to bear. He wanted intellectual comrades, not colleagues or students, and he thought ideas were best explored in an environment that was as open as possible. Universities, he was slowly coming to realize, could not provide that. They demand 'structure and bureaucratic responsibility'. (Engelke 2004: 31–2)

The 1960s was the time, Engelke notes, 'when the Turners developed their "Thursday Night Seminars", a kind of alternative classroom experience run out of their living rooms in Ithaca, Chicago, and Charlottesville that involved late nights, heated discussions, alcohol, ritual re-enactments, and as much communitas as they could muster' (Engelke 2004: 30).[2] More congenial, and a mode of being Turner continually sought to find or recreate around himself, was the research institute he knew first at the Rhodes-Livingstone Institute with its vibrant fieldworkers' gatherings, and which he later prized in the Manchester Department of Social Anthropology, with its staff and fieldworkers' seminars in its early years, before it had to take first-degree students.

At Manchester, there came to be a crisis, one might say the stuff of a social drama. The realist norm, pushed by some in the department who were not from the RLI, was that of the vice-chancellor, who backed undergraduate growth throughout the university for its survival. Turner was in the losing staff faction that claimed to be true to the principles of the RLI and its research ethos; he tried unsuccessfully to persuade Gluckman to maintain the department only for postgraduates. My guess is that Gluckman hoped to keep Turner by offering him the post of field director of a proposed Bernstein research scheme in Israel. In characteristically frank interviews with Matthew Engelke, Edith Turner later recalled: 'Vic was very devoted to Max [Gluckman] but also wanted to get out from under his thumb, so in 1960 he accepted an offer from the Center for Advanced Study in the Behavioral Sciences at Stanford to spend a year there' (Engelke 2000: 847). In the end, Turner found his new undergraduate teaching responsibilities at Manchester more than unwelcome, and following his year at the Stanford think-tank he was all the more attracted to the seemingly emergent possibilities of the New World. From Edith Turner, Engelke understood that, given 'the image of American life shaped by their encounters with the Beats in California – their fellow misfits and contrarians – Vic and Edie assumed America would be a promised land' (Engelke 2004: 30). The developing hippie era and the demonstrations and love-ins at Cornell in the 1960s did eventually figure prominently in Turner's work and form a source of reflection in his Morgan Lectures, *The Ritual Process* (1969).

For the second part of his Morgan Lectures, Turner's primary audience was, initially a seminar at Cornell, at that time of hippies' love-ins. He would have had his audience well with him when he spoke of *existential* or *spontaneous communitas* – approximately what the hippies would would call 'a happening' and William Blake might have called 'the winged moment as it flew' or, later, 'mutual forgiveness of each vice' (Turner 1969: 132). Even further, Turner offered a disclaimer, in the manner of a conversion narrative. He made the point in American universities, first Cornell and later Chicago, that he had turned away from what he represented as his British rearing:

> I was reared in the orthodox social-structuralist tradition of British anthropology, which, to put a complex argument with crude simplicity, regards a 'society' as a system of social positions … Field experience and general reading in the arts and humanities convinced me that the 'social' is not identical with the 'social-structural.' (Turner 1969: 131)[3]

In Chapter 3, my discussion of Elizabeth Colson's Morgan Lectures presents a contrast. Turner's Morgan Lectures and, after them,

Colson's register their opposed views on utopian quests and, in particular, those of the hippies. Approvingly on the hippies, Turner wrote: 'What they seek is a transformative experience that goes to the root of each person's being and finds in that root something profoundly communal and shared' (1969: 138). Doubting this, from a perspective on Berkeley hippies and Tonga witch-finding movements, Colson expressed her scepticism:

> Victor Turner, in his Morgan Lectures (1969), has seen in ritual the vehicle for creating 'communitas' that perfect world in which we know for the moment the expansion of ourselves into communion with others. This he contrasts with 'societas' that divided world of ordinary routines where life is measured out in roles and statuses. I, myself, am sceptical of the ability of ritual to produce this transformation if it is used consciously for this end. (Colson 1974b: 91)

The Turners themselves had to think again and again about America, and about utopian quests and hippies, and they found they could not go home; they were never to go back to live in England. It is perhaps even more surprising that after his early years of fieldwork, Turner never went back to Ndembu either. When I asked him why he did not return to Ndembu, he answered, 'What for? For another cult of affliction?' His indulgent twinkle and smile left me feeling I had asked a foolish question.

In his preface to the 1996 edition of *Schism and Continuity*, Turner noted 'a steadily broadening stream of studies in processual analysis' (1996: xxiii). It is remarkable that, influential as Turner has been in advancing that processual stream, he himself hardly followed Ndembu as people experiencing change after his early fieldwork. In the 1968 edition, Turner did report a surprising ethnographic fact, the news he received of an unexpected succession to village headmanship, more than a decade after he left the field. But Turner was not to be drawn into Ndembu re-analysis in the light of new theories or fresh ethnographic discoveries in the region. Ndembu remained *the* Ndembu.

Some basic facts about Turner's distinguished career are essential. He carried out his Ndembu fieldwork in two periods, between December 1950 and February 1952 and between May 1953 and June 1954, as a Research Officer of the RLI. At the University of Manchester, from 1954 to 1963, having been a research assistant, then a Simon Senior Fellow, he became a lecturer and quickly a senior lecturer, when he was slated to be the field director of Gluckman's last major research project, the Bernstein scheme in Israel (Gillon 1983: 5). From 1964 to 1968 he held his professorship at Cornell University. At the University of Chicago, from 1968 to 1977, he joined the prestigious Committee on Social Thought and became a professor, also, in the Department of Anthropology. His last decade he spent as William R. Kenan Professor of Anthropology and Religion at the University of Virginia, from 1977 until his death in 1983 (Babcock 1984: 462–3). He held fellowships in America, first at Palo Alto in 1961–62, at the Center for Advanced Studies in the Behavioral Sciences, and then at Princeton's Institute for Advanced Studies in 1975–76. Other fellowships later took him to Brazil and Japan, and finally to Israel as an Einstein Fellow at the Academy of Sciences and Humanities.

In the universities of Manchester, Cornell, Chicago and Virginia, Turner played intensely to his creative strength as a seminar man. I count myself among his pupils at Manchester who came away from his fieldwork seminar and his conversations at The Transport Café, a local pub, first with an article to write and then later a lifelong dialogue.[4]

I want to stress two things. The first is the importance of Turner's most productive and highly original period. Initially, he developed his ideas within a theoretical discourse on ritual to which Gluckman introduced him, and which the RLI director Clyde Mitchell encouraged him to pursue early, in his fieldwork: 'Vic *must* write up on ritual – he talks dreams and performs rituals all the time ... This is obviously going to be his major work so he may as well clear up in his own mind what shape it is going to take' (CM to MG, 27 February 1952, MPBL, cited in Gordon 2018: 394). Even further, a major source, deep in Ndembu realities and Lunda language, must have been the six early fieldwork seminars on ritual that he presented soon after returning to Manchester.

The second is that Turner reached this creative period, from 1955 onwards, while still based at Manchester. To reread his earliest review essay on 'A Revival in the Study of African Ritual' is to see the fine seeds of ideas already germinating; for example, 'Each crucial or pivotal symbol in the ritual system of a society evokes through a chain of association powerful feelings and wishes inherent in a number of social and cultural situations' (1955: 55). In the first decade, 1957 was the year when he wrote 'Symbols in Ndembu Ritual', and presented it with much acclaim to a meeting of the ASA in London in March 1958; 1959 saw 'Muchona the Hornet'; 1959/1960 'Ritual Symbolism'; 1960/61 *Chihamba*; 1961 'Three Symbols of Passage'; and 1963 'Colour Classification' and 'Betwixt and Between'. This evidence contradicts claims by Barbara Babcock and John MacAloon. In their view, Turner created his analyses primarily after he left England, supposedly when his 'transplanted iconoclasm took root and flourished' (Babcock and MacAloonr 1987: 8). The one major new field of research he opened later in life was pilgrimage (Turner 1973a; Turner and Turner 1978). Later in this chapter, I discuss Turner's personal fable, examine how far he 'rebelled against structural functionalism' and show the recurring affinities between his thought and Gluckman's.

The study of rites of passage, derived from Arnold Van Gennep and climaxing freshly in Turner's dominant idea of liminality, offers a telling example. The story turns on Gluckman's long-term interest in such rites. For Gluckman, Van Gennep's *Les Rites de passage* (1908) was 'one of the most important books written about ritual in the generation before the First World War' (Gluckman 1962b: 2).[5] To the memory of Arnold Van Gennep, Gluckman dedicated *Essays on the Ritual of Social Relations* (1962). In this collection, he assessed Van Gennep's achievements. He highlighted, among other things, how Van Gennep inspired the great missionary ethnographer Henri Junod to see Tsonga social life as a series of passages and movements 'through separation from normal life, into a marginal period, from which re-aggregation took place' (Gluckman 1962b: 9). Although Turner wrote, in this 1962 collection, about circumcision rites – 'typical *rites de passage* as characterized by Van Gennep' (Turner 1962: 124) – he said nothing about the marginal period or liminality as such. Turner did edge towards considering the rites as ontologically transformative only towards the end of his essay, when he reflected briefly on the move from initiatory death ending the 'indistinct and amorphous state of childhood' to rebirth into maturity. His focus was not on Van Gennep's model of transitions; it was, instead, on the symbols of passage and their associated levels of meaning, seen in a binary perspective, the passage being from one state to another. It was in 1963 that, following Gluckman's initiative, Turner addressed the familiar three-phase model from Van Gennep and Junod, and made his important breakthrough on the period of margin or liminality, full of confused categories and paradoxical ambiguities, as an interstructural situation. About it, in his essay 'Betwixt and Between', he offered the argument he continued to unpack tirelessly for decades:

> Liminality here breaks the cake of custom and enfranchises speculation. That is why I earlier mentioned Plato's self-confessed debt to the Greek mysteries. Liminality is the realm of primitive hypothesis where there is a certain freedom to juggle with the factors of existence. As in the works of Rabelais, there is a promiscuous intermingling and juxtaposing of the categories of event, experience, and knowledge, with a pedagogic intention. (Turner 1967: 106)

Turner went on to argue, or speculate, about how neophytes actually think during the liminal moment, when *sacra are* communicated: 'It intimately unites man and office. But for a valuable while there was an uncommitted man, an individual rather than a social *persona*, in a sacred community of individuals' (1967: 108).

If the positive resonance with what Turner later called *communitas* is striking, so too is a certain negative or oppositional resonance arising from Gluckman's 1962 collection. For example, whereas Turner refocused attention on promiscuity and the 'uncommitted man', Meyer Fortes had stressed moral obligation and the power of ritual at once to create individuality and at the same time commit the individual in a binding manner to moral norms.[6] Turner's departure was a redirection of theoretical interest, but one that gained its impetus from engagement or wrestling within a long-standing tradition in social anthropology.

Still based at Manchester, Turner became a semiotician in all but name, and in his own distinctive guise, influenced by neo-scholastic Thomist philosophy. His methical analysis reached the latent and even pre-conscious, inspired by Carl Jung on the 'living symbol' beyond conscious apprehension, and Sigmund Freud.[7] From Edward Sapir and linguistic anthropology, Turner developed his approach to symbols as stimuli of emotion. His appreciation of Sapir's idea of condensation symbolism and its roots in the unconscious was first presented in his 1958 essay on 'Symbols in Ndembu Ritual', in which Turner amended Sapir's formulation by stressing the importance of what Turner called the ideological or normative pole of meaning in ritual symbols (1967: 29). Among all his fellows in the early Manchester School, Turner was the only one who pioneered at this frontier: the exploration of the semantics of materiality and affective engagement.[8]

It became Turner's conviction that 'we have to put ourselves in some way inside religious processes to know them' (1975: 32). He believed in interpretive intuition – an approach, given intimate experience, through analysis, if need be highly formal; it culminates in interpretation open to public evaluation. Here Turner's personal history of religious experience is important. After a quest through ritual performances and intense religious experiences among Ndembu and in Britain, Turner, with his wife and family, had converted to Catholicism by 1959,[9] perhaps precipitated by the Russian invasion of Hungary in 1956 and his resignation from the Communist Party. He endured an ordeal, ridden with turmoil for him and his circles of significant others, including colleagues and leftist friends, who admired his charismatic personality. At the bitter height of the ordeal, recalled Edith Turner, 'Our socialist agnostic colleague Bill Watson said, "You've betrayed us. You've let us down. We were strong, and now you've given in – to the Papists." He saw the anthropological fight against illusion and bigotry as weakened – by us' (E. Turner 2006: 89). In 1959 Watson apologized. I was told in confidence that one good friend did say, 'Vic has gone from one religion to another.'

In response to a 'friendly and encouraging letter' from Gluckman on holiday in July 1959, Turner explained his conversion:

> I became a Christian … by reading the New Testament as a series of social dramas. In the course of this reading it came home to me that unless Jesus of Nazareth was what he claimed to be, i.e. God, he was either a lunatic, a criminal or a simpleton. The manner of his life and teaching, and especially the manner of his death, convinced me that he was none of these. Once I believed in the divinity of Jesus the rest followed. In a perfectly rational way. Catholicism is a rationalistic religion, and the Catholic claims to demonstrate by reason the existence of God, the deity of Christ, and the authority of the church, I find valid. But charity is at the heart of the whole thing: without it nothing. And it's heartening to believe that the 'non-spiralist'[10] qualities of humility and the like lie at the root of life.

In all this (while we are at it!) I have been totally uninfluenced by Oxford anthropology or anthropologists. My scientific and personal loyalties have always been, are and will be to Manchester. I am privately inclined to think that Oxford Catholics, like Oxford academics generally, lean to the heresy of Gnosticism, which as you know, is a revelation offered not to all mankind, but reserved as a privilege for elect souls. It is neither a Catholic (i.e. universal) nor a scientific (i.e. concerned with true knowledge) position; but it appeals to proud minds. I prefer the empiricism of Aquinas: 'No one perceives that he understands except through the fact that he understands *something*, for to understand something is prior to understanding *that* one understand.' In other words his view presupposes the fundamental role of sense-experience or sense-perception. We are not so different when we say that we 'start with social reality'. At Oxford one gets the impression that they start with a kind of detached ego or mind and then try to prove the existence of things other than this ego or mind, rather than in the Cartesian manner, oddly enough.

As regards authority and the individual, I personally find a great act of self-sacrifice 'compelling', innocence 'constraining' and love 'masterful'. It is in this sense I accept the teaching 'authority' of the Church in faith and morals.

She has learnt not to use prisons, brain-washing and secret police, for she develops in her human aspect and learns from science while teaching some scientists (VT to MG, 7 July 1959, GPRAI)

At the end of his letter, Turner added a handwritten note:

Let me finish by saying how proud I am to have the opportunity of working in a Department which under your guidance is going to make crucial discoveries about the Social aspect of human existence. I think some of these discoveries will surprise us, but we must go step by step, inch by patient inch, rejecting 'intuition' and subjectivism, until we have a corpus of theory that will stand. (VT to MG, 7 July 1959, GPRAI)

Working together on ritual was, at least still in 1959, a welcome prospect for Turner and Gluckman: they were planning a projected book together on circumcision rites, Gluckman on Wiko and Turner on Ndembu (VT to MG, 27 April 1959, GPRAI). Even further, they were planning to cooperate on research in 1963, just before Turner left for America.

The part I myself witnessed came late in 1959, when I was all too briefly Turner's supervisee. His infant daughter Lucy, born with Down Syndrome, died aged less than five months. Affirming their faith in the Roman Catholic Church, the Turners accepted, and asked others to join them, in facing her sin-free innocence in infancy, her goodness on the way to God. The Turners held a home celebration for redemptive joy, not grief, which I joined along with some who were still uneasy about the Turners' conversion to Catholicism. In consolation, Gluckman relieved Turner of some of his responsibilities, including me,[11] which gave him time to write *Chihamba*. Later, in her memoir, Edith Turner recalled: 'Back in 1960, during this trouble with the baby and at her death, the department of anthropology at Manchester University put out their richest human kindness to us, blessed us with as heavenly a love as from any church across the world' (E. Turner 2006: 91).

'British formed, American re-formed': the social drama in development

It was with a bit of truth, perhaps teasing banter, that Clifford Geertz called Turner 'a British formed, American re-formed anthropologist' (1980: 16). Turner was, Geertz recognized (and the recognition pleased Turner), in the very forefront of the current development of a ritual theory approach in the social sciences. This recognition came with an appreciation that marked Turner out among his fellows from the Manchester School – he was at the head of something like a school of his own, if not one formally institutionalized:

> Turner, in a remarkable series of works trained on the ceremonial life of a Central African tribe, has developed a conception of 'social drama' as a regenerative process that ... Has drawn to it such a large number of able researchers as to produce a distinct and powerful interpretive school. (Geertz 1980: 172)

Eventually, Turner appeared in some, but not all, American academic circles to be a rebel against British orthodoxy (Brunner 1986: 4) and his classic monograph appeared, according to a pupil of his, Barbara Babcock, to mark 'the beginning of his rebellion against structural-functional orthodoxy with its closed, static model of social systems, presenting society instead as a process, a field of forces and conflict, whose contradictions are expressed and redressed in social dramas' (Babcock 1984: 462). Against this caricature, Sherry Ortner, herself a Chicago-trained student of Geertz's, rightly argued, 'Despite the relative novelty of Turner's move to symbols, however, there is in his work a deep continuity with British social anthropological concerns' (Ortner 1984: 231).

Here I can only begin to trace Turner's reiteration of the social drama as the same yet somehow apparently refreshed when unpacked at new moments in his restless odyssey.[12] My account highlights certain key aspects of the critical or at least changing reception of Turner's dominant ideas, along with their reiteration.

If it is well known that one has to have a mentor, and perhaps even a circle of peers, in becoming a PhD in social anthropology, then the obscured role in an anthropologist's career is that of the age-mate who remains a lifelong interlocutor. Among Manchester anthropologists, the friend Turner seems to have eventually missed most was A. L. 'Bill' Epstein. Turner's age-mate as a contemporary RLI fieldworker in Zambia and the other of Gluckman's first two PhD students at Manchester, Epstein was the very close friend with the rare gift of being a listening yet deliberately forthcoming interlocutor. He must have brought to bear in conversations with Turner regarding village troubles and disputes the clarity in analysis of the phases in cases that is the hallmark of his work *Juridical Techniques and the Judicial Process* (1954).

Edith Turner told Matthew Engelke this story about the birth of the social drama:

> Vic was in the pub [in North Manchester] wondering what it was about anecdotes, episodes, and trouble cases that was so important … the very roots, the vital existence of the village was trembling and tottering all the time..Vic couldn't look at these events as just anecdotes or mere trouble cases … while still in the field he was taking notes, paying attention because of this hunch which he hadn't yet articulated – not until the pub with Bill Epstein. The hunch in Manchester was the concept of the social drama and the definable form: breach, crisis, redress and reconciliation. After the pub conversation, Vic wrote it all down and turned it in to Max as the major chapter in his dissertation. And Max liked it. (Engelke 2000: 846)

If Turner's 'rebellion' was true to the legend of the Americanized figure or his personal fable, in his own words 'reared in the ortho-dox social-structuralist tradition of British anthropology' (1969: 131), Turner's was a 'rebellion' that was victorious before it began. Or rather, he joined a rebellion against Oxford structuralism that was already fully developed under Gluckman's leadership, and with much support from the early RLI directors, Elizabeth Colson and Clyde Mitchell, both of whom influenced Turner during and after his fieldwork. Indeed, the fact that Mitchell had paved the way for Turner's analysis was well recognized at the time, by Turner himself (1968: 275) and by others. Mary Douglas noted that 'Many of the conflicts he [Turner] analyses are inherent in matrilineal systems and have been already adumbrated by Mitchell in his *Yao Village*. But he has carried the analysis to a far greater pitch of accuracy' (Douglas 1959b: 297).

My own assessment in my early review of the Manchester School argued for a perspective on further shifts in analysis:

> *Schism and Continuity* was at once the crest of one wave, on conflict resolution, and a force for movement in the alternative directions of transactionalism and more interpretive approaches such as sym-bolic interaction. If unmistakeably a part of the theoretical devel-opment from the Oxford structuralists, *Schism and Continuity* was a high watermark in that Manchester mainstream which derived from Malinowski's *Crime and Custom* (1926) and his notions of endemic conflict and the social or life situation. In *Crime and Custom*, the endemic conflict of principles was primarily between Mother-right and Father-love or paternal interest, in *Schism and Continuity* between matrilineality and virilocality. In both, the major conflict involved the choice between conflicting loyalties, the tension between selfish and social drives, and the antagonism between individuals or cliques seeking power or wealth.
>
> Malinowski can be read, of course, as if he meant to value practi-cal action over cultural norm. But that was not the received view in the early Manchester tradition. Malinowksi's lesson which *Schism and Continuity* took up was this. The full force of cultural reality is felt in crises: then governing norms are re-stated and upheld, not bent or manipulated to suit private interests. The point from *Crime and Custom* was, further, that compromises and adjustments are made beneath the surface of social life, until a crisis makes them public, when for the sake of redress people may bring 'ritual power' and 'its binding force'

(1926: 104) to bear. In *Schism and Continuity*, the radical advance was a highly systematic framework of processual analysis, built around the concept of the social drama with its pre- and post-crisis phases, and substantiated in the rich micro-histories of humanly rounded individuals. Sandombu confronted us, like a hero in a Greek drama, and it was as if we were witnessing the 'helplessness of the human individual before the Fates: but in this case the Fates [were] the necessities of the social process' (Turner 1957: 94).

But what were these necessities? The micro-histories in *Schism and Continuity* resonate with Turner's perceptions of human creativity and individual consciousness, his insights into the negotiation of cultural and social order, and his analysis of the power-seeking manipulations of self-interested individuals. In itself the interaction was generative on the micro-scale. Here the micro-historian seemed to be saying something more and other than the sociologist of the whole social system. Or rather, the insights implicitly called for a move away from the current structuralist paradigm of conflict resolution to conceptualize the nuances, even the ephemera, of micro-situations. (Werbner 1990b: 166–7)

It is worth saying also how Gluckman himself distilled *Schism and Continuity* for a popular audience in his general book on the problem of rule and disorder in social life (Gluckman 1965b: 238–42). In Gluckman's distillation, the monograph's extended case was about the Ndembu villagers' personal ambitions and self-interestedness, the rebalancing of power in their village, the enduring patterns of social relations, the contradictory principles in kinship and locality. But no less importantly, it was also about the grip of moral values invested with powerful sentiments and mystical beliefs – these held the main subject, the now-famous Sandombu, grief-stricken and having self-doubt to the point of not knowing if he was actually guiltless of sorcery and responsibility for suffering. And, in the culmination of the case, Gluckman stressed that, on the return of the prodigal Sandombu to his village, 'the most powerful values of Ndembu society prevented his rivals rejoicing permanently in his defeat. Their consciences began to trouble them over him. Was he not blood of their blood, born from the same "womb"?' (1969: 240). The perception that Gluckman caught was Turner's awareness of something among Ndembu that transcended the pragmatics of their power struggles, perhaps something deeply human beyond the division into factions.

Gluckman became convinced that the extended case method, his view of the social drama, was best grounded in statistics provided as a basis for the qualitative analysis of the sequences of actions in a series of cases. Hence his contention that Turner's ability to analyse his case material as social dramas depended upon the analysis of 'hard-nosed' data, that is, statistics (see MG to VT, 17 September 1974, 3 October 1974, GPRAI).

As is well known, the world little noted the quantitative data from Turner's Ndembu fieldwork. In his monograph, as in his dissertation, there are dozens of tables, and their analysis is in many chapters. It was the four pages on the concept of the social drama (1967: 91–4) and the narrative art in his following representation of a whole series of social dramas that attracted, and still attracts, the greatest interest. In fact, Edith Turner was the one, in their Ndembu fieldwork, who collected most of the 'hard-nosed' data, including the genealogies, took most of the photographs, and did the statistical analyses. Perhaps ironically, late in her long life she became, even more than her husband, not merely frustrated by the importance of 'hard-nosed' data in academia but ever more powerfully drawn, in her writing as a poetic novelist and as an anthropologist in her own right, to the expression of a 'spiritual' calling, the expression of what she felt to be 'the deeper realities of religious experience' (Engelke 2004: 29), ineffable mysteries. The collaboration, indeed teamwork, between the Turners was very close and mutually supportive, perhaps exceptionally so (see Engelke 2000, 2004).

Looking back in 1997, Edith recalled the production of her husband's thesis as a joint effort: 'And we began to build up the dissertation, chapter by chapter, very carefully, starting with the geography, means of subsistence, political systems and history, etc.' (Engelke 2000: 846).[13] Victor Turner did the main writing and Edith edited; he typed up his case material and checked his account of it against her statistical analysis, for confirmation. Not surprisingly, perhaps, Edith stressed this: '*Schism and Continuity* is in great part the statistical picture of a matrilineal people, including plentiful case material and a discussion of the implications of marriage and locality' (Engelke 2000: 846). Of course, she also recognized her husband's greater strength where it undoubtedly mattered most for the main case material in *Schism and Continuity*: 'He had a good eye for antagonisms in the village and the curious tangle of personalities that he wrote about in *Schism and Continuity*. I wasn't up to writing on the intricacies, or so I thought at the time' (Engelke 2000: 849). Edith praised Gluckman's fine editing of Turner's thesis and his monograph: 'Max Gluckman, when he finally got a complete draft in his hand, with great painstaking care went through every word of it, copyediting in detail' (Engelke 2000: 846).

The affinity between Turner's thought and Gluckman's: a genealogy of ideas

I find the affinity between Turner's thought and Gluckman's striking in at least two ways, often driven home in their writing. One is the frequent use of a characteristic expressive idiom, which is contrapuntal; and the other, the turn to the proposition which is dialectical but put in the form of an apparent paradox – apparent because its resolution is revealed. In brief, what Gluckman and Turner shared is a tendency to recursive thought which, sometimes in dazzlingly imaginative leaps, represents oscillations between extreme poles.

In his classic *Custom and Conflict in Africa*, Gluckman established the precedent: he conveyed the contrapuntal expression through many examples in oppositional terms, such as 'the peace in the feud', 'the logic in witchcraft', 'the frailty in authority'; and he put much of his analysis in such dialectical propositions as the following:

> conflicts in one set of relationships, over a wider range of society or through a longer period of time, lead to the establishment of social cohesion. Conflicts are a part of social life and custom appears to exacerbate these conflicts: but in doing so custom also restrains the conflicts from destroying the wider social order. (Gluckman 1956a: 2)

In Gluckman's footsteps,[14] Turner wrote contrapuntally on the centrifugal vs. the centripetal, overall ritual unity vs. fissile secular life, the liminal vs. the liminoid, structure vs. anti-structure; and in his turn, in his early work on Ndembu, originally written under

Gluckman's supervision, Turner argued, in a somewhat revisionist stance, for dialectical propositions, such as this:

> conflicts which split sub-systems tend to be absorbed by the widest social system and even to assist its cohesion by a wide geographical spreading of ties of kinship and affinity. Centrifugal tendencies prevail on the whole over centripetal tendencies at the level of corporate kinship and local groupings, but centrifugality is confined within the bounds of the total socio-geographical system of the Ndembu nation. (Turner 1957: xxiii)

I want to stress that the same mode of thought – not a radical rebellion against it – prevailed in the following decade in Turner's Morgan Lectures delivered in 1966 at the University of Rochester. Consider the following passage, given under the heading 'Dialectic of the Developmental Cycle':

> From all this [on communitas vs. structured society] I infer that, for individuals and groups, social life is a type of dialectical process that involves successive *experience* of high and low, communitas and structure, homogeneity and differentiation, equality and inequality. The passage from lower to higher status is through a limbo of statuslessness. In such a process, the opposites, as it were, constitute one another and are mutually indispensable. (Turner 1969: 97, italics mine)

This passage leaves no doubt about the long-term continuity in Turner's thought – his preference, like Gluckman's, for the contrapuntal idiom and the dialectical proposition. I italicize the word *experience*, because it conveyed a growing concern of Turner's, much accentuated by the influence of his wife Edith, to showcase the intimately felt swings, such as the highs and lows, in performance.

My genealogy of these key ideas and modes of thought, like any genealogy, is but one possibility among others. For a notable example, Raymond Firth showed his dissatisfaction with the whole notion of the social drama by putting it in the line not of his own teacher Malinowski, but Malinowski's rival, Radcliffe-Brown:

> 'The processual form' which Turner has identified in his 'social drama' (1957, 91–2): breach, redressive action; re-integration or recognition

of schism – seems not to be intrinsic to the notion of drama, but to be very much in line with Radcliffe-Brown's type of analysis of restoration of equilibrium after commission of an offence. (Firth 1973: 194–5; see also 1974: 1–2)

If for Firth this dominant idea came on the rejected line of his social anthropology genealogy, it was more on her own line for Douglas:

the originality of Turner's method lies in his notion of 'social drama'. Now and again in the life of a village, a crisis occurs, action is taken to restore harmony, and finally the group is re-integrated or permanently divided. The whole process, from the original breach of custom which provoked the crisis, to the redressive action and final resolution of conflict, is Turner's 'social drama' ... For English anthropology this technique has the ironic effect of taking another step away from the 'a-historical' approach favoured by Malinowski. In essence, the method is akin to that of the political historian. In any historical work, ten years of peace can be covered in one page ... while a single political crisis requires a whole chapter for its elucidation. The social drama is the political crisis, writ small... (1959b: 297–9)

What is striking is that the reception of 'drama' itself in Turner's dominant idea was polarized. At one extreme, for Douglas, it was unproblematic, to be taken at face value. At the other, Firth expanded his objections to question the utility of calling successive moments of crisis or conflict a *drama*, and he argued that it was more a suggestive metaphor for role-playing than a methodological tool (Firth 1973: 194). In response, and aware that for Gluckman, too, 'drama' ill fitted social processes, Turner reflected defensively on trenchant criticism in an essay written when he had turned to experimental theatre in collaboration with the director Richard Schechner (Turner 1982a: 106).

The doubts about Turner's drama analogy expressed by some senior British social anthropologists turned to a warm welcome in its reception within the mainstream of American social science, during the late 1970s and early 1980s. Having an eye to the meeting of the humanities and the social sciences, Geertz heralded this turn by repositioning Turner's dominant idea in an alternative genealogy of ideas (Geertz 1980). Out came the social drama from the sociological line of structural opposition. It suited Geertz's own turn towards 'humanistic' interpretation to reposition Turner's ritual drama in the line from Jane Harrison, Francis Ferguson, T. S. Eliot and Antonin Artaud. Their common interest, regarding affinities of theatre and religion, the temple as stage, was in drama as communion (not comedy).[15] In fact, however, apart from Harrison on the communication of *sacra* in initiation (Turner 1967: 122, citing Harrison 1903), and a marked departure from Eliot's ritual drama on Thomas Becket,[16] there is no trace of any of these other sources in Turner's own work, no direct engagement with any of them. He found his inspiration in William Blake, Samuel Taylor Coleridge, Walt Whitman, Herman Melville, Dante Alighieri, the French Symbolists, W. H. Auden, Rainer Maria Rilke, Jacob Boehme and Paracelsus.

For Geertz, or rather his view, Turner's thought, if new and original in reputation, was troublesome, tending to be universalist when it ought to have been relativist; it was perhaps tending to 'encyclopedic empiricism: massive documentation of a single proposition' (Geertz 1980: 174). Others might find Turner to be an ebullient, fun-loving *bon vivant* or a joyful bard, making the potency of symbols felt and heard; for Geertz, he was the one whose approach to social life as drama missed 'what exactly, socially, the poems say' (Geertz 1980: 174). Geertz deftly promoted Turner's approach – it was in the forefront of a mainstream – then exposed its weakness – 'A form for all seasons … making vividly disparate matters look drably homogeneous' (Geertz 1980: 173).

A 'Parthian shaft', Turner called it (Turner 1982a: 107), recognizing Geertz's tactic. Parthians were renowned for firing their arrows best while appearing to be in retreat. Geertz's sharp parting remark came over as if to strike down an enemy or a rival who has lowered his guard. In my view, Geertz's treatment of Turner's dominant idea, the social drama, was even more subversive, because it obscured the fact that Turner himself developed two ideas, the social drama and the ritual drama. While, for the social drama, Geertz managed to put in relief its focus on conflict resolution and regeneration, what got hidden in Geertz's treatment was how Turner perceived ritual drama and engaged distinctively with it. Geertz simply reconditioned one idea in terms of the other, or in other words, repackaged the ritual drama wrapped round the social drama.

Geertz's parting shot became not the last word in a put-down but a wind-up in schismogenesis. By opposition, accentuating against 'the massive documentation of a single proposition' the recognized accusation in Geertz's phrase (Geertz 1980: 174), Turner recycled the social drama all the more. He reiterated, as usual but with more illustration, its importance in 'simpler, preindustrial societies', then went on, loosely in full flood, to fresh guesswork about how and why the social drama in more 'complex, divided, industrialized' societies often does not run its full course through to reconciliation or mutual acceptance of schism, but may lead to critique and 'new ingenious cultural formulations of our human condition' (Turner 1982a: 111).

As part of an overview of mainstream currents, Geertz expanded his appreciation of the drama analogy by tracing a second line in its genealogy – that of symbolic action approaches which showcase persuasion and rhetoric, dramaturgical approaches influenced by Kenneth Burke and others. Geertz not only welcomed these approaches, he made synthesis his goal. In press was his book, *Nagara*, and Geertz promised that it would bring together both lines, from the ritual drama, with its 'power to shape experience', and also from the symbolic action dramaturgy, enacting an image of order. Turner would be surpassed, or so one might well be led to expect. It was as if Turner was boxed in by his approach to ritual theory at a time of sea change, when the 'reconfiguration of social theory' called for 'blurred genres' and moves to tack between different approaches and arguments.

Somewhat briefly, and in a perhaps over-compressed response, Turner met another challenge. It came in Geertz's campaign for what he insisted was already in mainstream approaches and yet still with much unexplored promise: the use of a text analogy. The campaign was the one he earlier heralded in and through his celebrated article on the Balinese cockfight – 'to understand symbolic forms in terms of how they function in concrete situations to organize perceptions (meanings, emotions, concepts, attitudes)' (Geertz 1973: 449 n.38). Where and how did Turner advance this understanding? Geertz's argument in the *American Scholar* article so greatly boxed Turner off from any use of a text analogy that he had to break into a 'me-too' rebuttal with a counter-claim. His was a better use of the text analogy, because he approached 'texts in context of performance' (1982a: 107). It might be argued, from a Turnerian view, that 'The Cockfight' stopped too short. The point is that by 'context of performance' Turner meant a situational approach, unlike Geertz's, and one somehow able to catch, in episodes of performance, profound and surprisingly emergent significance beyond the Geertzean understanding.

In Turner's situational approach, 'contexts of performance', we find foregrounded actors, who are participants from performance to performance, and well known to Turner as individuals, having their own interests and intrigue, loves and hates. With the actors, he attended to resonances, including subliminal resonances, through a whole repertoire of performances. For Geertz, the cockfight is a 'bloody drama of hatred, cruelty, violence and death', but it is a sacrifice without reference to the resonances or intertextual bits from other sacrifices and rites (Geertz 1975: 421).

If Turner's sociological roots were at first Durkheimian, in regarding 'social facts as things', he came to hold, towards the end of his life, that they

> gave little understanding of the motives and characters of the actors in these purpose-saturated, emotional, and 'meaningful' events [of the social drama]. I [Turner] gradually gravitated, with temporary pauses to study symbolic processes, theories of symbolic interaction, the views of sociological phenomenologists, and French structuralists and 'deconstructionists', towards the stance delineated by the great German social thinker ... William Dilthey. (1982a: 12)

Nevertheless, throughout this gradual gravitating or eclecticism, Turner held fast to a dominant idea of form, the four sequences in a linear process of conflict and crisis which he called the social drama; his unpacking of the process in successive, comparative studies foregrounded different facets, eventually including narrative and reflexivity, regeneration and generative emergence, but the form itself, he insisted, was universal.

Turner's thought embraced a paradox. He believed strongly that in the social drama there was a passage to a creative moment, the moment of liminality that took one somehow beyond the reach of society, even beyond thought, at least temporarily and with uncaptured, liberating potential. But he was also sure that the passage was highly regular in many, perhaps most societies. It was a paradox that he wrestled with endlessly: the formless essential in form, the thinking beyond thought.

Turner's personal fable and a moment of truth

Having followed Turner's dissemination of some of his key ideas, their wider reception, and his straddling of British and American anthropology, I want to try to make sense of a more problematic moment. It is the troublesome moment in Turner's personal voyage during which his personal fable, along with his close friendship with Gluckman, was called into question. This moment came in the late 1960s and early 1970s, at a time when Gluckman felt under attack, needing to defend himself, his old RLI colleagues and, more broadly, the autonomy of British social anthropology as a discipline in the colonial era. The context is critical, and I describe it very briefly before I unpack more of Turner's voyage story and his personal fable about his heroic emancipation from the intellectual and other shackles of his past, before becoming the enlightened born-again man in America.

Looking back on this period in the late 1960s and early 1970s, Gluckman argued:

> Many younger anthropologists, and indeed some of their elders, nowadays allege that the colonial situation dominated the work and theories of social anthropologists until, in the aftermath of the Second World War, most of the independent territories of Africa and Asia, and some in Oceania, were liberated. These allegations have not been supported by detailed analyses in the work of specific anthropologists. (1975: 21)

As Gluckman's biographer Robert Gordon documents, he was deeply offended and felt he had been slandered and the RLI's reputation badly damaged when such allegations were falsely made by Bob Scholte, in particular (Gordon 2018: 392–3). Gluckman was embattled in defence against this when he met Turner at a 1974 Wenner-Gren conference in Austria, and promised to reread and comment on Turner's *The Ritual Process*.

The year before Turner had written to express his strong support for Gluckman's defence of anthropology against 'smug philistines':

> In the course of our long (it seems that way!) variegated, and not always seeing eye-to-eye lives, we have joined forces over some issues

(not always theoretical – take the resistance to S. African Federation, for example) and split over others (possibly 'religious', though I think Western semantics are a fallacious obstacle here). But as against what in Scotland is called 'the dirt of gentry', in their anthropological manifestation or avatar, I 'believe' (pace Needham) we continue to stand shoulder to shoulder. The anthropology that we did together at Manchester and continue to do (in our different ways) is essentially a humanistic anthropology. It is not a 'class' or 'snob' anthropology. Both of us, in a weird way are interested only, in the end, in establishing the *facts*, 'the chiels that winna ding' and in a mode of (not unsophisticated) wonder, trying to figure out what they *mean* with our 'children' in mind, the progeny we teach. We may be corrupted with a hundred personal sins, but we have our own curious code of honour (like Samurai of the mind). We do not 'sell out' to those who have never lived, as we have, with the actual simple (and 'damnes') of the earth. We try to stay true to what actually happened to us. In this way, my faith is that our theory, such as it is, may be better than we know. (VT to MG, 17 September 1973, GPRAI)

A moment of outspoken and painful truth followed the 1974 conference in the exchange of letters about *The Ritual Process* between Gluckman and Turner. It was, primarily, about Turner's claim he had been blocked in his early interest in ritual, his contention that the RLI had a blind spot towards ritual, his discomfort with having had to busy himself with 'hard-nosed' data, and his claim about RLI policy work on labour migration and statistics, a claim by which he unintentionally seemed to support the stooges and handmaidens of the colonialism allegations. In all of these claims, Turner was elaborating what I have called his personal fable, and it was contrary to the truth as Gluckman and Mitchell knew it. Gluckman defended his supervision, in which he at first allowed Turner to try to find his own way, and then appealed to Evans-Pritchard's example as the best to follow. No one was to blame but Turner himself for his having to postpone his absorption with ritual. This runs counter to the better-known story, part of Turner's personal fable, that Gluckman simply insisted, somewhat dogmatically, that Turner had to follow a conventional model and address his dissertation analysis first to the social system, to social structure and social process (cf. Engelke 2000: 846; 2004: 24).

One comic, perhaps ironic, touch in the letters is the reversal of stances. Gluckman recalled his early argument on the autonomy of ritual, and being chided by Turner for that as the stance of a bourgeois idealist. Now Turner himself took pride in advocating his discovery of the same stance, contrary to the conventional wisdom of his elders and teachers.

Gluckman began the exchange on 17 September 1974. I quote his letter at length for its revealing mixture of frankness and great affection:

My Dear Vic,

As I said I would do, I have begun working through THE RITUAL PROCESS again to check what I said in my essay [at the Wenner-Gren conference] ... I have again been thrilled by the depth of your analysis of symbolism – but again shaken by your pages 5 to 6 about the RLI. I had meant to speak to you about this at the Schloss [the Wenner-Gren castle], but my annoyance was swamped in the pleasure of meeting you again. I think what you say there is just not true – and I am writing to say so, because if I accept the blandishments of some friends and publish a book on my view of the recent history of social anthropology to correct the growing body of myths, I shall have to deal with your statement.

If anything blocked your studying ritual it was nothing in the RLI directorship or atmosphere, but in yourself. You were a material dialectician – still are in many ways! Mary [Gluckman] is my witness to an argument I had with you and Peter Worsley (who has also spoken of this) at my home, before you went to the field. Peter and you were arguing that ritual and religion were superstructures; and almost regarding me as a bourgeois idealist, because I said they had their own autonomy, independently of any influence from technology, economy, etc.

Clyde had already published – at least in mss – stuff on Yao belief and ritual, as had Elizabeth on Tonga. When you came back from the field my rituals of rebellion was in preparation, and I taught you on Wiko circumcision ceremonies. What is true, is that when you returned to Manchester to do your thesis, you stopped on the way in Cape Town, where Monica was working on Nyakusa ritual, and you came here determined to write on ritual.

You were constantly getting blocked – and I told you the story of how EP [Evans-Pritchard] complained to me that because he was working on Nuer religion, a lot of students wanted to do so; but he felt he could write on religion and its social setting because he had published Nuer ecology, polity and domestic relations as well as many articles. I urged you therefore to work out Ndembu social organisation first – and when you agreed to this, the result was SCHISM AND CONTINUITY.

Many people see only the social dramas, but do not see that the first 80 pages are crucial to the analysis of these – and I consider crucial to your later work on ritual symbols. It is true that you made a great breakthrough on the analysis of symbols; I think far and away the greatest breakthrough yet, and that came out of your own creativity in combination with the kind of society you studied (at one time you said – perhaps flatteringly – that it was helped by work on the multivocality of legal terms and also the work I did, following Fortes and EP and Bateson – on conflict and ritual). Be that as it may, if I did not encourage you to jump into the study of ritual, it was only for your thesis; and I know because I had to get a renewal of your fellowship after your trying to jump into writing on ritual cost you a year.

As for your citing [in *The Ritual Process*] only the papers published in the RLI, what has that to do with the RLI itself? Godfrey Wilson published four good papers on subjects he was interested in plus the small THE STUDY OF AFRICAN SOCIETY which as you quote stresses the importance of studying ritual. And you would not question, I take it, that he contributed with field data to Monica's later work on ritual, would you?

I published on economy, law and land tenure – but the Lozi had no rituals to speak of (I had only enough for a paper and a lecture on mask dancers you heard, from my view of Wiko lodges, because I could not speak their language. But my first three articles from my thesis, were on rituals.) Ian Cunnison published an RLIP on ideas of history with stuff on ritual; John Barnes one on changing marriage, with accounts of ritual; you published on Chihamba ritual. Colson, van Velsen, Watson: none of them wrote for the RLI papers. But they did deal with rituals in essays and books. Also you were in a way lucky: Clyde has masses on ritual and beliefs; he moved from the Yao to the Copperbelt. In the time given you to study one society, Watson studied two. Cunnison left the Luapula to work on the Humr.

So you had a long spell in the field and in the study on the Ndembu against some of the others. You probably do have a temperamental ability to do this kind of study that I at least, and perhaps others, lack. That is something to be grateful for. As Meyer has to be grateful for a similar gift. It is no reason to concoct a thesis – at least implicit – that you were discouraged from studying rituals. The fault, dear Victor, lay not in your stars, but in your self.

I must say frankly that it was both unfair and ungrateful to myself, Elizabeth, and Clyde, as your teachers, for you to publish such a statement, as well as not the truth. The way it is phrased, with its reference to supplying knowledge, can only feed the Scholtes. And if I may say so it was also unfair to the Trustees of the Institute, who allowed you to work in perfect freedom as your teachers did: no-one tried to control what you did or thought or published, indeed you were encouraged to be an individual. Remember too you went into the field after working with Elizabeth and me through Mitchell's manuscript: you started from where he had worked years to get – so that when your first letter arrived after six weeks work, and I showed it to Worsley, he said: 'Finished his fieldwork I see.' I consider you owe us an apology.

Best regards to the family and you. (MG to VT, 17 September 1974, GPRAI)

Turner responded:

I grieved that almost all my words and works seem to rouse your ire these days. When I see a letter from Manchester I flinch from opening it, for I like rebukes and reproaches as much as the next man. I'm particularly sad and caught with my defences down in view of our (I thought) warm reunion at Burg Wartenstein [attending the Wenner-Gren Conference on Secular Ritual]. If I offended, forgive me. I assure you I intended nothing personal, *ad hominem*, in *The Ritual Process* when I pointed out (with my inveterate artlessness) that the RLI had put its official institutional imprimatur on few ritual studies. [F]ilial piety and personal friendship would prevent [me] from getting involved in one of those unedifying squabbles between former gurus and chelas of senior and junior colleagues that so disfigure anthropological journals. (VT to MG, 26 September 1974, GPRAI, cited in Gordon 2018: 394)

Writing again to Turner on 3 October 1974, Gluckman took great care to express his warmth and admiration for Turner himself and for his work. Gluckman's expressed intent was to be understood to criticize not the man or the work in general but specific issues. He offered this understanding while reassuring Turner, who had become fearful that their enduring bond might be at risk:

My dear Vic,
Your letter wrung my heart and my liver <as Bantu say [in Gluckman's handwriting]>, and I am horrified to think that you may open

this letter with trepidation. So let me begin by saying that my feelings for you are as warm, affectionate, and admiring as ever; you must never doubt that. Our reunion at the castle was in the fullest sense a happy reunion. As you yourself said, there is too much common feeling, from both celebration and suffering, between us, for it ever to be changed – and the feeling persists in the present, and will in the future. So let me assure that I would never have written to you as I did, save to someone whom I regard as one of my closest friends. (MG to VT, 3 October 1974, GPRAI)

In the rest of the letter, Gluckman recalled his expressed doubts about parts of Turner's *Ritual Process*, went further on the attack, reopened an old, even cherished argument going back to Turner's PhD thesis, and defended his stance as a teacher:

please remember that I always told my pupils that I would not regard criticism as an attack on me, the essential me – I would take it as an attack on my argument ... I have always expected my analyses to be criticised as severely as people can; that way one learns. And it was in that spirit that I felt I had at the schloss [the castle], and again in a letter, to write to you about my doubts ... In that spirit, I also wrote to you, if you think you are right, go ahead, whatever I or anyone else may say. Just what I told you about a part of your thesis I did not agree with, and also Meyer [Fortes, the external examiner expressed this criticism]. (MG to VT, 3 October 1974, GPRAI).

Here I want to highlight Gluckman's determination to be frank in criticism but to recognize that Turner, like any other of Gluckman's students, could be expected to stand his ground if he thought he was right. Finding himself under attack and misrepresented, Gluckman's response, characteristically, was to fight hard, though usually in public rather than privately, as in the correspondence with his dear friend. But Gluckman tried to put the record straight. His private fight was immediately with an earlier letter by Turner, which was something of a troubled personal history, with criticisms of the RLI and its priorities – too much on 'hard-nosed data', too little on ritual and symbolism:

I think you are wrong in your present letter when you suggest that the RLI policy was in any way (I quote you) 'undoubtedly influenced if not directed by the N.R. [Northern Rhodesia] Govt's feeling that the RLI should concern itself with "hard-nosed", measurable data and such topics as labour migration ... Etc.' That policy was laid down on theoretical grounds by Godfrey Wilson – he arrived in 1938, and by the time I got there in 1939 he was already discussing with me (Monica also, of course) the outlines of their book on THE ANALY-SIS OF SOCIAL CHANGE. And my choice of field, the Barotse, was made by me, with EP [Evans-Pritchard] and [Meyer] Fortes, purely on ethnographic grounds – it happened to be also one [?] picked by Godfrey for me. My research plan, in which you became involved, was based on trying to reconcile two different sets of variables: (1) filling in the ethnographic map; and (2) getting a variety of situations of adaptation to modern conditions. Did you think, after my work in Zululand, I was likely to change Godfrey's policy away from modern conditions? and do you believe theoretically, that it was impossible to overlook them in modern field studies? – obviously not, since you stress so much Sandombu's role as capitao, etc. So it was not the NRG which directed that we study hard-nosed facts and problems like labour migration, but the conditions in which we worked; and to have neglected them would have made our work vacuous...

Gluckman balanced his rehearsal of his specific criticism with general praise, the highest:

Now for the general admiration I have of your work. I will insist that your work on ritual and ritual symbols is outstandingly the most penetrating and original and path-breaking ever done. That as I said in my letter remains my impression from re-reading *The Ritual Process*...

I have already said that your ability to analyse social drama in SCHISM AND CONTINUITY depends on the initial 80-pages of analysis of hard-nosed data ... you and others benefitted from the training in collecting hard-nosed data ... No Director tried to control – so far as I know tried to control – what anyone did...

That means that subject to informal group pressures among ourselves, and the influence of teaching and technical methods developed together, on certain problems, everyone wrote about what he liked.

Is not law as important as ritual, if one is to understand people? And politics? You happen to have hit a ritually rich society (I know this from the Wiko). You happen not to have studied another society so that you have written the equivalent of 3½ books on the Ndembu – that makes a difference.

What I feel is unfair is that you say your teachers and RLI policy excluded the study of ritual. I have listed the work on /change/ [handwritten] [you] yourself drew [on], and of which you knew when you started.

Let me repeat, it is because of our friendship I write about this matter; I have never written privately to any one else who produced this /popular?/ [handwritten] rubbish about the RLI serving Government that goes round...

Please, dear Vic, do not think all this affects my feelings. Disagreements about history are inevitable: remember Sir Walter Raleigh tearing up his history of the world after he had seen different accounts of a riot in the prison yard. And I thought your history inaccurate; and I felt close enough to you to say so. As for the theoretical problems, I must out of admiration and respect for your brain and your work, and out of friendship and indeed love, warn you of my doubts. You are free to say I am wrong; I have often enough been wrong. (MG to VT, 3 October 1974, GPRAI).

In retelling the RLI history, Gluckman defended his own role as RLI director and the autonomy of RLI research. In accordance with that, and alert to the new, modern conditions in which they worked, the RLI researchers made methodological innovations,[17] some among which were quantitative methods, developed primarily by Clyde Mitchell as a statistician and also by John Barnes as a mathematician, along with Elizabeth Colson and Max Marwick. Anthropologists, not government, determined RLI policy, on the basis of their theoretical, ethnographic and sociological considerations. What is more, RLI fellows were free to pursue interests of their own choice, to fit the ethnographic riches. Gluckman strongly rejected the idea that he or any other RLI director dominated and imposed their will to control research interests. He insisted that it was unfair for Turner to say that his teachers and RLI policy excluded the study of ritual.

Having had his critical say, Gluckman reassured Turner, and thanked him for sharing his remembered experience of becoming personally transformed by being initiated among Ndembu. Finally, Gluckman expressed his respect – he too must be told when wrong, and he has often enough been wrong. Turner expressed his relief and, indeed joy:

It's quite clear that, as Ndembu say, 'Our livers are white towards one another'. This is a great joy to me, for you know how I prize our friendship – strongly reanimated on that magic mountain in Austria! (VT to MG, 17 November 1974, GPRAI)

Restless celebrity, personal fable

Celebrity for celebrity's sake, the mere making of fame, is not the most important thing for our purposes, of course. Turner himself would have us see a social process and from an insider's point of view. His huge efforts in itinerant communication were, in good measure, for fun and sociability with colleagues, mixing business with pleasure, he would claim. As Frank Manning recalled, 'If ritual was the "work of the gods" – one of his favourite phrases – scholarly sociability was analogously the "play of humans"' (Manning 1990: 173). It is perhaps not at all surprising that his restless celebrity and eclectic shifts provoked the taking of his measure, the new against the old, in gossip and correspondence among the intimates who had known him and his work throughout his striving.

In 1969, in a letter to Gluckman regarding the succession to Evans-Pritchard's chair in social anthropology at Oxford, Meyer Fortes gave this opinion about Turner as a potential candidate (he eventually refused to be considered):

> I agree with the remark in your letter to the V–C [Vice-Chancellor] that his work has shown signs of wooliness, latterly; but on looking again, as I have done in the past couple of days at this later work, I came to the conclusion that it is due to the kind of audience he addresses himself in America. He has not yet, it seems to me, fully succumbed to the seduction of the hero worship he is reported to enjoy ... However, there was first rate quality in his work until recently and there still is superb ethnography in what he writes; but it is the urge to be in the latest fashion and to wander into St. Francis and Martin Buber that bothers me, most of all. I should wish to be assured that he would take the job of organising, running and consolidating the Oxford Institute seriously. For remember that ever since he left Manchester he has been relatively free from administrative or even serious undergraduate teaching responsibility. (MF to MG, 1 November 1969, GPRAI)

After the 1974 Wenner-Gren seminar in Austria on 'Secular Ritual', Gluckman wrote to one of the conveners, Sally Moore:

> I must say that I was very saddened at the seminar to realise how much he [Turner] had deteriorated from our point of view. I think Elizabeth [Colson] is right – he is producing a kind of Dylan Thomas

flow of ideas – but it is not good poetry which at least Dylan wrote. They are just a string of association, with no firmness. With reference to what I said above about our seminar, he really has obviously not been criticised in the USA enough; what he used to say was very good indeed and there are germs of ideas in what he now says (though not in the last business about liminoid) ... His students have treated him with adulation instead of admiration and respect – respect including severe scrutiny of ideas. (MG to SM, 17 September 1974, GPRAI)

A 'maverick', an 'iconoclast', '*magister ludi*', 'a misfit and contrarian', or so it eventually appealed to Turner's fun-loving side to be labelled, for his personal fable. Attracted as he was by the liberating promises of the New World, particularly in the America of the 1960s, it was a changing Old World, an Ndembu world with all-too-human characters that he held closest. Its superabundance of symbols and vernacular Lunda idioms, its trees and their many bits and pieces dominated his anthropology, and to it he repeatedly reached back, not in later fieldwork but in his entranced imagination of symbols and in the re-enactment of ritual. The fascination had a peculiar, almost hypnotic drive. The more Turner was admired, particularly in America, for rebellion, for discoveries of emergent processes and marginal creativity, the more charmed he became by the siren call of his own early originality – charmed to reprint bits of his early and old work in the new, with some spin in commentary, to recite the old from his barrel chest and in his rich deep voice for fresh audiences, to replay Ndembu events, like an impresario, for theatrical performances; in brief, to parody, as the liminal playfully became the liminoid.

America did give him great opportunities to celebrate; and he made the most of one such opportunity in 1982 – he took on the role of guest curator for 'Celebration: A World of Art and Ritual' (Turner 1982b), a hugely popular and spectacular exhibition, exceeding any other in the history of the Smithsonian Institution's National Museum of Art in Washington DC. Its Turnerian richness enabled a vast audience, in the words of the secretary of the Smithsonian Institution, to 'learn something of America's celebratory heritage and experience the effervescence of communal feeling' (Ripley 1982: 6). Turner's fame as a cultural theorist, late in his career in America, put him in the forefront of his own 'school' in a sub-discipline called 'symbolic anthropology' – he called himself 'a comparative symbologist'.[18] He became a leading advocate for interdisciplinary creativity, bringing together the social sciences and the humanities.

There is, however, a noteworthy limit to Turner's exploration of the semiotics of performance. His colleagues at Chicago, led by Milton Singer and later Michael Silverstein, took the thought of Charles Peirce, the nineteenth-century philosopher of language, to be foundational; on that basis, Singer himself pioneered the analysis of cultural performance in a whole body of work (Singer 1972, 1984, 1991), influential for the very existence of 'semiotic anthropology' as a new mainstream more or less distinct from 'symbolic anthropology'. Against that mainstream emerging at Chicago, Turner seems never to have paid any attention to Peirce's thought – it may well have been unattractive, given Turner's own dialectical thought and his penchant for the moment of confused categories, be it liminal or liminoid. Even further, Turner was never drawn to revise or amend his dominant ideas of the social drama and liminality in the light of later debates in semiotic anthropology on how meaning, felt truth and communication are created in specific cultural and social contexts.

When Turner did seek in his later work to go beyond his rehearsal of the social drama or Ndembu ritual, he made no in-depth study of any cultural performance; programmatic statements became his metier. His final approach to cultural performance seemed to cram together a multitude of phenomena, almost any aesthetic or stage drama, so long as something liminal or liminal-like could be detected. Recent critics of performance studies, who now recognize the need for fine analytic distinctions, have cast doubt on the utility of Turner's over-generalizing approach to cultural performance (Beeman 1993; St John 2008: 12; Shepherd 2016: 45–6).

Turner promoted his influence systematically. He redeployed a few dominant ideas, most prominently the social drama and liminality, in a wide range of studies, from Brazilian carnival to Icelandic sagas, to Thomas Becket's difficulties with Henry II, to the American political upheavals in the 1960s.[19] Across disciplines, for a broad audience, the attraction of Turner's keywords and bits of his thought, if phenomenally popular late in his lifetime, became more uncertain after his death. A tide once fashionably in his favour has now slipped away, or bubbled up, oddly, as something hollow, for popular consumption, even a posthumous caricature.

Donald Weber recalled Turner's leading role as cultural theorist in the mid-1970s and 1980s:[20]

> I recall vividly a number of ASA [American Studies Association] sessions devoted to Turner's paradigm of ritual process: bibliographies were handed out along with a glossary, provided by Turner himself, defining his keywords ... Turner emerged as perhaps the most important (if not the most important, then at least the most readily invoked) cultural theorist for a host of disciplines: indeed, his specialized vocabulary of processual analysis had found a receptive place in religious studies, performance studies – the area that engaged him at the end of his career – literary theory, and, of course, American studies. (1995: 527)

Weber went on, however, to report:

> Turner's authority for current American culture studies has markedly diminished ... A telling sign of this striking displacement may be found in the mammoth volume of state-of-the-art essays entitled *Cultural Studies* which does not include even one reference to 'Victor Turner'. (1995: 527)

For a period from the 1960s onwards, Turner's 'liminality' was timely: a keyword fit for utopian expectations that desired creative release from normal constraints – the counter-culture. By the 1990s, the times were changing. 'Liminal' was displaced by 'border', and 'border theory' was branded an umbrella for passionate arguments over contested difference, above all ethnic, racial and gender difference, and for critiques in identity politics, in the politics of culture, and in the challenges Faye Harrison originally raised under 'decolonization' (1991; see my Chapter 9).

Soon after Turner's death in 1983, critique of his dominant ideas became sharper. The tide turned against the utopian, seemingly apolitical strands in his thought, particularly his notion of *communitas*, expressed as egalitarian fellow feeling, a liberating potential in ritual performance. Without the master's voice, his enduring work echoed all too mutely. And yet there has been a curious appropriation of his keywords, perhaps a problematic transfiguration of Turner himself as a visionary of extraordinary, liberating, even mystical experience.

According to the anthropologist Graham St John, Turner's theme of liminality had been

> developing a life of its own as an all-purpose tool. And, appropriated by New Age ritual and theatre practitioners, counterculturalists, Catholics, ravers, and other popular music fans, liminality (and ritual generally) would break free of its academic moorings. As Bell conveys, among all the significant theorists of ritual, Turner has been adopted as 'the authority behind much American ritual invention' legitimating ritual as a universal process that authenticates changes in traditional rites or empowers people to invent new ones. (St John 2008: 15, citing Bell 1997: 263)

In the edited collection honouring the 25th anniversary of Turner's death, St John finds Turnerian thought apparently undergoing a precarious revival in twenty-first-century 'performance studies' (St John 2008: 15).

Turner was a very conscious performer, a gifted lecturer, and later in life, the maestro for histrionic re-enactments of Ndembu rituals. The anthropologist Vincent Crapanzano, in a review of Turner's last book, *From Ritual to Theater* (1982), satirized Turner's collaboration with Richard Schechner and his laboratory, Performing Garage:

> It may be that a few months at the Performing Garage can turn any professor into a *porte-parole* for bohemia but Turner often had difficulty distinguishing the event from its gloss, its ideology, its exegesis. In a way, he was trapped in the fantasies of his own Anglo-American culture, with its modernist emphasis, its faith in the novel and the new, its celebration of inventiveness. He ignored the fact that the most subversive genres will still – in their very subversion – constitute the values they are trying to subvert. (Crapanzano 1984: 43)

Speaking for himself about Schechner's influence, and in a foreword to Schechner's commentary on his experimental practice in performance, Turner remarked, 'I learned from him that all performance is "restored behavior" that the fire of meaning breaks out from rubbing together the hard and soft firesticks of the past (usually embodied in traditional images, forms and meanings) and present of social and individual experience' (Turner 1985a: xi).

Turner had two funerals, one a requiem Mass; but the second, described by his wife Edie and son Frederick, was the performance everyone felt he intended:

> There was another funeral at home afterwards, with Vic's family, students, and anthropological and theatrical friends, re-enacting a full-scale Ndembu funeral for a tribal chief. All of this was done properly according to Vic's own field notes, with drums, masked dancers, ritual, and large quantities of beer and spirits. In that second funeral, we all felt Vic's spirit, dancing and singing among us as he would have done in life. (E. Turner and F. Turner 1985: 16)

In the next chapter, I will re-analyse Turner's classic study of *Chihamba* and criticize his concept of liminality in order the better to disclose and understand the creative force of his social and symbolic imagination, his ethnography and its living legacy.

Notes

1 For the best brief introduction to Turner's life and works, see Fardon 2004.
2 Robert Thornton, who was Turner's student at Chicago, recalls more dramatic and heroically staged sessions in the alternative classroom. With his students at his feet on a thick white rug, Turner would sit in a large, wing-backed chair in a room otherwise cleared of furniture. When studying pilgrimage, he would read from work in progress; and in a rare departure for Chicago, critical debate or heated discussion was rare (Thornton, personal communication, May 2018).
3 By rearing, Turner might have meant his undergraduate course for the BA at University College, London, where he studied with A. R. Radcliffe-Brown, Meyer Fortes, Raymond Firth and Edmund Leach, among others.
4 This dialogue ran through arguments in many of my articles and books on ritual and religion.
5 Gluckman made extensive notes on the French edition (RAI, n.d., translation of Van Gennep's classification of rites), and in negotiations with publishers from 1957 for more than a decade he planned its translation, to be accompanied by his introduction (RAI 25 February 1957 to Douglas West; December 1966 to James Cochrane). He never fulfilled this plan, but he kept the negotiations going until the 1970s, with

the intention of a new translation after one was published by Monika
Vizadom and Gabrielle Caffe in 1960.

6 Turner studied Fortes's ethnography closely, read it during his Ndembu
   fieldwork, responded to it in his PhD viva when Fortes was his external
   examiner, and enjoyed restating it to exemplify his own dominant ideas,
   such as *communitas* (Turner 1969: 113, 117, 121). In *The Ritual Process*,
   he explicitly addressed Fortes's argument on 'Ritual and Office' (1962)
   in Gluckman's collection, and objected to Fortes's reduction of the
   transition rites to 'giving a general stamp of legitimacy to a society's
   structural positions'. Instead, in his view the rite is 'giving recognition
   to an essential and generic human bond, without which there can be
   no society' (1969: 97). We are confronted by Turner's involvement in
   debate by assertion and counter-assertion, but it is clearly proceeding
   within an established tradition of social anthropology.

7 Victor and Edith Turner's reading during the Ndembu fieldwork of
   The Interpretation of Dreams was almost an epiphany, for ideas of multivocality and polysemy.

8 For the current salience of this exploration, see Svasek and Meyer 2016.

9 Turner himself began attending the Roman Catholic Mass in 1957
   (Engelke 2004: 26). For a detailed account of his and his wife Edith's
   involvement in the Church and its controversies, see Larsen 2014:
   ch. 5.

10 A reference to William Watson's notion of the spiralist, who gains
   upward mobility as a result of the efforts that others make to remove
   from one place to another a self-interested, troublesome manager or
   worker.

11 I then became Gluckman's supervisee.

12 For brief overviews of Turner's successive shifts in his redefinition of
   his dominant ideas of social drama and liminality, see Jules-Rosette
   1994; Shepherd 2016: 43–6.

13 See below on Gluckman's recall of Turner's blockage about ritual
   for his thesis and on the moment of truth between Gluckman and
   Turner.

14 Turner explicitly acknowledged his debt to *Custom and Conflict*, and its
   theory of a social system as 'a field of tension, full of ambivalence, of
   co-operation and contrasting struggle' (Gluckman 1956a: 21, cited in
   Turner 1957: xxii).

15 Geertz made no reference to seminal work on ritual drama by the
   American anthropologist Paul Radin (1957: 289–306). Radin stressed
   the importance of a plot and *dramatis personae*, but also found a variable
   connection to the re-enactment of a myth (1957: 293). Perhaps Turner
   would have found a strong resemblance between his 'ritual man' and
   Radin's priest-thinker and religious formulator of a fundamental principle in the cosmos. But missing from Turner's view is Radin's idea of
   the magician's role as a matter-of-fact man in tension with the priest-
   thinker and in bringing coercion and tricks, fantasy and familiar materials to the ritual drama. Perhaps also, Turner might have found some

resonances between his ideas, especially *communitas*, and, say, Harrison's ideas on merger and sinking one's own personality in ritual.

16 For a critical comparison of ritual drama in T. S. Eliot's play *Murder in the Cathedral* and Turner's use of the social drama for the decisive events in Thomas Becket's life, see Grimes 1985.

17 For the account of their methods, see Epstein 1967a.

18 Turner's colleague at Manchester, Emrys Peters, claimed that he was much influenced by the ideas of V. N. Volosinov, the Marxist philosopher of language. But to my knowledge, the earliest English translation of Volosinov's classic, *Marxism and the Philosophy of Language*, appeared in 1973, well after Turner's early work. Nevertheless, there is a convergence that is noteworthy, allowing that sign for Volosinov is symbol for Turner. The convergence can be seen in relation to Turner's view of the materialization of an idea and the polarization in a symbol, such as the *mudyi* tree, between the material (the mother's milk-like sap of the *mudyi*), and the ideological, the values of matriliny. For propositions on the sign as event in interaction with other events, and on ideology, affect and the materiality of the sign, see Volosinov 1989: chs 1 and 2; and in particular on 'the dialectical refraction of existence in the sign' (perhaps polarization in Turner's concept), see Volosinov 1989: 21. It is precisely where Turner's thought converges with that of Volosinov and Marxism that his approach to symbolism diverges from that of Freud and turns to ideology.

19 For a close examination of the shifts in Turner's approach, from the social drama presented in *Schism and Continuity* as a specific example in a case study to a 'universal processual form', see Jules-Rosette 1994.

20 Donald Weber is a professor of English and American studies.

9

The re-analysis of *Chihamba,*
the White Spirit

procreation depends on the duality of the two sexes, involving per-
petual strife, with only periodically intervening reconciliations.
(Nietzsche 1967: 33)

Victor Turner's *Chihamba, the White Spirit* (1975) is a much-cited
yet little-read ethnographic classic.[1] Its reception as a controversial
masterpiece about a ritual drama concerned with fertility and reproduction has largely neglected what distinguishes it, among all Turner's works, and makes it still very much an open text, fruitful for
re-analysis. Distinctively above all, *Chihamba* is a perspectival work,
one in which the author shifts his stance, more or less in succession,
for different parts of the work, in the effort to comprehend complexities otherwise inaccessible or, at least, hard to discern and
analyse. Of these stances, the four I find outstanding differ in their
utility for the benefit of Turner's understanding, and consequently
our own, as my re-analysis of each stance will show.

But why re-analyse *Chihamba* in depth? Even more generally,
why re-analyse the ethnography of the past,[2] especially if the ethnographer, apparently, is no longer among that select company in
which Richard Fardon places Mary Douglas, who 'uniquely among
her contemporaries, has become a factor in the discipline's wider
relevance' (2018: 26)? Here my aims are critical for ethnography
itself, rather than for the precious reputation of the ethnographer.

Quite simply, in following after Gluckman in a well-known
Manchester School tradition of re-analysis (Gordon 2018: 366), my
aim is to demonstrate that thoroughgoing, fine-grained re-analysis,
like comparison, must not be neglected if ethnography is to thrive in
knowledge that is cumulative. The more fine-grained the account, as

is Turner's, the more likely it is that details become scattered here and there in the ethnographer's own analysis, or merely recorded as an aside, perhaps in an obsession with the minutiae of the actual details. Hence I aim at integrated richness for the sake of the coherently fine-grained and theoretically informed literacy of future ethnographers. In a new generation, many anthropologists have little or no knowledge of classic twentieth-century ethnographies. Even further, my aim is to recover for fresh reading *Chihamba* as a classic whose theoretical value is all the more considerable seen in the light of current debate, regarding for example anthropology, theology and an anthropologist's own turn to religion. How did Turner's conversion to being a Catholic and an interpreter of Ndembu thought according to the Thomist theology of 'the primary act-of-being' skew his classic? Is it possible to amend that, and if so, how?

As is well known, for Turner *Chihamba* represented *the* ritual drama. Going beyond that, my aim is open out the interest in distinct genres of ritual drama, at the least tragedy and comedy. I will argue that Turner's approach mistakenly scripts a heroic tragedy around one leading character, the spirit known as *Kavula*, and above all, a perplexing moment, his beheading. Against that, my approach finds a comedy, from a male-biased perspective and with male body humour, in which a heroine is restored to well-being, beyond her obstacles, but still as a comic figure of fun, even derision.

Furthermore, I want to extend the theoretical value of *Chihamba* to arguments about ethical personhood, performance and gender. How does the course of the whole ritual turn subjection into a process of 'subjectivation' (see Faubion 2015: 4; Laidlaw 2014a: 101; Werbner 2017: 81), a process in which 'the self is incited or invited to become a moral subject' (Das 2015: 135) – here the caring person respectful of the dead? How does comic, playful sexuality arise from moment to moment in the ritual drama, and how, more or less, effectively from a male bias?

It hardly needs saying that a hallmark of so much of Turner's work is processual analysis. But Turner's very brilliance in semiotics, elaborated in a complicated framework of 'symbology' throughout the second chapter of *Chihamba*, left his classic almost blind to processual form. Barely mentioned is Van Gennep's familiar three-phase model.[3] Turner's ritual drama, unlike his social drama, surprisingly, has no model of phases, no culturally perceived or mimed course of transformations, no whole process comparatively conceptualized.[4] My aim is to take up the familiar three-phase model, while reconsidering conventional ideas of liminality by interrogating the transformative move and its significant reworking in the middle phase.

Pursuing this aim, I will disclose a course of ontological transformation, specifically in the exorcism of an aggrieved spirit that possesses her victim, the principal sufferer in the ritual. I will argue for transformations in *Chihamba* from adorcism, in Luc de Huesch's term for the accommodation of a spirit in a possessed person (1962), to liminal subjection, to exorcism, ending in sexy good humour. I will carry forward my early approach to 'the synergetics of ritual', 'how people use substances to modify their experience' and how 'metonymic transformations operate together and constitute some movement in the ritual, such as a modification in the moral condition or other state of being of a person or group' (Werbner 1989: 116).

This approach now converges with a turn in ethnographic analysis to consider substances as constitutive of persons and to theorize the importance of partibility for the composing and decomposing of persons as dividuals or partible persons (Strathern 1988: 122; 2018; Werbner 1996b, 2011a, 2011b; Busby 1997; Mosko 2010, 2015; Bialecki and Daswani 2015). But does such partibility have, so to speak, an 'author', a figure such as the magician, who has an imposing bent, recognizable in actual performance for the directed transformations of persons by means of substances? In much of the literature, 'No' seems to be the answer: partibility is held to be an emergent phenomenon, in accord with Strathern's original conceptualization of dividuality or partible personhood as seen in the Melanesian view (Strathern 1988: 324).

Against that, my re-analysis of *Chihamba* discloses a contrast. It shows how the men who are the Ndembu magicians direct the making of partible personhood in masculine terms, and in a process of decomposing and composing persons with a show of male dominance. In the ritual the creative fashioning of dividuality is according to an interested gender bias.[5] As dividuals themselves,[6] alongside priests, magicians, who perform tricks and other magical acts, share and distribute substances from within and outside themselves, undergo a change in being, and are thereby invested with power and dignity: they serve for the afflicted, who are yet to be substantially dividuated.

Finally, foregrounding the magician and his tricks and transformative substantiations enables us to re-envisage a creative figure
claimed by Turner to be a breakthrough in ethnographic discovery:
his discovery of 'the ritual man'. This is, for Turner, a universal yet
local figure. In his universal aspect, the ritual man is preoccupied
'in all places and ages' with that problem and dependence upon
a primal entity or 'primary act-of-being'. In his local aspect, his
problem was the specific expression 'of what cannot be thought of'
(Turner 1975: 187). But in both aspects, the ritual man appears singular, apart from a duo or any alternative, in particular the magician.

I want to shift the focus from the singular figure to a duo, while
interrogating, along with Robin Horton, the utility of the figure
as put by Turner. Horton questions the relation between *Kavula*,
a spirit, and the supreme being *Nzambi*. If ritual man is preoccupied with a primal entity or 'primary act-of-being', how is it that,
important as the supreme being is in Ndembu thought, apparently
as an otiose being, there is little or no preoccupation with the
supreme being in most if not all the Ndembu ritual in Turner's
works? 'Now if *Kavula* really is an attempt to represent pure act-
of-being, the primal entity that underlies and supports all things in
the world', asks Horton, 'why do Ndembu not identify him with
Nzambi or at least treat him as the latter's special manifestation?'
(Horton 1984: 92).

Of course, at the heart of the matter, for the argument about
ritual man, is the problem of Ndembu knowledge beyond words.
It was perceived by Ndembu themselves and expressed in a 'profound symbol' such as *Kavula*, yet 'impossible to catch … in any
of the terms or definitions Ndembu employ' (Turner 1975: 179).
This, Turner felt, raised a perplexing challenge for us in the study
of ritual. 'What are *we* to make of the character of *Kavula*?' (1975:
179, my italics). But whatever *we* might make of *Kavula*, how actually did Ndembu, in particular Turner's key informant, the magician
Muchona, take the question to be answered? Muchona's telling
answer is, '*Kavula* is the grandfather of all the people' (1975: 75).

This answer is in relational thought. It is not about one being
as he is alone or in isolation, but as related to others; his character
is known in his relationships involving a partner, the ancestress of
his descendants, and his children and grandchildren. Accordingly,
much of the ritual has to do with dealing with and propitiating an

afflicting ancestress; not dealing with her alone but also with the hard-to-get, even tricky and mischievous backing *Kavula* gives when he himself is pleased, despite his grandfatherly capacity for being cantankerous. To ask about *Kavula*, at least from an Ndembu viewpoint, is to ask above all about a *duo*, a pair of interrelated beings. The question of one alone is too difficult for Ndembu simply because it makes no sense in isolation, not because *Kavula* is many disparate things at once, 'an ambiguous and self-contradictory being who both conceals and reveals himself' (Turner 1975: 179). In the gendered pair, figured in sexual imagery is light, dominant and brilliant, like external lightning, striking with a big bang, the celestial male *Kavula* penetrating from above; the afflicting ancestress, grounded below, subordinate and dark, seems a troublesome, restless figure, like a rat scurrying on leaves in the wild with a soft sound, then a stealthy burrower, able wilfully to contain, to open or close her hole.

Here it is not Ndembu ethnography but scholastic philosophy that drives Turner's questions and arguments away from the plurality of social relations, both with people and spirits, and away from the duality of a pair of spiritual beings. This unsafe straying is from Ndembu dualism, pervasive in *Chihamba*,[7] towards misleading monism in Thomist and scholastic philosophy devoted to 'the essence' and 'the act-of-being'.[8]

Turner published no direct answer to Horton. But we may find a hint of a partial answer in *Lunda Rites and Ceremonies* (1953). This is Turner's earliest report, including his preliminary description of *Chihamba* after his first year of fieldwork. It shows the ethnographer already immersed in a 'vast and complicated system of ceremonial practices' (1953: 336). Found at the end of the description, and not reported in *Chihamba*, is the following last moment with a formulaic exchange between *Kavula* and 'the patient' in the 'curative ritual'. *Kavula* speaks to him throatily, asking him his business. '"I am very sick". "Good! *Nzambi* (the High God) helped you to me. Now go away. You are better. Don't forget to wash in the medicines I gave you every day"' (Turner 1953: 388). This formula hints at least at an implicit understanding among Ndembu: that *Kavula* acts for the High God *Nzambi* as his messenger whose agency the High God enables. Nevertheless, if there is a ritual man preoccupied in *Chihamba*, he seems too preoccupied with the messenger *Kavula* to have much to say or do about any representation of a 'primary act-of-being'. Turner's ritual man is a captive of Thomist theology, in need of liberating in a relation with the magician.

For that freedom, I want to turn to my first teacher on anthropology and ritual drama, Paul Radin (1957: 289–306).[9] Where Turner saw 'ritual man' in his essentialist dependence, Radin had the idea of 'the priest-thinker' who was the religious formulator of fundamental principles in the cosmos. But discovering a duo, in which the magician has a counterpart, Radin saw the magician's role in bringing coercion and tricks, fantasy and oddly familiar materials to the ritual drama; in Radin's view, the magician appears to be a matter-of-fact man[10] in tension with the priest-thinker. My aim in several parts of this re-analysis is to appreciate, in a comic ritual drama, cosmic understanding, so to speak the work of a 'ritual man' (not someone bothered in the main by a supreme being), and its casting in magic, the work of an artful and playful performer in ritual passages with transformative tricks and familiar materials.

The context of reception: scholarly tradition and authorial departure

Turner's *Chihamba* became highly controversial: sharply criticised by Robin Horton (1984: 92), much admired by Matthew Engelke (2004), Edith Turner (Engelke 2004: 850) and Timothy Larsen (2014),[11] and valiantly defended by Mary Douglas, as being about a joke rite (1968: 375).[12] In America, Clifford Geertz (1973) welcomed Turner's drama analogy. In accord with a strong tradition in social anthropology, Turner came to argue, in his *Drums of Affliction* (1968), that what ritual does is

> *dramatically* to represent the rights, obligations, and cultural context of a social status. This notion of 'drama' is crucial to the understanding of ritual. Both in its plot and its symbolism, a ritual is an epitome of the wider and spontaneous social process in which it is embodied and which ideally it controls. (Turner 1968: 273–4)

In *The Drums of Affliction*, argues Matthew Engelke, Turner 'pull[s] back from the repudiation of Durkheim, the "anti-sociological" method and the kind of "Dostoevskian mysticism" that characterizes

Chihamba' (2004: 28). On this view, contradictory or alternative tendencies prevailed in Turner's work, sometimes with one dominant or with both uneasily wrestling for abrupt shifts in stance.[13]

Engelke's thinking reflects Edith Turner's related but somewhat more critical view of two ways in which her husband wrote:

> Very hard-headed, but then sometimes – what's the word! – experiential and with an infinite respect for what was going on. Such is the way he wrote in *Chihamba, the White Spirit*. And in not a very different era he wrote *The Drums of Affliction*, in which he practically analysed away the true meaning of the Ihamba ritual. (Engelke 2000: 850)

For Edith, the more the analysis, the less the experience – the fun and the Bacchanalia – and the less the vision of the truly profound reality of ritual. There is a stark difference between Turner's later description in *Chihamba* (1962) and the earlier brief one in *Schism and Continuity* (1957), which under-represents playful sexuality, reconstructs liminal rites according to the 'traditional' narrative of a key informant, the magician Muchona, and offers exegesis before the performance, rather than reporting the actual performance as observed.

Perspectival stances

Here let me set out briefly the perspectival stances that I myself find in Turner's *Chihamba*, and then open out their importance more fully. These stances fit:

1) the documentary and textual ethnographer of the familiar kind, offering what Monica Wilson famously advocated (see Turner 1967: 13–14) – a rich record of local sources and vernacular texts, clearly in their own right, presented alongside the separate interpretations and observations of the ethnographer;
2) the situational semiotician of the kind who deploys a whole rather elaborate typology while he tracks the associations of symbols, more or less dominant and variably effective, from situation to situation;
3) the cognition comparativist of the kind who problematizes knowledge that is often not put into words or resists verbal

expression and, being hard to define, appears as paradox and enigma;

4) the transformational ontologist of the kind who regards the ritual process, from phase to phase, in terms of how persons, their states of being and experiences are dynamically constituted and reconstituted, above all by the deployment of substances, some bits or parts of the persons themselves or of others, some from organic matter, plants and animals.

It is in chapter 1 of *Chihamba* that Turner's *first stance* (documentary and textual ethnographer) is strongest. Turner meticulously gives local sources *not* from one key informant alone, such as Muchona the magician, but from various named specialists and laymen, separate from and followed by Turner's and his wife Edith's observations and interpretations.[14] Included are vernacular texts, a whole liturgy, followed by translations, lists (named rites, ritual episodes), and much exegesis on material bits in many rituals. Turner was lucky, he recognized, to have a rare educator as his influential key informant, Muchona the magician, who was eager to tell 'meanings', to say what each thing 'stands for'.[15]

As for the *second stance* (the situational semiotician): finely methodical in chapter 2, with a whole typology, Turner the semiotician disclosed that the more highly coded the ritual, the more powerful was the symbol. The coding, unlike an isolated structure, was actually incremental in situations – a recoding accumulating in and through events of performance in many rituals.[16] Here Turner's analysis foregrounded *formalism*, rather than *experience-based intuition*. Symbols were sorted according to many fine distinctions, their relative dominance,[17] their charge with affect, especially awe, their importance in categories of action.[18] The dominant symbol had senses hidden in performance, which 'fall within the province of the ontologist rather than the depth psychologist' (1975: 178), within the provinces of literature and comparative religion.[19] Accordingly, Turner aimed to comprehend 'symbolic actions which together constitute a ritual drama, with plot, role-enactment, and audience' (1975: 177).

The *third stance* (the cognition comparativist), focused on unspeakable knowledge, enigma and paradox, was positioned by Turner in relation to theory in philosophy and literary criticism.

Having himself become a Catholic, much preoccupied with the
Church's foundational teachings, Turner was attracted to Thomism,
to the legacy of thought of the medieval theologian Thomas
Aquinas about 'the essence' and 'the act-of-being'. In accordance
with this, Turner seemed to discern a single principle, profound
and essential, for Ndembu: the being they call *Kavula*, and who is
a main subject of *Chihamba*. Too rich in meaning, too provocative
in religious experience, this dominant spirit *Kavula* was not some
reflection of 'the social structure', expressing 'the ultimate unity of
Ndembu society' (1975: 181). *Kavula*'s 'being is an enigma, say,
a paradox' (1975: 179), of the one and the many, authority and
subordination, death and life. No one, no Ndembu and not even
Turner himself, could put fully into words what might be expressed
by *Kavula*, Turner held.

It was to Arthur Rimbaud's French surrealist theory of *voyance*
– the reasoned disordering of all the senses – that Turner appealed
for his cognitive stance on enigma and paradox. He argued:

> The aim appears to be, both for the poet and for Ndembu ritual man,
> to break through the habitual patterns formed by secular custom,
> rational thinking, and common sense, to a condition where the pure
> act-of-being is directly apprehended. The candidate is in a world
> where nothing follows in an expected sequence. (1975: 185)

What is remarkable, contrary to our own expectations *à la voyance*,
is that it is apart from ritual performance that the most licentious
moments burst upon *Chihamba*. On the very first night, on the
outskirts of the village, with the dark comes a popular festival.
The revelling, lavishly stoked to drunken ecstasy with endless free
beer, draws huge crowds, sometimes four hundred people, who
form their own circles, dance, court, choose partners and sneak
away to the bush for illicit sex. Jealous, their spouses often bring
the adulterous orgies to a head, by dawn, in drunken brawls. The
ecstatic intoxication could hardly be more fitting to welcome back
Kavula, the spirit who is the beer-loving grandfather of all, with
whom everyone jokes, using sexual swearing. Young revellers,
fearful and overawed by *Chihamba*, keep their distance from the
village. Their secret bush assignations are the profane realization of
Kavula's sexual intimacy in ritual, as are their brawls counterparts to
his. One ecstatic, intoxicated reality is temporarily normal for all:

not everyday reality, but life unbridled, running amok; and yet, in the village, it is instructed by priests and magicians, who defend, define and discipline their community against the very wildness which they incite, rework and transform ritually.

Contrary to the *voyance* theory, my re-analysis will disclose a sensible, coordinated, expected alternative, even at a sensuously sexual climax with hocus-pocus (perplexing for Turner, if tricky for Ndembu). Custom and common sense do make many acts appear matter-of-fact and following in expected sequences, according to organizing images and much more. Such acts remain grounded in familiar premises and axioms of sexual conduct even when the ritual licensees seem to be running amok.

Like Thomist philosophy, French surrealism is an unlikely source for illuminating Dionysian or Bacchanalian ritual drama, among Ndembu and perhaps elsewhere. Possibly Belgian surrealism, inspired by the painter René Magritte with his regard for the magical *and* everyday enigma, might be more illuminating.[20] Insofar as the magician in the Ndembu ritual drama commits to a disposition or a sensibility, we might say, after Magritte, it is that of maybe; not the neo-scholastic philosophy of the essence or the single cosmic principle, as Turner would have it, but the orientation to the possibility that what is seen is not the familiar thing it seems to be. Is it something in metamorphosis, turning into something else?[21]

For the *fourth stance* (transformational ontologist), there is a stumbling block, raised on the way by Turner himself: medicalization. Admittedly, Turner takes great care to record in fine detail and to inform his reader of the 'materialization of ideas', of the sequential use of specific ritual objects and substances and their actual or intended effects in transforming the states of being of persons, living and dead, human and spirit. But what limits his perspective is his marrying his drama analogy for ritual, awkwardly, with a medical analogy to medicines and doctors, patients and individuals. Nevertheless, Turner perceives an ontological transformation: that the therapeutic intention was to raise the sufferer of infertility or a reproductive disorder to a higher and better condition of being, free of spiritual affliction, above all, and remade whole, completely well.

For clarity, free of the medical analogy, I consider cosmetics and dividuals, priests and magicians, adepts and suppliants, including the *principal sufferers*, both of them women, one the main subject, the other her second in affliction. The Ndembu terms, translated as 'medicines', apply to 'everything that is thought to confer mystical benefit' (1975: 54).[22] In my usage of *cosmetics*, I follow Thomas Beidelman, who reminded anthropologists that, in its classical derivation from *cosmos*, cosmetics conveys 'the idea of making something orderly and therefore attractive and right' (1966: 376).

Situated performance: show-place for Ndembu, revelation for Turner

But where, according to Turner's cognitive stance, does *voyance* and revelation take place in *Chihamba*? For a moment of climax, the name of the important site, designated after a nearby tree, comes from *solola*, 'making visible' or showing. In Turner's view, 'the supreme representation of *Kavula* takes place in an *isoli*, "a place of revelation", near a *musoli*, "a revelatory tree"' (1975: 180). I call it a show-place, where magicians, who are make-believes, put on a histrionic, obviously exaggerated show, kidding the would-be adepts.

There is a high point, significantly exposing the presence of absence, after a moment when a rite requires women 'to kill' *Kavula*. A brilliant white covering is lifted to show nothing under it of the supposedly slain *Kavula*. 'He evaded definition', Turner would have us believe, 'and just when the candidates thought the mystery of his existence would be finally known by them, he became an emptiness, or something that had passed into the air' (Turner 1975: 197). But how did Turner, and thus how do we, know what they 'thought' or even what they were doing in 'killing' *Kavula*? Would it make a difference if they were play-acting at the 'kill' in sex? In fact, like Turner, we know not what the candidates thought, but what the man in charge of the whole show told Turner, perhaps in confidence, if somewhat in a boast. That man, Muchona, was, of course, a magician, up to his tricks, as befits the reputation magicians have, among Ndembu, for being liars.

Let me now pursue the ethnographic evidence in some detail, for the discussion of tricky, playful showing as against 'revelation'. Usually on the second day of *Chihamba*, away from public view, and not seen as a rite, preparation is made for the show-place. From about an hour before sunset, a magician takes charge of the show-place, setting the stage with props, including audio-visual effects gadgets, which convey sex and death. The exegesis of Muchona, who set the stage in the ritual Turner observed, admitted deception, but Muchona explained away an obvious appearance of the gadgets as tricky props by his secondary elaboration of their spiritual significance.

For the props inside the show-place, a mortar is turned upside, no longer available for pounding. Instead, it hides a razor for shaving and other bits of the procreative and productive mystery of *Chihamba*. Near this are priests' and magicians' prosthetic devices, their ball-bearing staffs. The main gadget has a frame of sticks, attached to smaller staffs and covered with a blanket, whitened with cassava meal. Hidden and protected under an arch is a flexible stick for moving the frame in sexual motion, like the belly dance or convulsive jerking until orgiastic exhaustion.

With his props in place, the magician, true to his reputation as a liar, makes his spiel. He play-acts histrionically (he demonstrated in melodramatic exaggeration for Turner) as if to instruct the candidates how to perform their roles, to greet and grovel in the presence of a great chief, the men to roll in the dirt and even bang their heads, like him; the women to crawl forward then squeeze their breasts, as if for milk. He does it all himself, play-acting with much pathos to frighten and impress candidates with the difficulty of visiting *Kavula*. For the principal, he even anticipates one rite later in the day and shaving on the last day, by bombastically miming extreme terror and going through an exaggerated pantomime of having a head cut off to show the principal 'the ghastly things that might happen to her' (Turner 1975: 103). Following the magician's example, the candidates perform also in the bush near the show-place.

The performance is informed by taken-for-granted assumptions about fertility, sex, food and ancestral affliction. Inside at the show-place, the candidates get to see what is said to be an apparition, the *mufu* of *Chihamba*, the ghost of an afflicting ancestress, materialized by the magicians' gadgets, above all the flapping white blanket over a *mortar*. With her, the candidates enjoy sensual dancing, capped by every candidate, with the women principals first, making sexual hits upon her apparition and its hidden 'head', the mortar. The rite is carried out using the priest's reproductive prosthesis, in the form of *Kavula*'s phallic staff with the seed-bearing ball.

The satisfying sexual hits, called 'kills', turn the ghostly movement deathly, in the convulsive shivers and shakes that a magician conjures, as if for ecstasy, we might say orgasm, making the ghost appear loved and adored and thus happy to haunt the living no longer. Traditionally, but not in the observed performance, the women go on to beat the exposed mortar itself with the seed-bearing ball of *Kavula*'s shaft. Having given up the ghost, the mortar yields, as if in a 'theft' from the body, handfuls of meal, shavings which are put on each initiate's head, and all are anointed with oil.

This account is subversive. It exposes a peak of enthusiasm, of understood satisfaction and fulfilment in performance with sexual objects and their familiar substances. There is sexual sensuality, not the 'disordering of the senses' *à la* Rimbaud. This exposure subverts the puzzling representation of paradox and enigma around a 'slain god', the almost neo-Frazerian comparison by which Turner draws similarities seemingly fundamental across religious traditions: first between *isoli*, the show-place and the empty tomb of Jesus, and second, between 'the disclosure of *Kavula*'s absence' and the Christian revelation of transfiguration.

Reviewing the second and liminal day's performance for Turner, his key informant Muchona dramatized, in a 'stagey' show, from the biased perspective of a conjuring magician, how much the candidates must be disoriented, mystified and deceived by their not knowing what they are actually seeing and doing. Perhaps Muchona *could* almost have been Rimbaud in Africa. It was as if even the mature women, the principals, were naive innocents, or rather dutifully playing that part. Muchona wanted Turner to accept that he knew better, but believed nevertheless in real truth, beyond mere chicanery. Even further, Muchona let Turner know that the whole performance is its subject: '*Kavula* is *Chihamba*. He is not really the lightning, that is just a name. The adepts are just deceiving the candidates at *Isoli*', the show-place (1975: 113). They *are* innocents.

Muchona's wily, male-biased exegesis made everything to be about something that Turner understood to be a shocking 'revelation': that after the 'killing', *Kavula* is *not dead*. Taking that 'revelation' at face value appealed to Turner. Further inspired by the scholastic thought of Thomism and Rimbaud's surrealist idea of *voyance*, Turner went on to gloss the action in terms of an enigma, a philosophy of the absurd, and an apprehension of 'the pure act-of-being'.

Against this, we must attend to a silence, to something missing in the telling of the key informant, with his magician's male bias. By contrast to Muchona's plain-speaking exegesis about an earlier rite of copulation by men, entirely unmistakable, with a mortar and pestle, Muchona is silent about the women's sexy acts in the show-place. Breaking that silence, I suggest that the women are given a role in the playful sexuality that has them bringing the seed-bearing balls of *Kavula* to bear on the outside, not the inside, of the blankets, where the mortar hides: getting together under blankets is a widely used expression in Central Africa for sexual intercourse. If there is a joke here, it is a joke on foolish women in their use of *Kavula's* balls, for spent sexuality. They are 'killers', the ones keeping back the fertility, until the ghost collapses, dead: the sex has got to her.

Liminality: subjection, submission and disengagement

By contrast to Turnerian liminality, apparently a phase of detach-ment or utopian liberation, indeed a rare moment to think with freedom, what prevails publicly in the liminal phase of *Chihamba* is a jokey put-down. Women are made fools of, dominated and made out to be mere *kids*, who really have no clue about a man's magic.

Turnerian liminality envisions the 'betwixt-and-between' with the liberating promise of the ludic, throwing off even the poet Blake's 'mind-forged manacles'. Against that in the ritual process, at least in *Chihamba*, what liminality forwards is domination. Mani-fest slavery is enacted with manacles. Subjugation prevails in *Chi-hamba* under the command of the magician and ritual expert in the service of a double-dealing master, the unknowable *Kavula*. Where is Turner's liminal realm, having a 'certain freedom to juggle with the factors of existence' (Turner 1967: 106)?

In the procreative rites, the men who are the magicians and priests indulge in *kidding* – and I mean by this both senses, making *kids* of captives in agonistic ordeals and *kidding* by playful teasing with them. The ordeal for the kids is attractive play for the spirits.

For the *sufferers*, above all the women who are the ritual's prin-cipals, the agonistic ordeals appear, I suggest, to proceed towards being born again by the end of *Chihamba* with a new name and a new identity, and free of a possessing spirit, the ancestress manifest as a ghost. For the *spirits*, the attractive appeals are made with playful sexuality very differently: in the village for *Kavula* and in the wild for the ancestress as ghost. There are circulating processions with whiteness – on thanksgiving supplicants and on various ritual paraphernalia. Later I give in detail the village rites first, then the ghost's in the wild, numbered in order of performance.

My criticism points beyond liminality to the related concept, *communitas*, which Turner elaborated after writing *Chihamba*, and to engage with that elaboration would be a major task in itself. For the present, it must suffice to indicate the insight on 'the dark side' of liminality, which Roy Willis perceives in his deeply felt obituary for Turner: 'As presented by Turner, it [*communitas*] often tended to have a somewhat Pollyanna-ish air, a result of his comparative neglect of the complementary destructive and terrifying aspect of liminality, the dark side of Shiva' (Willis 1984: 75). If having its joyous time of shared licence, liminality is no less dark and binding.

This liminal phase plays out an ordeal of *public* subjection to virility, magic make-believe and conciliation, under the priests' and magicians' direction. Here the gendered division of perspectives – *public* and *backstage* – among Ndembu themselves is significant. Only in public is the performance seen from a perspective of male dominance; backstage, in secluded privacy, woman disengage and find the performance *funny, even ridiculous*, from their own perspective.

First, the afflicted principals, along with a good number of captured others, undergo subjection, here submission to power that is external: the procreative force of *Kavula* is perceived to be *active* in opposition to his mate. She is now the white, female ghost who has to be put down again, to rest in the grave, and anyone under her influence must undergo an ontological transformation, with a new identity and yoked like a slave to *Kavula*.

I want to discuss here two exemplary rites in this liminal phase, and I refer to them by number (8 and 9) according to a sequence I consider more fully later. In the eighth rite, chased from the bush to the village and back to an esoteric space of the initiated, captives become slaves of the master *Kavula*, to be disciplined and subjected to violent beatings. Stripped to the waist, abased like infants held by the arm by a priest, they trot in rhythm with songs repeating *mpanda*, the yoke used by Chokwe slave traders. Struggling around a site that is *Kavula*'s marginal point, they are grilled, jeered or ululated for, according to their answers to riddles or cryptic questions about the names and nature of *Kavula*. Like newly born *kids*, they are about to take on a mature identity, with their new names. Like *kids*, they have to tell their grandfather *Kavula* that they are sick, and like *kids*, they even have to learn his correct name and their own. They must not fiddle with grass, lest they appear to be playing with themselves in childish masturbation, in 'things of sin', *yuma yinshidi*, which displease the spirit.

Next, in the ninth rite, the principal sufferers try unsuccessfully to rush towards the show-place, but have to trot towards the main principal's hut. Hustled inside, they are ordered to stand, like manacled slaves, by a wall with their hands spread above their heads.

The action divides, for a brief moment of respite and disengagement, between front stage and back, between what men demand publicly and what, as Edith Turner discovered, only women know they are doing stealthily. Safely, behind the door, unseen and unheard by men, they clap and cheer until told by a priestess to stop. An appearance of deference must be maintained. The women have to be silent, bide their time and keep themselves from laughing out loud at the priests' antics, because now when they stamp their feet and bang their staffs, aroused, and as if to force their way in, the hut's door is securely closed against them. The play keeps up appearances.

If not a sexual game of hide-and-seek, say by analogy to the cultic image of the burrowing rat, then perhaps it is fittingly, from the exhausted women's point of view, a happy, calm moment of denial of access for men. It comes after rites of endurance in enactments of spent copulation, the tiring dragging of reproductive paraphernalia in the form of mortars, and 'the runs' in the manner of incontinent infants. Male dominance does not mean men always have it their own way, appearances to the contrary.

An alternative semiotic stance: ritual coordination, pivotal icons

Having examined in relation to subversive evidence in Turner's ethnography his cognitive stance towards ritual man, revelation and liminality, I want to go beyond his situational semiotic stance.

To do so, I turn to a semiotic stance alternative to his symbology – the stance of the American semiotician Charles Peirce – in
order to make more sense of the relation between the pursuit of
fertility and sexual playfulness in *Chihamba*. On this basis, I seek
also to clarify ritual coordination, important for the ritual process,
and largely neglected by Turner in *Chihamba*. In its elaboration,
Turner's symbology is cumbersome and unwieldy. His tracking of
significant associations is overwhelming, so much so that the symbol
looms large at the expense of the *mimetic action* and the organizing
image.[23] For clarity, I rely on Peirce's distinctions between icon,
index and symbol.[24]

Let me illustrate some of this, and then put it in general terms,
according to Peirce's distinctions. Close attention to the specif-
ics is essential. Things have to be seen, visualized in use, to be
believed by us, as felt to be effective by Ndembu. The detailed
analysis discloses the familiar, easily known means of coordination,
phase organization, sequencing, boundary marking, expected sensual
interaction – all of which Turner's adoption of the *voyance* filter
occludes.

To start with icons, the material means of reproductive healing
for the restoration of fertility: I offer a gendered, dualist view of an
outstanding pair of fertility icons for the pair of main spirits, *Kavula*
and his wife. Turner was, frankly, sometimes bewildered: 'I could
not make much sense of this at the time' (1975: 52). He recalled
remaining puzzled about 'a dominant symbol', the 'medicine pouch'
and its fearsome sound. His puzzle is an artefact of his symbology:
the dominant symbol with its associations by symbol, rather than as
part of a pair, by gendered *likeness*. Seen as an icon with feminine
likeness, the pouch is the counter to an icon with male likeness,
Kavula's ball-bearing shaft; and so too are their sounds opposites, a
big bang for the active male, and for the restless female, soft rustling.
This pair of icons, male and female, materializes the opposition
between husband and wife, *Kavula* and the restless ancestress, the
afflicting spirit. A bit of the icon for the male is the arrowhead,
cut out-of-joint with its counterpart, the shaft, uniquely carved
by lightning-like adze strokes, along with its ball bearing maize
seeds in their noisy kernels – thus able, in their potentially fertile
big bang, to arouse a spirit. *Kavula* fertilizes by watering seeds (an
ejaculation?).

A phallic icon, in my view, with vital, reproductive virtue, *Kavula*'s shaft is never simply handed over; rough horseplay achieves its release. *Kavula*'s shaft is the priest's phallic prosthesis for the extension of his capacity for reproductive healing.[25] Turner calls the shaft with its ball a rattle. The female icon, the pouch, is from the skin of a giant, fearsome rat, dangerous for reproduction; its meat must not be eaten, lest it make babies unable to control their defecating.[26]

Further, there is a *pivotal icon* in operation for sequential organization during ritual, marking and coordinating phase after phase. I speak of a pivotal icon because it conveys spiritual presence in imaged *likeness*, such as *Kavula*'s in something shot like lightning; upon it pivot *transitions and boundary marking* as well as the organization of precedence and sharing in a performance. Such an icon becomes an index also, when a certain connection is established, for example, ownership or belonging and protection. The arrowhead, feathered and associated with *Kavula*'s shaft and ball, provides *an organizing image* for ritual sequences which are meant to *quicken* and take flight, like an arrow – for *Chihamba*, adepts supplicate, 'let it fly'– let life be in motion.

Kavula's arrowhead serves highly important organizational purposes. With it, the village headman signals his willingness – the performance may start – and, by sending it to a priestess, he appoints her to be the senior female organizer; with it also, the senior male organizer orders precedence – he gets each adept in turn to dip the arrowhead in beer and then lick it – and accordingly, they also substantially share dividuality. *Kavula*'s icon[27] is kept safe for making transitions around the afflicted principal's hut: first, inserted for *Kavula*'s possession of her, in front, during the first day; on the second day, for *Kavula*'s protection through penetration, in her doorway thatch; and, on the last day, concluding the ritual in a return to the place where it began, now transformed for a personal shrine. In addition, other arrowheads are carved by a female adept for boundary making, with aggressive threats to exclude uninitiated persons.

The ritual process: after rehearsal

Having focused upon familiar things in use as icons and indexes, I want to turn now to an account of the ritual as a movement from phase to phase: the ritual process. It is hard to explain, I would argue, why Turner reached no perspective from any of his stances on the transformational movement as a whole in *Chihamba*, despite his well-known theoretical preoccupations. In my processual analysis, the ritual begins with a rehearsal, an afternoon episode. After it come three days, one for each of the ritual's main phases.

Held in the senior organizer's kitchen, the rehearsal makes preparations, creating the gendered pair of pivotal icons, the male arrowhead and the female pouch. The rehearsal turns from planning the arrowhead usage to conversation about participants' degrees of ritual status and the assignment of ritual tasks and privileges, such as access to an esoteric site. Order is essential. Preparation is to ensure this. The ritual has moments of licence, within discipline.

After a maize beer drink, sometimes gatecrashed by the uninitiated merely wanting beer, the rehearsal ends when the male organizer discusses 'the procedural form of the ritual' (1975: 45). Surprisingly, Turner did not report the performers' own delineation of 'the procedural form of the ritual'. If I am right, and the afternoon episode is a rehearsal, then rethinking the whole ritual drama is possible through processual analysis with a model of three phases, on three days.

Food and sex: production and reproduction

My model covers the move from adorcism, in Luc de Huesch's sense as given earlier, to exorcism in playful sexuality, and it is informed by a cultural axiom, widely held in Africa and already recognized in the Introduction. To repeat, for clarity, it is the axiom by which the production and consumption of food and the reproduction of life are two sides of the same thing. In outline, some of the means for food production and consumption, along with cassava shavings, are:

1 the winnowing basket for arousal, sifting the good from the bad, for carrying cosmetics along with *Kavula*'s ball-bearing shafts, and then once pierced through, left to rot in the bush;
2 the mortar for pounding away in virile copulation, dragged in labour for delivery and during feminized copulation, overturned to hide goods for sacrifice, including a razor; and finally a mortar

never used for cosmetics, hence empty; it serves for threats about provision during a final mock battle;

3 the roots for erections, exposed, made vulnerable, and then preserved for a personal memorial;

4 the poultry for communion through sacrifice and exorcism by beheading in a series of rites, turning to a cock that is a red male elder,[28] to a blanketed white mock-up with a drop of red blood on its mortar head, to a whitened female, a hen identified with the sufferer being exorcised;

5 the pestle for *ku-jika Chihamba*, 'the stopping of *Chihamba*', comes in *danse du ventre* (Turner's term, used for African belly dance since 1860), which climaxes in a mock brawl, *wusensi wa Chihamba*, the joking of *Chihamba*, in the *finale*.[29]

Phase one, day one: adorcism in the village and the wild

In the following I outline the rites, except those already discussed, at the *isoli* show-place:

1 *Kavula* takes mastery of the principal sufferer, when a priest inserts *Kavula*'s arrowhead in front of her hut. The principal waits inside.

2 Thank-offering is given by whitening with white clay, first whitening *Kavula*'s balled shafts in a winnowing basket (where they

	VILLAGE	WILD
1 *Mastery by Kavula*	**hut, arrowhead, root**	
	winnowing basket with balled shafts	
2 *Thank-offerings*	**white clay**	
3 *Arrival of ancestress, invoked libation, cosmetic collection* >--------------------→		
	circled elder tree root, leaves, white beer	
4 *Shaving exposure of erection* ←--<		
	winnowing basket, erection root, staffs	
5 *Orgiastic dance*	**young women in orgiastic dance**	
6 *Erotic stimulation*	**eating shavings, banging staffs**	
7 *Invocations, offerings, libations, after dark*		
	redwood fire, pots, winnowing basket	
8 *Sexy intimacy*	**darkened hut**	
9 *Purification, white cosmetics in night vigil*		
	redwood fire, pots, winnowing basket	

Figure 9.1 Phase one: adorcism in the village and the wild

are tested for good sound and licked), and second, whitening adepts, some of whom cross themselves in gratitude for fertility.

3 Next comes an act of care and erotic foreplay in sexual intimacy, like a married couple's shaving of their pubic hair elsewhere in Zambia.[30] Once *Kavula*'s erection roots are uncovered in a winnowing basket by the hut, the priest places them carefully, scraped by him to bare whiteness. Children, who are driven away violently, must not witness this act of intimacy. Some shavings are put in the iconic female pouch, to be kept until the second day's rite for contact with each supplicant's head, and in anticipation of the final day's rite of hair-shaving. All of the shaving is, I would venture to guess, sexual: rites for making the female reproductive organ attractive and thus having the promise of fertility.

4 The female adepts' dance becomes ever more orgiastic around this exposure. Adepts crowd around, making *Kavula*'s shafts bang.

5 In erotic stimulation, other shavings are eaten by supplicants, mixed with salt as a sweetener or stimulant, a renowned luxury, and as such, a sexual offering that pleases *Kavula*. Eating food and having sex are, of course, the same thing.

6 After dark, before the hut, by a wood fire, strikingly red and thus in a condition that is the opposite of whiteness, an elderly priest makes an attractive invocation.[31] Libations from a calabash are for the named and remembered ancestress who had come out as a ghost in *Chihamba*. Made well beyond the ritual fire are libations and offerings from a winnowing basket for the unnamed spirits of the sterile, the malevolent dead, because, after all, they were once human beings.[32]

7 Late in the evening, along with an afflicted companion, the principal enters her hut guided by senior priestesses. The door is left open; no need to bang on it, as in the next day's rites, having women apparently trapped. Now priests enter the hut backwards. The mood, like the music from *Kavula*'s shafts, is sexy; in the dark the women tremble. It is whispered, '*Kavula* had come', entering from on top, from the sky through the topknot of the hut. One priest, said to act *Kavula* (1975: 87), does a sexual belly dance, at least miming intercourse. *Kavula* is not seen. What matters is not what *Kavula looks like*, as Turner puzzled, but how he is *felt*, when the harmonizing women, the

two principals, *vibrate*, and *Kavula* is *aroused*. *Kavula's* felt *sexual intimacy* is secret: an experienced mystery (*mpangu*).

8 Afterwards, the principals, now *Kavula's* intimates, are led outside again, to sit near the redness from the special redwood of the ritual fire; there they are repeatedly washed and purified with whitening cosmetics from clay pots, and given some to drink throughout a night vigil, when adepts sometimes ululate and dance in circles. For the female ghost in the wild, her grounds, centred on an icon, are surrounded by encircling and fortified with apt cosmetics, mostly blown and sprayed from the mouth (the most common dividual act of sharing substance).[33] Over an offering of white clay and beer, she is asked for the release of the supplicants' today, once caught in *Chihamba*; and tomorrow, given the good increase in their cosmetics, to *quicken Chihamba*, giving the afflicted their strength back. It is an appeal to the female ghost to move from adorcism to exorcism.[34]

Phase two, day two: liminal subjection and subjugation

The following gives the order of rites on the second day.

1 During the second day, villagers are alerted to the promise of help from *Kavula*, according to their needs, for crops and for sickness, once he is pleased with the vital offer of blood and eats his sacrificial red cock. Before this, still alive, it is brought by priests singing its song, *chokolo choko*, to the threshold of every hut. To testify that everyone is awakened and has seen it, its plucked feathers, associated with the feathered arrow icon, are left. Later sacrificed, it is eaten by priests and magicians in *Kavula's* presence.

2 In seduction, around 7.30 a.m., the afflicted women display themselves, pleasing *Kavula*. They dance sensuously, bare-breasted and, for the whole day, ravenously desirous of food and thus more likely, when *Kavula* possesses them, to be desirously intoxicated by beer-drinking, while other women, allowed to eat, carry sacred food, later taken into the bush for a rite of getting the afflicted on the run.

3 Protective fertility is indicated when *Kavula's* pivotal icon is thrust into the principal's doorway thatch. Turned into a

moving index of birth, it goes wrapped in the leaf of the castor oil plant used on the fontanelles of a newborn baby. The leafy arrowhead flies in a mimetic motion, a spiritual action without the aid of human hands, not touching the ground, and wrapped in the birthing leaf, not in contact with human flesh. *Kavula*'s agent is the high priest, who hops with the wrapped arrow between his toes, and then is lifted up to thrust the arrow into the thatch with his foot.

4 A barrier at a fork in a path demarcates the space of the uninitiated from that of the initiated. Candidates pass by on their way to the nearby scene of the main rites, usually at a tree called *isoli*, 'show' or 'expose', and a site named after the tree, the show-place.

5 Kavula's dominion over a site called the *ishikenu* is asserted by grounding his arrow, and laying down around it, as life-giving, the blood of the red sacrificial cock and, again, its feathers. Usually, the site has a marginal archway where candidates would be washed with cosmetics before greeting *Kavula*, and where they later rest briefly in seclusion, apart from the uninitiated.

6 Extraordinarily virile and rapid copulation is performed by priests together, as *Kavula*'s one body, in the motions of sex with a feminine food container, a much-pounded cosmetics mortar. They pass it from one to another between each crotch, *ipanza*, 'the place where children come from', without it ever touching the ground. Following this quickening motion above ground, as befits *Kavula*, the drudgery of labour is left to a principal's husband, who has to drag the mortar along the ground, sometimes too long an ordeal for an impatient, hardly virile husband, say with yellow semen, like the convener Sandombu, who shows his impotence by carrying the mortar in his hands rather than keeping it up in the air. From life flying like an arrow comes the drag; and vice versa.

7 A magician, like a hunter, shoots an arrow into the bush. It starts the rush of bush runs for kids, as the candidates are. This leads to much display of male subjugation, discipline and rearing, as if from infancy, following the previous day's rite of thrusting fontanelle cosmetics into the doorway. Inferiors are forcefully put down, seniority is asserted and the superiority of

cult elderhood is enforced, with much abusive fun and extor-tionate payments from the uninitiated.

8 and 9 Earlier, in commenting on liminality, I discussed these rites of enslaving captives and the divide between front and back-stage in performance.

10 By the archway, the identity testing begins with candidates having to solve riddles.

11 Flagellation, subjugation and joking prevail towards mid-morning. Humiliating mayhem breaks out among the men, in an exaggeration of subjugation. In turn by seniority, priests and adepts armed with branches threaten or actually beat, terrify and abuse others, often with sexual joking. Sometimes, priests with a grudge take advantage of the moment to beat someone they hate, and senior female adepts, like *tulama*, police messengers, serve the priests with great vigour, helping in their attacks by aggressively crowding around potential captives.

The humbling of the pretentious, including lesser priests and magicians themselves, reaches a pitch. It brings comic relief, seen in a grin on the high priest's face, when the humiliated are gatecrashers, or someone who tries to buy his way out too easily or a shamed village headman who for years has pretended to be a senior adept.

12 After several hours of pursuit of the candidates, at the command of the high priest, each of the magicians is ignominiously pushed all the way to the principal's hut. The village is now 'crowded with spectators who laughed and jeered uproariously as these "liars" (*ukwakutwamba*) were chased by [the senior priest's] other adepts, who shouted *sho, sho,* as if their victims were dogs', and blew piercing blasts on whistles to please the spirit (1975: 98). The magicians, having a slave's yoke around their necks, are also felt, at least by themselves, to be the born-again, the pure, who have been through slavery. For the prin-cipals, too, the yoke, like a cross, is worn in remembrance of a sacred passage from suffering. They are becoming redeemed slaves of *Kavula*. Before the magicians' greatest part at the show-place, they are held in suspicious irreverence, at the pleas-ure of their master, *Kavula*. In my view of this ordeal, they too bear the yoke, must be disciplined, must endure, like dogs

whistled for, the passion of submission and penitence, and face ridicule from everyone around them for not being able to tell the truth which, of course, they cannot reveal.

On the way home, villagers remain silent at first, respectfully keeping their thoughts to themselves, until they are past *Kavula*'s sacred archway. Consecrated and returning to the village, they are halted by the high priest who strikes a firebrand from the sacred fire at the principal's hut, announces the ghostly death with a great shout, and declares the end of the show-place ritual. In the village, the high priest recognizes their innocence and inveighs against sorcerers who use familiars.[35] The supplicants, treated with cosmetics through the night, sleep by their sacred fire.

Phase three: exorcism

In this phase, in my view, the ghost and the afflicted undergo a metamorphosis together, away from the show-place. Exorcism prevails. Then, as we might expect on Van Gennep's model, though surprisingly not conceptualized by Turner, there comes the aggregation of supplicant and ancestress in the desired moral relationship, which is memorialized by a personal shrine.

1   Recovered in well-being and in moral remembrance, supplicants appear renewed. Early in the morning of the last day, aided by

WILD	VILLAGE
1 *Redressed*	root shrine, white cosmetics
2 *Identity testing*	riddles
3 *Mimed beheading, exorcism*	shavings
4 *Memorial sacrifice*	white hen, personal shrine
5 *Passing away, Chihamba traces of ghost*	
mound, skeleton, arch	
6 *Spiritual healing of Kavula, affliction*	
root, *Kavula*'s wounds	
7 *Regeneration*	planted beans, cassava
8 *Joking of Chihamba*	
pestle	

Figure 9.2   Phase three: exorcism

magicians and the wife of a man who impersonates *Kavula* in his dialogues, the high priest creates a personal memorial, a shrine with a bit of a small root branching off from the taproot of a tree, called cassava root of *Chihamba*. Adepts, marked with cosmetics from the pouch, use *Kavula*'s ball-bearing staffs to lift out an axed bit of the root and put it in a winnowing basket, with other cosmetics. The supplicants, waiting nearby, are also so marked, by the high priest, and dressed in clean clothes, with white beads of the spirit.

2 Tests are made of the candidates and their knowledge of their new identities. It is an ordeal through riddles, through their greetings with obeisant crawling, and then through their being splashed with cosmetics.

3 Said to terrify the principal into a sense of fear and awe, the high priest mimes beheading, the sacrificial act, as if the principal were the victim. He passes a knife menacingly over each of her shoulders and her head, feigning to kill her. But also, I suggest, he performs an act of exorcism to get her substance, bits of her hair. He shaves the hair over her brow and at back of her head, apparently in imitation of a genet cat. Jeered at, the principal slinks away. The priest leaves bits of hair for the spirit, to whom he later sacrifices a white hen along with some hair at the personal memorial shrine, *kantong'a*, by the original place of beginning at the principal's hut and by each candidate's hut.

4 The winnowing basket is emptied on top of the skeletal figure, as I described earlier. Brought together and called *yibi*[36] are a mound, the figure and an arch through which everyone and the whole of *Chihamba* passes; and *yibi* is abandoned in the wild.

5 An exposed tap root's injuries, *Kavula*'s wounds,[37] are anointed and buried by a magician, who bundles cosmetics, against all afflictions, for burial also.

6 Nearby are planted beans and cassava, whose growth manifests the departure of both of the spirits. Finally, the whole comic ritual drama ends in the 'joking of *Chihamba*', with a crescendo of badinage and horseplay, capped by a sexy belly dance with a long pole, like a pestle but perhaps an erection as long as *Kavula*'s, stretched between the organizer and his chosen female adept. Everyone enjoys the lewd humour.

Conclusion

In this re-analysis of *Chihamba*, I have taken up the bits in Turner's ethnography, some found together, others scattered here and there in the rest of his work. Much of my argument, disclosing the importance of certain stances in this perspectival work, establishes how we need to reconsider the basics in Turner's thought and the received wisdom about, among other things, liminality and ritual process.

If, as I argue, Turner's *Chihamba* stances in his perspectival work are four, the underlying advocacy is one, the conviction in religious experience through ordeal and turmoil towards the extra-ordinary perception 'of realities we cannot perceive by means of the senses alone' (Turner 1975: 195). Part of my response, while inspired by this perspectivalism, is oppositional; for example, taking up, counter to his symbology, a semiotic stance derived from Peirce, and turning from medicalized individuals to attend to dividuality as it is constituted through things and substances. Further, Turner's ritual drama is tragic; against that, my re-analysis of *Chihamba* shows another genre of ritual drama: the comedy, teasing and making fun of the subjected, while revelling in Bacchanalian moments and much playful sexuality, and while allowing somewhat muted, alternative fun backstage, gendered for women only.

Turner as the ethnographer intends to illuminate, in specific cultural expressions, universals of the human condition; and as the theologian/literary critic, he seeks to convince us of profound truths of religion and the religious imagination. Hence, in my view, to re-analyse *Chihamba* is more to renew an ongoing, wider debate than to be dogmatic and have the final say about it.

One outcome is a question. How useful, for comparison, is Turner's notion of 'the ritual man'? After all, like the reasonable man, as a supposed universal, and thus a much-challenged notion (see Epstein 1973), his ritual counterpart may be transfigured, with very different preoccupations in unlike 'places and ages'. It is distinctive of *Chihamba* that the preoccupation is informed by a cosmic premise according to which social harmony, cosmic order and personal well-being, including fertility, are one.[38] The expressed intent in performance is, of course, to bring well-being, not merely personal but communal, and for people drawn from many villages.

Certain kinds of disturbance, such as neglect of ancestrality, ramify and call for an ontological transformation from adorcism to exorcism. Ancestrality is eroticized and conciliated, for the sake of fertility and other mystic benefits, with mysteries of masculinity and femininity under male dominance, and from a traditional perspective acutely publicized, at least apart from women behind closed doors, according to a male bias. I am tempted to guess, therefore, that only where this cosmic premise prevails along with the making of an ontological transformation are we likely to find a ritual man like the one in *Chihamba*. And only where he is accompanied by and works hand in glove with the wily magician is their accomplishment likely to be comic ritual drama. Here our interest turns from the 'slain god' to the play of magic, tricks and lustful fantasy.

The liminal phase, in my view, is, in one aspect, *extravagant*, rich in licensed playful excess, being out of control, and yet, in another aspect, also rich in *agonistic* ordeals, submission to *dominant order*. As for *extravagance*, the playful excess, *Chihamba* affords, I suggest, the momentary experience of an infantile, unbridled existence, being on the go, running amok – the disorderly counter to orderly movement in procreation; it is started by the troubling, restless ancestress; it is catchy and, in a rude joke with an infant's bowels as the organ of generation, it means having the runs; whoever gets it has been caught, like a kid, on the run, under attack. Ndembu men joke in body humour, turning *Chihamba* into a coarse, bawdy, male chauvinist pun on the relaxation of control. Evocative of infantile awkwardness and the ritual's feminine pouch (a vulva?) in its rat origins with shitty meat, the pun has the term *Chihamba* coming from *ku-hambuka*, 'to defecate as infants do' (1975: 52 n.4), having the runs, out of control.

Mere excess prevails in the popular festival, accompanying *Chihamba* and held beyond sacred sites and the village. Young revellers enjoy getting wildly drunk, having an orgy of adulterous sex, and joining in a brawl. It is apt in tenor for youth breaking free of sexual and social constraints, well away from the scenes directed by the priests and magicians. Under their direction, however, the running amok and playful sexuality serves subjection, imaged in infantile captives coming under the yoke of a master, *Kavula*.

In its second aspect, liminality turns into an *agonistic ordeal* through which male dominance, elderhood and seniority are *publicly* asserted, and identities are refashioned within an order of *subjugation*. Intoxicated supplicants undergo tests and challenges, indeed playful, comic ones, to please *Kavula* and get him on their side. A force for recuperation, he takes pity on his people, and all at *Chihamba* are his grandchildren, whom he nurtures and disciplines.

Turner's legacy, including his actual fieldwork notes (Turner 2017) is promising, not for keywords such as liminality or interdisciplinary truisms, but as open texts for critical and deep dialogue.[39] Hence, rather than being the last word, my conclusion is liminal: for a passage to the disturbing moment of undoing much more of the received wisdom about Turner's legacy, and yet not losing our sense of welcome surprise in the familiar.

Notes

1 Written in 1960, published in 1962 in the Rhodes-Livingstone Papers, reprinted in 1969, but not widely available until the Cornell University Press edition in 1975 (Turner 1975). This edition brought together *Chihamba* and Turner's study of divination, with an introduction that loads diviners with paranoia, is weak on séances, and empties divination of poetry and philosophical speculation. For my view of the fieldwork and substantial shortcomings in his seminal study of divination, see Werbner 2015: 289–95.

2 For a discussion of the value of re-analysis in distinction from deconstruction, and for a brief review of re-analyses in British and European anthropology, particularly in Manchester School studies, see P. Werbner 2018: 80–1.

3 The ritual drama involved 'the performance of two successive rituals [first *ilembi*, then *ku-tumbuka*], separated by a period in which the patient undergoes partial seclusion from secular life' (Turner 1975: 38). Turner did not observe the first ritual and concentrates primarily on the second. Accordingly, I focus my re-analysis on the second ritual.

4 For my comparative analysis of considerable variation in such passages, see Werbner 1989.

5 I developed this argument earlier for creative dividualism and reproductive care in Zimbabwe (Werbner 1996b), for Lunda basket diviners' possessive dividualism (Werbner 2015: 191–3), and for charismatic Apostles in their oscillations between dividuality and individuality (Werbner 2011a, 2011b).

6 Anointed with oil, covered in the white meal of cassava from *Kavula*'s shrine, together having eaten cassava (the basic staple) and beans (the food of love and intimacy), and drunk the sacralized maize beer of *Chihamba*, they are honoured and privileged. For their services, magicians exact final payments, held to be so extortionate that the bargaining goes

on with much indignation, surprise and fooling. In shared, empowering participation as dividuals, both priests and magicians together eat cosmetics in pursuit of fertility from a special and feminine container, the *Chihamba* pouch.

7 Throughout *Chihamba* expressions of dualism, extensive, sensational and salient in ontological transformation, appear in binary oppositions, including very prominently the chromatic (white vs. red), the auditory (loud bang vs. soft rustling), the spatial (celestial vs. underground) and the kinetic (being given over to an external force vs. being contained and inaccessible). Reproductive capacity (*lisomu*) is white, and someone whose semen (*matekela*) is yellow lacks the virtues of whiteness, 'purity, health, strength, piety towards the ancestors' (Turner 1957: 107). Yellow Ndembu call red, the colour often linked with witchcraft, aggressiveness and evil power. Although Ndembu present the milk tree (*mudyi*) as iconic for human breast milk, no icon is explicitly given for semen, perhaps an omission to fit Ndembu taboo.

8 From his stance as a cognitive comparativist, but blinkered by Thomist thought and thus over-focused on the singularity of one ritual character, Turner obscured duality and, even more significantly, pervasive dualism. There could hardly be a greater contrast to this shortcoming, and thus an argument by Turner against himself as a monist, than his regard for the 'Dialectic of the Developmental Cycle' (1969: 97) and the rest of his main approach to opposites in *The Ritual Process* (1969).

9 Radin stressed the importance of a plot and *dramatis personae*, but also found a variable connection to the re-enactment of a myth. He applied ritual drama to 'the performance of a ritual belonging to a clearly defined non-public organization, in other words, to some society or club whose membership is restricted; and, secondly to such rituals as are theoretically supposed to be enactments of a series of events generally embodied in a myth or myth-poem and in which specific individuals or groups definitely impersonate the original actors' (1957: 293). For a richly insightful biography of Radin, along with life histories of former slaves, see Glazier, in press.

10 Muchona, the magician and key informant, expressed the disposition of the 'matter-of-fact man' when he rationalized the efficacy of a cosmetic in terms of experience through trial and error; if it worked for recovery from affliction, it was adopted for use, if not it was said to be worthless (Turner 1975: 156).

11 Timothy Larsen is Professor of Christian Thought at Wheaton College, Illinois, which was founded by abolitionist evangelicals in 1860. In *The Slain God*, Larsen devotes a chapter to spirituality in the interwoven lives and works of Edith and Victor Turner (Larsen 2014: 43–84).

12 In an intimately informed article, Engelke calls *Chihamba* 'the most radical piece Victor Turner published in his lifetime' (2004: 28).

13 A similar point was made by Ronald Grimes in his view of a Janus-like aspect in Turner's work which appeared to face 'towards semantics and

semiotics' on one side, and on the other, towards 'political anthropology or processualism' (Grimes 1985: 19).

14 Turner acknowledges that his textual method was influenced by Monica Wilson during a fieldwork break in Cape Town in the 1950s (see Turner 1967: 19–20).

15 For example, Muchona went on to explain what the symbols stood for. When the adepts go through the legs this means *ipanza*, the place where children come from. It means that a child enters a woman's body and comes out alive. It is just the same in *Mukanda* (another ritual). A cock is used (for killing in the ritual) because he is an elder and awakens everybody. For sacrifice (literally 'cut', *ku-ketula* – always by beheading) means life (*wami*) (Turner 1975: 84–6).

16 Turner also cited his earlier work showing how ritual symbolism becomes 'a force in a field of social action' (1967: 44).

17 On this basis, Turner considered Susanne Langer's thoughts on 'meaning' (Langer 1958) and argued in the light of his analysis of the semantics of Ndembu ritual symbolism how her model of 'the symbol-function' might be modified.

18 'Death in these cases', remarked Turner, 'may be real or symbolic – in either case it represents a major, qualitative change in the status and state of being of the subject' (1975: 177).

19 The turn to literature was to images of whiteness, to 'Melville's white whale and the white symbolism in Judaism and Christianity … Coleridge's albatross and Mallarme's swan, the Unicorn and Virgin myths of the Middle Ages, the sacrifice of white or unblemished beasts in many societies' (1975: 178). In none of these comparisons does a ghost figure, as in *Chihamba*. Nor is there any consideration of whiteness to counteract a familiar in sorcery, which the *mufu* could be.

20 On Magritte and thought rendered visible, see Paquet 2015: 85–92.

21 For my re-analysis of metamorphosis and playful sexuality in Melanesian performances, see Werbner 1989, 1992. The interest in comparison of Melanesian and African performances that foreground playful sex calls for much discussion, which is largely beyond my present scope.

22 The Ndembu term *yitumbu* is used for components of shrines and sacred fences, as well as for potions, poultices and various external applications. *Nyitondu*, 'trees', is used for vegetable potions (Turner 1975: 54).

23 On this, see Fernandez 1986: 215; Werbner 1990a.

24 According to this, 'there are *likenesses*, or icons, which serve to convey ideas of the things they represent simply by imitating them … *indications*, or indices which show something about things on account of their being physically connected with them … *symbols* or general signs, which have become associated with their meanings by usage' (Peirce 1998). See also my discussion of icons, indices and symbols in divination in Werbner 2015.

25 For my comparative discussion of prosthesis between healer, patient and spiritual powers among Tswapong and Angolan refugees, related to Ndembu, see Werbner 2015: 62–3, 289, 295, 300.

26 The pouch is a powerful container for leaves and roots, associated with the rat's stealth, and used to activate *cosmetics*. The staff's ball, bearing its seeds, is smeared with fertility cosmetics from the pouch and is licked. Cosmetics, like satisfying food, are collected in a winnowing basket.

27 It is draped with a necklace of white beads (a counter to a pain in the neck of the childless).

28 This is the red cock for *Kavula*, with its feathers, including bits from the head, for everyone, the blood for *Kavula*, and the flesh that the adepts eat with *Kavula*.

29 I quote Turner's description at length, because it is a revelation of mockery of *Chihamba itself*: 'all the adepts and candidates gathered near [the principal] Nyamukola's hut and started to revile and jeer at one another. Then they started a mock battle, snatching up brands of firewood and cindered logs from the sacred fire to throw them at one another. [A senior magician] Sakutoha threatened people with the meal mortar that had not been used for for pounding medicines. This behaviour was called *wutensi wa Chihamba*, the joking of Chihamba. During this joking, [the organizer and principal's husband] Sandombu and a woman adept danced, facing one another with a long pole stretched from the shoulder of one to the shoulder of another, making the suggestive movement of the *danse du ventre*' (1975: 133).

30 On shaving pubic hair, see Simpson 2009: 88–9.

31 He invokes, 'Completely white [is] that white clay, you yourself grandfather, all of you, [naming ancestress], all of you come, our dead. Today, if you are making this person sick, today we will sing your drum [perform your ritual], this person must become strong. Completely white [is] that white clay' (Turner 1975: 63).

32 The calabash has white beer for libations and for offerings, the winnowing basket holds maize, grains, beans, sweet potatoes and cassava.

33 Her icon is a root, itself become flaccid (not the tap root). Taken from an uprighted tree with a likeness to an erection, it is attractive and pleasing for the female.

34 In the wild, when cosmetics are collected, arguments sometimes reach acute disagreement. Should, as a sterile organizer would claim, the root be from *mudyi*, milk tree? If so, the cosmetic would bear unity, on the likeness of breast to breast, closeness between mother and daughter. Or should, as most adepts insist, the needed source be the *mucheki* tree? Its root serves best, being completely white, like the white clay, which makes a person seen, thankful and mindful of the spirits.

35 I refer the reader again to Turner's early translation of *mufu* as the dangerous familiar of a sorceress. Given that, this would be the moment when the familiar is dead and the innocence of harbouring a familiar is established. The interpretation gives further support to the importance of exorcism in the ritual.

36 The skeletal figure is an image said to be like an animal's skin stretched out to dry, and it is by a mound of earth with an arch of forked sapling from the *musoli*, the show tree, an index of the show-place.

37 The wounding is made out to be an 'accident' due to the cutting by the wife of the impersonator of *Kavula*, who exposes, for about eight feet, the dorsal portion of the tree known as the cassava root of *Chihamba*. The *mukishi*, spirit, is said to be in the ground at the foot of the tree.

38 For a further discussion of a cosmic premise for ritual, see Werbner 2015: 171–2.

39 Although a recent collection is dedicated to 'The Intellectual Legacy of Victor and Edith Turner' (Salamone and Snipes 2018), the only one of the essays to mention *Chihamba, the White Spirit* merely reports that 'Edie valued *Chihamba* the most highly of all of Vic's publications' (Glazier 2018: 39), and it says little more than that about the ritual drama itself.

10

Anthropology and the postcolonial

The story of ethnic difference in Africa has threatened to overwhelm larger debates about postcolonial identity politics across the continent. Once told in terms of tribe, now ethnicity and ethnogenesis, this narrative apparently remains spell-binding. Yet as in the colonial politics of everyday life that we saw shown in early Manchester School studies, so too ethnic identities are only a small fraction of the identities mobilized in the postcolonial politics of everyday life, and anthropology has faced a major challenge to analyse how postcolonial strategies improvise multiple, shifting, intersecting identities over time, some of which may be promoted as if authentically natural or intensely primordial.

Postcolonies are radically unalike. Hence the need is for postcolonial studies to illuminate correspondingly disparate identity strategies emerging in everyday life. More or less deliberate, 'rational' or 'irrational', these identity strategies have put distinctive imprints upon postcoloniality through local languages, with their cultural richness of specific idioms, images, metaphors and metonyms that must be understood in the historic specificity of their contribution to making postcoloniality. Anthropologists have located postcolonial utterances in changing sociopolitical contexts, opening the possibility of tracing the emergence of arguments in a new politics of identity and belonging, which centres within the postcolony on who represents whom, to whom, and for whom. Anthropological accounts in this vein have addressed reflexive issues ranging from anthropologists' textual authority, to the consequences for postcolonial theory of analysts' own languages, and claims to use universal concepts and transcultural knowledge in representing postcolonial realities (Fardon 1990; Englund 2006). How classifications of identity and difference are defined, contested and revalued over the *longue durée* of South African history, from pre-colonial to postcolonial times, is the question Adam Kuper addresses in a brief yet highly informative survey (2005). Kuper discerns enduring dilemmas and contradictions which, if unexpected and troublesome for the people themselves, are no less problematic for the anthropologists who claim scientific authority for their classifications. There is a further challenge, which Wale Adebanwi raises specifically for the postcolonial anthropology of elites and the ethnographic gaze in Africa (Adebanwi 2016), but which recent critical studies raise very broadly, for example the post-socialist studies by anthropologists based in the former socialist region (Kurti and Skalnik 2009). It is the challenge of anthropology at home and the knowledge claims of insiders as against outsiders or strangers abroad. I return to this challenge later in a discussion of Adebanwi's critical ethnography, *Yoruba Elite and Ethnic Politics in Nigeria* (2014).

Postcolonial anthropology has revealed just how wide the range of identity strategies is: from the defence of moral agency, respect and respectability, in the face of catastrophe, such as the AIDS pandemic (Ogden 1996; Whyte 1997, 2002; Simpson 2003, 2009), to promised novel Christian or Muslim identities, which redefine boundaries of morality (Masquelier 1996, 2001; van Dijk and Pels 1996), and the 'identity giving power of the land' (Thornton 1996; Fontein 2006), or emancipation of the 'sovereign subject' (Fisiy and Geschiere 1996) which make subjectivities powerfully felt as occult realities (see also Comaroff and Comaroff 1993, 1999; De Boeck 1996; Englund 1996b; Moore and Sanders 2001; Niehaus 2001; Sanders 2003; West 2005; Kiernan 2006). Still others disrupt the very grounds of perception, identity and subjectivity, and even threaten the existence of moral agency (van Dijk and Pels 1996; De Boeck 1996; Fisiy and Geschiere 1996; Thornton 1996). The postcolonial imagination, as a highly specific and locally created force, has reconfigured personal knowledge in everyday life, shaping subjective, moral and religious realities around the uses and abuses of power (Worby 1998).

The occult imaginary and degradation through witchcraft victimization are among the most contentious problematics of postcolonial anthropology (Niehaus 2001). Much has been written about the perceived resurgence of witchcraft as a topic of both academic and public discourse, and about the ambiguous topic of damage to others by occult means.[1] Fisiy and Geschiere have been among those who have helped redirect theoretical interest in witchcraft discourses from ahistorical questions of social control, responsibility or micropolitics in interpersonal relations towards historical questions of moral and political economy within the state under changing conditions of capitalism (Fisiy and Geschiere 1996; Geschiere 1997, 2013; for a critique of the modernist paradigm of witchcraft, see Werbner 2015: 48–9). The trend is represented as if it were a major departure from, in particular, the Manchester School studies of accusations in Central African villages. Some earlier anthropology, however, had indeed analysed how the colonial state criminalized and dealt with witchcraft. Isaac Schapera's account of 'Witchcraft Beyond Reasonable Doubt' is an outstanding, albeit neglected, analysis tracing the introduction and impact of demands for 'tangible proof' of witchcraft in courts under the indirect rule of strong chiefs in colonial Botswana (Schapera 1955, 1969).

The force of state violence against ethnic groups in the postcolony explains why anthropologists have problematized states and state-created domains in order to illuminate identity politics (Fukui and Markakis 1994). As a liberation struggle against colonial domination, nationalism encouraged identification between nation and state. In many parts of Africa, it also brought with it a 'quasi-nationalism' which, while energized by ancient hostilities and a myth of priority to the nation-state, differs from ethnicity and operates in various situations, irrespective of any dominant cleavage dividing the nation (Werbner 1991: 159). As I observed for Zimbabwe, the catastrophe of quasi-nationalism

> is that it can capture the might of the nation-state and bring authorised violence down ruthlessly against the people who seem to stand in the way of the nation being united and pure as one body. In such times, agents of the state, acting with its full authority, carry out the violation of the person. It is as if quasi-nationalism's victims, by being of an opposed quasi-nation, put themselves outside the nation, indeed beyond the pale of humanity. They are dealt with ferociously not merely for the sake of political dominance by one part of the nation over another, but importantly also for the sake of moral renewal of the nation as a whole. (Werbner 1991: 159–60)

Such a catastrophe in postcolonial Zimbabwe has left many survivors alienated from their nation-state, some of them deeply convinced that the war for Zimbabwe failed to make it one nation. In the words of a member of the family I knew well in western Zimbabwe, 'Mugabe says he fought and won the country. But has he got a country? No, he has no country.' Like the colonial legacy of which it is a reinscription, the quasi-national legacy lives as an unfinished moral narrative, and it motivates survivors to call repeatedly for political debts to be met and moral violations put right, especially by the state and its agents, most recently in the regime under Mugabe's successor President Munagagwa (Werbner 1995: 102, 106; Fontein 2010).

Jessica Ogden's study of the AIDS crisis in Kampala discloses an uneasy transformation in postcolonial intimacy and domesticity, expressed in contested assertions about *omukyala oumutumfu*, the 'proper woman' (1996). Stereotypes stigmatizing town women with spoilt identities were a colonial legacy. Identity strategies that were empowering during colonialism gave rise to disempowering contradictions in postcolonial contexts. Ogden clarifies the historicity of identity politics and the changing impact for town women not merely of negative stereotypes but of their own strategies, and personal and moral defences against stereotyping (see also Salo 2016).

Vulnerable subjectivities: subjection and subjectivation

With such analysis of identity politics and accompanying appeals to authentic and essential belonging or autochthony has come an exploration of the ways that subjectivities are changing, often in ephemeral ways, while remaining constrained by intractable conditions, some of very long duration. In analytic terms, subjectivities are *political*, a matter of subjugation to state authority; *moral*, reflected in the conscience and agency of subjects who bear rights, duties and obligations; and *existentially realized*, in the subjects' consciousness of their personal or intimate relations.

Subjugation and subjection are slippery as common terms for subjective processes. Usually but not consistently, subjugation is about the power of the state to dominate and make the subject, while subjection, often associated with disciplinary processes, has become an umbrella term for the making of the subject in almost any sense, and usually in several senses at once. Postcolonial anthropologists cannot claim to have resolved these ambiguities or standardized their own vocabulary; the literature is too richly engaged, and the ambiguities brought together by the multiple senses of the basic terms too much the stuff of actual discourses to allow that.

Recognizing that subjectivity is an ambiguous concept, which includes reflexivity and intersubjectivity, and that it has various senses, postcolonial anthropology has problematized relations between the personal, the political and the moral across remarkably different postcolonial transformations. None of these relations is amenable to being understood through simplistic dichotomies, such as citizen vs. subject.[2] As originally proposed in subaltern postcolonial studies and later elaborated by Mahmood Mamdani (1996), the citizen was a rights-bearing person entitled to justice and living under the rule of state law. By contrast, the subject lived under despots, customary authorities deployed by the colonial state under indirect rule. Against this simplification, Francis Nyamnjoh argues that Africans 'are both citizens and subjects ... sometimes they are more citizen than subject and sometimes more subject than citizen' (2001: 364).

A theoretical interest in the contingency and ambiguity of subjectivity lies at the heart of postcolonial analysis by Susan Reynolds Whyte, who is concerned to understand how people in eastern Uganda survive the ravages of the AIDS epidemic (1997, 2002). Her analysis turns on a concept of the subjunctive: that is, the tentative and the conditional mood which is responsive to the *if* and *maybe* of experience, and looks to an uncertain future with both hope and doubt. In people's own terms, it is a matter of *ohugeraga*, of trying out alternatives, one plan of action then another. This subjunctive mood, Whyte suggests, prevails in subjection to the insufficiencies of healthcare systems in postcolonial African states. Related to the subjunctive is the concept of 'civility' which, following Richard Rorty, Whyte defines as a virtue people themselves recognize in their practical wisdom, of attending to others, showing them respect and recognizing 'their moral privilege to an account of how things are'. In everyday life, this exercise of civility – which relates to a sense of mutual dependence – qualifies realization of the subjunctive mood, as people cope with the chanciness of postcolonial healthcare.

Conviviality, its dark and light sides: Mbembe and Nyamnjoh

Achille Mbembe has argued for a dark view of conviviality, which he found linked to a distinctively postcolonial style of political improvisation. It is a style that materializes within 'a series of corporate institutions and a political machinery which, once they are in place, constitute a distinctive regime of violence' (Mbembe 1992: 5). In the light of his insights from Cameroon, Mbembe carried this argument further by taking seriously the obscene laughter *with* and not merely *against* the regime.[3] Doing so, he made us recognize a link between domination and the grotesque in what he called the banality of power in the postcolony, and he moved our understanding of playfulness in the face of tyranny – whether bureaucratic, charismatic, domestic, nationalist or other – from the overemphasis on resistance typical of sociopolitical theory, towards recognition of connivance. 'Precisely because the postcolonial mode of domination is as much a regime of constraints as *a practice of conviviality and a stylistic of connivance*, the analyst must be attentive to the myriad ways in which ordinary people bridle, trick, and actually *toy* with power instead of confronting it directly' (Mbembe 1992a: 22, italics in original).

The smile on the face of the tyrant has been a ubiquitous postcolonial icon standing midway between consensus and coercion. Anthropologists might detect resonances with Max Gluckman's argument about 'rituals of rebellion' (1963c), but Gluckman's theoretical interest was in what he regarded as 'an instituted *protest* demanded by sacred tradition, which is seemingly against the established order, yet which aims to bless that order to achieve prosperity' (1963c: 114, my italics). For Gluckman, under certain ritualized conditions identities were persuasively formed in support of established values by open, yet highly formalized expressions of conflict. The *toying* with power Mbembe described has taken the postcolony beyond such familiar formulations applied to pre-colonial or colonial conditions.

Mbembe called upon Bakhtin only to stand Bakhtin on his head: when writing at the height of the Stalin era, Bakhtin suggested that unofficial humour scoffed at the deity, opposed the official world, unmasked its pretence of reality and opened 'a second world and a second life outside officialdom' (Bakhtin 1984: 6). For Mbembe, however, the divide between official and unofficial collapsed into a baroque style of political improvisation in which everyone indulged. To bend Geertz's argument (1973) to Mbembe's postcolonial purposes, the 'wink' and the 'thick description of the wink' has become the postcolonial work *par excellence*; along with conviviality, connivance reigns.

Writing on Banda's oppressive era in Malawi and its aftermath, Harri Englund (1996a) qualified Mbembe's view to argue that however authoritarian the founding postcolonial regime, it did not entirely colonize the imagination of its subjects. Connivance in simulacra may have been real and far-reaching, yet not complete or unqualified; hence, it is liable to challenge in moments of crisis by persuasive appeals to locally axiomatic morality and by people strategically using already available identities.

The consequences of changes in postcolonial subjectivities for human vulnerability have been underlying concerns of different anthropological approaches: shared human vulnerability has a global context in 'a world of hegemonies of all kinds', to use Francis Nyamnjoh's phrase. We are all at risk, when it comes to being able to be who we are as agents in relationships with others, and when it comes to articulating and defending our collective interests. Building on public debate in Cameroon about *convivialité culturelle*, Nyamnjoh introduced his own concept of 'conviviality' (Nyamnjoh 2002; see also Nkwi and Nyamnjoh 1997; Nyamnjoh 1999) as a matter of interdependence and intersubjectivity: the congenial fellowship – often light-hearted, merry, even hilarious – that is created between active agents who are otherwise in competition or conflict with each other yet determined to empower and not marginalize each other. Nyamnjoh's aim in writing of conviviality has been to understand how postcolonial subjects can transcend their vulnerability while negotiating their subjection through relationships with others. Conviviality is the light side of subjectivity in the postcolony, the darker side being the one Nyamnjoh foregrounded in much of his other writing, including his remarkable novel, *Mind Searching* (1991).[4]

'Cameroon constantly needs', Nyamnjoh observed, 'to balance the tensions of a triple colonial heritage and other multiple identities that have made it "Africa in miniature" and also, a paradise of paradoxes' (2002: 112). The question that Cameroonian academics, journalists, writers, politicians and clergy now ask is: how can Cameroon survive in 'harmonious co-existence', when it is 'threatened by political, religious, ethnic and economic differences and inequalities'? What can keep such a postcolony united 'despite its internal contradictions and differences' (Nyamnjoh 1999)? How can its people realize their agency and subjectivity while drawing upon multiple and disparate cultural repertoires (Nkwi and Nyamnjoh 1997)? No one believes there are simple answers, but such questions are being raised publicly and answered openly in a conscious quest for a survival strategy in the face of war and turmoil in the postcolony.[5]

The relative autonomy of social actors, like the very category of the subject, becomes problematic under changing postcolonial conditions, argues Pnina Werbner (2009), examining the dialogical subjectivities of women in Botswana. The argument carries forward, also, the regard for 'fun spaces' (P. Werbner 1996, 2001) where, as in rap music and smartly dressed portrait photography, people indulge in the pleasures of playful self-fashioning (Behrend 2002; Stroeken 2005; Weiss 2009). The resonance is with our discussion of colonial popular culture in the *kalela* dance, in Chapter 4. Taking the fun as seriously as the apocalyptic pronouncements in popular practice leads to a deeper insight into what Brad Weiss calls, in relation to the postcolonial life-world of youth in urban Tanzania, 'the fugitive character of reality' (2009: 207).

Violence or civility?

The reconfiguration of personal agency has rarely been entirely peaceful. 'Culture-as-political struggle' has all too often been waged by brutal violence, whether colonial or postcolonial. The postcolonies are 'societies recently emerging from the experience of colonisation and the violence which the colonial relationship, *par excellence*, involves' (Mbembe 1992b: 3). For different postcolonies, anthropologists have shown how traumatic identities have been formed in intergenerational struggles, and how personal transformations have been made through political violence or human violation (Englund 1996a; Fisiy and Geschiere 1996; Hutchinson and Jok

2002; Argenti 2007). Their accounts have revealed the redefinitions of identity, self and other that occur in processes of postcolonial subjection when civility ends. They have confronted brutal realities, when subjects of mutual respect, friends and neighbours, become objects of violation in interethnic or intercommunal conflict (Van der Veer 1994; Holtzman 2017), yet they also show careful regard for the saliences of civility, honour and respect (Whyte 2002; Klaits 2005, 2010).

War-torn southern Sudan is one region where remaking post-colonial subjectivities has been accompanied by escalating violence directed by the people against themselves. As Sharon Hutchinson and Jok Madut Jok show (2002), the political violence which over-whelmed the rural communities of Nuer and Dinka was largely driven from outside by pressures from international petroleum com-panies and by the postcolonial state's ruling regime. In a new version of an old colonial policy, Nuer and Dinka endured the efforts of the postcolonial state to divide and rule by funding rival military elites to achieve control over this oil zone. During rapid polarization and militarization from 1991 to 1999, the ethnic other ceased to be the subject of ethical restraints during interethnic conflict between these neighbouring, intermarried peoples who recognize common ancestry. Previously, the lives of women, children and the elderly were sacrosanct, and they were never intentionally killed in battle. Slaying them was an affront to God as the ultimate guardian of human morality, which would visit the slayer or some member of his family with divine anger in the form of terrible illness, sudden death and other affliction. Hutchinson and Jok show the devastat-ing consequences for Nuer and Dinka postcolonial subjectivities of devaluing the ethnic other from ethical subject to brutalized object, and how this has led to a vicious increase in gendered and inwardly directed aggression. The power of men over women has been magnified, and with that the vulnerability of women to violence and rape, not merely by enemy troops but even by male 'protectors' from their own ethnic group. Ending interethnic civil-ity brought about a profound shift in moral reasoning and personal consciousness that altered the very concepts of ethnicity. Militari-zation, and political violence against unarmed non-combatants, has sealed the ethnic divide from both sides, making it less permeable.

Concurrently, the Nuer concept of ethnicity gravitated towards what Hutchinson and Jok termed 'a more "primordialist", if not "racialist" way of thinking about their "essence"' (Hutchinson and Jok 2002: 105). Notwithstanding, Hutchinson and Jok also found signs of a potential reversal of this trend, and their hope remains to be fulfilled: that interethnic peace would 'continue to reawaken Nuer and Dinka men and women to the historical fluidity and permeability of their ethnic identities for the greater good of the South' (2002: 106).

The reappropriation of the state, reciprocal assimilation, political hybridity

The cultural politics of everyday life, whether within or against state-created domains, is another concern that anthropologists have foregrounded in postcolonial studies. Quoting Gramsci, the political scientist Jean-François Bayart notes of 'the reciprocal assimilation of elites' that '[i]n the case of Caesar and Napoleon I, it could be said that A and B, whilst being distinct and opposed entities, could after a molecular process, still end up in an "absolute" fusion and reciprocal assimilation' (Gramsci 1983: 503, cited in Bayart 1993: 322–3 n.78). In Bayart's usage, reciprocal assimilation describes the relations between new and traditional elites, their encompassing identities, and their potential social inclusion or even political fusion. Elites were typically distinct, even if historically related, sometimes sharing familial or local origins. For Bayart, 'reciprocal assimilation' argues the importance of the *longue durée* for hybridity in political culture, which involves both continuity *and* change. Applied to the postcolony, 'reciprocal assimilation' highlights the problematic agency of dissimilar political actors in the selective alliance of disparate postcolonial elites, and draws attention to the hybridity of postcolonial political culture, as the active and changeable synthesis/ anti-synthesis of renewable pre-colonial and colonial legacies.[6] With such assimilation and hybridity potentially come acquiescence or resistance to state power, or indeed both, in specific sociopolitical contexts.

Given Bayart's stress on the *longue durée*, it would be mistaken to read into his argument the implication that political hybridity is distinctively postcolonial. This false contrast between the colonial and the postcolonial is rejected by most anthropologists who prefer to accept Bayart's challenge to analyse the reworking of traces of colonial political hybridity in the postcolonial.[7] Even further, anthropologists, faced with the idea of 'the end of the tribe', have recently had to rethink the postcolonial robustness and the 'modernity' of chiefs, surprisingly strategic and authoritative in their neo-traditional entanglements with their personal and communal property within the postcolony (Comaroff and Comaroff 2018; Geschiere 2018).

Post-conflict societies, grassroots ecumenism and the state

In a recent special issue of the *Journal of Southern African Studies* (2018), we put forward a broad argument, particularly with regard to post-conflict societies. The argument is that grassroots ecumenism tends to change radically, and yet ambiguously, with far-reaching shifts in the political interventions made by the state. Andrea Grant (2018) discloses the ecumenical uncertainties in post-genocide Rwanda through a substantial analysis of struggles involving an autocratic state regime and between the new Pentecostal churches and the historically dominant Catholic Church. Her close observation of a public occasion, meant to be a showcase for thanksgiving and reconciliation in unity but inadvertently overcome by bitter controversy, tellingly grounds the broad argument in nuanced first-hand evidence.

Carrying our argument forward to post-war Angola, Ramon Sarro (2018) illuminates the formidable hurdles in the way of coexistence and the very possibilities for grassroots ecumenism, where the remembered burden of troubling and brutal wartime legacies, even from the ancient past, threatens to sink people in religious polemic. His fine case study provides the rare evidence for southern Africa of a problematic in-gathering of exiles from wartime sanctuary in a foreign city. They are the would-be homecomers having inherited citizenship who are actually cultural strangers, foreign in their language. They have to be accommodated, along with their imported and numerous, ever-fragmenting churches; but, as Sarro shows, what is still very much in doubt is inclusion, whether the accommodation will bring the homecomers together with other

Angolans in the same churches or in some everyday forms of religious fellowship.

The state itself is intervening to regulate the proliferation of churches, by demanding unity in federations. Such top-down unity is contested and arouses suspicion that the institutional ecumenism is a mere trap. It is seen to be a political move for dominance by one church over others, perhaps to return to rejected colonial control, say by Catholics, or perhaps for new advantage in state or party politics; and by subverting grassroots ecumenism among tiny churches, it is counterproductive. The very upholding of Christian public culture is radically called into question. Some of the counter-publics that arise aggressively demand a public place for what Sarro calls anti-Christianity. The counter-publics' claim that Christianity is alienating speaks to an impulse for restoration, getting back to oneself in a truly authentic way of belonging and revitalization. According to Sarro, new churches hugely multiply, turn away from the white Jesus, and devote themselves to a black as a martyr, mediator and prophet, truly theirs in a continuous tradition of their own.

For South Africa, and based on very long-term, frank and intimate research among Afrikaners, Annika Teppo (2018) offers a fresh perspective on powerfully felt moral and religious upheavals in their post-apartheid lives. There is a remarkable shift from anti-ecumenism to ecumenism. Teppo reveals that when the Afrikaners' historically anti-ecumenical church ceased to be the state at prayer, so to speak, they found themselves no longer able to take many things for granted which, in their past, they understood, almost as an obsession and subject to much surveillance, to be *ordentlikheid* (being proper or decent).[8] What is now emerging is a considerable variety of forms of grassroots ecumenism. Of those that Teppo documents, perhaps the most innovative are the Cape Town ecumenical walks, virtually pilgrimages, when South Africans, including Afrikaners, celebrate together in visiting all the local places of religion, churches, mosques and synagogues. Very broadly, Teppo traces the dynamic engagement of disparate publics and counter-publics in the reconstruction of Christian public culture in South Africa.

Ilana van Wyk (2018) carries our broad argument forward to one of the most controversial churches in South Africa, the

Brazilian-derived Universal Church of the Kingdom of God (UKGC). Unmotivated by humanitarian interest in the public good and hardly given to charitable support for public welfare, this increasingly popular church faces exclusively in the very opposite direction, under post-apartheid conditions, to that of now more inclusive Afrikaner churches. Christian scholars might well argue that the teachings of the UKGC are quite extraordinary and stand in contradiction to orthodoxy on fellowship, kinship, solidarity, trust and unity within the Christian traditions in Africa and beyond. Two of South Africa's major ecumenical bodies, the South African Council of Churches (SACC) and the Evangelical Alliance of South Africa (TEASA), got the South African Human Rights Commission to investigate the church, but under pressure from the UKGC's lawyers the Commission had to end its investigation and retract statements it had made to the media about the church. Clearly, the UKGC mobilized to protect its interests and public image, but van Wyk draws our attention also to the church's deeply and aggressively anti-ecumenical theology with its apocalyptic vision. From the UKGC website, she cites the warning of the coming of the anti-Christ that the head of the UKGC in Brazil, Bishop Macedo, gave his congregants in South Africa against ecumenism: its supposed emphasis on 'love and peace' masked a dark ambition to establish a world order in which 'one government led by the antichrist and assisted by his beast (the false prophet)' held sway. To contextualize this anti-ecumenical appeal, van Wyk traces the responses to earlier intolerant battle cries of the head of another Brazilian Pentecostal church, Igreja Universal do Reino de Deus (IURD). These polemical attacks, which provoked violence against people of other faiths, especially Afro-Brazilians, were opposed by non-violent protests, when Afro-Brazilians were joined during grassroots ecumenical marches by Catholics, Muslims, Jews, Protestants, Buddhists and Baha'is.

What van Wyk makes plain is that the Pentecostalism imported from Brazil is extreme, devoted not to Christian peace but to religious intolerance, opposition to reconciliation, and an unforgiving divisiveness – it is the extreme in which members are as strangers, anonymous to each other and potentially estranged from kin and friends. This extreme of Brazilian Pentecostalism is the same one that, following van Wyk, Linda van de Kamp now finds in

Mozambique. In her acutely sensitive account of women becoming strangers in urban Pentecostalism, van de Kamp observes:

> Converts rarely participate in a community of engaged brothers and sisters with checks and balances where trust can be built. In contrast to Englund (2007) who concluded that Pentecostalism in Malawi was an important source for the development of civility and trust, Brazilian Pentcostalism in Mozambique (and the Universal Church in South Africa, van Wyk 2014) enhanced anonymity and distrust. Converts with problems are avoided by fellow converts. Little to no personal information is shared and Pentecostal[s] generally do not establish contact with others in church, in contrast to to the AICs [African Independent Churches] and the Assemblies of God Churches I frequented. (van de Kamp 2016: 182)

In a debate with mainstream academic literature, van Wyk questions whether it has focused adequately on the anti-ecumenical strand in South African Christianity, now promoted fiercely by the new Pentecostalism from Brazil – or whether it has sufficiently appreciated the enthusiasm with which many believers are embracing this strand's tenets of spiritual war and its transactional approach to personal salvation and prosperity. But can we interpret their spiritual war as a fight to right a world of economic and social precarity, a fight by the unforgiving poor in their own self-interest and without misguided 'empathy' for others? This is a central challenge that van Wyk confronts in her article, which advances the critically engaged yet still truly empathetic account in her recent monograph on the UKGC (2014).[9] Part of her argument is that not all UKGC members could openly 'fight' this world. Instead, many resorted to a covert dual engagement. On the one hand, they did not break with local traditions held to be demonic by the church; on the other, they clandestinely attended the church. Van Wyk calls this tactic, somewhat loosely and ironically, a practical make-do 'ecumenism from below'; and she finds that for the believers themselves it was unsatisfactory – if they did retain important social ties, they knew that they were exposing themselves to enormous spiritual dangers. The make-do tactic actually hinders grassroots ecumenism; it obviates an ideology of a more inclusive ecumene or an *ekklesia*; and van Wyk argues that it is an inadequate form of immediate social risk management.

These essays on grassroots ecumenism reach a recognized frontier where there is a challenging agenda for even more broad research (Jules-Rosette 2018). It is now more than a decade since the landmark publication on *Muslim–Christian Encounters in Africa* edited by Benjamin Soares (2006). More recently, a special section of *Africa* has brought the broader research agenda up to date (Janson and Meyer 2016). Reflecting there, more recently, in a substantial state-of-play review, Soares observes, 'Among historians, social scientists, and scholars of religion, there has been increased recognition of the importance of studying Islam and Christianity in Africa not separately but together, as lived religions in dynamic interaction over time' (2016: 673). In agreement with this, while advocating a bolder comparative analysis, the special issue editors, Marloes Janson and Birgit Meyer, appreciate that the making of productive analytical perspectives on the dynamic interactions of Islam and Christianity in Africa is still in a very early stage.[10] Hence Janson and Meyer call for 'an encompassing conceptual framework that is devoted to drawing out similarities, differences and entanglements.' (2016: 615). Arguably, in relation to our own regard for grassroots ecumenism, this call needs to put a further item on the research agenda, or at least shift the weight in debate from too much on mutual transformations, with 'similarities, differences', and too little on entanglements. Even further, if it is useful to start the conceptualization of entanglements with Brian Larkin's view of a range of 'modes of borrowing, mutual confrontation or reciprocal exchange' (2016: 655), then an important question still remains. How are we to open out a better perspective on what, under the gross rubrics of 'interfaith dialogue' and 'interfaith relations', has been poorly documented and little analysed for Christian–Muslim encounters in Africa?

Although the answer is well beyond my present scope, it is worth saying that the very question itself calls for even more rethinking of alternatives in religion. There is a familiar perception of a widespread shift in direction from openness to exclusion. Michael Lambek sees this in terms of an opposition between two religious logics, one of 'both/and' which accommodates and includes certain alternatives; and the other of 'either/or' which suppresses and excludes them (Lambek 2008). 'What appears to be happening in *some parts of Africa*', remarks Lambek, 'is a shift from accepting

Christianity or Islam within an inclusive both/and universe to accepting them in an exclusive either/or paradigm' (2008: 124, my italics). *Some parts of Africa* – it is as if Lambek is challenging us to foreground more of the other parts, or even to reconsider the familiar appearance, perhaps to allow for *reprise*, for a turn away from either/or exclusion and towards another version of both/and inclusion. This is the postcolonial challenge that takes us to an important frontier where grassroots ecumenism is itself unbound and calls for a perspective on a shift to being both Christian and Muslim, to being not of one religion or another but of both.

Perhaps the most outstanding study to address this postcolonial challenge is Marloes Janson's account of the West African Chrislam movement (Janson and Meyer 2016). Its leaders call for 'unity between Christians and Muslims', while at the same time they vie in rivalry for followers, for their own separate centre (mosque/church). There is, of course, a special religious context in which Chrislam emerges. In Nigeria, Chrislam thrives only in the context of enduring, long-term and highly valued religious tolerance among Yoruba in south-western Nigeria, which John Peel's monumental work so profoundly illuminates (2015). In accord with that, Janson argues that 'Chrislam can be considered a Yoruba phenomenon: it is the shared ethnicity that makes the mixing between Islam and Christianity possible' (2016: 652). Janson shows that the movement cannot be comprehended merely in familiar terms of interfaith dialogue or syncretism or the fusion of elements from two world religions, Christianity and Islam. Instead, as the movement's self-designation, Chrislam, declares, with membership comes the insistence on a dual religious identity, being both a Christian and a Muslim.

It is, of course, hardly novel to speak of the religious pluralism which sometimes appears communal in public occasions for participation irrespective of religious difference, and which sometimes appears personal in that the same person undergoes conversion from one religion to another, sometimes in a series back and forth. But what now calls for more attention in postcolonial studies, extending beyond the frontiers of present research on grassroots ecumenism, is the entanglement which proceeds through a process of religious straddling; a process that is not *either* Christian *or* Muslim, but, in Lambek's terms, a religious process of *both/and*.

Finally, mention of Yoruba and their creative agency brings me to the collaboration in postcolonial anthropology that is the most outstanding example of path-breaking achievement in ethnography by a mentor, John Peel, and his pupil, Wale Adebanwi. The achievement is all the more remarkable and inspiring because each writes his own landmark ethnography on a distinctive field and from a distinctive perspective, and yet both shed fresh light on phenomena of ethnogenesis and ethnicity among the same people (Adebanwi 2014; Peel 2015). As I mentioned earlier and as is richly examined in the special issue of *Africa* (Janson and Meyer 2016), Peel's masterwork, *Christianity, Islam, and Orisa Religion* (2015), explores innovative interrelations across religious frontiers. It is *somewhat* away from religion and towards politics and statesmanlike, progressive leadership, most importantly to the example of Chief Obafemi Awolwo, that Adebanwi turns in *Yoruba Elite and Ethnic Politics in Nigeria* (2014). I stress *somewhat*, because Adebanwi examines the hallowing process in politics, while documenting crisis events at death and burial, which are significant for transforming an elder into a hallowed, guiding ancestor – and here, Adebanwi acknowledges, he places his own argument and ethnography in the Cambridge anthropological tradition from Meyer Fortes. In a core chapter on the extraordinary idealization of Awolwo as 'the secular ancestor', Adebanwi illuminates the contested spirituality of the 'ethno-national figure' who emerged as Nigeria's most controversial political leader, even in death, in practices of veneration and through the intensely renewed, highly contentious narration of heroic excess in his life.

Peel's perspective is that of the stranger who becomes an intimate through a lifetime of devotion, first to the fieldworker's firsthand observation and later to the unrivalled mastery of archival and other documentary sources for the Yoruba. Complementing this is Adebanwi's perspective, extremely rare in postcolonial anthropology – he writes as the consummate insider who enters into a 'cult of power', becomes a leading activist, even a passionate, captivating orator in the public fray of factional politics, keeps its 'secrets' and confidences, yet cogently discloses, in rich evidence – *among the richest we have so far* – the 'co-ordination of corporate activities' by which an elite fosters *with* 'the masses' an elective affinity, rather than a divorce in subjugation. It is hardly surprising that of the two

Yoruba experts, the postcolonial insider is the one who takes greatest care to position himself reflexively and to locate the critical arguments in his ethnography comparatively, as in the waves to and from class and elite theories (Adebanwi 2016). Adebanwi leaves us in no doubt that he knows he must speak not only *for* Yoruba but *with* the social scientists and social historians of elites and state formation not only in Africa but in many other parts of the world. I must confess a very strong sympathy with his basic view of an elite as a progressive force, given my own advocacy of an Afro-optimistic agenda in *Reasonable Radicals and Citizenship in Botswana* (2004). Here postcolonial studies reaches beyond our past to promising insights into the change and continuity we still need to face together in a troubled world that now appears in many ways increasingly polarized and threatened by denials of our shared humanity. This challenge makes the regard in the earlier colonial studies for overlapping relations in complex social fields all the more important. Here what is important in the tradition from Gluckman and his circle is not a body of received answers but a critical approach, reopening problems and asking fresh questions for analysis in shifting and open-ended contexts.

Notes

1 On the resurgence of academic interest in witchcraft and a critique of the modernist paradigm of witchcraft, see Werbner 2015: 47–9.
2 Partha Chatterjee argued that 'the colonial state could confer only subjecthood on the colonized; it could not grant them citizenship' (1993: 237; see also Nyamnjoh 2016: 187–208, 229–58).
3 On postcolonial derision and hollow laughter, see Bayart 1993: 293.
4 On connivance and the *commandement* in Cameroon and other postcolonies, see also Mbembe 1992a, 1992b; and Werbner 1996a.
5 For an appreciation of the challenges to liberalism that are, hopefully, being met by reimaginings of difference in everyday life, see Comaroff and Comaroff 2004: 200; they see the challenge coming from a contradiction in apartheid South Africa as an exemplary postcolony: 'There is no resolution to the antinomy between the "One Law for One Nation," with its unremitting commitment to legal universalism under the new South African Constitution and the primordially sanctioned demands of heterodoxy in this policultural society'.
6 On the parallel of syncretism/anti-syncretism, see Stewart and Shaw 1994; Werbner 1994.

7 See Werbner 1969; on the salience of a colonial political legacy for a post-apartheid youth elite, see also Fumanti 2016. On the historicity of the reciprocal assimilation of elites in the face of the virtual collapse of the state in Zaire, see De Boeck 1996.

8 See Salo 2016 on transformations among Afrikaans-speaking 'coloureds' on the urban margins of Cape Town: the reworking by teenagers of *ordentlikheid* and the crossing of the boundaries of apartheid classification.

9 See Salo 2016 on transformations among Afrikaans-speaking 'coloureds' on the urban margins of Cape Town: the reworking by teenagers of *ordentlikheid* and the crossing of the boundaries of apartheid classification.

10 See Salo 2016 on transformations among Afrikaans-speaking 'coloureds' on the urban margins of Cape Town: the reworking by teenagers of *ordentlikheid* and the crossing of the boundaries of apartheid classification.

Conclusion

This book began by positioning Max Gluckman within his personal
and intellectual history. His father, a progressive lawyer who served,
among other roles, as a controversial advocate for African clients
and their politically sensitive causes, was a much-admired role
model for Gluckman. I offered an analysis of his father's most celebrated case, against Paramount Chief Khama, in order to shed light
on aspects of Gluckman's family that were formative not only for
his interest in problematic rationality, uncertainty, ethics and judicial
process but also for his liberal and cosmopolitan disposition.

My account from Chapter 2 and throughout much of this book
documents Gluckman's lasting commitments as a public intellectual
and his highly responsive, critical approach to human problems
during the colonial to postcolonial transformation. There was no
moral disconnect between him and his subjects, the fault-line among
early modern social anthropologists, according to Geertz (1988:
152). Gluckman wrote in consultation *with* the people he studied
and expected to be read *by* them; reaching broader publics was an
achievement he made in radio talks and popular texts.

Anthropology after Gluckman discloses the vicissitudes and entanglements in the intense, argument-rich collaborations and dissen-
sions among his circle that came to be known as the Manchester
School. It reminds the reader of Gluckman's theorization of conflict
resolution, of the frailty of authority, of order and rebellion, of the
social situation and the changing social field. It shows also that he
had an acute historical consciousness, and pursued a transformational
project over the series of studies which I discuss most closely in
Chapter 2. He anticipated many of our continuing efforts to explore

the force of opposition in history; ahead of his times, he wrote auto-ethnography; he was reflective about his own practice, situating it within his intellectual debts, both to older and younger generations of ethnographers, and self-consciously problematizing his own objectivity, according to his changing social relations. Gluckman practised the re-analysis of ethnography, and he cultivated this practice among his students – fine rethinking of the arguments in an ethnography in the light of a close examination of the evidence presented and, by *comparison* to other works, missing. I stress comparison here, and in Chapter 2 I show how Gluckman carried forward different modalities of comparison in social anthropology, according to the varied problems and questions he pursued in a long-term comparative project, which is now all the more important for renewed interest in the distinct illumination that diverse modalities of comparison afford (see Candea 2019). If currently phrased in terms of state violence, power and globalization, of the politics of custom and indigenization, of gender, cultural hegemony and resistance, of civic culture and civility, of ethical and moral anthropology, and now with fierce divisiveness in terms of decolonization, the urgent problems resonate with challenges in theory and practice that Gluckman confronted.

Focused on Elizabeth Colson's life and breakthroughs as a pioneering member of the Manchester School, Chapter 3 contributes at least two things which are basic in the book. One is the regard for interdisciplinary contributions; the other, for academics as themselves outsiders or 'people on the move' and yet somehow deeply concerned with their own belonging and identity. In particular, Chapter 3 reveals how as a transatlantic social scientist, Colson excelled in her boundary-crossing accomplishments; she built bridges between American sociology, British social anthropology and British moral philosophy. Having herself been a research assistant at Harvard in the early 1940s, she knew of work by the sociologist George Homans, and she encouraged Gluckman to invite him to Manchester and consider his ideas on small group research. Some of these became even more fruitful in the turn to relational thought and networks by members of the Manchester School, above all John Barnes, Clyde Mitchell and A. L. 'Bill' Epstein.

Colson's bridges are among the most important ones that sustained intellectual mobility rather than closure in the making of the Manchester School. But if a cosmopolitan, with a cultivated sense of our human comedy, Colson was not the anthropologist as rootless cosmopolitan. Instead, she was the reflexive, home town anthropologist, returning again and again over a very long career to certain human problems of dislocation familiar to her from her own home town in the American Midwest. It was a place of uneasy coexistence between Ojibwa Indians and white settler Americans, mainly farmers like her grandparents, Colson's own parents being educators. For Colson, with her home town reflexivity, and as an avowedly moderate liberal in politics, came her radical commitment to the fight against discrimination and bullying in academic life. Very highly productive, Colson wrote richly empathetic ethnographies, some on social dislocation and misguided development, at troubling times of postcolonial crisis. Her critical essays offer a great stream of topical insights. Throughout her work runs a hopeful moral imagination.

Chapter 3 makes plain a further aspect of the book as a whole. It is at once both an intellectual and personal history and also a contribution to the sociology of knowledge. Hence Chapter 3 follows Colson's networking, her alerting of her American colleagues to Manchester works 'hot off the press', and her generosity to her old colleagues' students, including myself. Colson's importance is shown for the reception by the Manchester School of what might be called travelling theories, perhaps most importantly Kurt Lewin's field theory. The account advances a fresh understanding of arguments within the Manchester School. To these, Colson contributed as a *systems sceptic* in deeply sustained dialogue and enduring friendship with Max Gluckman, *the systems builder* who towered over the School and profoundly influenced the received wisdom about the School, its programme in influential pronouncements, and its ideas of crisis and conflict resolution.

If I am right that Colson was a home town anthropologist, then Clyde Mitchell could be said to be the one whose lack of a home town in his early life may well have been formative in another direction, one that was very much his own, and then highly influential in certain Manchester School studies, as I discuss in Chapter 4. Neither Pietermaritzburg, Natal where he was born in 1918, nor any other South African town became a place of deep roots for Mitchell. Instead, he moved in Natal from place to place and had to learn from early on to navigate his way along routes and the railway line, perhaps becoming familiar with the numbers on the timetables, because his Scottish father worked on the railway. Significantly, his first urbanization paper maps 'The Distribution of African Labour by Area of Origin in the Copper Mines of Northern Rhodesia' (1954). I am tempted to speculate on a lifelong disposition of Mitchell's – it is the one having both affinity with mapping, navigating and finding a way through flux and complexity, and also a fascination with empirical bits of the kind a mathematician might parse, or the maker of a timetable might locate on a graph.

Having this disposition in mind, I consider mainly two things in Chapter 4. One is the distinctiveness of Mitchell's original contributions as an urban anthropologist, often calling himself a sociologist. The other is the nature of an interdependent, if ambivalent, relation with his mentor and friend, Max Gluckman, from whom he learned and whom in turn he taught, in good measure through restatements and revisions of Gluckman's work and ideas.

Collaboration with A. L. Epstein during Mitchell's most creative period in Africa is very much a part of both of these considerations, and in this and following chapters, I examine some of this, too. I also reopen the debate about anthropology and the encounter with colonial and settler states, because of the part of Mitchell's work that became fiercely controversial in its time and, further, because of the pressing need in our postcolonial times to illuminate Mitchell's role as a *socially aware* institution builder and a *critically engaged* anthropologist. In Chapter 5, I follow the trail of links important for Mitchell's and Epstein's pioneering and long-term contributions to the field now known as social network analysis. I also raise questions about diffusion and independent development in the advancement of relational thought in Africa and Melanesia.

One assumption might seem hard to contest: that anthropology deeply honours our shared humanity the more we shed light on how, in the face of adversity, people still celebrate living. Fun, joy, playful creativity, even people showing off how smartly they can dress: the fact is that precisely for illuminating all of this in his study of *The Kalela Dance* (1956) in colonial Zambia (then Northern Rhodesia), Clyde Mitchell came under fierce attack, indeed an *ad hominem* polemic against even his personal motives, from the South African sociologist Bernard Magubane. This was at a time when the affinity between rising nationalism and the liberation struggle in Africa seemed more certain than it now does; and in the USA's African diaspora, while based at the University of Connecticut, Magubane had the moral authority of a prominent African National Congress activist in the forefront of the campaign against disinvestment from South Africa. Magubane had a meta-narrative about class and race, with a strong thesis of imperial economic domination and disempowerment, which allowed no room for such relational and processual concepts as the social situation and the social field. Worse still, implied Magubane, was what we now call 'speaking for': that is, to be a white social scientist claiming expertise on Africa was in itself suspect and to focus on interpersonal relations and everyday life was to be open all the more to the charge of hiding the class struggle and being an agent, perhaps unwittingly, of 'white supremacy'.

Aware of the serious resonance with the renewed debate about decolonization and indigenous knowledge (Allen and Jobson 2016; Nyamnjoh 2016), I seek in Chapter 4 to trace certain implications for urban ethnographic research of the trenchant Marxist critique in Magubane's polemic. This chapter follows the development by Mitchell along with Epstein of their approach to social and cultural *innovation* and change in Copperbelt towns; in the foreground is Epstein's analysis of urban Africans' continuous struggles for power and improved positions within the new industrial society. More broadly, on that basis I devote a major part of the discussion to problems of engaged and contested social science in the eye of the storm, and here I show how, for Mitchell, engaged anthropology was *public* anthropology, which takes critical stands on pressing social and political issues, including academic freedom.

Chapter 5 examines the turn by Epstein, Mitchell and others to relational thought, at first primarily about ties of friendship or kinship and about the structures of these ties. Where an earlier generation of anthropologists in the 1930s had turned to science for physicists' ideas of process theory, in the 1950s, led by Barnes and later Mitchell, anthropologists fostered an approach to science through mathematics (for a brief introduction, see Barnes 1974). After Barnes, Mitchell reformulated mathematical concepts in sociological language and brought graph theory and algebraic ideas and methods to bear on the data of interpersonal relations. Chapter 5 shows, also, how Mitchell responded when the tide of social network analysis turned in a fresh direction, sometimes called 'The Harvard Renaissance', and towards 'block modelling', in part stimulated by very much faster computers and exponentially more powerful computer programs. This chapter thus helps to explain why, as John Scott suggests, at least in Mitchell's time, social network analysis in Britain 'largely failed to attract adherents from outside community studies' (Scott 2017: 34).

Of all the interdisciplinary contributions by members of the Manchester School, the ones that are best known, especially in sociology, are their pioneering parts in the development of this huge growth industry: the field of social network analysis. It remains an open problem to understand and explain how and why it is that the growth in the development of this field stopped short when it came to influence on comparable, now robust mainstreams under rubrics of 'relationality' (Strathern 1995, 1996) and Actor-Network Theory (Latour 2005).

Now, with a good measure of credibility, a leading exponent, the mathematical sociologist Linton Freeman, can make this inclusive claim:

> Network analysis cuts across the boundaries of traditional disciplines. It brings together sociologists, anthropologists, mathematicians, economists, political scientists, psychologists, communication scientists, statisticians, ethologists, epidemiologists, computer scientists, both organizational behavior and market specialists from business schools and recently, physicists. (Freeman 2004: 5)

It began small, of course. There was first in 1953 work by John Barnes and in 1954 Elizabeth Bott's work, which was influenced by Barnes and by the Manchester seminar, and which in turn was later taken up by Epstein and Mitchell. In the early 1950s also present at Manchester seminars was the American sociologist George Homans, who had been working on the re-analysis and theoretical framing of small group research, carried out by sociometric social psychologists led by Jacob Moreno and by anthropologists, colleagues of W. Lloyd Warner (Homans 1950).

Through my own research on elites in Botswana, Chapter 6 carries forward some of Mitchell's and Epstein's ideas of networks, but without Mitchell's formal analysis in a mathematical model. In part, my agenda is set in opposition to a toxic version of Afro-pessimism. It is the version that finds Africa doomed by the klep-tomania of elites, ungovernable because of the self-seeking of Big Men, and inevitably victimized by liberators who reveal themselves to be tyrants. Against that, in *Reasonable Radicals and Citizenship in Africa* (2004), I documented some of the facts that show that Bot-swana does have its share of wider postcolonial conflicts and pre-dicaments – and indeed, as I write in 2019, following the landslide electoral victory of the country's fifth president, Mokgweetse Masisi, a major public debate is in progress, calling for constitutional reform, for successful investigation of large-scale corruption and crony capi-talism, and for far-reaching accountability for scandalous abuse of power under the fourth president, Ian Khama (see Ditsheko 2019). But I argued earlier, and still do, for the strength of the concern for the public good; I do so on the basis of substantial evidence that strong and resilient values of civic virtue and civility have been and are being sustained in the public sphere; that progressive elites have been making constructive contributions to state and nation building; that good governance continues to be advanced through the deliberately developed and well-sustained political structures and practices of a strong state.

In this chapter, my own approach extends the network studies questions to social mobility and the accomplishments through which elites emerge, constitute cliques, participate in interlocking directo-rates, generate convivial subjectivities and sustain long-term friend-ships. Raised on that basis are further arguments regarding the importance of elite friendship for the constituting of openness and public trust in postcolonial state formation (see also Adebanwi 2014). Following a familiar example in Manchester School studies, I turn to events and a public occasion, the funeral of Richard Man-nathoko, to reveal the actual practice I observed among elites. Here I bear testimony to Mannathoko as a great friend of mine; and at the funeral itself, as I report in Chapter 6, I acknowledged how much my understanding of life in Botswana owed to our dialogue over many years from our shared youth to elderhood.

The funeral brought to the foreground Mannathoko's life as a senior civil servant turned big businessman, who took the lead in struggles for good governance and yet who also nurtured his roots among Kalanga in his own ethnic community. This chapter thus

seeks to further our understanding not only of interpersonal relations and interlocking directorates among elites but also their cosmopolitanism. Perhaps for any cosmopolitan, but certainly for the
public cosmopolitan, the cosmopolitan who engages actively with
the state and contributes to the public sphere, the question of how
to be patriotic and cosmopolitan at the same time is sensitive and
pressing. If never a merely academic question, it is arguably inescap-
able for the scholarly understanding of the changeable force that
public cosmopolitanism has in civic culture and civil life in postcolonial Africa, no less than post-imperial Europe. Later in Chapter
10, I return to this argument in my discussion of the important
analysis of the corporate agency of Yoruba elites by Wale Adebanwi
as a postcolonial insider (Adebanwi 2014, 2016).

So far, much of my account foregrounds the considerable extent
to which Manchester School members complemented in their own
work the work of their fellows, despite acknowledged critical disagreements – it was as if they avoided stepping on each other's toes
by allowing room for each to make disparate inquiries, to turn to
another interface with different disciplines in the social sciences and
humanities. In Chapter 7 I consider the work on law by A. L. 'Bill'
Epstein, the only one among Gluckman's students who engaged
publicly in sustained, critical and sensitive dialogue with Gluckman
about certain of the most cherished ideas of his great mentor, even-
tual colleague, and lifelong cherished friend. In Chapters 4 and 5,
I show how, alongside Clyde Mitchell, Epstein came to be a leading
ethnographer and theorist of urbanism. Ulf Hannerz (1980: chs 4
and 5) has very fully and acutely illuminated more of that contribution, and I refer the reader to Hannerz's discussion for a further
essential understanding of Epstein's outstanding contributions to
urban studies in British social anthropology. Given that as background, I focus in Chapter 7 on the development of Epstein's own
approach to law and courts.

It is a tribute to Epstein's rare capacity for careful disagreement
without being disagreeable that, in the midst of his critique of
Gluckman's core arguments, he and Gluckman remained on the
very best of terms, free of acrimony or any breach of their mutual
respect. They continued, also, to share a mode of thought which
always sought to make the most of actual cases, the very stuff of
everyday hearings in court. With this in mind, I disclose in Chapter

7 how they brought their case method to bear in their own interpretive and ethical reasoning, and I locate their arguments in a
wider discussion of the critique of Gluckman's legal studies. In
1975, shortly before Gluckman's death that year, Epstein was planning a Festschrift in his honour.

Epstein made his contributions with characteristic deliberation,
step by step, at first in one move that was the relatively fine, small
step of the faithful student, and much later in the more critical and
significant departures of a mature scholar of international distinction.
His move was not only in ethnographic area – from his fieldwork
in Zambia and his interest in Central African courts to his research
on dispute settlement in Melanesia – but also in a turn from problems of the importance of reason and reasonableness, morality and
ethics, in the affordance of justice. In this later turn he took up a
comparative study in the anthropology of affect, *The Experience of
Shame in Melanesia* (reprinted in his collection *Gunantuna*, 1999),
and finally he focused on law and affect in his last monograph,
subtitled *Affect and Ideation in the World of the Tolai* (1992). In
Chapter 7, I unpack the deliberation in Epstein's scholarship on the
figure of the reasonable man, starting with the early and mainly
Zambian part of his revisionist response to Gluckman's stance,
which he offered during Gluckman's lifetime. Through a closer
discussion of Epstein's Melanesian work, I examine later in this
chapter his perhaps more radical departure, after Gluckman's death.
My discussion shows that posing questions came to be no less
important in Epstein's anthropology than reaching sure answers.

Above all, one strength is unmistakable in Epstein's many
monographs, from 1958 with his first on the Zambian Copperbelt, *Politics in an Urban African Community*, to his last in 1992 on
the Tolai of Matupi Island in Papua New Guinea, *In the Midst of
Life*. He persists in the provision of evidence. It is always rich and
relevant to an argument. Having had the gift of some of his notes
from his Copperbelt fieldwork (and Epstein was known for such
open generosity to younger scholars), I am a witness to his ear for
the choice bit of gossip that later excites the analyst in moments of
insight. Even without such insider knowledge, no one can doubt
that what always nourished his broader reasoning was his abundant
harvest of germane particulars from fieldwork with people whose

language he spoke, people he knew very well, often as close, mutually trusted friends.

Epstein's readers can feel the fieldworker's passion for 'being there' in the immediacy of moments and places, for us unfamiliar, even distant, yet shown by him to be connected to us in our shared human condition, including the faces we make in disgust or delight. *In the Midst of Life* lives up to its title most forcefully through fine cases of dispute. These Epstein recounts with the lawyer's feel for the nicely salient details which clinch an argument.

But why is it that page after page of his last book puts forward questions? Is this a mere rhetorical device? A Socratic style of dialogue to make the reader wonder, reflect and then rethink? Perhaps! Epstein himself might well have responded, with a twinkle and characteristic wit that if the question has an answer, then first the question has to have a question. Even further, when looking back on his long career, he reflected, 'I think I was always more interested in questions than in answers: there was no finality to our enquiry and every conclusion reached served only to raise further questions' (Epstein 1992a: xxvi).

Documenting his observation through case after case, *In the Midst of Life* gave Epstein the means to show the specific dynamics of reason and emotion in hearings. His contribution reopened the frontiers of psychological and legal anthropology; it disclosed where emotive persuasion meets moral and value judgement, and it did so by making us understand a process of deliberation, namely how people seek through cogent argument with each other to have compassion in order to temper overreaching emotion, especially rage. On this basis, Epstein located his analysis within an important change in the wider intellectual climate. This was a turn in the social sciences to the subject and subjectivity, and he suggested that it was energized by or perhaps gives impetus to a paradigm shift 'from an image of man as a role-player to one of meaning-maker' (1992a: 278).

Epstein's perception leads me to a broader conclusion about his anthropological legacy. In Chapter 7 I say relatively little about his contribution as an ethnographer and theorist of urbanism, or even about what is widely considered his most popular work, *Ethos and Identity* (1978). The reason is that attention to the importance of that has largely overshadowed much that we now need to appreciate in his other work, especially work produced late in his life, when he advanced the radical study of law and passion. Important as this is for the history of the anthropology of law, his advance is currently becoming all the more significant, because it speaks to the very frontiers of a new interdisciplinary field across the social sciences and the humanities. It is the field that has recently come to examine and theorize how emotion animates, as Susan Bandes and Jeremy Blumenthal note, 'legal reasoning, legal doctrine, the behavior of legal actors, and the structure of legal institutions' (Bandes and Blumenthal 2012: 161). As in Epstein's late work, so too in this field, a central debate addresses emotional issues of compassion and moral reason (see Werbner and Werbner, 2020). Hence the present challenge is to develop the emerging study of law and emotion on a more comparative basis in the light of Epstein's insights grounded in ethnography from New Guinea and inspired by deep reflection on the differences and the similarities, as well as the transformations with and within the judicial process in Central Africa.

Chapter 8, locating Victor Turner's brilliant creativity in a Manchester School context, follows his remarkable odyssey through which he emerged as one of the most influential, widely cited social anthropologists of his generation. Turner became a celebrity, with an extraordinary and interdisciplinary world reputation and with a flock of admirers, more uncritical than his fellows at Manchester, and with something of a 'school' of his own. What the price for his celebrity was is a question I consider in much of this chapter.

If, in British anthropology and as Gluckman's PhD student, Turner was once an avowed structuralist, foregrounding crisis in social relations along with their realization in ritual and symbolic performances, he saw himself later, in America, as fathering an 'anthropology of experience'. Even further, as if returning to a legacy long repressed, from his mother's role as a Scottish actress, he pioneered theatre research in collaboration with Richard Schechner, the American performance theorist and theatre director. And yet, as I document, even at the height of Turner's fame and in his most popular work, including *Ritual Process* (1969), he carried forward not only the paradoxical literary style but even the dialectical thought of his mentor Max Gluckman.

My understanding of Turner's distinctive approach, especially in his semantic project and his study of ritual and the social drama, starts from something obvious. His deepest ethnographic encounter, with Ndembu in Zambia, was with people who relished interpretation. They got him drawn to an interpretive approach during his fieldwork and in his early writing up at Manchester, well before his welcome as a star in America among fellow interpretivists as cultural anthropologists. Ndembu not only had lots of ritual but had, or came to have in interaction with the ethnographer, lots of capacity to speak of meanings in representation; the Ndembu with Turner were at ease in significance talk – some thing (a material, a quality like a colour, or even an action) 'stands for', they would say, something else. If their ritual got beyond the visible to the invisible, it did so through the symbol that represented what lies beyond itself. However magical, it was 'revelation', accessing 'the inside view', for Turner, who found a process of symbolism he called 'the materialization of an idea' (1969: 26).

I suggest that Turner's earliest paper on 'Symbols in Ndembu Ritual', written in 1957, established his distinctive voice with his Ndembu interlocutors, and positioned the situational stance – symbols *in relation* to events and *in relation successively* from event to event, but not symbols merely *in configurations with each other* – to which he kept returning:

> I found that I could not analyse ritual symbols without studying them in a time series in relation to other 'events', for symbols are essentially involved in social process. I came to see performances of ritual as distinct phases in the social processes whereby groups become adjusted to internal changes and adapted to their external environment. From this standpoint the ritual becomes a factor in an activity field. (Turner 1967: 20)

Turner showed how a silent language of things – the bits used in ritual performance – is made to speak significantly, to be felt powerfully, to move and motivate actors in the presence of what they glimpse but momentarily, an awesome reality beyond human speech.[1]

Hence this continuity: Turner echoed Ndembu voices, above all, from his original work in the 1950s and early 1960s to his later period of apparently 'straddling' British social and American

cultural anthropology. He did so whether addressing the Association of Social Anthropologists in 1958 or in the first two and best
chapters of his Morgan Lectures for 1966, perhaps his most accessible, popular work (Turner 1969). Ndembu voices guided his study
of the semantics of ritual symbolism by making the silent language
of things resound with manifest meanings. The latent meanings
were the ones Turner, again and again, dared to imagine for us,
if speculatively, more or less cogently, then at least as evocatively
as possible.

This leads me to the close, detailed re-analysis, which I explore
in Chapter 9 through my account of Turner's *Chihamba, the White
Spirit* (1975), his masterpiece on ritual drama in an Ndembu fertility
cult. In the Introduction, I review this account when I contextualize the very strategy of re-analysis relative to other important and
substantial strategies of ethnographic critique.

In order to present a broader perspective on certain underlying
transformations largely implicit in much of my main discussion, I
turn to comparison, perhaps as Gluckman might have engaged for
postcoloniality. In Chapter 10, I pursue comparative arguments
from postcolonial Africa to ask how anthropologists have understood the postcolonial, and how their understandings relate to those
of mainstream postcolonial studies. History conceived as linear progress has had little bearing on most anthropological approaches to
the postcolonial; these have not been underwritten by a simple
narrative periodization of pre-colonial, colonial and postcolonial.
Both the nature and impact – indeed, the active *sedimentation* – of
the colonial legacy have instead been taken as problematic and
contested, to be understood in the light of deepening social inequality across the postcolonial continents, and in consequence sometimes freighted with nostalgia for an imaginary past of colonial or
pre-colonial sociality (Werbner 2002a; Fontein 2006; De Jong and
Rowlands 2007; Argenti and Schram 2009). This understanding
runs contrary to theories of globalization which give short shrift to
postcoloniality and, thanks to an undue focus on a contemporary
local–global binary, consign the fermenting legacies of empire to
the shadows.

Thanks in part to widespread disenchantment with liberation
struggles, and with the postcolonial fruits of nationalism, many
anthropologists of Africa have looked to the *longue durée* to periodize

the postcolonial (Comaroff and Comaroff 1999, 2004; Ferme 2001; Shaw 2002; Ntarangwi, Mills and Babiker 2006; Argenti 2007). Some of them share a sense that a second postcolonial era has begun, which may take the form of a recently emerging counter-view to the prevalence of toxic Afro-pessimism, particularly in the study of elites and the civil service (Lentz 1994; Werbner 2004a, 2008, 2014a; Fumanti 2016: 98–123; Adebanwi 2014, 2016).

Views on the general direction of change vary between the extremes of the over-optimistic Polyannas and the cheerless Cassandras, with their relentless rehearsals of disorder and apocalypse now; and their disagreement is not due entirely to differences between the postcolonies they address.[2] Some anthropologists prefer to see the present hopefully, as the promised fulfilment of Africa's Second Liberation Struggle after the passing of the founding tyrants. Others claim that people themselves fear an apocalypse, the ominous signs of which intensify most violently in genocide (for the extreme in Rwanda, see De Waal 1994; Malkki 1995), in brutal crime, in vigilantism (Kirsch and Gratz 2010), in public injustice (Comaroff and Comaroff 2004) and in catastrophic social contradictions. Disagreements extend to opposed analyses of the local impact of global discourses on human rights and democracy (Wilson 2001; Mitchell and Wilson 2003; Englund 2006; Hodgson 2011), to debates about 'decolonization' (Harrison 1991; McGranahan, Roland and Williams 2016; Nyamnjoh 2016; Allen and Jobson 2016), and beyond this to an ocean of postcolonial debate about poverty and 'development' (Allen and Thomas 2000; Ferguson 2006).

Political independence in Africa and elsewhere has all too rarely come with freedom from the imperial grip, even if the alien hands in effective, if mediated, command have changed. Debate has been growing among anthropologists about the interpretation of China's expanding influence, especially in Africa. Does this portend a new colonial era? Or is the pervasive condition still better understood as late capitalist domination by Western metropolitan powers, including metropolitan-based transnational corporations and global agencies?

There are, in my view, four main reasons, which I discuss in Chapter 10, why anthropologists, analysing the cultural politics of identity and the shaping of subjectivities in everyday life in postcolonies, have foregrounded the state and state-linked or state-created domains. Briefly, these are the 'retreat of the state' or its transformation; the importance of political violence and state genocide; the reappropriation of the state, reciprocal assimilation and political hybridity; and the change in identity degradation, stereotyping and the occult imaginary of the postcolony. But is the state itself in a challenging crisis?

If 'the retreat of the state' is a global phenomenon (Comaroff and Comaroff 2001: 633–4) in postcolonies, especially in Africa, the extremes have been and still are great. They are changeable from one historical moment to another, towards the overriding importance of non-governmental organizations and their transnational alliances, as Ferguson contends (2006: 89–112), or to an expansion of the state whose officials penetrate such organizations in the public sphere (Fumanti 2016).

Anthropological points of departure to locate the changing horizons of identity politics across the postcolonies have been as variable, not necessarily privileging hybridity or the working class. Conventional class analysis has led all too readily, in the past, to the dubious thesis of the single dominant class for the postcolony, the state bourgeoisie, which, as a unity, is effectively in command of state power. Against that, fruitful anthropological arguments about cultural politics in diverse postcolonies have started from the distinctive postcolonial realities of multiple arenas, fluid, intersecting identities, and positional relations of power, all of which are at once within and also, through negotiation, constitutive of the state. As postcolonies, some African nation-states, marked by their swelling state salariats, are still on the march. In many, the government is still the largest single employer in the national economy. Africa is yet to see the end of oppressive regimes which, like Mugabe's and now Monagagwa's in Zimbabwe, coerce their subjects through state terror, intimidation by the security services, and more innocuous everyday controls.[3]

Africanists have much to say about postcolonies in ever more rapid decay or virtual collapse; and anthropologists, recognizing the greater potential for self-alienation, have opened out a series of problems in the cases where the state has failed – the modes of local resiliency, the cultural assertion of social identities for survival, the recuperation of moral and political agency. With this in view, anthropologists have problematized the importance of grassroots ecumenism in postcolonial societies (Werbner 2018a). Chapter

10 shows that grassroots ecumenism depends upon efforts to bring people together in local settings, despite and without effacing their religious differences. I see it as often a yearning, an ideal, and a hope of highly valued religious unity and spiritual fellowship. Rarely is it a firm, unchallenged accomplishment. Indeed, ecumenism itself, seen as a modern idea in religious debate, is what the philosopher W. B. Gallie calls 'an essentially contested concept' (Gallie 1956), which significantly shifts with the times and under pressure, if within arguably reasonable limits. If usually precarious or somewhat awkward in many societies, grassroots ecumenism is acutely contested or politicized in post-genocide and post-apartheid societies. The conflict emerges perhaps most acutely in efforts towards reconciliation and forgiveness, and in post-war ordeals over silence, the said and the unsaid. That is at the heart of the argument in Chapter 10 in my discussion of a collection of recent articles on 'Grassroots Ecumenism in Conflict', which I co-edited with Anthony Simpson (Werbner 2018a, 2018b; Grant 2018; Sarro 2018; Teppo 2018; Cabrita 2018; Golomski 2018; Jules-Rosette 2018).

Even beyond the arguments about religion and conflict, anthropologists have shown the constructive and the destructive force that identity strategies have had in postcolonies. Much anthropological research has redirected postcolonial studies away from its mainstream diasporic concerns back to arenas within the postcolonial states themselves. On this basis, anthropologists have engaged critically with postcolonial subjects themselves in the past and now continue to reflect upon our own participation in the making of postcoloniality.

Anthropology in colonial history and postcolonial myth

In historical anthropology – a growing field in itself – there is an emerging mainstream quest for critical knowledge on the recent making of modern social anthropology. Arguably, the increasing open access to archives of mid-to-late twentieth-century personal correspondence, field notes and long-closed disciplinary documents has whetted the appetite for a peek at the back-stage to get a more revealing perspective on front-stage contrivance.

Taking others' origin myths with a pinch of salt is customary among anthropologists, although a myth of our own still gets naive rehearsal, that is, that apparently in the 1920s and 1930s, an original generation of ancestors, primarily Radcliffe-Brown and Malinowski, made their headway by studying 'the underside of modernity' found in timeless, isolated, small-scale, homogeneous, self-reproducing societies (Comaroff and Comaroff 2012: xxxi). Notice that this rehearsal could appear authoritative, despite the facts to the contrary, in highly influential contributions by the 'founding fathers', Radcliffe-Brown and Malinowski. In his 1921 Inaugural Lecture as professor at Cape Town, Radcliffe-Brown famously espoused the radical concept of 'one whole society' including Africans and white settlers in South Africa, this single society thesis being the one that Gluckman advanced in his celebrated 'Bridge' essay, the very thesis regarding which, as Adam Kuper notes, 'Gluckman published some of the most innovative analyses of *rural* society' (Kuper 2005: 290, italics mine).[4] It was in 1922 also that Malinowski revealed the remarkably risky border-crossing in trading networks across vast distances among thousands of individuals from many communities in the Kula Ring.

Against that dip into origin mythology, *Anthropology after Gluckman* advances an intellectual history that turns in a social biography, with personal portraits, from the discipline's founding generation to some of its immediate successors in the Manchester School. If the origin myth evokes nostalgia for a Golden Age, it is the shock of recognition that we have to experience, looking back at the successors' survival through times, like ours, of turmoil and troubled by crises. Encountering fascism, the Second World War, the End of Empire, decolonization and challenges to racial domination, the last gasps of settler societies, and much instability in scientific thought – all this almost inevitably demanded the Manchester School's turn to experiment and transformative projects. Even further, insofar as theirs can be seen to have been one project, it was a cosmopolitan project. Where outsiders saw dominating leadership and unity with a common stock of problems, chiefly about conflict – an image that owed much to Gluckman's public representations and forceful programmatic statements – the consciousness insiders had was that they were drawn to explore many new frontiers in fieldwork and ethnography, because they themselves in class, gender, national and ethnic origins were inclusive. For the sake of heightened clarity, and perhaps at the risk of caricature, in the chapters with their fuller portraits I have represented them in these contrasted figures: the public intellectual and systems builder, the systems-sceptical home town anthropologist attuned to dislocation, the railway navigator with the empirical sensibility of the mathematical sociologist, the advocate of justice with a curious sense of both reason and passion, and the ethnographer become Americanized celebrity and hostage to fickle fashion. Innovation – in research methods and techniques, in the people's praxis and social relations, and in the expansion of social anthropology as a dynamic, open discipline, with many fathers, many mothers – became their hallmark, and now their living legacy. The School's distinctiveness and distinction, this book argues from an insider's perspective, speak to our times in the active force of creative difference in cutting-edge ideas, interdisciplinary approaches, and travelling theories of the intimate circle around Max Gluckman.

Notes

1 For the current salience of this exploration, see Svasek and Meyer, 2016.
2 On certain stark realities in Zimbabwe, see Werbner 1991, 1995, 1998, 1999; Brickhill 2019; and, by contrast in Botswana, see Werbner 1977d, 1981, 1993, 2002b, 2002c, 2004a, 2008; R. Werbner and P. Werbner 2000, 2018, 2019, 2020.
3 An outstanding example of anthropological research through long-term fieldwork on agrarian politics in the face of postcolonial violence, economic crisis and transformations in nationalism is Blair Rutherford's ethnography of Zimbabwean farmworkers (2016).
4 Kuper also makes the point that another of Gluckman's teachers, Isaac Schapera, published in 1934 his *Western Civilization and the Natives of South Africa*, which focused on 'culture change, land shortages, labour migration, Christianity, and urbanization' (Kuper 2005: 288).

Bibliography

Unpublished sources

Abbreviations

ALE   A. L. 'Bill' Epstein
ALEPSD   Arnold Leonard and T. Scarlett Epstein Papers, University of
            California, San Diego Library
CM   Clyde Mitchell
EC   Elizabeth Colson
GPRAI   Gluckman Papers, Royal Anthropological Institute
GPJRUML   Gluckman Papers, John Rylands University of Manchester
            Library
JB   John Barnes
MF   Meyer Fortes
MG   Max Gluckman
MPBL   Mitchell Papers, Bodleian Library
RW   Richard Werbner
SM   Sally Moore
UCSD   University of California at San Diego
VT   Victor Turner

Colson, E. (1961), letter to MG, 28 February, GLU/1/16, GPJRUML
Colson, E. (1963), letter to MG, GLU/1/3, GPJRUML
Colson, E. (1966b), letter to MG, GLU/1/43, GPJRUML
Colson, E. (1973), letter to ALE, 28 September, MSS 22, ALEPSD
Epstein, A. L. (1955), letter to CM, 30 March, MPBL
Epstein, A. L. (1958b), letter to CM, 24 January, MPBL
Epstein, A. L. (1960a), letter to MG, 17 February, GLU/2/42, GPJRUML
Epstein, A. L. (1960b), letter to MG, 7 April, GLU/2/6, GPJRUML
Epstein, A. L. (1973b), letter to MG, 8 September, MSS 22, ALEPSD
Epstein, A. L. (1973c), letter to EC, 9 October, MSS 22, ALEPSD
Fortes, M. (1969), letter to MG, 1 November, A7, GPRAI
Gluckman, M. (1956c), letter to CM, 17 January 1956, MPBL
Gluckman, M. (1956d), letter to CM, 5 February, MPBL

Gluckman, M. (1957), letter to CM, 24 January, MPBL

Gluckman, M. (1958a), letter to Registrar, University of Sydney, 5 February, GPRAI

Gluckman, M. (1958b), letter to Registrar, University of Sydney, 13 February, GPRAI

Gluckman, M. (1960c), letter to EC, 14 November, GLU/1/7, GPJRUML

Gluckman, M. (1960d), letter to ALE, 22 May, GLU/2/8, GPJRUML

Gluckman, M. (1960e), letter to ALE, 22 June, GLU/2/8, GPJRUML

Gluckman, M. (1961c), letter to EC, 28 February, GLU/1/16, GPJRUML

Gluckman, M. (1962c), letter to CM, 12 June, GPJRUML

Gluckman, M. (1964a), letter to EC, 21 February, GLU/1/35, GPJRUML

Gluckman, M. (1964b), letter to RW, 17 August, GPRAI

Gluckman, M. (1965c), letter to CM, 17 March, MPBL

Gluckman, M. (1968b), letter to ALE, UCSD, box 4, folder 19

Gluckman, M. (1974d), letter to VT, 17 September, GPRAI

Gluckman, M. (1974e), letter to VT, 3 October, GPRAI

Gluckman, M. (1974f), letter to SM, 17 September, GPRAI

Mitchell, J. C. (1952), letter to MG, 27 February, MPBL

Mitchell, J. C. (1956c), letter to ALE, 28 February 1956, MPBL

Mitchell, J. C. (1956d), letter to MG, 4 October, MPBL

Mitchell, J. C. (1958), letter to JB, 2 February, MPBL

Mitchell, J. C. (1965a), letter to MG, 17 February, GPJRUML

Mitchell, J. C. (1965b), letter to MG, 28 March, GPJRUML

Peters, E. (1967), letter to the Chair, Anthropology, University of California, Berkeley, GLU/1/54, 2 April, GPJRUML

Turner, V. (1959a), letter to MG, 27 April, GPRAI

Turner, V. (1959b), letter to MG, 7 July, GPRAI

Turner, V. (1973b), letter to MG, 17 September, GPRAI

Turner, V. (1974a), letter to MG, 26 September, GPRAI

Turner, V. (1974b), letter to MG, 17 November, GPRAI

Published works

Adebanwi, W. (2014), *Yoruba Elites and Ethnic Politics in Nigeria* (Cambridge : Cambridge University Press).

Adebanwi, W. (2016), 'Elites, ethnographic encounters, and the "native" ethnographer in contemporary Africa', in R. Boswell and F. Nyamnjoh (eds), *Postcolonial African Anthropologies* (Cape Town: HSRC Press).

Aginsky, B., and E. Aginsky (1947), 'A resultant of intercultural relations', *Social Forces* 26(1): 84–7.

Allen, J., and R. Jobson (2016), 'The decolonizing generation', *Current Anthropology* 57(2): 129–48.

Allen, T., and A. Thomas (eds) (2000), *Poverty and Development into the 21st Century* (Oxford: The Open University in association with Oxford University Press).

Appiah, K. (1992), *My Father's House* (Oxford: Oxford University Press).

Appiah, K. (1998), 'Cosmopolitan patriots', in P. Cheah and B. Robbins (eds), *Cosmopolitics* (Minneapolis, MN: University of Minnesota Press).

Appiah, K. (2005), *The Ethics of Identity* (Princeton, NJ: Princeton University Press).

Appiah, K. (2006), *Cosmopolitanism* (London: Allen Lane).

Argenti, N. (2007), *The Intestines of the State* (Chicago: University of Chicago Press).

Argenti, N., and K. Schram (eds) (2009), *Remembering Violence* (Oxford: Berghahn).

Argyle, J. (1991), 'Kalela, Beni, Asafo, Ingoma and the rural-urban dichotomy', *African Studies* 50(1): 65–86.

Babcock, B. (1984), 'Obituary: Victor W. Turner', *The Journal of American Folklore* 97: 461–4.

Babcock, B., and J. Macaloon (1987), 'Victor W. Turner (1920–1983)', *Semiotica* 65: 1–27.

Bachignani, N. (2016), 'A new bibliography of Elizabeth Colson', EScholarship Program, University of California, http://escholarship.org/uc/item/9j45p150 (accessed 4 November 2019).

Bakhtin, M. (1984), *Rabelais and His World*, trans. Hélène Iswolsky (Bloomington, IN: Indiana University Press).

Bandes, S., and J. Blumenthal (2012), 'Emotion and the law', *Annual Review of Law and Social Science* 8: 161–81.

Bank, A. (2016), *Pioneers of the Field* (Cambridge: Cambridge University Press).

Barber, K. (2006), 'Introduction: hidden innovators in Africa', in K. Barber (ed.), *Africa's Hidden Histories: Everyday Literacy and Making the Self* (Bloomington, IN: Indiana University Press).

Barnard, H. (1985), 'Victor Witter Turner: a bibliography (1952–1975)', *Anthropologica* n.s. 27: 207–33.

Barnes, J. (1954), 'Class and committee in a Norwegian island parish', *Human Relations* 7: 39–58.

Barnes, J. (1969a), 'Networks and political process', in J. C. Mitchell (ed.), *Social Networks in Urban Situations* (Manchester: University of Manchester Press for Institute for Social Research, University of Zambia).

Barnes, J. (1969b), 'Graph theory and social networks', *Sociology* 3: 215–32.

Barnes, J. (1974), *Social Networks*, Module in Anthropology, 26 (Redding, MA: Addison-Wesley).

Barnes, J. (1983), 'Foreword', in P. Hage and F. Harary, *Structural Models in Anthropology* (Cambridge: Cambridge University Press).

Barth, F. (1959), *Political Leadership among the Swat Pathans* (London: University of London, Athlone Press).

Barth, F. (1966), *Models of Social Organization* (London: Royal Anthropological Institute).

Barth, F. (2005), 'The golden age 1945–1970', in F. Barth et al., *One Discipline, Four Ways* (Chicago: University of Chicago Press).

Bateson, G. (1935), 'Culture contact and schismogenesis', *Man* 35: 178–83.

Bateson, G. (1958) [1938], *Naven*, 2nd edn (Stanford, CA: Stanford University Press).

Bayart, J.-F. (1993), *The State in Africa* (London: Longman).

Beeman, O. (1993). 'On the anthropology of theater and spectacle', *Annual Review of Anthropology* 22: 369–93.

Behrend, H. (2002), 'I am like a movie star in my street', in R. Werbner (ed.), *Postcolonial Subjectivities in Africa* (London: Zed Books).

Beidelman, T. (1966), 'Swazi royal ritual', *Africa* 36(4): 373–405.

Beidelman, T. (1986), *Moral Imagination in Kaguru Modes of Thought* (Bloomington, IN: Indiana University Press).

Bell, C. (1997), *Ritual: Perspectives and Dimensions* (New York: Oxford University Press).

Bell, C. (2009), *Ritual Theory, Ritual Practice* (New York: Oxford University Press).

Bernard, H. R. (1990), 'Interview with Clyde Mitchell', Human Studies Film Archive, Smithsonian Institute, Washington DC, UFDC.UFL.EDU/HA00012783/0001.

Bialecki, J., and G. Daswani (2015), 'What is an individual? The view from Christianity', *HAU: Journal of Ethnographic Theory* 5(1): 271–94.

Blau, P. (1964), *Exchange and Power in Social Life* (New York: John Wiley & Sons).

Bohannon, P. (1957), *Judgement and Justice among the Tiv* (London: Oxford University Press for the International African Institute).

Boissevain, J. (1974), *Friends of Friends. Networks, Manipulators and Coalitions* (New York: St Martin's Press).

Bott, E. (1957), *Family and Social Networks* (London: Tavistock).

Brickhill, P. (2019). 'ZVAKAPRESSER (We are under pressure)', *Zimbabwe Review* 19 January: 1.

Brunner, E. (1986), *The Anthropology of Experience* (Urbana, IL: University of Illinois Press).

Busby, C. (1997), 'Permeable and partible person: a comparative analysis of gender and body on South India and Melanesia', *JRAI* n.s. 3(2): 261–78.

Cabrita, J. (2018), 'Christian ecumenism, Swazi nationalism, and a unified church for a united nation, 1920s–1970s', *Journal of Southern African Studies* 44(2): 283–98.

Campbell, N. (1921), *What is Science?* (London: Methuen).

Candea, M. (2019), *Comparison in Anthropology: The Impossible Method* (Cambridge: Cambridge University Press).

Candea, M., et al. (eds) (2015), *Detachment: Essays on the Limits of Relational Thinking* (Manchester: Manchester University Press).

Chabal, P. (1994), *Power in Africa* (London: Macmillan).

Chabal, P. (1996), 'The African crisis', in R. Werbner (ed.), *Postcolonial Identities in Africa* (London: Zed Books).

Channock, M. (2001), *The Making of South African Legal Culture 1902–1936* (Cambridge: Cambridge University Press).

Chatterjee, P. (1993), *The Nation and its Fragments* (Princeton, NJ: Princeton University Press).

Clifford, J. (1986), 'On ethnographic allegory', in G. Marcus and J. Clifford, *Writing Culture* (Berkeley, CA: University of California Press).

Cocks, P. (2001), 'Max Gluckman and the critique of segregation in South African anthropology', *Journal of Southern African Studies* 27(4): 739–56.

Cohen, A. (1965), *Arab Border Villages in Israel* (Manchester: Manchester University Press).

Colson, E. (1940), *A Study of Acculturation among Pomo Women* (Ann Arbor, MI: University of Michigan Press).

Colson, E. (1943), 'The family in Poston', *Poston Community Analysis Sections* 15–17.

Colson, E. (1945), 'The Makah', PhD thesis, Radcliffe College.

Colson, E. (1950a), '*Dynamics of Clanship among the Tallensi* by Meyer Fortes', *African Studies* 9: 203–6.

Colson, E. (1950b), 'Director's report to the trustees of the Rhodes-Livingstone Institute on the work of the years 1947–1948–1949', *Human Problems in British Central Africa* 10: 75–94.

Colson, E. (1953), *The Makah Indians: A Study of an Indian Tribe in Modern American Society* (Minneapolis, MN: University of Minnesota Press).

Colson, E. (1954), 'The intensive study of small sample communities', in R. Spencer (ed.), *Method and Perspective in Anthropology* (Minneapolis, MN: University of Minnesota Press).

Colson, E. (1958), *Marriage and the Family among the Plateau Tonga of Northern Rhodesia* (Manchester: Manchester University Press).

Colson, E. (1960), *The Social Organization of the Gwembe Tonga* (Manchester: Manchester University Press).

Colson, E. (1962), *The Plateau Tonga of Northern Rhodesia* (Manchester: Manchester University Press).

Colson, E. (1966a), 'The alien diviner and local politics among the Tonga of Zambia', in M. Swartz, V. Turner, and A. Tuden (eds), *Political Anthropology* (Chicago: Aldine).

Colson, E. (1967), 'Intensive study of small sample communities', in A. L. Epstein (ed.), *The Craft of Social Anthropology* (London: Tavistock).

Colson, E. (1968), 'Wallis, Wilson D.', in *International Encyclopedia of the Social Sciences* 16 (New York: Macmillan and Free Press), 445–7.

Colson, E. (1969), 'African society at the time of the scramble', in L. Gann and P. Duignan (eds), *The History and Politics of Colonialism, 1870–1914* (Cambridge: Cambridge University Press).

Colson, E. (1970), 'The assimilation of aliens among the Zambian Tonga', in R. Cohen and J. Middleton (eds), *From Tribe to Nation in Africa: Studies in Incorporation Processes* (Scranton, PA: Chandler Publishing).

Colson, E. (1971a), 'Heroism, martyrdom, and courage', in T. Beidelman (ed.), *The Translation of Culture* (London: Tavistock).

Colson, E. (1971b), *The Social Consequences of Resettlement* (Manchester: Manchester University Press).

Colson, E. (1974a), *Autobiographies of Three Pomo Women* (Berkeley, CA: Department of Anthropology, University of California).

Colson, E. (1974b), *Tradition and Contract* (London: Aldine/Heinemann).

Colson, E. (1976), 'Culture and progress', *American Anthropologist* 78(2): 261–71.

Colson, E. (1977), 'The institute under Max Gluckman, 1942–47', *African Social Research* 24: 285–96.

Colson, E. (1979), 'Max Gluckman', in *International Encyclopedia of the Social Sciences* 18 (New York: Free Press), 242–6.

Colson, E. (1980), 'Scale and diversity', *Reviews in Anthropology* 7(2): 229–34.

Colson, E. (1986), 'Obituary: Lucy Mair', *Anthropology Today* 2(4): 22–4.

Colson, E. (1988), 'David G. Mandelbaum (1911–1987)', *American Anthropologist* 90(2): 411–12.

Colson, E. (1989), 'Overview', *Annual Review of Anthropology* 18: 1–16.

Colson, E. (1996), 'The Bantu Botatwe', in D. Parkin, L. Caplan, and H. Fisher (eds), *The Politics of Cultural Performance* (Oxford: Berghahn).

Colson, E. (2002), 'Anthropology and a lifetime of observation: interview by Suzanne B. Riess' (Berkeley, CA: Bancroft Library, University of California).

Colson, E. (2006), *Tonga Religious Life in the Twentieth Century* (Lusaka: Bookworld Publishers).

Colson, E. (2007a), 'Biases: place, time, stance', in C. Lancaster and K. Vickery (eds), *The Tonga-Speaking Peoples of Zambia and Zimbabwe: Essays in Honor of Elizabeth Colson* (Lanham, MD: University Press of America).

Colson, E. (2007b), 'Interview with Professor Elizabeth Colson, by Anna Schmidt' (Oxford: Department of International Development).

Colson, E. (2007c), 'Linkages methodology', *Journal of Refugee Studies* 20(2): 320–33.

Colson, E. (2008a), '*The Manchester School* by T. M. S. Evens and Don Handelman', *Current Anthropology* 49(2): 335–7.

Colson, E. (2008b), 'The founding moment', in P. Werbner (ed.), *Anthropology and the New Cosmopolitanism* (New York: Berg).

Colson, E. (2012), 'Happiness', *American Anthropologist* 114(1): 7–8.

Colson, E., and M. Gluckman (eds) (1951), *Seven Tribes of British Central Africa* (Oxford: Oxford University Press).

Colson, E., and M. Gluckman (1952), 'Reply to review by Mary Douglas', *Africa* 22(3): 271–4.

Colson, E., and T. Scudder (1988), *For Prayer and Profit* (Stanford, CA: Stanford University Press).

Comaroff, J., and J. L. Comaroff (eds) (1993), *Modernity and Its Malcontents* (Chicago: University of Chicago Press).

Comaroff, J., and J. L. Comaroff (1999), 'Occult economies and the violence of abstraction', *American Ethnologist* 26(2): 279–303.

Comaroff, J., and J. L. Comaroff (2001), 'Naturing the nation', *Journal of Southern African Studies* 3: 627–51.

Comaroff, J., and J. L. Comaroff (2018), 'Chiefs, capital and the state in contemporary Africa', in J. Comaroff and J. L. Comaroff (eds), *The Politics of Custom* (Chicago: University of Chicago Press).

Comaroff, J. L., and J. Comaroff (2004), 'Criminal justice, cultural justice', *American Ethnologist* 31(2): 188–203.

Comaroff, J. L., and J. Comaroff (2012), *Theory from the South* (London: Routledge).

Comaroff, J. L., and S. Roberts (1981), *Rules and Processes* (Chicago: University of Chicago Press).

Coplan, D. (2003), 'Land from the ancestors', *Journal of Southern African Studies* 29(4): 977–93

Coser, L. (1984), *Refugee Scholars in America* (New Haven, CT: Yale University Press).

Crapanzano, V. (1984), 'Liminal recreations', *Times Literary Supplement*, 27 April: 473.

Darnell, R., and S. Murray (2018), 'Series editors' introduction', in R. Gordon, *The Enigma of Max Gluckman* (Lincoln, NE: University of Nebraska Press).

Das, V. (2015), *Affliction, Health, Disease, Poverty* (New York: Fordham University Press).

De Boeck, F. (1996), 'Postcolonialism, power and identity', in R. Werbner (ed.), *Postcolonial Identities in Africa* (London: Zed Books).

De Huesch, L. (1962), 'Cultes de possession et religions initiatiques de salut en Afrique', *Annales de Centre d'etudes des Religions* 2: 226–44.

De Jong, F., and M. Rowlands (2007), *Reclaiming Heritage: Alternative Imaginaries of Memory in West Africa* (Walnut Creek, CA: Left Coast).

De Waal, A. (1994), 'Genocide in Rwanda', *Anthropology Today* 10(3): 1–2.

Derrida, J. (1974), *Of Grammatology* (Baltimore, MD: Johns Hopkins University Press).

Devisch, R. (1995), 'Frenzy, violence and ethical renewal in Kinshasha', *Public Culture* 7: 593–629.

Devons, E. (1961), *Essays in Economics* (London: Allen and Unwin).

Ditsheko, E. (2019), *Wrestling Botswana from Khama* (Gaborone: Yearbook Publications).

Douglas, M. (1952), 'Review of M. Gluckman and E. Colson (eds), *Seven Tribes of British Central Africa*', *Africa* 22(1): 59–65.

Douglas, M. (1957), 'Review of J. Clyde Mitchell, *The Yao Village: a Study of a Nyasaland Tribe*', *Africa* 27(3): 290–2.

Douglas, M. (1959a), 'Review of William Watson, *Tribal Cohesion in a Money Economy*', *Man* 59(270): 168

Douglas, M. (1959b) 'The spirit of contradiction. Review of V.W. Turner, *Schism and Continuity in an African Society*', *Zaire* 13(3): 295–300.

Douglas, M. (1960), 'Review of *Marriage and the Family among the Plateau Tonga* by Elizabeth Colson', *Africa* 30(2): 196–97.

Douglas, M. (1963), 'Review of Max Gluckman (ed.), *Essays on the Ritual of Social Relations*', *Africa* 33(3): 271–2.

Douglas, M. (1968), 'The social control of cognition', *Man* n.s. 3: 361–76.

Douglas, M. (1970), 'The healing rite', *Man* n.s. 5: 302–8.

Durham, D., and F. Klaits (2002), 'Funerals and the public space of sentiment in Botswana', *Journal of Southern African Studies* 28(4): 777–98.

Engelke, M. (1996), '"Dear Max": Victor Turner from the field in 1951', *History of Anthropology Newsletter* 23: 3–6.

Engelke, M. (2000), 'An interview with Edith Turner', *Current Anthropology* 41: 843–52.

Engelke, M. (2004), 'The endless conversation', in Richard Handler (ed.), *Significant Others* (Madison, WI: University of Wisconsin Press).

Englund, H. (1996a), 'Between God and Kamuzu', in R. Werbner (ed.), *Postcolonial Identities in Africa* (London: Zed Books).

Englund, H. (1996b), 'Witchcraft, modernity and the person', *Critique of Anthropology* 16(3): 257–79.

Englund, H. (2002a), *From War to Peace on the Mozambique-Malawi Borderland* (Edinburgh: Edinburgh University Press for the International African Institute, London).

Englund, H. (2002b), 'The village in the city, the city in the village', *Journal of Southern African Studies* 28(1): 137–54.

Englund, H. (2006), *Prisoners of Freedom* (Berkeley, CA: University of California Press).

Englund, H. (2007), 'Pentecostalism beyond belief', *Africa* 77(4): 477–99.

Englund, H. (2011), *Human Rights and African Airwaves* (Bloomington, IN: Indiana University Press).

Englund, H. (2018), 'From the extended case method to multi-sited ethnography (and back)', in M. Candea (ed.), *Schools and Styles of Anthropological Theory* (London: Routledge).

Englund H., and T. Yarrow (2013), 'The place of theory: rights, networks and ethnographic comparison', *Social Analysis* 57(3): 132–49.

Epperson, M. (2004), *Quantum Mechanics and the Philosophy of Alfred North Whitehead* (New York: Fordham University Press).

Epstein, A. L. (1951), 'Urban native courts on the Northern Rhodesian Copperbelt', *Journal of African Administration* 3: 117–24.

Epstein, A. L. (1953), *The Administration of Justice and the Urban African*, Colonial Research Series 7 (London: HMSO).

Epstein, A. L. (1954), *Juridical Techniques and the Judicial Process*, Rhodes-Livingstone Paper 23 (Manchester: Manchester University Press).

Epstein, A. L. (1958), *Politics in an Urban African Community* (Manchester: Manchester University Press).

Epstein, A. L. (1959), 'Linguistic innovation and culture on the Copperbelt, Northern Rhodesia', *Southwestern Journal of Anthropology* 15: 235–53.

Epstein, A. L. (1961), 'The network and urban social organization', *Rhodes-Livingstone Journal* 24: 29–62. Reprinted in J. C. Mitchell (ed.), *Social Networks in Urban Situations* (Manchester: Manchester University Press, 1969).

Epstein, A. L. (ed.) (1967a), *The Craft of Social Anthropology* (London: Tavistock).

Epstein, A. L. (1967b), 'The case method in the field of law', in A. L. Epstein (ed.), *The Craft of Social Anthropology* (London: Tavistock).

Epstein, A. L. (1969), *Matupit* (Canberra: Australian National University Press).

Epstein, A. L. (1970), 'Autonomy and identity', *Anthropological Forum* 2(4): 427–43.

Epstein, A. L. (1973a), 'The reasonable man revisited: some problems in the anthropology of law', *Law and Society Review* 7: 643–66.

Epstein, A. L. (1981), *Urbanization and Kinship* (London: Academic Press).

Epstein, A. L. (1984), *The Experience of Shame in Melanesia*, Royal Anthropological Institute Occasional Paper 40.

Epstein, A. L. (1992a), *In the Midst of Life: Affect and Ideation in the World of the Tolai* (Berkeley, CA: University of California Press).

Epstein, A. L. (1992b), *Scenes from African Urban Life: Collected Copperbelt Essays* (Edinburgh: Edinburgh University Press).

Epstein, A. L. (1999), *Gunantuna* (Bathurst: Crawford Publishing).

Epstein, T. (1968), *Capitalism, Primitive and Modern* (Manchester: Manchester University Press).

Eriksen, T., and F. Nielsen (2013), *A History of Anthropology*, 2nd edn (London: Pluto Press).

Evans-Pritchard, E. (1937), *Witchcraft, Oracles and Magic among the Azande* (Oxford: Clarendon Press).

Evans-Pritchard, E. (1940), *The Nuer* (Oxford: Clarendon Press).

Evens, T., and D. Handelman (eds) (2006), *The Manchester School* (Oxford: Berghahn).

Fairweather, I. (2006), 'Heritage, identity and youth in postcolonial Namibia', *Journal of Southern African Studies* 32(4): 719–36.

Fanon, F. (1967) [1961], *The Wretched of the Earth*, trans. Haakon Chevalier (Harmondsworth: Penguin).

Fanon, F. (1986) [1952], *Black Skins, White Masks*, trans. Charles Markmann (London: Pluto Press).

Fardon, R. (ed.) (1990), *Localizing Strategies* (Edinburgh: Scottish Academic Press).

Fardon, R. (1999), *Mary Douglas* (London: Routledge).

Fardon, R. (2004), 'Turner, Victor Witter (1920–1983), social anthropologist', *Oxford Dictionary of National Biography* (Oxford: Oxford University Press).

Fardon, R. (2018), 'Immortality yet?', *Anthropology Today* 34: 23–4.

Fassin, D. (2014), 'The ethical turn in anthropology', *HAU: Journal of Ethnographic Theory* 4: 429–35.

Fassin, D. (2015), *A Companion to Moral Anthropology* (Malden, MA: Wiley Blackwell).

Faubion, J. (2011), *An Anthropology of Ethics* (Cambridge: Cambridge University Press).

Faubion, J. (2014), 'Anthropologies of ethics', *HAU: Journal of Ethnographic Theory* 4: 437–42.

Faubion, J. (2015), 'Foucault and the genealogy of ethics', in D. Fassin (ed.), *A Companion to Moral Anthropology* (Malden, MA: Wiley Blackwell).

Ferguson, J. (2005), 'Decomposing modernity', in Ania Loomba et al. (eds), *Postcolonial Studies and Beyond* (Durham, NC: Duke University Press).

Ferguson, J. (2006), *Global Shadows* (Durham, NC: Duke University Press).

Ferme, M. (2001), *The Underneath of Things* (Berkeley, CA: University of California Press).

Fernandez, J. (1986), *Persuasions and Performance* (Bloomington, IN: Indiana University Press).

Fernandez, J. (1990), 'The body in Bwiti', *Journal of Religion in Africa* 20: 92–111.

Firth, R. (1973), *Symbols, Public and Private* (London: George Allen and Unwin).

Firth, R. (1974), 'Society and its symbols, review of Victor Turner, *Dramas, Fields, and Metaphors*', *Times Literary Supplement*, 13 September: 967–8.

Fisiy, C., and P. Geschiere (1996), 'Witchcraft, violence and identity', in R. Werbner (ed.), *Postcolonial Identities in Africa* (London: Zed Books).

Fontein, J. (2006), *The Silence of Great Zimbabwe* (London and Harare: UCL Press, Weaver Press).

Fontein, J. (2010), 'Between tortured bodies and resurfacing bones', *Material Culture* 15(4): 423–48.

Fontein, J. (2015), *Remaking Mutirikwi* (Rochester, NY: Boydell and Brewer).

Fortes, M. (1940), 'The political system of the Tallensi', in M. Fortes and E. Evans-Pritchard (eds), *African Political Systems* (Oxford: Oxford University Press).

Fortes, M. (1945), *The Dynamics of Clanship among the Tallensi* (Oxford: Oxford University Press).

Fortes, M. (1949a), *The Web of Kinship* (Oxford: Oxford University Press).

Fortes, M. (ed.) (1949b), *Social Structure: Essays Presented to A.R. Radcliffe-Brown* (Oxford: Oxford University Press).

Fortes, M. (1970), *Kinship and 'the Social Order* (London: Routledge and Kegan Paul).

Fortes, M. (1978), 'An anthropologist's apprenticeship', *Annual Review of Anthropology* 7: 1–30.

Fortes, M. (1983), *Rules and the Emergence of Society*, Occasional Papers 39 (London: Royal Anthropological Institute).

Fortes, M. (1987), 'Towards the judicial process', *Social Analysis* 22: 132–46.

Fortes, M., and E. Evans-Pritchard (1940), 'Introduction', in M. Fortes and E. Evans-Pritchard (eds), *African Political Systems* (Oxford: Oxford University Press).

Foster, B., and S. Seidman (1981), 'Network structure and the kinship perspective', *American Ethnologist* 2: 329–55.

Foucault, M. (1980), *Power/Knowledge*, ed. C. Gordon (New York: Pantheon).

Frankenberg, R. (1957), *Village on the Border* (London: Cohen and West).

Frankenberg, R. (1966), 'British community studies', in M. Banton (ed.), *The Social Anthropology of Complex Societies* (London: Routledge).

Frankenberg, R. (1978), 'Economic anthropology or political economy?', in J. Clammer (ed.), *The New Economic Anthropology* (New York: St. Martins).

Frankenberg, R. (ed.) (1982), *Custom and Conflict in British Society* (Manchester: Manchester University Press).

Frankenberg, R. (2006), 'A bridge over troubled waters – or what a difference a day makes', in T. Evens and D. Handelman (eds), *The Manchester School* (Oxford: Berghahn).

Freeman, L. (2004), *The Development of Social Network Analysis* (North Charleston, SC: BookSurge).

Freeman, L., and C. M. Webster (1994), 'Interpersonal proximity in social and cognitive space', *Social Cognition* 1: 223–47.

Fukui, K., and J. Markakis (eds) (1994), *Ethnicity and Conflict in the Horn of Africa* (London/Athens, OH: James Currey/Ohio University Press).

Fuller, C., and V. Benei (eds) (2001), *The Everyday State and Society in Modern India* (London: Hurst).

Fumanti, M. (2007), 'Burying E.S.', *Journal of Southern African Studies* 33(3): 469–83.

Fumanti, M. (2016), *The Politics of Distinction* (Canon Pyon: Sean Kingston Publishing).

Gallie, W. (1955–56), 'Essentially contested concepts', *Proceedings of the Aristotelian Society* 167–98.

Garbett, G. K. (1970), 'The analysis of social situations', *Man* 5: 214–27.

Gates, H., Jr (1991), 'Critical Fanonism', *Critical Inquiry* 17: 457–70.

Geertz, C. (1973), *The Interpretation of Cultures* (New York: Basic Books).

Geertz, C. (1980), 'Blurred genres', *The American Scholar* 49: 165–79.

Geertz, C. (1988), *Works and Lives* (Stanford, CA: Stanford University Press).

Geschiere, P. (1997), *The Modernity of Witchcraft* (Charlottesville, VA: University Press of Virginia).

Geschiere, P. (2013), *Witchcraft, Intimacy, and Trust* (Chicago: University of Chicago Press).

Geschiere, P. (2018), 'African chiefs and the post-cold war moment', in J. Comaroff and J. L. Comaroff (eds), *The Politics of Custom* (Chicago: University of Chicago Press).

Gillon, P. (1952), *Frail Barrier* (New York: Vanguard).

Gillon, P. (1983), 'All the world's a stage', *Jerusalem Post*, 19 June: 5.

Glazier, J. (in press), *Anthropology and the Radical Humanism of Paul Radin* (East Lansing, MI: Michigan State University Press).

Glazier, S. (2018), 'From dissection to discernment', in F. Salamone and M. Snipes (eds), *The Intellectual Legacy of Victor and Edith Turner* (Lanham, MD: Lexington Books).

Gluckman, M. (1935), 'Zulu women in hoeculture ritual', *Bantu Studies* 9(3): 255–72.

Gluckman, M. (1936), 'The Realm of the Supernatural among the South-Eastern Bantu', DPhil thesis, University of Oxford.

Gluckman, M. (1940a), 'Analysis of a social situation in modern Zululand', *Bantu Studies* 14(1): 1–39, 14(2): 147–74; reprinted (1958, 1968, 1971) with a foreword by J. Mitchell (Lusaka: Rhodes-Livingstone Institute).

Gluckman, M. (1940b), 'The kingdom of the Zulu of South Africa', in M. Fortes and E. Evans-Pritchard (eds), *African Political Systems* (Oxford: Oxford University Press).

Gluckman, M. (1941), *Economy of the Central Barotse Plain*, Rhodes-Livingstone Papers (Livingstone: Rhodes-Livingstone Institute).

Gluckman, M. (1942), 'Some processes of social change illustrated from Zululand', *African Studies* 1(4): 243–60.

Gluckman, M. (1943), *Essays on Lozi Land and Royal Property*, Rhodes-Livingstone Paper 11 (Livingstone: Rhodes-Livingstone Institute).

Gluckman, M. (1944a), 'The difficulties, limitations and achievements of social anthropology', *Rhodes-Livingstone Journal* 1(1): 22–45.

Gluckman, M. (1944b), 'Director's report to the trustees on the work of the years 1941–42–43', Rhodes-Livingstone Institute.

Gluckman, M. (1945a), 'Seven-year research plan of the Rhodes-Livingstone Institute of Social Studies in Central Africa', *Rhodes-Livingstone Institute Journal* 1(1): 22–45.

Gluckman, M. (1945b), 'Zambesi river kingdom', *Libertas* 5(8): 20–39.

Gluckman, M. (1946), 'Human laboratory across the Zambesi', *Libertas* 6(4): 38–49.

Gluckman, M. (1948), 'Director's report to the trustees on the work of the years 1944–45–46', *Human Problems in British Central Africa* 6: 64–79.

Gluckman, M. (1949), 'The role of the sexes in Wiko circumcision ceremonies', in M. Fortes (ed.), *Social Structure: Essays Presented to A.R. Radcliffe-Brown* (Oxford: Oxford University Press).

Gluckman, M. (1950), 'Kinship and marriage among the Lozi of Northern Rhodesia and the Zulu of Natal', in A. Radcliffe-Brown (ed.), *African Systems of Kinship and Marriage* (Oxford: Oxford University Press).

Gluckman, M. (1955), *The Judicial Process among the Barotse of Northern Rhodesia* (Manchester: Manchester University Press).

Gluckman, M. (1956a), *Custom and Conflict in Africa* (Oxford: Basil Blackwell). Reprinted 1961.

Gluckman, M. (1956b), 'Social anthropology in Central Africa', *Rhodes-Livingstone Journal* 2(2): 1–27.

Gluckman, M. (1960a), 'The rise of a Zulu empire', *Scientific American* 202(4): 157–69.

Gluckman, M. (1960b), 'Tribalism in modern British Central Africa', *Cahiers d'Etudes Africaines* 1.

Gluckman, M. (1961a), 'African jurisprudence', *The Advancement of Science* 75: 439–54.

Gluckman, M. (1961b), 'Ethnographic data in British social anthropology', *The Sociological Review* n.s. 9: 5–17.

Gluckman, M. (1962a), ' Foreword', in E. Colson, *The Plateau Tonga of Northern Rhodesia: Social and Religious Essays* (Manchester: Manchester University Press).

Gluckman, M. (ed.) (1962b), *Essays on the Ritual of Social Relations* (Manchester: Manchester University Press).

Gluckman, M. (1963a), 'Gossip and scandal', *Current Anthropology* 4(3): 307–16.

Gluckman, M. (1963b), *Order and Rebellion in Tribal Africa* (London: Cohen and West).

Gluckman, M. (1963c), 'Rituals of rebellion in South-East Africa', in M. Gluckman, *Order and Rebellion in Tribal Africa* (London: Cohen and West).

Gluckman, M. (1965a), *The Ideas in Barotse Jurisprudence* (New Haven, CT: Yale University Press). Repr. with new preface, Manchester: Manchester University Press, 1972.

Gluckman, M. (1965b), *Politics, Law and Ritual in Tribal Society* (Oxford: Basil Blackwell).

Gluckman, M. (1966a), *The Judicial Process among the Barotse of Northern Rhodesia*, 2nd edn (Manchester: Manchester University Press)

Gluckman, M. (1966b), 'Reasonableness and responsibility in the law of segmentary societies', in L. Kuper and H. Kuper (eds), *African Law: Adaptation and Development* (Berkeley, CA: University of California Press).

Gluckman, M. (1967), 'Introduction', in A. L. Epstein (ed.), *The Craft of Social Anthropology* (London: Tavistock).

Gluckman, M. (1968a), 'The utility of the equilibrium model in the study of social change', *American Anthropologist* 70(2): 219–37.

Gluckman, M. (1971), 'Preface', in E. Bott (ed.), *Family and Social Network: Roles, Norms and External Relationships in Ordinary Urban Families* (New York: Free Press).

Gluckman, M. (ed.) (1972), *The Allocation of Responsibility* (Manchester: Manchester University Press).

Gluckman, M. (1973a), 'Limitations of the case-method in the study of tribal law', *Law and Society Review* 7: 611–41.

Gluckman, M. (1973b), *The Judicial Process among the Barotse of Northern Rhodesia* (repr., Manchester: Manchester University Press).

Gluckman, M. (1974a), *African Traditional Law in Historical Perspective* (London: Proceedings of the British Academy).

Gluckman, M. (1974b), 'The individual in a social framework: the rise of King Shaka', *Journal of Modern African Studies* 1: 113–44.

Gluckman, M. (1974c), 'The philosophical roots of masked dancers in Barotseland (Western Province), Zambia', in *Memoriam: Antonio Jorge Dias* (Lisbon: Instituto di alti cultura).

Gluckman, M. (1975), 'Anthropology and apartheid: the work of South African anthropologists', in M. Fortes and S. Patterson (eds), *Studies in African Social Anthropology* (London: Academic Press).

Gluckman, M., with E. Devons (eds) (1964), *Closed Systems and Open Minds* (Chicago: Aldine).

Gluckmann, E. (1922), *The Tragedy of the Ababirwas, and Some Reflections on Sir Herbert Stolley's Report* (Johannesburg: Central News Agency).

Golan, D. (1990), 'The life story of King Shaka and gender tensions in the Zulu state', *History in Africa* 17: 95–111.

Golomski, C. (2018), 'Work of a nation', *Journal of Southern African Studies* 44(2): 299–314.

Gordon, R. (2018), *The Enigma of Max Gluckman* (Lincoln, NE: University of Nebraska Press).

Gramsci, A. (1975), *Letters from Prison*, trans. Lynne Lawner (London: Jonathan Cape).

Gramsci, A. (1983), *Cahiers de prison*, vol. II (Paris: Gallimard).

Grant, A. (2018), 'Ecumenism in question', *Journal of Southern African Studies* 44(2): 221–38.

Gray, G. (2019), '"In my file, I am two different people': Max Gluckman and A. L. Epstein', *Cold War History* 2: 1–18.

Grillo, R. (2004), 'Arnold Leonard [Bill] Epstein, 1922–1999, social anthropologist', *Oxford Dictionary of National Biography* (Oxford: Oxford University Press).

Grimes, R. (1985), 'Victor Turner's social drama and T.S. Eliot's ritual drama', *Anthropologica* 27: 79–99.

Gulliver, P. (ed.) (1978), *Cross-Examinations* (Leiden: Brill).

Hage, P., and F. Harary (1983), *Structural Models in Anthropology* (Cambridge: Cambridge University Press).

Hall, S. (1991), 'Introductory Essay', in R. Simon (ed.), *Gramsci's Political Thought* (London: Lawrence and Wishart).

Handelman, D. (1990), *Models and Mirrors* (Cambridge: Cambridge University Press).

Handelman, D. (2006), 'The extended case', in T. Evens and D. Handelman (eds), *The Manchester School* (Oxford: Berghahn).

Hannerz, U. (1980), *Exploring the City* (New York: Columbia University Press).

Harary, F., and R. Norman (1953), *Graph Theory as a Mathematical Model in Social Science* (Ann Arbor, MI: Institute for Social Research).

Harary, F., R. Norman and D. Cartwright (1965), *Structural Models* (New York: John Wiley and Sons).

Harrison, F. (ed.) (1991), *Decolonizing Anthropology* (Washington DC: American Anthropological Association/Association of Black Anthropologists).

Harrison, J. (1903), *Prolegomena to the Study of Greek Religion* (Cambridge: Cambridge University Press).

Hickel, J. (2015), *Democracy as Death* (Berkeley, CA: University of California Press).

Hodgson, D. (ed.) (2000), *Rethinking Pastoralism in Africa* (Oxford: James Currey).

Hodgson, D. (2011), *Being Maasai, Becoming Indigenous* (Bloomington, IN: Indiana University Press).

Hollinger, D. (2002), 'Not universalists, not pluralists', in S. Vertovec and R. Cohen (eds), *Conceiving Cosmopolitanism* (Oxford: Oxford University Press).

Holtzman, J. (2017), *Killing your Neighbors* (Oakland, CA: University of California Press).

Homans, G. (1950), *The Human Group* (New York: Harcourt, Brace).

Horton, R. (1984), 'Ritual man in Africa', *Africa* 34: 85–104.

Hutchinson, S., and J. Jok (2002), 'Gendered violence and the militarisation of ethnicity', in R. Werbner (ed.), *Postcolonial Subjectivities in Africa* (London: Zed Books).

Janson, M., and B. Meyer (2016), 'Introduction', *Africa* 86(4): 615–18.

Jules-Rosette, B. (1994), 'Decentering ethnography', *Journal of Religion in Africa* 24: 160–81.

Jules-Rosette, B. (2018), 'From grassroots ecumenism to global entanglements', *Journal of Southern African Studies* 44(2): 361–4.

Kapferer, B. (1972), *Strategy and Transaction in an African Factory* (Manchester: Manchester University Press).

Kapferer, B. (ed.) (1976), *Transaction and Meaning* (Philadelphia: Institute for the Study of Human Issues).

Kapferer, B. (1987), 'The anthropology of Max Gluckman', *Social Analysis* 22: 3–21.

Kapferer, B. (2006), 'Situations, crisis and the anthropology of the concrete: the contribution of Max Gluckman', in T. Evens and D. Handelman (eds), *The Manchester School* (Oxford: Berghahn).

Kelly, E., J. C. Mitchell and S. Smith (1990), 'Factors in the length of stay of homeless families in temporary accommodation', *Sociological Review* 38: 621–33.

Kiernan, J. (ed.) (2006), *The Power of the Occult in Modern Africa* (Berlin: Lit).

Kirsch, T., and T. Gratz (2010), *Domesticating Vigilantism in Africa* (Oxford: James Currey).

Klaits, F. (2005), 'Postcolonial civility', *Journal of Southern African Studies* 3(3): 649–62.

Klaits, F. (2010), *Death in a Church of Life* (Berkeley, CA: University of California Press).

Kuper, A. (1973), *Anthropologists and Anthropology: The British School 1922–1972* (London: Allen Lane).

Kuper, A. (1994), 'Culture, identity and the project of a cosmopolitan anthropology', *Man* n.s. 29(3): 537–54.

Kuper, A. (2005), '"Today we have naming of parts": the work of anthropologists in southern Africa', in B. de L'Estoile, F. Neiburg and L. Sigaud (eds), *Empires, Nations and Natives* (Durham, NC: Duke University Press).

Kuper, A. (2015), *Anthropology and Anthropologists: The British School in the Twentieth Century*, 4th edn (London: Routledge).

Kuper, A. (2016), 'Meyer Fortes, the person, the role, the theory', *The Cambridge Journal of Anthropology* 34(2): 127–39.

Kuper, A. (2019), 'Deconstructing anthropology', *HAU: Journal of Ethnographic Theory* 9(1): 10–22.

Kurti, L., and P. Skalnik (eds) (2009), *Postsocialist Europe* (New York: Berghahn).

Laidlaw, J. (2014a), *The Subject of Virtue* (Cambridge: Cambridge University Press).

Laidlaw, J. (2014b), 'Significant differences', *HAU: Journal of Ethnographic Theory* 4: 497–506.

Lambek, M. (2008), 'Provincializing God?', in H. de Vries (ed.), *Religion* (New York: Fordham University Press).

Lambek, M. (2010), 'Introduction', in M. Lambek (ed.), *Ordinary Ethics* (New York: Fordham University Press).

Lancaster, C., and K. Vickery (eds) (2007), *The Tonga-Speaking Peoples of Zambia and Zimbabwe* (Lanham, MD: University Press of America).

Langer, S. (1958), *Philosophy in a New Key* (Cambridge: Harvard University Press).

Larkin, B. (2016), 'Entangled religions', *Africa* 86(4): 633–9.

Larsen, T. (2014), *The Slain God* (Oxford: Oxford University Press).

Latour, B. (2005), *Reassembling the Social* (Oxford: Oxford University Press).

Lears, T. (1985), 'The concept of cultural hegemony', *The American Historical Review* 90(3): 567–93.

Lebner, A. (2017), 'Introduction', in A. Lebner (ed.), *Redescribing Relations* (Oxford: Berghahn).

Lentz, C. (1994), 'Home, death and leadership: discourses of an educated elite from northwestern Ghana', *Social Anthropology* 2(2): 149–69.

Lévi-Strauss, C. (1966), *The Savage Mind* (London: Weidenfeld and Nicolson).

Lupton, T. (1963), *On the Shop Floor* (Oxford: Pergamon).

Macintyre, A. (1981) [1967], *After Virtue: A Study in Moral Theory* (London: Duckworth).

Macmillan, H. (1995), 'Return to the Malungwana Drift – Max Gluckman, the Zulu nation, and the common society', *African Affairs* 94(374): 39–65.

Magubane, B. (1971), 'A critical look at indices used in the study of social change in colonial Africa', *Current Anthropology* 12: 419–45.

Magubane, B. (1979), *The Political Economy of Race and Class in South Africa* (New York: Monthly Review Press).

Magubane, B. (1987), 'The current situation in South Africa: a sociological perspective', *Journal of Law and Religion* 5(2): 473–93.

Magubane, B., and J. Faris (1985), 'On the political relevance of anthropology', *Dialectical Anthropology* 9(1): 91–104.

Magubane, B., and W. Minter (2004), 'Interview', in W. Minter, G. Hovey and C. Cobb Jr (eds), *No Easy Victories: African Liberation and American Activists over a Half Century, 1950–2000* (Trenton, NJ: Africa World Press).

Makgala, J. (2001), 'The Policy of Indirect Rule in Bechuanaland Protectorate, 1926–57', DPhil thesis, University of Cambridge.

Makgala, J. (2004), 'Taxation in the tribal areas of Bechuanaland Protectorate, 1889–1957', *Journal of African History* 45(2): 279–303.

Malinowski, B. (1926), *Crime and Custom in Savage Society* (London: Routledge and Kegan Paul).

Malkki, L. (1995), *Purity and Exile* (Chicago: University of Chicago Press).

Mamdani, M. (1996), *Citizen and Subject* (London: James Currey).

Manning, F. (1990), 'Victor Turner's career and publications', in K. Ashley (ed.), *Victor Turner and the Construction of Cultural Criticism* (Bloomington, IN: Indiana University Press).

Marcus, G., and J. Clifford (eds) (1986), *Writing Culture* (Berkeley, CA: University of California Press).

Marcus, G., and M. Fischer (1986), *Culture as Critique* (Chicago: University of Chicago Press).

Marx, E. (1975), 'Anthropological studies in a centralized state', *Jewish Journal of Sociology* 17(2): 131–50.

Marx, E. (2014), *Max Gluckman*, Oxford Online Bibliographies (Oxford: Oxford University Press).

Masquelier, A. (1996), 'Identity, alterity and ambiguity in a Nigerian community', in R. Werbner (ed.), *Postcolonial Identities in Africa* (London: Zed Books).

Masquelier, A. (2001), *Prayer Has Spoiled Everything* (Durham, NC: Duke University Press).

Masselos, J. (1992), 'The dis/appearance of subalterns', *Journal of South Asian Studies* 15(1): 105–25.

Matongo, A. (1992), 'Popular culture in a colonial society', in S. Chipungu (ed.), *Guardians in Their Time* (London: Macmillan).

Maundeni, Z. (2004), *Civil Society, Politics and the State in Botswana* (Gaborone: Megi Publishing).

Mazonde, I. (1994), *Ranching and Enterprise in Eastern Botswana* (Edinburgh: Edinburgh University Press for the International African Institute).

Mbembe, A. (1992a), 'Notes on the postcolony', *Africa* 62(1): 3–36.

Mbembe, A. (1992b), 'The banality of power and the aesthetics of vulgarity in the postcolony', *Public Culture* 4(2): 1–30.

Mbembe, A. (2002), 'African modes of self writing', *Public Culture* 14(1): 239–73.

McGranahan, C., K. Roland and B. Williams (2016), 'Decolonizing anthropology: a conversation with Faye. V. Harrison, part I', https://savageminds.org/2016/05/02/decolonizing-anthropology-a-conversation-with-faye-v-harrison-part-i (accessed 21 November 2019).

Mills, D. (2006), 'Made in Manchester?', in T. Evens and D. Handelman (eds), *The Manchester School* (Oxford: Berghahn).

Mills, D. (2008), *Difficult Folk* (Oxford: Berghahn).

Mitchell, J. C. (1954), 'The distribution of African labour by area of origin in the copper mines of Northern Rhodesia', *Rhodes-Livingstone Journal* 14: 3–36.

Mitchell, J. C. (1956a), *The Kalela Dance*, Rhodes-Livingstone Communications 6 (Livingstone: Rhodes-Livingstone Institute).

Mitchell, J. C. (1956b), *The Yao Village* (Manchester: Manchester University Press).

Mitchell, J. C. (1957), 'Aspects of African marriage on the Copperbelt in Northern Rhodesia', *Rhodes-Livingstone Journal* 22: 1–30.

Mitchell, J. C. (1964), 'Occupational prestige and the social system', *International Journal of Comparative Sociology* 5.1: 78–9.

Mitchell, J. C. (1966), 'Theoretical orientations in African urban studies', in M. Banton (ed.), *The Anthropological Study of Complex Societies* (London: Tavistock).

Mitchell, J. C. (1969), 'The concept and use of social networks', in J. C. Mitchell (ed.), *Social Networks in Urban Situations* (Manchester: Manchester University Press for Institute for Social Research, University of Zambia).

Mitchell, J. C. (1971), 'Response to Magubane', *Current Anthropology* 12: 434–6.

Mitchell, J. C. (1973), 'Networks, norms and institutions', in J. Boissevain and J. C. Mitchell (eds), *Network Analysis: Studies in Human Interaction* (The Hague: Mouton).

Mitchell, J. C. (1974a), 'Social networks', *Annual Review of Anthropology* 3: 279–99.

Mitchell, J. C. (1974b), 'Distance, transportation and urban involvement in Zambia', in A. Southall (ed.), *Urban Anthropology: Cross-Cultural Studies of Urbanization* (Oxford: Oxford University Press).

Mitchell, J. C. (1979), 'Networks, algorithms, and analysis', in P. Holland and S. Leinhardt (eds), *Perspectives on Social Network Research* (New York: Academic Press).

Mitchell, J. C. (1987), *Cities, Society, and Social Perception – A Central African Perspective* (Oxford: Clarendon Press).

Mitchell, J. C. (1994), 'The marks of prestige of Yao village headmen', *Zeitschrift fur Ethnologie* 119: 267–72.

Mitchell, J. C. (2006), 'Case and situational analysis', in T. Evens and D. Handelman (eds), *The Manchester School* (Oxford: Berghahn).

Mitchell, J. C., and F. Critchley (1994), 'Configurational similarity in three class contexts in British society', *Sociology* 19(1): 72–92.

Mitchell, J. C., and A. L. Epstein (1959), 'Occupational prestige and social status among urban Africans in Northern Rhodesia', *Africa* 29(1): 22–39.

Mitchell, J. C., and S. Irvine (1965), 'Social position and the grading of occupations', *Rhodes-Livingstone Journal* 38: 42–54.

Mitchell, J., and R. Wilson (eds) (2003), *Human Rights in Global Perspective* (London: Routledge).

Molosiwa, P. (2013), '"The Tragedy of the Ababirwas": Cattle Herding, Power and the Socio-Environmental History of the Ethnic Identity of the Babirwa in Botswana, 1920 to the Present', PhD thesis, University of Minnesota.

Moore, H. (2011), *Still Life* (Cambridge: Polity).

Moore, H., and T. Sanders (eds) (2001), *Magical Interpretations and Material Realities* (London: Routledge).

Moore, S. (1973), 'Law and social change: the semi-autonomous social field as an appropriate subject of study', *Law & Society Review* 7(4): 719–46.

Moore, S. (1978), 'Archaic law and modern times on the Zambezi', in P. Gulliver (ed.), *Cross-Examinations* (Leiden: Brill).

Moore, S. (1987), 'Social and symbolic elements in an instrumental negotiation', *Social Analysis* 22: 118–20.

Moore, S. (1994), *Changing Perspectives on a Changing Scene* (Charlottesville, VA: University of Virginia Press).

Moore, S. (2006), 'From tribes and traditions to composites and conjunctures', in T. Evens and D. Handelman (eds), *The Manchester School* (Oxford: Berghahn).

Morewagae, I. (2011a), 'Big shots seek out of court settlement', *Mmegi Online* 28(179), 29 October, http://www.Mmegi:bw/index:php?Sid=1&aid=296&dir/October/Tuesday29 (accessed 30 January 2013).

Morewagae, I. (2011b), 'Jamali Rantshabeng acquitted', *Mmegi Online* 28(179), 30 October, http://www.Mmegi:bw/index:php?Sid=1&aid=296&dir/OctoberWednesday30 (accessed 30 January 2013).

Morton, F., and J. Ramsay (1987), *The Birth of Botswana: A History of the Bechuanaland Protectorate, 1910–1966* (Gaborone: Longman Botswana).

Mosko, M. (2010), 'Partible penitents: dividual personhood and Christian practice in Melanesia and the West', *Journal of the Royal Anthropological Institute* 1(2): 215–40.

Mosko, M. (2015), 'Unbecoming individuals: the partible character of the Christian person', *HAU: Journal of Ethnographic Theory*, 5(1): 361–93.

Mudimbe, V. (1988), *The Invention of Africa* (Chicago; University of Chicago Press).

Muzvidziwa, V. (2006), 'The teaching of anthropology in Zimbabwe over the past forty years', in M. Ntarangwi, D. Mills and M. Babiker (eds), *African Anthropologies* (London: Zed Books).

Myhre, K. (2013), 'Introduction: cutting and connecting', *Social Analysis* 3: 1–24.

Nader, L. (1997) [1969], 'Preface', in L. Nader (ed.), *Law in Culture and Society* (repr. Berkeley, CA: University of California Press).

Nader, L. (2002), 'Introduction. Interviewed by Suzanne B. Riess' (Berkeley, CA: Bancroft Library, University of California).

Niehaus, I. (2001), *Witchcraft, Power and Politics* (London: Pluto Press).

Nietzsche, F. (1967) [1872], *The Birth of Tragedy*, trans. Walter Kaufman (New York: Vintage).

Nkwi, P., and F. Nyamnjoh (1997), *Regional Balance and National Integration in Cameroon* (Yaounde: ASC/ICASSRT).

Ntarangwi, M., D. Mills and M. Babiker (eds) (2006), *African Anthropologies* (London: Zed Books).

Nussbaum, M. (1994), 'Patriotism and cosmopolitanism', *Boston Review* 19(5): 3–6.

Nyamnjoh, F. (1991), *Mind Searching* (Awka, Anambra State: Kucena Damian Nigeria).

Nyamnjoh, F. (1999), 'Cameroon: a country united by ethnic ambition and difference', *African Affairs* 98: 101–18.

Nyamnjoh, F. (2001), 'Expectations of modernity or a future in a rearview mirror?', *Journal of Southern African Studies* 27: 363–9.

Nyamnjoh, F. (2002), '"A child is one person's only in the womb": domestication, agency and subjectivity in the Cameroonian grassfields', in R. Werbner (ed.), *Postcolonial Subjectivities in Africa* (London: Zed Books).

Nyamnjoh, F. (2006), *Insiders and Outsiders* (London: Zed Books).

Nyamnjoh, F. (2016), *#Rhodes Must Fall – Nibbling at Resilient Colonialism in South Africa* (Mankom, Bamena: Langa Research and Publishing).

Ogden, J. (1996), '"Producing" respect: the "proper women" in post-colonial Kampala', in R. Werbner (ed.), *Postcolonial Identities in Africa* (London: Zed Books).

Ortner, S. (1984), 'Theory in anthropology since the sixties', *Comparative Studies in Society and History* 26(1): 126–66.

Parry, J. (2009), '"Sociological Marxism" in Central India', in C. Hahn and K. Hart (eds), *Market and Society* (Cambridge: Cambridge University Press).

Paquet, M. (2015), *Magritte* (Cologne: Taschen).

Peach, C., and J. C. Mitchell (1988), 'Marriage distance and ethnicity', in C. Mascie-Taylor and A. Boyce (eds), *Human Mating Patterns* (Cambridge: Cambridge University Press).

Peel, J. (2015), *Christianity, Islam, and Orisa Religion* (Berkeley, CA: University of California Press).

Peil, M. (1988), 'Review of Mitchell, *Cities, Society and Social Perception*', *Urban Studies* 15: 263–4.

Peirce, C. (1998), *The Essential Pierce*, The Pierce Edition Project (Bloomington, IN: Indiana University Press).

Peters, E. (1990), *The Bedouin of Cyrenaica*, ed. J. Goody and E. Marx (Cambridge: Cambridge University Press).

Pina Cabral, J., and A. Pedroso de Lima (eds) (2000), *Elites: Choice, Leadership and Succession* (London: Bloomsbury).

Polanyi, M. (1950), 'Scientific beliefs', *Ethics* 61: 27–37.

Polanyi, M. (1952), 'The stability of beliefs', *British Journal for the Philosophy of Science* 3: 217–32.

Polanyi, M. (1958), *Personal Knowledge* (London: Routledge and Kegan Paul).

Powdermaker, H. (1959), '*Marriage and the Family among the Plateau Tonga* by Elizabeth Colson', *American Anthropologist* 61(6): 1119–21.

Pritchett, J. (2007), '*The Tonga-Speaking Peoples of Zambia and Zimbabwe* by Chet Lancaster and Kenneth P. Vickery', *African Studies Review* 50(3): 135–42.

Rabinow, P. (1995), *French Modern* (Chicago: University of Chicago Press).

Radcliffe-Brown, A. (1957), *A Natural Science of Society* (Chicago: University of Chicago Press).

Radin, P. (1957) [1937], *Primitive Religion* (New York: Dover).

Raheja, G. (1988), *The Poison of the Gift* (Chicago: University of Chicago Press).

Ranger, T. (1975), *Dance and Society in East Africa 1890–1970* (Berkeley, CA: University of California Press).

Ranger, T. (1983), 'The invention of tradition in Colonial Africa', in E. Hobsbawm and T. Ranger, *The Invention of Tradition* (Cambridge: Cambridge University Press).

Rew, A. (1999), 'Obituary: Professor A.L. Epstein', *The Independent*, 19 November, https://www.independent.co.uk/arts-entertainment/obituary-professor-a-l-epstein-1127117.html (accessed 21 November 2019).

Ripley, S. (1982), 'Foreword', in S. Ripley (ed.), *Celebration* (Washington, DC: Smithsonian Institution Press).

Rosaldo, R. (1986), 'From the door of his tent', in G. Marcus and J. Clifford (eds), *Writing Culture* (Berkeley, CA: University of California Press).

Rutherford, B. (2016), *Farm Labor Struggles in Zimbabwe* (Bloomington, IN: Indiana University Press).

Ruud, A. (1999), 'The Indian hierarchy', *Modern Asian Studies* 33(3): 689–732.

Salamone, F., and M. Snipes (eds) (2018), *The Intellectual Legacy of Victor and Edith Turner* (Lanham, MD: Lexington Books).

Salo, E. (2016), 'Men, women, temporality and critical ethnography in Africa', in R. Boswell and F. Nyamnjoh (eds), *Postcolonial Afrian Anthropologies* (Cape Town: HSRC Press).

Sanders, T. (2003), 'Reconsidering witchcraft', *American Anthropologist* 105(2): 338–52.

Sapir, E. (1935), 'Symbols', in *Encyclopedia of the Social Sciences* 14 (New York: Macmillan).

Sarro, R. (2018), 'Religious pluralism and the limits of ecumenism in Mbanza Kongo, Angola', *Journal of Southern African Studies* 44(2): 239–52.

Savage, M., and K. Williams (eds) (2008), *Remembering Elites, Sociological Review* 2, special issue.

Schapera, I. (1955), 'Witchcraft beyond reasonable doubt', *Man* 55: 72.

Schapera, I. (1969), 'The crime of sorcery', *Proceedings of the Royal Anthropological Institute*, 15–23.

Schechner, R. (1985), *Between Theater and Anthropology* (Philadelphia: University of Pennsylvania Press).

Schumaker, L. (2001), *Africanizing Anthropology* (Durham, NC: Duke University Press).

Scott, J. (2017), *Social Network Analysis*, 4th edn (New York: Sage).

Scudder, T. (2005), *The Future of Large Dams* (London: Earthscan).

Shaw, R. (2002), *Memories of the Slave Trade* (Chicago: University of Chicago Press).

Shaw, T. (1982), 'Beyond neo-colonialism', *Journal of Modern African Studies* 20(2): 239–61.

Shepherd, S. (2016), *The Cambridge Introduction to Performance Theory* (Cambridge: Cambridge University Press).

Shokeid, M. (2000), 'A. L. Epstein (1924–1999)', *American Anthropologist* 102(4): 858–60.

Simpson, A. (2003), *'Half-London' in Zambia* (Edinburgh: Edinburgh University Press for the International African Institute).

Simpson, A. (2009), *From Boys to Men in the Shadow of Aids* (New York: Palgrave Macmillan).

Singer, A. (1981), 'Preface', in E. Evans-Pritchard, *A History of Anthropological Thought*, ed. A. Singer (New York: Basic Books).

Singer, M. (1972), *When a Great Tradition Modernizes* (New York: Praeger).

Singer, M. (1984), *Man's Glassy Essence* (Bloomington, IN: Indiana University Press).

Singer, M. (1991), *Semiotics of Cities, Selves, and Cultures* (Berlin: Mouton de Gruyter).

Smith, S. J. (2019), 'J. Clyde Mitchell', *Biographical Memoirs of Fellows of the British Academy XVIII*, www.thebritishacademy.ac.uk/publications/ biographical memoirs-fellows-british-academy (accessed 4 November 2019).

Soares, B. (2006), *Muslim–Christian Encounters in Africa* (Leiden: Brill).

Soares, B. (2016), 'Reflections on Muslim–Christian encounters in West Africa', *Africa* 86(4): 673–97.

Solway, J. (2002), 'Navigating the "neutral" state', *Journal of Southern African Studies* 28(4): 711–30.

Spencer, J. (1997), 'Post-colonialism and the political imagination', *Journal of the Royal Anthropological Institute* n.s. 3(1): 1–19.

St John, G. (2008), 'Introduction', in G. St John (ed.), *Victor Turner and Contemporary Cultural Performance* (Oxford: Berghahn).

Starr, J. (1984), 'Scholar in controversy', in J. Glazier (ed.), *Opportunity, Constraint, and Change* (Berkeley, CA: Department of Anthropology, University of California).

Stewart, C., and R. Shaw (eds) (1994), *Syncretism/Antisyncretism* (London: Routledge).

Stoller, P. (1987), *In Sorcery's Shadow* (Chicago: University of Chicago Press).

Strathern, M. (1972), *Official and Unofficial Courts: Legal Assumptions and Expectations in a Highlands Community*, New Guinea Research Bulletin 47 (Port Moresby and Canberra: New Guinea Research Unit).

Strathern, M. (1986), 'The limits of auto-anthropology', in A. Jackson (ed.), *Anthropology at Home* (London: Tavistock).

Strathern, M. (1988), *The Gender of the Gift* (Berkeley, CA: University of California Press).

Strathern, M. (1992), *After Nature: English Kinship in the Late Twentieth Century* (Cambridge: Cambridge University Press).

Strathern, M. (1995), *The Relation* (Cambridge: Prickly Pear).

Strathern, M. (1996), 'Cutting the network', *Journal of the Royal Anthropological Institute* n.s. 2(3): 517–35.

Strathern, M. (2005), *Partial Connections* (Walnut Creek, CA: AltaMira Press).

Strathern, M. (2015), 'Detaching and situating knowledge: comment', in M. Candea, J. Cook, C. Trundle and T. Yarrow (eds), *Detachment: Essays on the Limits of Relational Thinking* (Manchester: Manchester University Press).

Strathern, M. (2018), 'Persons and partible persons', in M. Candea (ed.), *Schools and Styles of Anthropological Theory* (London: Routledge).

Stroeken, K. (2005), 'Immunizing strategies', *Africa* 75: 488–509.

Svasek, M., and B. Meyer (eds) (2016), *Creativity in Transition* (Oxford: Berghahn).

Tambiah, S. (1966), 'Tribal society as seen from Manchester', *Nature*, 5(3): 951.

Tambiah, S. (1986), *Sri Lanka – Ethnic Fratricide and the Dismantling of Democracy* (London: I.B. Tauris).

Tambiah, S. (1990), *Magic, Science and Religion, and the Scope of Rationality* (Cambridge: Cambridge University Press).

Teppo, A. (2018), 'Moral radicals', *Journal of Southern African Studies* 44(2): 253–68.

Thornton, R. (1996), 'The potentials of boundaries in South Africa', in R. Werbner (ed.), *Postcolonial Identities in Africa* (London: Zed Books).

Thornton, R., and P. Skalnik (eds) (1993), *The Early Writings of Bronislaw Malinowski*, trans. Ludwik Krzyzanowski (Cambridge: Cambridge University Press).

Tlou, T., and A. Campbell (1997), *A History of Botswana* (Gaborone: Botswana).

Tomkins, S. (1963–64), *Affect, Imagery, Consciousness*, vols 1 and 2 (London: Tavistock).

Turner, E. (2006), *Heart of Lightness* (Oxford: Berghahn).

Turner, E., and F. Turner (1985), 'Victor Turner as we remember him', *Anthropologica* n.s. 27(1/2): 11–16.

Turner, V. (1953), *Lunda Rites and Ceremonies*, Occasional Papers of the Rhodes-Livingstone Museum 10 (repr. Manchester: Manchester University Press for the Institute for African Studies, University of Zambia, 1974).

Turner, V. (1955), 'A revival in the study of African ritual', *Rhodes-Livingstone Journal* 17: 51–6.

Turner, V. (1957), *Schism and Continuity in an African Society* (Manchester: Manchester University Press).

Turner, V. (1962), 'Three symbols of passage in Ndembu circumcision ritual', in M. Gluckman (ed.), *Essays on the Ritual of Social Relations* (Manchester: Manchester University Press).

Turner, V. (1967), *The Forest of Symbols* (Ithaca, NY: Cornell University Press).

Turner, V. (1968), *The Drums of Affliction* (Oxford: Clarendon Press and the International African Institute).

Turner, V. (1969), *The Ritual Process* (London: Routledge and Kegan Paul).

Turner, V. (1971), *Colonialism in Africa, 1870–1960* (Cambridge: Cambridge University Press).

Turner, V. (1973a), 'The center out there: pilgrim's goal', *History of Religions* 12(3): 191–230.

Turner, V. (1975) [1962], *Revelation and Divination in Ndembu Ritual* (Ithaca, NY: Cornell University Press).

Turner, V. (1982a), *From Ritual to Theatre* (New York: Performing Arts Journal Publications).

Turner, V. (1982b), 'Introduction to the exhibition', in S. Ripley (ed.), *Celebration* (Washington, DC: Smithsonian Institution Press).

Turner, V. (1985a), 'Foreword', in R. Schechner, *Between Theater and Anthropology* (Philadelphia: University of Pennsylvania Press).

Turner, V. (1985b), *On the Edge of the Bush*, ed. E. Turner (Tucson, AZ: University of Arizona Press).

Turner, V. (1996) [1957], *Schism and Continuity in an African Society*, 2nd edn (Oxford: Berghahn).

Turner, V. (2017), *Victor Witter Turner Papers*, https://alexanderstreet.com/products/anthropological-fieldwork-online (accessed 4 November 2019).

Turner, V., and E. Turner (1978), *Image and Pilgrimage in Christian Culture* (Oxford: Basil Blackwell).

Uberoi, J. S. (1962), *Politics of the Kula Ring* (Manchester: Manchester University Press).

Van Binsbergen, W. (2007), 'Manchester as the birthplace of modern agency research', in M. De Bruijn, R. Van Dijk and J.-B. Gewald (eds), *Strength Beyond Structure* (Leiden: Brill).

Van de Kamp, L. (2016), *Violent Conversion* (Oxford: Berghahn).

Van der Veer, P. (1994), *Religious Nationalism* (Berkeley, CA: University of California Press.

Van Dijk, R., and P. Pels (1996), 'Contested authorities and the politics of perception', in R. Werbner (ed.), *Postcolonial Identities in Africa* (London: Zed Books).

Van Velsen, J. (1964), *The Politics of Kinship* (Manchester: Manchester University Press).

Van Velsen, J. (1967), 'The extended case method and situational analysis', in A. Epstein (ed.), *The Craft of Social Anthropology* (London: Tavistock).

Van Wyk, I. (2014), *The Universal Church of the Kingdom of God in South Africa* (Cambridge: Cambridge University Press for International African Institute, London).

Van Wyk, I. (2018), 'Fragile wars', *Journal of Southern African Studies* 44(2): 269–82.

Veblen, T. (1950), *The Theory of the Leisure Class* (New York: Macmillan).

Viveiros de Castro, E., C. Fausto and M. Strathern (2017), 'Within the limits of language: interview with Marilyn Strathern', in A. Lebner (ed.), Redescribing Relations (Oxford: Berghahn).

Volosinov, V. (1989) [1973], *Marxism and the Philosophy of Language*, trans. L. Matejka and I. R. Titunik (Cambridge, MA: Harvard University Press).

Wagner, R. (1975), *The Invention of Culture* (Englewood Cliffs, NJ: Prentice-Hall).

Wallis, W. (1930), *Culture and Progress* (New York: McGraw Hill).

Wasserman, S. (2005), 'Introduction', in P. Carrington, J. Scott and S. Wasserman (eds), *Models and Methods in Social Network Analysis* (Cambridge: Cambridge University Press).

Watts, D. (2003), *Six Degrees: The Science of a Connected Age* (New York: W.W. Norton).

Weber, D. (1995), 'From limen to border', *American Quarterly* 47: 525–36.

Weiss, B. (2009), *Street Dreams and Hip Hop Barbershops* (Bloomington, IN: Indiana University Press).

Werbner, P. (1990), *The Migration Process* (Oxford: Berg).

Werbner, P. (1996), 'Fun spaces', *Theory, Culture and Society* 13(4): 53–79.

Werbner, P. (2001), 'The limits of cultural hybridity: on ritual monsters, poetic licence, and contested postcolonial purifications', *Journal of the Royal Anthropological Institute* (incorporating *Man*) 7(1): 133–52.

Werbner, P. (2003), *Pilgrims of Love* (London/Bloomington, IN: Hurst/Indiana University Press).

Werbner, P. (2008), 'Introduction', in P. Werbner (ed.), *Anthropology and the New Cosmopolitanism* (Oxford: Berg).

Werbner, P. (2009), 'Dialogical subjectivities for hard times', *African Identities* 7.3: 299–325.

Werbner, P. (2010), 'Appropriating social citizenship', *Journal of Southern African Studies* 36(3): 693–710.

Werbner, P. (2014), '"The duty to act fairly": ethics, legal anthropology, and labor justice in the Manual Workers Union of Botswana', *Comparative Studies in Society and History* 56(2): 479–507.

Werbner, P. (2017), 'Barefoot in Britain – yet again', *The Sociological Review* 65: 4–12.

Werbner, P. (2018), 'Rethinking class and culture in Africa', *Review of African Political Economy* 45(155): 7–24.

Werbner, P., and R. Werbner (2018), 'Divorce as process, Botswana style: customary courts, gender activism and legal pluralism in historical perspective', *Legal Anthropology* 2(2): 1–23.

Werbner, P., and R. Werbner (2019), 'A case of insult: emotion, honour and witchcraft accusations in a Botswana village customary court', *Social Analysis* 63(3): 89–113.

Werbner, P., and R. Werbner (2020), 'A case of inheritance: from citizens' forum to magisterial justice in Botswana's customary courts', *Anthropology Southern Africa* 43(1).

Werbner, P., and R. Werbner (forthcoming, 2020), 'Adultery redefined: changing decisions of equity in customary law as "living law" in Botswana', *PoLar, Journal of Political and Legal Anthropology Review* (May).

Werbner, R. (1967), 'Federal administration, rank, and civil strife among Bemba royals and nobles', *Africa* 37(1): 22–49.

Werbner, R. (1969), 'Constitutional ambiguities and the British administration of royal careers among the Bemba of Zambia', in L. Nader (ed.), *Law in Culture and Society* (Chicago: Aldine).

Werbner, R. (1972), 'Sin, blame and ritual mediation', in M. Gluckman (ed.), *The Allocation of Responsibility* (Manchester: Manchester University Press).

Werbner, R. (1973), 'The superabundance of understanding', *American Anthropologist* 75: 414–40.

Werbner, R. (ed.) (1977a), *Regional Cults* (London: Academic Press).

Werbner, R. (1977b), 'Introduction', in R. Werbner (ed.), *Regional Cults* (London: Academic Press).

Werbner, R. (1977c), 'Continuity and policy in southern Africa's high god cult', in R. Werbner (ed.), *Regional Cults* (London: Academic Press).

Werbner, R. (1977d), 'Small man politics and the rule of law', *Journal of African Law* 21: 24–39.

Werbner, R. (1979a), 'Totemism in history', *Man* 14: 163–83.

Werbner, R. (1979b), 'Richards, Audrey I.', in *International Encyclopedia of the Social Sciences, Biographical Supplement* 18 (New York: Free Press), 658–60.

Werbner, R. (1981), 'The quasi-judicial and the experience of the absurd', in R. Werbner (ed.), *Land Reform in the Making* (London: Rex Collings).

Werbner, R. (1984a), 'World renewal', *Man* n.s. 19: 267–90.

Werbner, R. (1984b), 'The Manchester School in South-Central Africa', *Annual Review of Anthropology* 13: 157–85.

Werbner, R. (1989), *Ritual Passage, Sacred Journey* (Washington, DC: Smithsonian Institution Press).

Werbner, R. (1990a), 'Bwiti in reflection', *Journal of Religion in Africa* 20: 2–25.

Werbner, R. (1990b), 'South-Central Africa: the Manchester School and after', in R. Fardon (ed.), *Localizing Strategies* (Edinburgh: Scottish Academic Press).

Werbner, R. (1991), *Tears of the Dead: The Social Biography of an African Family* (Edinburgh: Edinburgh University Press).

Werbner, R. (1992), 'On dialectical versions', in B. Juillerat (ed.), *Shooting at the Sun* (Washington, DC: Smithsonian Institution Press).

Werbner, R. (1993), 'From heartland to hinterland: elites and the geopolitics of land in Botswana', in T. Bassett and D. Crummey (eds), *African Agrarian Systems* (Madison, WI: University of Wisconsin Press).

Werbner, R. (1994), 'Afterword', in C. Stewart and R. Shaw (eds), *Syncretism / Antisyncretism* (London: Routledge).

Werbner, R. (1995), 'Human rights and moral knowledge: arguments of accountability in Zimbabwe', in M. Strathern (ed.), *Shifting Contexts* (London: Routledge).

Werbner, R. (1996a), 'Multiple identities, plural arenas', in R. Werbner and T. Ranger (eds), *Postcolonial Identities in Africa* (London: Zed Books).

Werbner, R. (1996b), 'Creative dividualism: reflections on "Mwana Ndi Mai"', *Svensk Missionstidskrift* 84: 86–93.

Werbner, R. (1997a) [1969], 'Constitutional ambiguities and the British administration of royal careers among the Bemba of Zambia', in L. Nader (ed.), *Law in Culture and Society*. (repr. Berkeley, CA: University of California Press).

Werbner, R. (1997b), 'The suffering body: passion and ritual allegory in Christian encounters', *Journal of Southern African Studies* 23: 311–24.

Werbner, R. (ed.) (1998), *Memory and the Postcolony* (London: Zed Books).

Werbner, R. (1999), 'The reach of the postcolonial state', in A. Cheater (ed.), *The Anthropology of Power* (London: Routledge).

Werbner, R. (2001), 'Truth-on-balance: knowing the opaque other in Tswapong wisdom divination', in G. Bond and D. Ciekaway (eds), *Witchcraft Dialogues* (Athens, OH: Ohio University Press).

Werbner, R. (2002a), 'Introduction', in R. Werbner (ed.), *Postcolonial Subjectivities in Africa* (London: Zed Books).

Werbner, R. (2002b), 'Introduction', *Journal of Southern African Studies* 28(4): 667–80.

Werbner, R. (2002c), 'Cosmopolitan ethnicity', *Journal of Southern African Studies* 28(4): 727–49.

Werbner, R. (2004a), *Reasonable Radicals and Citizenship in Botswana* (Bloomington, IN: Indiana University Press).

Werbner, R. (2004b), 'Sacred centrality and flows across town and country', in P. Probst and G. Spittler (eds), *Between Resistance and Expansion* (Berlin: Lit).

Werbner, R (2004c), 'Epilogue', in H. Englund and F. Nyamnjoh (eds), *Rights and the Politics of Recognition in Africa* (London: Zed Books).

Werbner, R. (2005), *Séance reflections with Richard Werbner* [film], Manchester: International Centre for Contemporary Cultural Research; London: Royal Anthropological Institute.

Werbner, R. (2008), 'Responding to rooted cosmopolitanism', in P. Werbner (ed.), *Anthropology and the New Cosmopolitanism* (Oxford: Berg).

Werbner, R. (2009), 'Safe passage for well-being', *Cambridge Anthropology* 29(3): 45–68.

Werbner, R. (2011a), 'The charismatic dividual and the sacred self', *Journal of Religion in Africa* 41: 180–205.

Werbner, R. (2011b), *Holy Hustlers, Schism and Prophecy* (Berkeley, CA: University of California Press).

Werbner, R. (2012a), 'Anthropology and the postcolonial', in R. Fardon et al. (eds), *The Sage Handbook of Social Anthropology* (London: Sage).

Werbner, R. (2012b), 'Africa's new public cosmopolitans', in G. Delanty (ed.), *The Routledge Handbook of Cosmopolitan Studies* (New York: Routledge).

Werbner, R. (2014a), *Burying Hallelujah* [film], Manchester: International Centre for Contemporary Cultural Research; London: Royal Anthropological Institute.

Werbner, R. (2014b), 'Down-to-earth', in M. Guichard (ed.), *Friendship, Descent and Alliance* (Oxford: Berghahn).

Werbner, R. (2014c), 'Empathy and sympathy', *Archivio di Etnografia* 2: 27–46.

Werbner, R. (2015), *Divination's Grasp: African Encounters with the Almost Said* (Bloomington, IN: Indiana University Press).

Werbner, R. (2017), 'The poetics of wisdom divination', *Journal of the Royal Anthropological Institute* 23(1): 81–102.

Werbner, R. (2018a), 'Grassroots ecumenism in conflict – introduction', *Journal of Southern African Studies* 44(2): 201–20.

Werbner, R. (2018b), 'Botswana's ecumenical funerals in the making', *Journal of Southern African Studies* 44(2): 315–30.

Werbner, R., and T. Ranger (eds) (1996), *Postcolonial Identities in Africa* (London: Zed Books).

Weyl, H. (1932), *The Open World* (New Haven, CT: Yale University Press).

West, H. (2005), *Kupilikula* (Chicago: University of Chicago Press).

White, H. S., S. Boorman and R. Breiger (1976), 'Social structure from multiple networks, I. Block models of roles and positions', *American Journal of Sociology* 81(4): 730–80.

Whyte, S. (1997), *Questioning Misfortune* (Cambridge: Cambridge University Press).

Whyte, S. (2002), 'Subjectivity and subjunctivity', in R. Werbner (ed.), *Postcolonial Subjectivities in Africa* (London: Zed Books).

Williams, R. (1977), *Marxism and Literature* (Oxford: Oxford University Press).

Willis, R. (1984), 'Victor Witter Turner (1920–1983)', *Africa* 54(4): 73–5.

Wilson, R. (2001), *The Politics of Truth and Reconciliation in South Africa* (Cambridge: Cambridge University Press).

Winch, P. (1972) [1964], *The Idea of a Social Science* (London: Routledge and Kegan Paul).

Wolfe, A. (1970), 'On structural comparisons of networks', *Canadian Journal of Social Anthropology* 7(4): 244–66.

Wolfe, A. (1978), 'The rise of network thinking in anthropology', *Social Networks* 1: 53–64.

Worby, E. (1998), 'Tyranny, parody and ethnic polarity', *Journal of Southern African Studies* 24(3): 560–78.

Wylie, D. (1990), *A Little God: The Twilight of Patriarchy in a Southern African Chiefdom* (Johannesburg: Witwatersrand University Press).

Yelvington, K. (1997), 'An interview with A. L. Epstein', *Current Anthropology* 38(2): 289–99.

Yngvesson, B. (1978), 'The reasonable man and the unreasonable gossip', in P. Gulliver (ed.) *Cross-Examinations* (Leiden: Brill).

Yoshida, K., and J. Mack (2008), *Preserving the Cultural Heritage of Africa* (Woodbridge/Muckleneuk: James Currey/Unisa).

Young, M. (2000), 'A.L. ("Bill") Epstein', *The Asia Pacific Journal of Anthropology* 1(1): 119–29.

Zappia, C. (2001), 'Equilibrium and disequilibrium dynamics', *Journal of the History of Economic Thought* 23(1): 55–75.

Zeller, E. (1957) [1931], *Outlines of the History of Greek Philosophy* (New York: Meridian Books).

Index

EU authorised representative for GPSR:
Easy Access System Europe, Mustamäe tee 50,
10621 Tallinn, Estonia
gpsr.requests@easproject.com